SCOTTISH RECORD SOCIETY

NEW SERIES 10

PROTOCOL BOOK OF JOHN FOULAR

SCOTTISH RECORD SOCIETY

Since its foundation in 1897, the Scottish Record Society has published numerous volumes of calendars and indices of public records and private muniments relating to Scotland. A list of the Society's publications is available on request.

Membership of the Society is open to all persons and institutions interested in its work. Further particulars may be obtained from the Honorary Secretary.

PRESIDENT

Professor Emeritus Gordon Donaldson
Ph.D., D.Litt., F.B.A., F.R.S.E.
H.M. Historiographer in Scotland

TREASURER

The Reverend Duncan Shaw, Ph.D., Th.Dr.
4, Sydney Terrace, Edinburgh, EH7 6SL

SECRETARY

James Kirk, Ph.D.
Department of Scottish History
University of Glasgow, Glasgow, G12 8QQ

SCOTTISH RECORD SOCIETY

NEW SERIES 10

Protocol Book of John Foular 1528-1534

edited by

JOHN DURKAN, D. Litt.

Edinburgh
1985

*Published in 1985 by the
Scottish Record Society
Edinburgh*

Copyright © Scottish Record Society
and
John Durkan 1985

ISBN 0 902054 07 4

ISSN 0 143-9448

*Printed in Great Britain by
John Geddes (Printers) Irvine*

CONTENTS

	Page
Preface	v
Introduction	vii
Abbreviations	xxvii
The Text	1
Appendix	189
Index	191

PREFACE

This is the last part of the Protocol Book of John Foular, an enterprise begun half a century ago when part of the manuscript first volume was published with Latin transcripts accompanied accompanied by English abstracts. The transcriber was the Rev. Walter Macleod, and, while the transcript was accurate, the translation was sometimes less so.

Subsequent parts appeared without the Latin originals, and were expertly edited by Dr Marguerite Wood, former City Archivist.

There remained only manuscript volume IV, of which neat handwritted abstracts were compiled by Miss Helen Armet. These have required the minimum of revision and are now made available, with her consent, to a wider public. The editor wishes to thank Dr Walter Makey, present Archivist, for facilities afforded while this final volume was in preparation.

JOHN DURKAN

University of Glasgow,
November, 1983.

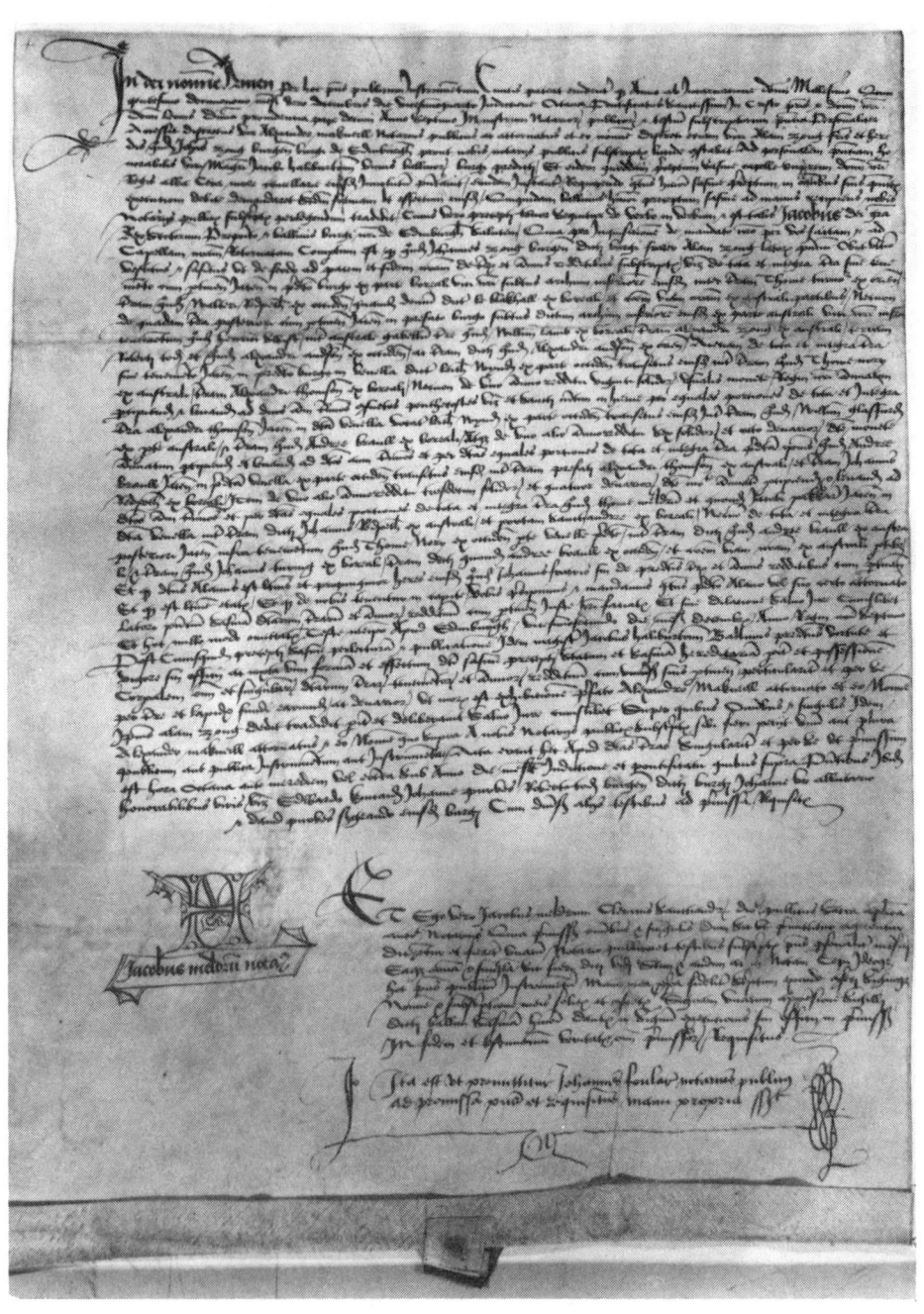

24 December, 1519. Three Edinburgh notaries are involved in this transaction: Alexander Makneill, as attorney, produces a precept of chancery; the instrument is in the hand of James Meldrum; and John Foular also subscribes. SRO, GD28/387.
(By courtesy of the Scottish Record Office, Edinburgh)

INTRODUCTION

It is appropriate to begin the introduction to the final protocol book of an Edinburgh notary with some considerations on the light thrown on Edinburgh itself in the sixteenth century, and perhaps not inappropriate later to cast the net wider with some specimens garnered from a wider selection of Scots notaries of the time.

This is the fourth and last of the surviving protocol books of the Edinburgh notary and town clerk, John Foular. In spite of the name, protocol books seldom give the actual protocols in their complete legal form, but as can be seen from the first section of volume I, published by Edinburgh corporation in 1930 and presented to the Scottish Record Society, they are mostly made up of memoranda from which the protocol itself can be reconstructed. This volume exceptionally gave the Latin original as well as an English abstract and is here referred to as Ia, to avoid confusion with the Scottish Record Society series proper, which confines itself to abstracts. It has a useful preface by the late Dr Marguerite Wood, mainly on Edinburgh topography.

That a lost first book formerly existed can be demonstrated by sixteenth-century references to our present book III as 'Jhone foularis fourt bwk' and our present book IV as his 'fyift bwk', references to be found in extracted items made for the so-called 'cartulary' (and obit-book) of St Giles, a manuscript that also contains protocols from the lost books of another Edinburgh notary, Henry Strathauchin, as copied in his own hand by Foular's co-notary, Vincent Strathauchin.[1] Other Edinburgh protocol books for the period to the Reformation are in the hand of the following notaries: Vincent Strathauchin, 1507-53; Henry Strathauchin, 1513-17 (not Mr Thomas as it says on the spine); Mr Adam Otterburn, 1515-19; Andrew Brounhill, 1536-44; James Stevenson, 1547-49; Alexander King, 1548-63; John Guthrie, 1557-59; Alexander Guthrie senior, 1556-1561; William Stewart, 1558-1566 (a transcript only). Even so, there were many other notaries in Edinburgh whose books are not among these burgh records (now deposited in the Scottish Record Office) or have failed to survive because their compilers did not hold burgh office. The protocol book of James (often referred to mistakenly as William) Meldrum is out of place, among the Haddington burgh records, for Meldrum lived in Edinburgh, and its entries mostly concern Newhaven and the principal bailie of the king there, Robert Leslie of Inverpeffer. Meldrum was certainly not so busy a notary as Foular.[2] The Canongate notaries also naturally have much material that concerns Edinburgh. Foular often worked with Vincent Strathauchin, both in 1522 being described as 'notaris and clerkis to the toun for the tyme'.³

Who was John Foular? The sources do not reveal much of him. He signed his individual protocols as 'cleric of St Andrews diocese, notary public by apostolic authority'.⁴ His sign manual was not distinctive being a scroll with his name surmounted by a few intertwining curves set on a round base, from which emerge two quills on either side and topped by a 'tau' or Greek cross (illustrated in volume Ia). We know nothing of Foular's date of creation as notary, nor who was responsible. His father may have been a certain John Foular who is known as an importer of books, and who was paid in 1502 for three printed mass-books destined for the household of James IV.⁵ The notary must be distinguished from another of the same name, a merchant, who like the notary was a burgess, but whose reception was not at the time recorded in the burgess roll, though he had been bailie and had 'keipit oppen buith and taverne be the space of xx or xxx yeris'.⁶ It was this John Foular whose wife was recorded as a secret Lutheran around 1539 and her brother, Mr James Lindsay, was in 1551 curator to their son.⁷ John Foular, notary, and his namesake are clearly distinct persons, a point settled by the presence of notary and merchant together in one deed of the period This was in 1536, two years after his last protocol book.⁸ On 25 September, 1520, the notary was himself received as a burgess and gild brother because he was acting then as the town's clerk-substitute.⁹ Like some other notaries of the period, John Foular was a married clerk, his wife being Alison Lawson, sister of Mr Robert Lawson, vicar of Ecclesgreig or St Cyrus in the Mearns, who in 1526 was himself a scribe in St Andrews to the court of the priory.¹⁰ It would seem to have been his wife's second marriage, as in 1548 a married stepdaughter is on record, Christine Craufurde, with her husband, James Stirk. This was on the occasion of Foular's widow surrendering to them in Edinburgh land on the south side of the High Street along with six acres in the neighbourhood of Dundee inherited from her brother the vicar. However, Christine only got these properties in the interim, for it was laid down that, if the widow's lawful son, Mr Alexander Foular, were to come home and lease the Dundee lands, the Edinburgh property would become his.¹¹ It is likely that this young man had departed to England with the English troops under the earl of Hertford who laid much of Edinburgh waste in 1544 during King Henry VIII's invasion of Scotland termed the 'Rough Wooing'. In the event, the Governor, Arran, on 24 March 1550/1 granted remission to the youth for his treasonable absence in England in war-time. ¹² The notary's son in fact got repossession and remission, but only by promising the Dundee lands to one of the royal officials in return.¹³ From the fact that Alexander had graduated at St Leonard's college in St Andrews in 1540, it can be deduced that his father, the notary, had been married at least since 1520.¹⁴ Later in 1556, Alexander is found as servitor to James Balfour, later of Pittendreich, but then official of St Andrews in Lothian and parson of

INTRODUCTION

Snow.[15] In Alexander's absence James Stirk, John Foular's son-in-law, was termed in March 1550 'keeper for the time' of the dead notary's protocols, but when exactly John Foular, notary, died is not clear.[16] From a number of entries we gather that John Foular sometimes used 'the booth of the common clerk of the burgh' (nos. 192, 571 for instance) and sometimes his own home (e.g. no. 96 : in those days the town clerkship was temporary, 'for the time'.

The technicalities of notarial documentation have been described elsewhere and it would be inappropriate to repeat that description.[17] It might be enough to indicate that the situation never remained static, not even in the matter of self-description. For instance the Henry Strathauchin cited above, in a docquet of 1490, described himself as 'cleric of St Andrews diocese, public notary by imperial and royal authority'.[18] Notaries 'by royal authority' seldom recur in the period to 1560 when Queen Mary revived them in the post-Reformation abolition of 'apostolic (i.e. papal) authority'. Though a cleric, Strathauchin was married and in August 1513 took over his son's account book for his protocols. His son was Mr Thomas Strathauchin, vicar of Boncle, who pre-deceased his father leaving incidentally a small bequest of ten merks to 'margaret lany his barnys moder ... till hyr marriage, sua that scho mary with faderis consent and nocht ellis and all the ger that scho hes of his at this tym siclik sua that scho mary with his fadir counsale'.[19] There are signs of discomfort with the claim to clerical status on the part of the married laity, for although both Foular and Vincent Strathauchin continue as clerics, notaries of St Andrews diocese by apostolic authority, Andrew Brounhill and Alexander King, in their docquets, while retaining the diocese, both omit the clerical designation.[20] Men from other dioceses are known to have moved east to the capital: one Canongate notary, John Makneill, was a cleric of Glasgow diocese.[21]

Several Edinburgh notaries are recorded in post-Reformation registers of admission to office by the Lords of Council on the abolition of papal authority. These registers included not only old notaries being confirmed in possession but new ones being presented either by Queen Mary or by the Regents. For instance John Lokart, admitted in 1564, was, we learn, aged 63 at that time: he was a priest born in Edinburgh and created in February 1547 by the protonotary apostolic, John Steinston, chanter of Glasgow. Similarly John Logie, advocate, admitted the same year, was unmarried, 37, born in Fife and created in November 1548 by Mr David Henderson, protonotary. Logie can by identified as the St Andrews student of 1550, and his notarial career was evidently interrupted by further studies before his admission as an advocate.[22] The usual notary's training, however, was invariably by apprenticeship. Some men admitted claimed to have the learning that sufficed for notaries and to be well exercised in the art of writing. Some were servants of other notaries or of writers to the signet, or, like Mr Alexander Hervy of Aberdeen, lived in Edinburgh with a lord of session.[23] It is notable that in neither of these books is there a single applicant from the western highlands where nevertheless we know notaries were exercising. The problem of provision of Protestant notaries must have been acute. The 'Irishman', John Torquillie, found in Linlithgow in 1561, was presumably Protestant, though created notary by 'apostolic authority'. His creator was Alexander Gordon, archbishop of Athens, who had been newly recruited by the Reformers and had then as one of his servitors Mr John Craig, apparently the Canongate minister of that name. Though described as an 'Irishman', Torquillie was in fact, it would seem, a Macleod of Lewis or Raasay.[24]

From 1400 on, we see a great increase in the number of notaries, partly because of increasingly rigorous requirements from central government in the proving of titles to property, and thus the need to record sasines: a requirement that in time would make protocol books little more than sasine registers. Foular's book, as his career advanced, became largely a conveyancing record. His legal vocabulary is thus limited by that need, recording regularly the giving and breaking of sasine; conjunct infeftment; hesp and staple and other symbols of transfer; liferent; escheat of goods because of absence in England; cognition and entry on sasine; and constitution of procurators. Less frequent are references to: the books of the official of Lothian (no. 85); 'good neighbourhood' law (96); letters of apprising (97); poinding by burgh officials (97); templar bailie (209); burgh usage in entering heirs (187); precise boundaries (164); franktenement (168); courtesy of Scotland (120); oath de fideli (107); retour of apprising (103); free burgage (221); procuratory of resignation (485); possession pro indiviso (550), regress to annualrent (448); hypothec and obligation (377); fencing of court (306); resignation in the King's presence (362); and letter of division (367). How profound was the average notary's knowledge of the law in these matters is a subject that still remains to be investigated.

For those interested in the economic ties of Edinburgh with places abroad, the harvest from protocol books is fairly meagre. Leaving aside such matters as banking and the issue of letters of credit, we have to recognise that Leith was only one of many Scots North-Sea ports trading overseas then, so that the total shipping in such good sea-going months as the period June-October 1556 was only 19. Of that number 7 ships went to Dieppe, 4 to other French ports; 3 to Danzig; and 5 to Flanders. Mostly they carried Edinburgh merchants.[25] Some crumbs of information about Scots factors in Dieppe are found in Foular and one Frenchman even witnesses an Edinburgh sasine of 1520 (ii, 72). The master mariner of a ship the 'Nicholas' of Dieppe is found bargaining with a citizen in 1508 over the price of wine (Foular i, 426). The executor for a dead Edinburgh trafficker relaxed a decree of arrestment of his cash held abroad, either in the hands of two named Scots who were burgesses of Dieppe or in the hands of Jerome Frescobaldi, the Italian banker (i, 345). A local trader in 1531 is found delivering to a Scottish ship's clerk the documents in a legal process between him and a certain Robert Monchell, that is, both the commissions and articles sent from Dieppe and the depositions given in Edinburgh concerning them, all fortified with the burgh's seal of cause (no. 342 *infra*). In 1505 there is mention of the carved 'Trinity' from La Rochelle; while another dispute concerned the nearby Ile de Rhé (i, 118; iii, 92). Other ports mentioned are Antwerp, because Andrew Barton, the famous sailor, had taken the ship called 'Fasterinsevin', the skipper and crew acknowledging in 1509 that they had been paid in full for captured goods with which the piratical Barton had intromitted and thus they quitclaimed the King (i, 569); and Veere, the staple port, in 1533 gave its backing to the arrest of an Edinburgh merchant's goods there in view of a lawsuit against all Scots traders then under way in Middelburg (498, *infra*); in this deed the reference to 'lib. greit' relates to Scots money as evaluated in respect of the Flemish groat. A burgess of Greifswald in 'Denmark' is mentioned in 1514, 'Denmark' being a loose usage as Greifswald was a Hanse port (ii, 11). The price of a French ship's whole freight of 15 measures of barley was accepted by a Scots buyer at 3 francs, 5 sous, 6 deniers, but the master promised to be prepared to refund the surplus if it should turn out that the Scots factors in Dieppe did not place on it a value 'sa dere' (ii, 77). This shows the importance of the correspondence between these agents overseas and their fellows at home.

Quite a few deeds in these books concern church matters, but at first sight they can be confusing rather than illuminating. However, George Hay's most helpful study on late medieval St Giles, based on a building still extant as, of course, Kirk o' Field and Trinity College are not, demonstrates how a skilful jig-saw reconstruction can show us the lay-out of a medieval burgh church.[26] One or two altars on his accompanying plan, however, are given by the author without orientation, whereas it is fairly certain that in Scotland all altars, like the kirks themselves, were 'oriented', that is, the altars were backed by pillars or small partitions, and faced east. Exaggerated estimates of the number of altars might seem confirmed by the evidence in Foular and other manuscript protocols. But, as Hay shows, we must allow for single altars with multiple dedications. Even so there must have been about forty altars. To Hay's list of chaplainries we must add: one of Saints Simon and Jude (at St Duthac's altar);[27] one of the Holy Spirit at the overcrowded St Salvator's altar;[28] and probably one of St Jerome, for which altar the factor was Quentin Cadzow identifiable as chaplain of St Sebastian's altar in St Giles Kirk.[29] Contemporary piety reasoned that, as the mass was important, there should be altars stationed at every pillar. Nobody had as yet concluded that, because God's Word was important, therefore there should be a pulpit at every pillar, though during the Restoration, a stranger in Edinburgh reported that the collegiate kirk, then turned cathedral, 'is now divided into six sermon houses'.[30] The pillars were important as props for the reredos or altarpiece; after the Reformation, £5 was paid for the 'back' to the altar of St Christopher, the skinner's patron.[31]

There were separate chaplains attached to each dedication,

so that a number might be competing to serve the one altar, and the fashions in dedications changed with fashions in devotion. Moreover, there was occasionally more than one foundation honouring the same saint, for instance, the Virgin Mary's altar was served by chaplains on both the Craigcrook and Ravelston foundations.[32] There was a limit on the number of canonries or prebends however, though it is possible that in course of time their numbers rose slightly. The known prebendaries on the collegiate establishment at the Reformation are worth listing: the provost (James Chisholm), the vicar or curate (James Johnston), Ravelston (Ninian Hamilton), Craigcrook (William Gray), Merchiston (Patrick Douglas), Grotall (Henry Mow), St Andrew (Robert Craig), St Michael (John Symson), St Michael *de Monte Tumba* (Thomas Gray), Holy Cross (James Crawford), St Salvator (Patrick Douglas), St John Baptist (John Beir), St Nicholas (Walter Haliburton), Holy Cross *de Lucano* (George Manderston), St Sebastian (William Johnston). In addition there was a sacrist (Henry Loch), a 'minister chori' or choirmaster (Edward Henryson) and a bedel (unnamed). The 'de Lucano' dedication would be symbolised by a figure or painting representing the famous 'il santo volto' or image of the suffering Christ at Lucca in Italy. But that same altar was a veritable clutter of dedications of which one, that to our Lady of Loreto, introduced in the sixteenth century by the city goldsmiths, can now be recorded at greater length.[33]

The trades had their own altars scattered throughout the church, both in nave and choir. They were St Anne (tailors), St Anthony (taverners and wine-merchants), St Blaise (? wool traders), St Aubert or Hubert (baxters), Sts Crispin and Crispinian (cordiners), St Christopher (skinners, cf., *infra* no.399) St Eloy (hammermen), Sts John Evangelist and Baptist (wrights, etc.), Sts Mark, Philip and James (waulkers, shearers, hatmakers), St Mungo (surgeons, barbers), St Cuthbert (fleshers), Sts Severin and Bartholomew (weavers, glovers), Holy Blood (merchants), our Lady of Loreto (goldsmiths). There was also a confraternity called *pietas pauperum*, not to be confused with that of our Lady of Pity (? candlemakers), an altar which stood to the right of the choir entrance.[34]

The goldsmiths' minute-book is a neglected source in this regard.[35] On 31 January 1526, 'Adame Lies deacon wes in great cummor throw the depairting of the smithes altar, always we got our intent ouir thame before the counsell.... In his tyme the yle was reapperralit and the glassin window wes put up'. From this we can infer that up till then the hammermen or smiths had shared Eloy's altar with them, hence the embarrassment of the goldsmith's deacon, though at this point the hammermen had not yet moved to the Magdalene chapel in Cowgate.[36] The new goldsmiths' altar was to be fixed at the east end of the consistory aisle, hence conflict arose with the official of Lothian whose consistorial court was held there. Under deacon Thomas Rynd, on 15 October 1526, 'the yle wes maid closs with the stawyes and tymber wark and the brasin pillaris wes sent to flanderis for, and the image of our lady of lorret wes brocht home by hym and we had that tyme great stop of the cheising of the yle be the officiall and his cwrttis with great pley, nochtheless we gatt our desyris and he wes deacone twa zeiris and sauld sanct aloj to outred their adois this samyn tyme'. Obviously such litigation was an expensive business. Michael Gilbert was elected in 1529 and it was only in his time that 'the pillaris cam hame and wes put up' (doubtless curtain-supports). The importation of the 'arrass frunt tyle (Arras frontal) of our lady of loreithe' had to await 1532. The hammerman's book implies additional dedications to St Lucy and our Lady at St Eloy's altar, and there were certainly three foundations there, by Nicholas Spethy, John Dalrymple and Elizabeth Wood, the chaplains of which are at no time identical with the smiths' chaplains.[37] Little is known of the Magdalene altar in St Giles itself, except that it was there already in 1468 and that the founder was an Aberdonian: thus it was in 1582 before the local collectors of kirk lands could lay their hands on the deed of foundation (now missing).[38]

The friars in the burgh appear less frequently in sasines, because, apart from the Black Friars or Dominicans, they are less involved in property deals. Hence it is impossible to reconstruct the Franciscan Observant community at Greyfriars and little is known of the small Carmelite friary in Greenside of which their provincial accepted custody from the town in 1525. [39] Many friars, however, were sons of Edinburgh burgesses and a number of small annuals were due to the Black Friars from Edinburgh properties, as their provincial, John Grierson, describes in a letter to the prior of Paris on 6 October 1555. This letter was being delivered by Michael Bassandyne, son of an Edinburgh merchant, James, and brother of the future printer, Thomas. Attacks on friaries had taken place before that date and Grierson painted a gloomy picture of friars who had gone into hiding or who lived with parents and others: in his letter he claimed that the Edinburgh house had been burnt in part and sacked completely. As provincial of his order in Scotland, Grierson resided mostly in this priory, though at the Reformation he was in St Andrews. [40] The single names of friars conscientiously gathered mainly from protocols by W. Moir Bryce can be positively misleading as to the numbers maintained in the Edinburgh priory, and he was mistaken in thinking there were no more than four friars in the Dominican priory at the Reformation as compared with thirteen in 1479, which would indeed have pointed to a calamitous decline.[41] Being a mobile body, seldom attached to any one priory for long, and, having continental contacts, friars were the first to feel Reformation winds of change. In 1509 there were ten, including the prior provincial of the Scottish province but that was before there arose the need to provide friar chaplains to the newly founded convent of Dominican sisters in Edinburgh, the nunnery at Sciennes.[42] Attached to the latter in 1558 appear to be Friars Andrew Layis (an octogenarian in 1564), James Richardson and Thomas Liston.[43] Moir Bryce has been followed by others in accepting from a list of friars pensioners two more Black Friars, namely James Hopper and a Friar Blyth, plus an uncertain quantity called 'Hopparis marrow' of doubtful gender. But a careful reading of the list of 'aucht freiris' Black and Grey who were pensioned shows that to get the number eight we must read 'Blyth, Hopparis marrow' not as two persons but as one, that is Blyth was the *socius* or friar-companion of Hopper. Both these men were in fact not Dominican but Carmelite or White Friars, visitors to Edinburgh from Linlithgow where both appear together early in 1559/60.[44] The correct use of 'marrow' in this context can be paralleled elsewhere.[45] Again, the mention of Grey Friars in this Edinburgh group of pensioners is misleading, unless James Stevenson was one. Nor were all the Black Friars listed either: some may have forgone pensions or gone to live with parents or with sympathetic noblemen. Friar Layis was known at Roslin and two others are found at Castle Semple.[46] The Edinburgh Black Friars of 1560 were eight in number: Bernard Stewart, prior; James Johnston, subprior; followed, probably in order of seniority, by William Simson (formerly of Perth), John Black, John King, William Struthers, John Chalmer and John Chepman.[47] An Edinburgh deed of 1554 concerning this community lists as many as in 1479, including one, possibly a novice, who could not write: friar James Richardson.[48] Prominent Edinburgh friars on the Catholic side are mentioned in literary sources, by Knox, Calderwood and Leslie: Friars John Black, Andrew Abercromby and Andrew Leich notably. John Rough who was with Knox in the castle of St Andrews and who died a Protestant martyr in England, is found as an Edinburgh friar. His name appears in the form 'Rucht', on an occasion when, along with a companion, he was visiting Linlithgow on 11 October 1530.[50]

A recent work gives a useful list of Edinburgh and Leith 'heretics' c 1534 – c 1557, not exploring the possibility of others at earlier dates. Some of these names, such as George Aldjoy and Henry Henryson, schoolmaster, occur in this volume. However, it would be useful and should be possible to establish the family links between the early Scottish Reformers with the aid of Edinburgh protocols. Apart from his birth in the city, no details up to the present were available, for instance, of Alexander Alane, or Alesius, as he was known in Luther's Wittenberg, and his parentage and kin. We knew merely that Alesius was born in Edinburgh, became an Augustinian canon of St Andrews and fled abroad to escape the fate of the first Scots Protestant martyr, Patrick Hamilton. Yet there is a group of Allans in Edinburgh, including Henry Allan abbot of Jedburgh (died 1512) who began life as a chaplain to the canons of Holyrood. Though his father's name does not appear in protocols we do find there Alesius' mother, still alive on 2 May 1514. Her name was Christine Bigholm. She is described in a protocol book entry as 'gud moder' or mother-in-law to a certain James Matheson who quitclaimed her of some items of women's clothing that she held or holds from Matheson's wife, her daughter; for which she is to foster his bairn called Vincent for three years. Presumably therefore the daughter was ill. However, by 13 August 1515 Alane's mother was dead. On that day one of the Edinburgh bailies cognosced and entered Alexander Alane,

son and heir of the late Christine Bigholm, sister and one of
the heirs of Dene John Bigholm, canon of the monastery (Augustinian) of Jedburgh in and to his late mother's part of the whole
and entire tenement of land lying in the said burgh on the
south side of the high street near the collegiate church of St
Giles between Robert Vaus's land on the north and the Cowgate
on the south, by delivery of earth and stone; which done, the
aforesaid Alexander of his own will resigned his portions of
the annual rent and the waste land situated at the end of the
said tenement in the hands of the bailie in favour of his dear-
est sister, Katherine Allane, and this in view of the marriage
to be contracted solemnly between her and Andrew Wood. On
22 December following, Marion Bigholm resigned her fourth part
of this tenement, described as formerly of Mr Richard Robertson,
bounded, it is stated, 'as in the protocol of Alexander Alane of
13 August preceding', in favour of Euphamie Adamson.[51] Another
of the heirs was John Baron, chaplain (Foular, i, 897, cf. 895)
presumably owner of the third part acquired by Euphamie Adamson and her husband (ii, 67). Euphamie again resigned the
lands in favour of Katherine, the sister of Alesius, and her
husband (*infra*, 385). This resignation must have been res-
cinded, as by August 1536, Euphamie Adamson, now a widow,
obliged herself to resign the same lands to a neighbour as she
could not pay the annual rents with which they were burden-
ed.[52] It is noteworthy that the Barons and Adamsons of a later
generation were contacts of Knox in his pre-Reformation visits
to Edinburgh.

At the date when Alesius was being served heir of his
mother, he was still an undergraduate at the university of St
Andrews in the college of St Leonard, and soon to become a
canon of St Andrews. Marion Bigholm, his aunt, was the wife
of James Richardson, near kin if not father to Robert Richardson, himself an Augustinian canon of Cambuskenneth, who was
born about 1491. After James Richardson's death about 1502,
Marion married Nichol Macbrair, alderman of Dumfries, and,
of course, he is a link with another associate of John Knox,
an exile at the time in Frankfurt, John Macbrair.[53] The latter,
a former monk of Glenluce, joined the Reformers a decade and
more after Alesius.

In a passage seldom adverted to, the historian, Calderwood speaks of secret sympathisers with the Reformation in Edinburgh in 1539. Whether these were all outright Lutherans could
be debated, but he refers to 'manie profesors ... houbeit
secreit ... as Sibilla Lindsay, spous to Johne Fouler....'
Sibilla, of course, was spouse, not to the notary, but to the
other John Foular, for she appears in a 'good neighbourhood'
protest of 1541 about the bounds of her husband's lands being
infringed.[54] She obviously ties up with Patrick Lindsay, goldsmith, and his brother 'frier Alexander, a great mathematician
and maker of horologes'. both of whom Calderwood names also
as sympathisers with reformation. Friar Alexander is obviously
the Black Friar of 1537 whom we find in Aberdeen mending the
town 'knok'.[55] Other names given by Calderwood include John
Maine, merchant (*infra*, 511) and Francis Aikman, apothecary

(434). The Maine or Mayne family is worth especial attention. Katherine, daughter of Jasper Mayne, notary and his wife, Alison Rouch or Rough, kinswoman of John, the Reformer, are present in this volume (see *infra*, 92, 353-4). Katherine Mayne later took refuge in England and married Alesius. She was the widow of Alexander Cant and we find that her former property in Peebles Wynd was, with the express consent of Alesius, made over to her daughter, Elizabeth Cant, conjointly with her goldsmith husband, Edward Bassandyne.[56] Alesius is then described as rector of the university in Meissen (i.e. Leipzig) and his authorisation was given under that city's common seal.

Besides being the age of the first Scots Reformers, this century is also that of the Renaissance. The name of our earliest Renaissance Latin poet, James Foulis, recurs in several protocols, as also that of our earliest printer, Walter Chepman. Contrary to belief, Chapman came from the west and was initially a cleric, notary of Glasgow diocese, who married in Edinburgh. It may have been the present notary's father, John Foular (dead by 1504) who was importing books from Thomas Richard in Rouen, for which firm Ursin Monyer was agent in Edinburgh. Ursin Monyer is better known to British bibliographers as an early bookseller in York and it is confidently asserted that he was born there. The designation 'Frenchman', however, (*Foular*, i, 67) would rule that possibility out. Another of our Latin poets was Adam Otterburn, himself a notary, but his hexameters have not survived. Buchanan himself praised his work but with some overtones of implied mockery. There was at least one Greek speaker in town, the exiled bishop of Elphin, a native of Athens.[57] John Scot, the printer, is not identifiable in Foular's protocols, though a few facts are recorded by another Edinburgh notary. He was stationed in the city from 1539-1544 near Borthwick's Close to the north of the Cowgate, and certainly his wife, Margaret Leis, occupied a house there in 1527. This might be identical with one that Scot was granted in 1539 on the death of the previous owner, and that Scot held later in conjunct fee with Margaret. It is good to know, with the aid of such examples, that the faces behind these transactions were not just mere names on a page.[58]

In view of the notaries' claim to universal jurisdiction, it can only have been in big cities that their linguistic abilities were ever tested. In Scotland relations with France were still important in August 1548, when an Edinburgh notary who claimed to understand French was approached by two French merchants engaged with the French forces in Scotland. Their mission was to report an incident of three days before when a quarrel broke out in a private house between a Frenchman from Lyons called Schane and Cargyllyng, a Breton, from 'Leschevenyng' (? Lesneven) in the diocese of St Pol, over money owed. The Breton lifted a lighted candle from the table and threw it: it hit instead the landlord, Robert Melville. In the darkness Cargyllyng then slipped out, returning with a Jedwart staff or javelin, exclaiming probably 'Qui m'en veut?' (The notary took it to be, 'Quis me vult?') Schane responded

INTRODUCTION

by unsheathing sword and dagger to strike the Breton, inflicting instead a mortal blow on another Frenchman, Jean Barron, interposing himself between the combatants. Subsequently suspicion fell on the host, whose name was cleared by witnesses including a French skipper, an Orleans merchant and a French-speaking Scots priest. With his last breath, the victim had relieved the landlord of all responsibility and also forgiven the two men of war for taking his life, and the matter may have rested there.[59] Passing over an Avignon creditor claiming some Scottish debts and a Provencal's will, we turn to the financial risks of foreign trade, evidenced in a transaction concerning Penmarch, then a rival to Nantes, now an insignificant fishing port in Brittany. In March 1472, Jean Gilbert, agent for the ship 'Maria' from Penmarch, accepted three Dumbarton burgesses as customary pledges for the cost of some red and white wine purchased by Alexander Cunningham, burgess of Irvine. The dangers of shipwreck were greater at the exposed Buchan Ness; we learn that the emperor of Russia lost a fortune when an English ship, the 'Edward Bonaventure', ran into trouble there on a stormy November day in 1556. The Russian envoy had appointed English proxies to recover the goods, one of the Englishmen acting as his interpreter to the Edinburgh notary.[60] Again in 1551, the uncertain national status of Henry Courtes as a 'German or Dane' may have arisen from language problems. Courtes appointed some Edinburgh lawyers as his procurators to recover 400 crowns of the sun, Scots, from Robert Barrie, skipper of the 'Matho'. Barrie was alleged to have robbed him of certain jars of wine and aquavita belonging to George and Henry Schrever, 'Danes', inhabitants, however, of Hamburg which might account for the linguistic confusion.[61]

Scots abroad figure occasionally in transactions. Oswald Porteous wrote home from Regensburg in Germany to his native Peebles. John Darg, 'induellar in the toun of danskyne' was the son of a Haddington burgess and a witness was Robert Liell, vicar in Danzig. In 1556 we learn that David Logan had died in Poland, leaving his brother John in Restalrig his sole heir; a Scots merchant in Poland, however, John Langlands, bought the right to the inheritance from Logan's brother for certain unspecified sums. A different type of Scot abroad was the student, and it is perhaps as such that Robert Stewart, commendator of Holyrood, is found at Orleans on 14 July 1551, calling on a foreign notary's services; this notary was Jean Damyte who also returned to Scotland.[62] The existence of Italian merchants in Edinburgh is sufficiently attested by the altar in St Giles dedicated to the holy rood ('il santo volto') of Lucca, but Italian domestic fashion was not neglected either, as we find in January 1545 when an Edinburgh goldsmith received from Mr Alexander Mauchan two pieces of silver of $17\frac{1}{2}$ ounces, with the obligation of making the same 'in new forme of Italie callit Italiane cowpis ingravit in the bak syde haldelie'.[63]

The quirks of a particular age with which social historians are fascinated seldom come to light in state documents, but here too protocols can be revealing. Changing fashions in architecture seem to be indicated when in August 1531 an

Edinburgh burgess specifies that a workman must 'mak ane squair wyndo in the south part of his nether hall quhar the round oo is now'. A fashionable word is found in a deed at Samuelston, to which Knox as his master was witness, where the notary referred to his pupil as an 'elegant junior'.64 Medieval churches especially in burghs, were often flooded with altars, sometimes, as we saw, with multiple dedications, and with fashions not only in the latter but in their very siting. It is of interest then that the site of St Blaise's altar in St John's kirk, Perth, should have been 'next to the choir'. The parish altar did not always have the same dedication as that of the church; for instance we hear of, 'St Ninian's altar in the cathedral church of Dunblane which is called the parish altar'.65 Kirk burial was a continuous bone of contention in both pre-Reformation and post-Reformation days. For instance, in 1557 Andrew Alexander wished to bury his father in a place awkwardly defined as the 'southern pedestal' (crepido) of his uncle's grave in the porch of the collegiate kirk of Peebles, right in mid-threshold. Leave was requested at the funeral, too late, one would think, for decent refusal, but it was made clear that it was not to be a precedent. In Peebles, too, the honest minor (infans), William Peblis of Cruxton, explained how in childhood he studied under his teacher, David Crichton, when his uncle Adam, ever since a fugitive from justice, had accidentally killed John Brounton in Hallyards, but that he, the boy, then as now was an innocent party. Crichton must himself have been a mere 19 at the time, and added notarial duties to his schoolmastering.66 Another person pledged to the paths of righteousness, Robert Schurtuss, younger, of Haddington, promised his elders in return for an honest bribe ('a stane of lint') 'neuer to play at dyice or cartis in na maner of place weder by hand or pak with no man quhill this day tuelfmonth'.67 The notary's specialisation in composing latterwills might lead to his presence at a moment of truth, as at the confession of Robert Wardlaw's impersonation of his spouse at the gallows foot on the Boroughmuir, Edinburgh. Wardlaw confessed that he arranged it at the time of a sasine to Clement Litill of land in the mealmarket on behalf of someone else's spouse, whom he persuaded 'till pass and cleid hir till similitud of his awne wife', who herself could not be persuaded to participate, and admitted at the end that nobody knew of the deceit but himself. Another notary witnessed a legal act of quite a different nature at sea in the Kyles of Bute on 20 October, 1514, when the serjeant of the Lord High Admiral was declared to have 'fenced' a Breton ship whose master was a certain Jacob Evan with the command that goods belonging to the Glasgow merchants should remain with the master till the Glaswegians finally met their debts.68

Notaries as scribes of literary material need separate investigation, but it was not unknown for them to be in the literary market themselves. After the evidence adduced above and in 'The early Scottish notary', there is no cause for hesitating to believe that a notary could act in the same town as schoolmaster and poet, and even be a licentiate in decreets, despite the scepticism of certain biographers of Robert Henryson. Another poet, Richard Holland, was successively an imperial notary of Caithness, Moray and Orkney dioceses, and was also described as parson of Abriachan (or Bona) and canon of Orkney. His pro-Douglas partisanship is well-known, but nobody has noted that it even invaded his Latin cross sign manual, flanked as it was with Douglas 'heart' emblems.[69] A minor poet of the sixteenth century was John Rolland, often described as 'of Dalkeith' where he spent his latter days under the patronage of the earl of Morton, publishing his first work during his Regency. Rolland was also a priest-notary and some evidence of his activity as such has been garnered by his editors. Hitherto, however, his place and date of birth have remained undiscovered. But Rolland was born in 1504 or thereabouts in Ayr, 'alleluia' on his sign manual being a pun on 'Alloway'. His father was a Hugh Rolland. Created notary in 1528 by John Bull, who had delegated power to make 32 notaries, he soon left the Ayr area, practising at Melrose and Dalkeith among other places; at the former place his instrument of creation and first protocol book were burnt 'in robene wallace hous' and at the latter place another was destroyed in 1548. He had land from the earl of Morton in Dalkeith in 1554, by which date he was parson of Ettletown, and as such owned a Nuremberg Chronicle now at Glamis. He too was a Douglas partisan. A Douglas 'heart' symbol heads the monogram in his sign manual.[70]

Testaments often give something of the flavour of the times, as does that of August 1558 of William Tunno of Manor, who assured the notary that he was much troubled by the devil and his angels, but that like Lazarus he hoped soon to be received to Abraham's bosom: an intimate brief shot of the last battle of his soul with death. By contrast the household of James Syme, 'pottinger' or apothecary of Edinburgh, was plainly Protestant. Syme's will, first drawn up on 6 March 1559, was recited on 19 March in the presence of David Forest 'generall' (that is, master of the mint). Syme left his soul to God and his body to be buried 'at my christeane bretheris will as ane christeane man'. His brother, Mr Alexander Syme, a well-known lawyer, was to be at hand to advise his widow and children. He left £20 to the 'poor brether' and £10 to William Harlaw (minister).[71]

John Carswell, who became the first superintendent of Argyll, began his career as a notary in close association with Donald Dubh, Lord of the Isles, who died in Ireland at Drogheda during a treasonable campaign in support of the earl of Lennox, 'secund persoun' of the realm, on the side of Henry VIII against Governor Arran. As one of two notaries he was present at the council of the Isles at Ellencarne, Eigg, which took that decision, in July 1554. He was also present in the following August in the Greyfriars church, Carrickfergus, in Ireland, when the oath supporting Henry's purposes was taken by the commissioners of Lennox, the same who referred to Henry as the church's 'supreme hed', and all present concurred in Henry's plan for a Rough Wooing between the young Mary, Queen of Scots, and Prince Edward. As clerk of the diocese of the Isles, John Carswell certified the commission in the 'second year of our princess' (*nostre principis anno secundo*).[72] A final document concerns no less a person than John Knox in his role as arbiter between two lay patrons. On 21 October 1561, as minister of Edinburgh, Knox approached the notary in connection with a dispute over the lands of Abernethy along with patronage rights of the collegiate kirk and its annexed kirks, a dispute between George Douglas, illegitimate son of the late earl of Angus, and the young heir and present earl, Archibald. 'In hoip of aggreance to haf bene dressit' between the earl and his tutors and George, the latter had handed over to Knox a letter of renunciation, a letter he now demanded back. The First Book of Discipline had envisaged abolition of lay patronage; but, despite that, Knox claimed to have 'bestowit his faithfull labouris besyde the travellis tane be diuerss noblemen' to bring about a settlement, adding that various reasonable offers made by them had been turned down and that the newest offer was more reasonable 'nor be belevis'. Reluctantly therefore Knox handed back the renunciation in the study of James McGill, clerk register, and in the presence of Mr George Hay, then vicar of Eddleston.[73] Even so, however we interpret this incident, it is still clear that Edinburgh's religious situation had already changed somewhat since the days of John Foular, notary.

NOTES

1. ECA, 'Cartulary' of St Giles, fos 3v–11v (Foular), 13 (Strathauchin); 12v (17 prebendaries signed).

2. SRO, Haddington Burgh Records, PB James Meldrum (B30/1/1), passim.

3. *Reg. Sancti Egidii*, 216.

4. SRO, Register House Calendar of Charters, RH6/973a.

5. *ALHT*, ii, 68.

6. *Edin. Burgesses*, 191.

7. D. Calderwood, *The History of the Kirk of Scotland*, ed. T. Thomson (Wodrow Society, 1842–49,) i, 134, SRO, EBR, PB Alexander King (B22/1/15), ii, fo 163.

8. SRO, EBR, PB Vincent Strathauchin (B22/1/7), iii, fo 37v.

9. *Edin. Burgesses*, 191.

10. SRO, EBR, PB Alex King (B22/1/14, i, fo 16; *RMS*, iii, 897, 1982.

11. PB King, *ibid*.

12. *RSS*, iv, 1156.

13. *Ibid*., iv, 1219, 2099; SRO, Register of Acts and Decreets (CS7/4), iv, fo 345. The royal officer was Neil Laing.

14. *Acta Facultatis Artium Universitatis Sanctiandree* (SHS and St Andrews University Publications, Edinburgh 1964), ed. A.I. Dunlop, ii, 39.

15. PB King (B22/1/18), v, fo 53v.

16. *Reg. Sancti Egidii*, 255.

17. J. Durkan, 'The early Scottish notary', in *The Renaissance and Reformation in Scotland: Essays in honour of Gordon Donaldson* (Edinburgh 1983), edd. I.B. Cowan and D. Shaw, 22–40.

18. ECA, Bundle of miscellaneous early writs, no 10.

19. SRO, PB Henry Strathauchin (B22/1/9), flyleaf facing fo 1. The meaning is that she should marry by her own father's consent and also by the counsel of Henry Strathauchin, father of Mr Thomas, who survived him.

20 ECA Bundle of misc. early writs, nos 18–20, 27.

21 Ibid., no 26.

22 Register of Admissions of Notaries (NP2/1), fos 196v, 198; *The Faculty of Advocates in Scotland* (SRS, 1944) ed. F.J. Grant, 126.

23 SRO, NP2/1, fo 215.

24 *Protocol Book of Nicol Thounis, 1559-1564* (SRS, 1927), no 46.

25 M. Wood, 'The domestic affairs of the burgh', *BOEC*, xv, 15–16. I have not traced the source of this statement, but some records of foreign shipping appear in ECA, Council Register, ii (1151–58), mentioning Dieppe, Bordeaux, Koenigsberg, Flanders and 'Danskyne' (the last a word sometimes used loosely for Baltic ports). Total shipping for various years is given in D. Robertson and M. Wood, *Castle and Town* (Edinburgh, 1928), 279.

26 G. Hay, 'The late medieval developement of the High Kirk of St Giles, Edinburgh', *PSAS*, cvii (1975–6), 240–60.

27 PB Alex King, v, no 189.

28 SRO, PB Edward Dickson (Np1/5B), 167 (the MS is paged).

29 *PB Foular*, iii, 286, 234.

30 P.H. Brown, *Early Travellers in Scotland* (Edinburgh,1891),83.

31 W. Angus, 'The incorporated trades of the Skinners of Edinburgh', *BOEC*, vi, 78.

32 RMS, ii, 887; *CPL*, vii, 136. The SRO Craigcruik writs only begin in 1540 (GD252).

33 The list of prebendaries is compiled from various sources, including SRO, Books of Assumption (E48/1/2), ii, ECA, 'Cartulary' of St Giles and protocol book references.

34 SRO, EBR, PB Andrew Brounhill (B22/1/12), ii, fo 156v.

35 Details of the Loreto altar come from the goldsmiths' minute book in SRO, GD1/482/1, fo 7. The entries are copies, slightly anglicised, made in the 17th century.

36 Cowan and Easson, 176.

37 J. Smith, *The Hammermen of Edinburgh and their altar in St Giles Church* (Edinburgh, 1906), 47, 85 etc. Smith has noted 8d paid for a copy of 'ane bill of John Fular', i,e, our notary (*ibid*., 80). The editor's transcripts need

to be checked with the original in ECA. For Dalrymple's foundation, *Reg Sancti Egidii*, 120; Spethy's, PB V. Strathauchin, fo 1; Elizabeth Wood's, J.C. Lees, *St Giles, Edinburgh* (Edinburgh, 1889), 341.

38 *REG*, ii, 416; Alexander Knollis, burgess of Aberdeen had patronage in 1537, London, Public Record Office, PRO, 31/9/33, 60 (paged); ECA, Accounts of Collectors of Kirk Land, i, under 13 March 1581/2 (unfoliated).

39 Cowan and Easson, 136; *PB Foular*, iii, 641.

40 My note, 'The Dominicans at the Reformation', *Innes Review*, ix, 216–7, attempted to re-date this letter, now, I believe, mistakenly; *Register of the minister, elders and deacons of the Christian congregation of St Andrews*, ed. D.M. Fleming, (SHS, 1890), 16–8.

41 For 1479 members, J. Anderson, *Calendar of the Laing Carters* (Edinburgh, 1899), 177; Cowan and Easson, 118.

42 SRO, Elibank writs, GD32/21/14; one friar in this list of Black Friars appears also in *PB Foular*, i, 453, without indication of order.

43 SRO, Haddington Burgh Recs., PB Thomas Stevin (B30/1/5), fo 205v.

44 W. Moir Bryce, *The Black Friars of Edinburgh* (Edinburgh 1911) 65; *Accounts of the Collectors of Thirds of Benefices, 1561-72* (SHS, 1949), ed. G. Donaldson, 153 and note; *Laing Charters*, 715.

45 *Aberdeen Recs.*, i, 189; compare Andrew Leich, subprior, and Henry Smith, his *confrater* in October 1553, SRO, EBR Canongate, PB John Makneill, iii (B22/22/23), fo 112.

46 *Extracta e variis cronicis Scocie* (Abbotsford Club, 1842), ed. W.B.D.D. Turnbull, 249, among the 'notanda Rossliniana.' *Essays on the Scottish Reformation*, ed. D. McRoberts (Glasgow, 1962), 228 note.

47 SRO, Elibank writs, GD 32/8/11–12; R. Milne, *The Blackfriars of Perth* (Edinburgh, 1893), 64.

48 ECA, Inventory of Documents re Church Lands no 8, & August 1554 lists: Andrew Abercromby prior, Andrew Leich subprior, James Skene, Mark Hamilton, John Rolly, Andrew Philip, Henry Smith, John King, John Chalmers, Allan Peter, George Penny, William Logan, John Chepman, James Richardson. Mobility is shown by the presence of 3 of these at Ayr in 1557, *Charters of the Friars Preachers of Ayr* (Edinburgh, 1881), 98.

49 *Protocol Books of Dominus Thomas Johnsoun* (SRS, 1926), no 17.

50 M. Lynch, *Edinburgh and the Reformation* (Edinburgh, 1981), 276–80.

51 SRO, PB Henry Strathauchin (B22/1/9), fos 13, 45, 50.

52 *Edin. Recs.*, ii, 77–8.

53 SRO, Acta Dominorum Concilii (C55/14), fo 56. On April 1513, Francis Towris, in the name of his wife Jonet Richardson and Marion Bigholm, wife of McBrair, granted the receipt of a box containing 300 merks belonging partly to him as husband of Jonet and partly to Marion, SRO, EBR, PB V. Strathauchin, i, fo 62. For Robert Richardson and Alesius, see my 'Scottish "evangelicals" in the patronage of Thomas Cromwell', *RSCHS*, xxi, 134–9.

54 Above, note 7; PB V. Strathauchin, iii, 140v.

55 P.J. Anderson, *Aberdeen Friars: Red, Black, White, Grey* (Aberdeen, 1909), 81.

56 *RSS*, ii, 1782, 2009; SRO EBR, PB Alexander Guthrie senior (B22/1/23), fo 3v: J.T. McNeill, 'Alexander Alesius, Scottish Lutheran, 1500–65', *Archiv für Reformationgeschichte*, lv (1964) 179.

57 J.A. Inglis, *Sir Adam Otterburn of Redhall, King's Advocate* (Glasgow, 1935) cites the poem; D. McRoberts, 'The Greek bishop of Dromore', *Innes Review*, xxviii, 22–38.

58 SRO. EBR, PB Brounhill, i, fos 20v (M. Leis), 105, 121, 123v; PB V. Strathauchin, iii, fo 103.

59 SRO, EBR, PB John Stevinson (B22/1/13), fo 16, of which there is a transcript not quite accurate (e.g. 'habitum' for 'halitum') in *Edin. Recs.*, ii, 137–40.

60 SRO, PB Thomas Kene (NP1/2A), fos 81v–82v (Avignon); PB James Harlaw (NP1/12), fo 22 (will); NLS, Advocates MS, 19.2.23 is PB John Kerd, fo 9v (Penmarch); *Antiquities of Aberdeen and Banff, Illustrations* (Spalding Club, 1848–69), iv, 108–9 for the envoy, who as 'ambassador of Muscovia' was regaled with a council banquet, *Edin. Recs.*, the *Burgh Accounts*, i, 203.

61 PB Harlaw, fo 84v (Barrie was a Dumbarton merchant).

62 SRO PB John Scott (B58/1/5), fo 108v; PB Alexander Symson (B30/1/4), iii, fo 69 (Darg); PB Harlaw, fo 123 (Logan); NLS, Acc. 3142, Wigtown Papers, vol. i, no 241.

63 PB Harlaw, fos 95v, 119. Of Italians in Edinburgh at the

JOHN FOULAR xxv

time only Timotheo Cagnioli can be identified as from Lucca.

64 *Infra*, fo 117; PB Symson iii, fo 33.

65 SRO PB Robert Lauson (NP1/96), fo 67v. SRO, Stirling Burgh Recs., Old Charters, Protocols etc 1544-1590, fo 47v.

66 PB John Scott, fos 117v, 148; Admissions of Notaries (NP2/1), fo 47.

67 PB Alexander Symson, iii, fo 12v.

68 PB V. Strathauchin, i, no. 390; NLS, Old Dumbartonshire Protocols in Adv. MS, 19.2.23, fo 27.

69 For example, D. Gray, *Robert Henryson* (Leiden,1979), 3. Master Robert Henryson is notary in Adv. MS, 34.1.3A (Dunfermline Register), fos 98 (twice),99. A long list of schoolmaster-notaries could be drawn up (Andrew McCormel, John Kendal, Gavin Ross, all in Ayr; George Lorn, in Glasgow; Matthew Forsyth in Dumbarton, are a few examples). Holland's sign manual is reproduced in D. Laing *Adversaria* (Bannatyne Club, 1867), 12-15 and for his Douglas partisanship, M. Stewart, 'Holland's "Howlat" and the fall of the Livingstons', *Innes Review*, xxvi, 67-79.

70 Holland's sign manual is illustrated in Laing, *Adversaria*, 16. See also *PB Gavin Ros* (SRS, 1907), nos 941-2; SRO PB Thomas Stevin (B30/1/50), fo 88 (Ettletown reference); for book, Earl of Strathmore papers at Glamis in National Reg. Archives Scotland, 0918. He was witness at Dryburgh with John Bull who made him notary, *Liber S. Marie de Dryburgh* (Bannatyne Club, 1847) page xxii, and his biographical details are in NP2/1 (Admissions) fo 164.

71 PB John Scott, fos 131v-114; SRO, PB James Nicolson (NP1/10), fo 67.

72 *Letters and Papers Foreign and Domestic, Henry VIII* (London 1894—), xx (part 1), no 1298 and (part 2), no 42: A. and A. Macdonald, *The Clan Donald* (Inverness, 1896), i, 371-386; D.E. Meek and J. Kirk, 'John Carswell, Superintendent of Argyll: a reassessment', *RSCHS*, xix, 1-22.

73 PB James Nicolson, fo 79v.

ABBREVIATIONS

Aberdeen Recs.	Extracts from the Council Register of the Burgh of Aberdeen, 1398-1570 (Aberdeen Spalding Club, 1844)
ALHT	Accounts of the Lord High Treasurer of Scotland, edd. T. Dickson et al.(Edinburgh, 1877—)
BOEC	The Book of the Old Edinburgh Club (Edinburgh, 1908—)
CPL	Calendar of entries in the Papal Registers, Letters, edd. W.H. Bliss et al. (London, 1893—)
Edin. Burgesses	Roll of Edinburgh Burgesses and Guild Brethren 1406-1700, ed. C.B.B. Watson (Edinburgh SRS, 1929)
EBR	Edinburgh Burgh Records
Edin. Recs.	Extracts from the Records of the Burgh of Edinburgh, 1403-1589, ed. J.D. Marwick (Scottish Burgh Records Society, 1869-1892)
Edin.Recs.,Accounts	Edinburgh Records: The Burgh Accounts, ed. R. Adam, 2 vols. (Edinburgh, 1899)
Laing Charters	Calendar of the Laing Charters, ed. J. Anderson (Edinburgh, 1899)
NLS	National Library of Scotland
PB	Protocol Book
PSAS	Proceedings of the Society of Antiquaries of Scotland (Edinburgh, 1851—)
REG	Registrum Episcopatus Glasguensis, 2 vols. (Bannatyne and Maitland Clubs, 1843)
Reg. Sanct Egidii	Registrum cartarum ecclesie Sancti Egidii de Edinburgh: A series of charters and original documents connected with the church of St Giles, Edinburgh (Bannatyne Club, 1859)

RMS	*Registrum Magni Sigilli Regum Scotorum: The Register of the Great Seal of Scotland,* edd. T. Thomson *et al.* (Edinburgh 1882—)
RSCHS	*Records of the Scottish Church History Society*
RSS	*Registrum Secreti Sigilli Regum Scotorum: The Register of the Privy Seal of Scotland,* edd. M. Livingstone *et al.* (Edinburgh 1908–)
SRO	Scottish Record Office, Edinburgh
SRS	Scottish Record Society
Yester Writs	*Calendar of Writs preserved at Yester House, 1166–1625,* edd. C.C. Harvey and J. Macleod (SRS, 1930)

1. Resignation by John Cannon, nephew and heir of the late Gilbert Cannon, in favour of James Ur, burgess of Edinburgh, of his land now occupied by James Gilry, lying in the burgh on the north side of the High Street, within a tenement of the late Alexander Lauder of Blyth, knight, between the land of the late James Ross on the south and a waste land of the said Alexander Lauder on the north, of all terms preceding, from the time of the death of the late Jonet Piper, conjunct-fiar thereof, up to the date of the present instrument. The said John Cannon grants and transfers from himself, his heirs and assignees, all right and title in favour of James Ur and his heirs, with full power to receive and apply to his own use all fermes and profits therefrom for all terms past, to grant discharges on receipts and, if need be, to convene in judgement, sue, prosecute and defend all interested parties as the course of law requires: and generally to do whatever is customary for cessioners and assignees to do. Moreover he promised to hold firm and stable whatever the cessioners, etc., were bound to do in the premises, in his name and in their own interest, and this under hypothec and obligation of all his goods present and future. Witnesses, William Adamsone, John Marjoribanks, John..... ..., ...Ure, James Stevinstoune, Thomas Arnot and Hugh Wallas, serjeant. 1529/30 Feb. 15.

2. 1528 April 18. William Rynde, one of the bailies of Edinburgh, passed to a tenement of land of the late Patrick Richartson, lying in the said burgh, on the south side of the High Street thereof, between a land of the late Patrick Scot on the east, and a land of John Cant on the west; and there James Home burgess of the said burgh, with consent and assent of Elizabeth Cokburne his spouse, surrendered and purely and simply resigned by delivery of earth and stone, in the hands of the said bailie, all and whole his land and mansion, built and waste, with pertinents, lying within the said tenement, on either side of the close thereof, between a land of the said Patrick Scot on the east, and the lands of the said John Cant and Maurice Coupland on the west, a land of the said Maurice on the south, and a land of the late John Broune, now pertaining to Clement Litill, on the north: which done, the said William Rynde, bailie, gave heritable sasine and conjunct-infeftment of the said land and mansion, by delivery of earth and stone, to a prudent man, James Cokburne, and Marion Creichton his spouse, the longer living of both, and the heirs lawfully procreated or to be pro-

created, between them; whom failing, to the lawful and nearest heirs of the said James Cokburne whomsoever. Moreover, in a full and open court held before the said bailie, upon the ground of the said mansion, the foresaid Elizabeth Cokburne, in the absence of the said James Home, her husband, led not by force or fear, nor fallen into error, but of her own free will, as she affirmed, assented and consented to the doing of all and sundry before written, and gave her bodily oath, the holy scriptures of God touched, not to revoke in time to come. Witnesses, James Johnston, Robert Mason, William Cokburne, John Johnston and Thomas Arnot, Serjeants.

3. 1528 April 22. Sasine on resignation by James Forstar, son and heir of the late Philip Forstar, burgess, given by William Lauder, bailie, to Master Adam Ottirburne of Auldhame, attorney and in name of Archibald Douglas, Lord of Kilspyndie, Treasurer of our Sovereign Lord the King, and Isobel Hoppar, spouse of the said Archibald, of a land and mansion of the said late Philip Forstar, lying on the south side of the High Street, near the Nether Bow, between a land of the late Andrew Mowbray on the north, and another land or yard of the said Andrew on the south, the lands of William Lauder and Robert Tod on the east, and a certain transe of a tenement on the west. Witnesses, David Kincaid, James Kincaid, Edward Kincaid, William Forous, Sirs William Broune David Rannyk and Robert Liddaill, chaplains, Symon Richartson, and Patrick Lithqw, serjeant.
The same day, etc., Edward Kincaid declared and alleged, that the foresaid land and mansion, built and waste, pertains to him in liferent, and protested, that the sasine thereof, given by William Lauder, bailie, after resignation thereof by the said James Forstar, to Master Adam Ottirburne, attorney of Archibald Douglas and Isobel Hoppar, his spouse, hurt not him in his liferent thereof, and for remeid of law when and where it effeiris, and asked instruments.

4. 1528 April 23. Sasine on resignation by James Uddart, with consent of Cristiane Towris his spouse, and of Robert Gray, assignee of the late William Bell, in favour of Sir John Lauson, chaplain, in name of the Church, and his successors in office, chaplains of the service founded by John Glen at the altar of Saint Salvator, situated in the foresaid church of Saint Giles, of an annual-rent of 13s.4d., out of a land of the late Alexander Gray, lying on the south side of the High Street and Tolbooth of Edinburgh, between the cemetery of the collegiate church of Saint Giles on the east, a land of the late John Barcar on the north, and the lands of the late John Best on the south and west: which annual-rent the said James Uddart and his spouse confess is now redeemed from them by the said Robert Gray. Witnesses, Robert Bruce, Sirs Alexander Cùnynghame and Thomas Paterson, chaplains, William Cokburne, William Nesbet and Patrick Linlithqw, serjeants. William Rynde is bailie.

5. 1528 May 8. Sasine to Alexander Bruse, son of the late John Bruse, burgess, on resignation in his favour by Jonet Adamson, relict of the said John, of her conjunct-fee, and on his cog-

nition by John Mauchane, bailie, as heir of his said father, of the said late John Bruse's land or tenement on the south side of the High Street, between a land of the late Edward Bonkle on the east, and a land of the late Walter Blaklok on the west, a land of Patrick Baroun, now pertaining to the heirs of the late William Ker, on the south, and the public king's highway on the north: Reserving the liferent of the said land or tenement, to the said Jonet. Witnesses, Vincent Strathauchin, notary public, Sir George Roger, chaplain, William Uddart, William Farquhar, Robert Law, James Gilry, and Hugh Wallas, serjeant.

6. 1528 May 12. Sasine on resignation by John Hog, in favour of William Huntroddis, burgess, and Cristiane Cossar his spouse, of the said John's land or tenement, lying beyond the Bow of "the most blessed virgin Mary", west side the High Street thereof between a land of James Pacok on the south, and the lands of the said James Pacok and Walter Chapman on the north, the cemetery of the church of the Friars Preachers on the west, and the king's common way on the east. Witnesses, Sir William Gothrason, Robert Lyndesay, Adam Lyndesay, William Tod, James Galloway, and David Purves, serjeant. William Lauder is bailie.

7. 1528 May 15. William Rynde, bailie, passed to a certain fore-land and back-land of the late William Cranston of Rathobyris, lying on the north side of the High Street, between a land of the late John Tyndaill, now pertaining to George Gude, on the east, and a land of the late Walter Young on the west, the land of Patrick Creichtonn of Kynglassy, and le penteis on the east side of the trause thereof, on the north, and the king's common way on the south; and there Robert Douglas of Pomfra-stoun, procurator and in name of Elizabeth Cranston, daughter and one of the heirs of the late William Cranston of Rathobyris, whose procuratory is under the sign and subscription manual of Sir William Kempioun, notary public, resigned in the hands of the bailie the foresaid fore-land and backland: The said bailie passed also to a land or tenement of the late John Tweedy, on the north side of the High Street, between a land of the late John Dun, now pertaining to the heirs of the late Alexander Lauder of Blyth, knight, on the east, and a land of the late Alexander Bonkill on the west; and there the said Robert Douglas, procurator and in name of the said Elizabeth Cranston, resigned her half of an annual-rent of 6 merks out of the foresaid land or tenement, in the hands of the said William Rynde, who, as bailie, gave heritable sasine and conjunct-infeftment of the said Elizabeth Cranston's half of the foresaid fore-land and back-land; and also of her half of the said annual-rent of 6 merks, to Mungo Tennent, burgess, and Marion Harlaubankis, his spouse. Witnesses Mungo Stevinson, Sirs Patrick Powok and John Young, chaplains, James Douglas, Robert Dennun, James Balgarvy and David Purves, serjeant.

8. 1528 May 16. Sasine on resignation by Geills Cranston, daughter and one of the heirs of the late William Cranston, with consent of Edward Affleck her spouse, in favour of Mungo Tennent, burgess, and Marion Harlaubankis his spouse, of the said Geills's

half of a fore-land and back-land of the late William Cranston of Rathobyris, lying on the north side of the High Street, and bounded as described in the preceding sasine. With court and the oath of the said Geills not to revoke in time to come. Witnesses, Thomas Weir, Mungo Stevinson, Robert Douglas of Pomfraston, Robert Dennun, William How, Thomas Russall, James Uddart, and David Purves, serjeant.

9. 1528 May 16. Sasine on resignation by Alexander Towris, brother and heir of the late Andrew Towris of Moshouschelis, in favour of James Uddart and Cristiane Towris his spouse, of an annual-rent of 40s., out of a land of the late William Ferry, on the south side of the High Street, in the vennel of Peebles Wynd, on the east side of the trause thereof, between a land of the blessed Mary Magdalen on the north, and the Cowgate on the south: Also of an annual-rent of 10s., out of a land of the late William Howison, now pertaining to the prebendaries of the Kirk o' Field, lying in the vennel of the said Kirk, on the east side of the transe thereof, between a land of Francis Inchecok on the east, the said trause on the west, a land of the late John Dee on the north, and the cemetery of the said Kirk on the south. Winesses, Sir William Braidfut, Archibald Robisone, Robert Mason, Robert Uddart, and David Purves, serjeant. William Rynde is bailie.
The same day, etc., William Lauder protested, that the sasine of an annual-rent of 40s., given by William Rynd to James Uddart and his spouse, out of a land of the late William Ferry, lying as above, hurt not him nor his heirs, nor his lands lying within the said bounds, and for remeid of law as effeirs.

10. 1528 May 18. Sasine on precept of chancery, in favour of Patrick Creichtoun, as son and heir of the late Patrick Creichtoun of Cranstoun Riddaill, of a back-land, under and above, with halls, chambers, cellars and houses thereof, in which James McCalzeane now dwells; together with the kitchen above the close and pend, with all their pertinents, lying on the north side of the High Street, within a tenement of the late William Cranston of Rathobyres, between the fore-land of the said late William on the south, and a land of the late William Adamson on the north; which tenement lies on the north side of the High Street, between a land of the late Walter Haliburton, now pertaining to George Gude, on the east, and a land of the late Walter Young on the west. Witnesses, Sir David Young, curate of Saint Giles Kirk, George Ur, John Lyntoun, Robert Adamson, Alexander Rynde, Robert Mason, John Bartilmo, and David Purves, serjeant. William Rynde is bailie.

11. 1528 May 18. William Rynd, bailie, passed to the back-land of Patrick Creichtoun, son and heir of the late Patrick Creichtoun of Cranston Riddaill, in which James McCalzeane now dwells, on the north side of the High Street, within a tenement of the late William Cranston of Rathobyres, and bounded as before described; and there the said Patrick Creichtoun resigned the foresaid back-land, with halls, chambers, etc., in the hands of the bailie, who gave sasine of the foresaid back-land, halls,

chambers, cellars and kitchen thereof, to a prudent woman, Jonet Turing, relict of William Adamson, in life-rent, and to Alexander Adamson, son of the said Jonet, his heirs and assignees, in fee; under reversion of £140 by the said Alexander and his heirs to the said Patrick, upon the redemption being made of the said back-land. Witnesses aforesaid.

The same day, etc., Patrick Creichtoun obliged himself and his heirs, that whensoever it should happen him and his heirs to loose the said back-land from the foresaid Alexander Adamson, his heirs or assignees, by payment of the said sum of £140, that then he shall resign the said land, and shall infeft Katherine Turing, his mother, therein in liferent. And thereupon Sir David Young, curate, asked instruments.

12. 1528 May 20. Sasine on resignation by Walter Chapman, in favour of himself, and Agnes Cokburne his spouse, of the said Walter's fore-land lying immediately above the entrance of the vennel of the Friars Preachers, between a land of the late Thomas Ramsay on the east, and another fore land of the said Walter on the west. Witnesses, George Towris of Bristo, Edward Bissait, William Rutherfurd, Robert Haithwy, Robert Ker, William Nesbet and Patrick Lithqw, serjeants. William Lauder is bailie.

13. 1528 May 23. Sasine on resignation by John Preston, son and heir of the late Archibald Preston, in favour of Richard Nicholson and Elizabeth Henrison his spouse, of the said John Preston's back-land in which the said Richard now dwells, containing hall, chamber and kitchen, lying between the foreland of a tenement of the said late Archibald Preston on the south, and a land of John Lowrison on the north; and which tenement lies on the north side of the High Street, between a tenement of the late Stephen Knox on the east, and a tenement of the late James Towris on the west: Paying yearly the said Richard and his spouse, the survivor of them and their heirs, to the foresaid John Preston, his heirs and assignees, in name of feuferme, 4 merks usual money of Scotland. Moreover, the said John Preston resigned the remaining part of his said tenement in the hands of the bailie, William Lauder, who gave sasine thereof to the foresaid Richard Nicholson and his spouse, in special warrandice of the foresaid back-land. Witnesses Andrew Uddart, Thomas Coupland, James Gourlaw, John Preston, Robert Haithwy, William Nesbet, and Patrick Lithqw, serjeants.

14. 1528 May 24. William Lauder, bailie, passed to a tenement of the late Archibald Preston, on the north side of the High Street, between a tenement of the late Stephen Knox on the east, and a tenement of the late James Towris on the west; and there John Preston, son and heir of the said late Archibald, resigned in the hands of the bailie the following annual-rents, (1) An annual-rent of 40s out of a chamber or cellar of the back-land of the said tenement, in which David Young and Jonet Nory his spouse now dwell, lying between the land of John Lowreson on the north, and another cellar of the foresaid back-land on the south. (2) An annual-rent of 13s4d, out of the said land of

John Lowreson, lying within the said tenement, between the said back-land thereof on the south, and a land of Andrew Uddart on the north. (3) An annual-rent of 6s and 8d, out of the east part of a certain waste-land or yard of John Anderson, lying in the north end of the said tenement, between the waste lands of the said tenement on the south and north, which bailie gave sasine of said annuals to Richard Nicholson and Elizabeth Henrison his spouse. Moreover, the said John Preston resigned his foresaid tenement, back and fore, etc., in the hands of William Lauder, bailie, who gave sasine thereof to the foresaid Richard Nicholson and Elizabeth his spouse in special warrandice of the said annual-rents, extending in whole to 4 merks 6s8d. Witnesses aforesaid.

15. 1528 May 26. Elizabeth Cranston, daughter and one of the heirs of the late William Cranston, of her own free will, sealed her charter made to Mungo Tennent and his spouse, of and upon her part and half of the fore-land and backland lying on the north side of the burgh, and of her part of an annual-rent of 6 merks, out of the land of John Tweedy; and that she would never come in the contrary thereof in judgement nor outwith the same in time to come; and affirmed and ratified her said charter in all points. And in like manner Geils Cranston and Edward Affleck, her spouse, sealed their charter made to the said Mungo Tennent and his spouse, of and upon her part of the foresaid foreland and backland, and ratified the same in all points and clauses contained therein. Upon which the said Mungo Tennent asked instruments, in presence of Robert Douglas of Pomfraston, Mungo Stevinsone, Thomas Hamilton in Alderston, and Sir Thomas Wallas, chaplain, with divers others.

16. 1528 May 29. Obligation by James Uddart, burgess, of Edinburgh, to seal and deliver to Alexander Towris, his heirs, etc., a letter of reversion under the proper seal, containing the sum of £20, for redemption of an annual-rent of 2 merks, alienated to the said James out of a land of the late Sir John Rynd, lying in the Buithraw, on the south side of the High Street. Likewise the said James obliged himself to make and deliver to the said Alexander another letter of reversion containing the sum of £16 upon redemption of another annual-rent of 2 merks, out of a land of the late William Ferry lying in the lower end of Peebles Wynd, to be extended in the surest form. Alexander Towris asked instruments. Done beside the merchant booth of the said James, in presence of Thomas Wardlaw, William Mow, Mathew Irland and ( ) Uddart. (This entry has been cancelled).
On the margin:-
22nd. April 1530. This prothogoll was distroyit be command of Alexander Towris; and renunsit all rycht that he had to the ij annuellis fra him and his airis for evir to james Uddart and his airis becaus he grantis that he had resavit thankful payment tharfor. This was done at the Merket Cros befor Thomas Cuike and John Litill.

17. 1528 June 8. William Lauder, bailie, passed to a Tenement of John Davidson, on the north side of the High Street, near the

Nether Bow, between a land of Alexander Cant on the east, and a land of Patrick Fleming on the west; and there Francis Spottiswode, with consent of Margaret Davidson his spouse, resigned an annual-rent of 40s., out of the foresaid tenement, in the hands of the bailie, who gave sasine thereof to the said John Davidson, his heirs and assignees: with court, and oath of the said Margaret not to revoke in times to come. And forthwith the said John Davidson, with consent of Isobel Kyle his spouse, resigned the said annual-rent of 40s, in the hands of the bailie, who gave heritable sasine of the same to Sir David Young, curate of Saint Giles Kirk, in name and on behalf of the church, for an anniversary and "le daile" for the poor to be done yearly, for the souls of the said John and his spouse, according to the tenor of a charter of foundation to be made thereupon: Reserving the liferent of said tenement to the said John and his spouse. John Davidson and Sir John Young asked instruments. Likewise the bailie passed to another tenement of John Davidson, lying on the south side of the High Street, between a land of John Purves on the east, and a land of the late William Fawsyde on the west; and there the said John, with consent of Isobel his spouse, resigned an annual-rent of 40s, which done, William Lauder, bailie, gave sasine of said annual-rent to the foresaid Sir David Young, curate, in name of the church, for an anniversary and "le daill" for the poor to be done yearly for the souls of the said John and Isobel: Reserving to them the frank tenement of said annual during their lifetimes. Moreover, the bailie passed to a certain land of the said John Davidson, on the south side of the High Street, lying within a tenement of the late Archibald Todryk, east side the transe thereof, between a land of the late Andrew Watson on the north, and a land of the Friars Preachers on the south; and there Elizabeth Spottiswode, lady fiar of the foresaid land, with consent of Francis Spottiswode her father, resigned an annual-rent of 2 merks in the hand of the bailie, who thereupon gave sasine of the said annual of 2 merks to the foresaid John Davidson, which annual-rent he immediately resigned in the bailie's hands, who at once gave sasine thereof to the said Sir David Young, chaplain, curate and in name and behalf of the church, for an anniversary and "le daill" for the poor yearly to be done for the souls of the said John and his spouse, according to the tenor of a charter of foundation to be made thereupon: saving all rights, and reserving as aforesaid. Witnesses, Alexander Young, notary public, William Lyndesay, Archibald Donaldson, George Bell, Rolland Donaldson, and James Johnston *alias* Edinburgh, serjeant.

18. 1528 June 8. Sasine on resignation by John Davidson, with consent of Isobel Kyle his spouse, in favour of John Spottiswode, son of Francis Spottiswode, of the fore-land of the resigner's tenement, lying on the south side of the High Street, between a land of John Purves on the east, and a tenement of the late William Fawsyde on the west: Reserving the frank-tenement of the paid foreland to the said John Davidson and his spouse and the survivor of them. Sasine given by William Lauder, bailie,

in presence of George Maxwell and the witnesses aforesaid.

19. 1528 June 8. Sasine on resignation by John Davidson, with consent of Isobel Kyle his spouse, in favour of Margaret Spottiswode, and the heirs of her body lawfully to be procreated, etc., always and until the said Margaret be paid the sum of 200 merks, of the back-land of the said John's tenement, lying on the south side of the High Street, between a land of John Purves on the east, and a tenement of the late William Fawsyde on the west: Reserving to the resigner and his spouse as before reserved. Witnesses the same.
The same day,etc.,Francis Spottiswode, in name of Margaret his daughter, obliged himself to cause the said Margaret to make and deliver to the said John Davidson a letter of reversion, containing the sum of 200 merks, upon redemption of the said back-land.

20. 1528 June 17. Sasine on resignation by Robert Gray, with consent of Helen Keith his spouse, of an annual-rent of 40s, out of a tenement of the said Robert, beyond the Bow or West Port, on the south side of the High Street thereof, between a land of John Nicholson on the west, and a land of the late Alan Wait on the east, the lands of Hieriggis on the south and the king's public street on the north, in favour of William Rowat, burgess, and Marion Cunynghame his spouse: with the usual oath of the woman, and an obligation by the said William and Marion his spouse to make and deliver to the said Robert Gray a letter of reversion upon redemption of the paid annual-rent of 40s., and of another annual-rent of 40s. alienated to the paid William, extending in whole to 6 merks, containing the sum of £43.10s. Witnesses, Sir William Braidfut, George Gray, Robert Gray, John Bartilmo, John Dyksone and Patrick Lithqw, serjeant.

21. 1528 June 19. Renunciation by John Smyth, son and heir of the late william Smyth, of a letter of reversion made by Sir William Brown to the said late William his father, upon redemption of an annual-rent of 40s., out of his land, lying upon the castle-hill, on the north side of the High Street; and this for certain favours and sums of money bestowed upon him by the said Sir William. Done in St. Giles church in presence of Sir James Baroun, and Patrick Lithqw, serjeant.

22. 1528 June 26. Sasine on resignation by Robert Bruse, burgess, in favour of David Boithuell, of an annual-rent of 40s, out of a land of the late Alexander Barcar, now pertaining to Francis Boithuell, lying on the north side of the High Street, between a land of the Henry Cant elder on the east, and a land of Gilbert Lauder on the west.Witnesses, Master James Lausone, Mr. Francis Boithuell, John Coldane, David Purdy, and John Johnston, serjeant. William Rynde is bailie.

23. 1528 June 26. Sasine on precept of chancery, under testimonial of the great seal, in favour of Master Francis Boithuell, burgess, of two waste lands, with pertinents, lying on the north side of the High Street, within a tenement of the late John Bar-

car; the one of which waste lands lies on the east side of the transe of the said tenement, sometimes inhabited by the late John Lilly; and the other lies on the west side of the transe thereof, sometime occupied by the late Andrew Burrell, between the lands of the John Barcar on the south, and the North Loch on the north, which tenement lies between the lands of Gilbert Lauder on the west, and the lands of the late Henry Cant on the east, now in His Majesty's hands by escheat as ultimate heir, by reason of the ultimate heirs of the foresaid waste lands going into England and remaining there in time of peace and war, without licence of His Majesty or his predecessors, or their guardians for the time being, and without having any other excuse whatsoever, as in the crown charter to the said Mr Francis Boithnell is more fully contained. Witnesses, Master James Lauson, John Coldane, David Purdy, and John Johnston, serjeant. William Rynde is bailie.

24. 1528 June 30. Sasine on resignation by Robert Haithwy, brother and heir of the late Alexander Haithwy, with consent of Patrick Lithqw his curator, in favour of George Leithe, burgess, and Marion Dee his spouse, of the said Robert's half of the backland lying within the easter tenement of Alexander Cant, on the north side of the High Street, between a land of the late John Blakstok on the east, and the wester tenement of the said Alexander Cant on the west; between the fore land of said tenement on the south, and a land of the late David Gill on the north, a land now pertaining to Edward Litill on the east, and the transe of the said tenement on the west. Witnesses, Alexander Cant, William Sym, Sir George Litiljohne, chaplain, John Bayne, James Henrison, John Cowane, Hugh Wallas, Thomas Arnot and John Johnston, serjeants.

25. 1528 July 8. William Rynde, bailie, passed to a certain land newly built, lying on the south side of the Tolbooth, in the vennel of Bestis Wynd, in the lower end and west side the trause thereof, between the street of the Cowgate on the south, and a waste land of the late Andrew Litill on the north, and there cognosced and entered John Vaiche, attorney and in name of friar Archibald Hynde, son and heir of the late John Hynde, in and to the foresaid land, by delivery of earth and stone thereof to the attorney, in name of the said friar Archibald. Witnesses, Robert Coupland, Robert Heriot, William Carwode, George Karnis, David Purves and John Johnston, serjeants.
1528 July 8. John Vaiche procurator and in name of friar Archibald Hynde, resigned the above mentioned land, in the end of Bestis Wynd, in the hands of William Rynde, bailie, who gave heritable sasine and conjunct-infeftment thereof to George Karnis, attorney and in name of William Henrison, burgess, and Agnes Forest, his spouse in presence of the witnesses aforesaid.

26. 1528 July 14. Sasine on resignation by John Colquhoun of Luss, Knight, in favour of Francis Spottiswode, burgess, and Margret Davidson his spouse, of an annual-rent of 4 merks, out of a land of the late Robert Neill, lying within a tenement of John

Davidson on the north side of the High Street, west side the trause thereof, between a land of the late Alexander Turnour, now pertaining to Thomas Schott, on the south, and the common passage of Trinity College on the north, the land of Alexander Cant on the east, and the land of Patrick Flemyng on the west. Witnesses, John Marjoribanks, Alexander McNeill, Master James Colquhoun, rector of Luss, Sir James Dennystoun, chaplain, Thomas Schort, William Mow and Thomas Arnot, serjeants. John Mauchane is bailie.

27. 1528 July 16. Sasine on resignation by John Kirkhop in favour of William Stevinson, notary, of an annual-rent of 6s8d. out of the two south cellars of the late John Bannatyne, lying within a tenement of the late Charles Levingtoun on the south side of the High Street, west side the transe thereof, between a land of the late Agnes Gibson, now pertaining to Jonet Reid, on the south, and a land of John Foular on the north; a land of the Laird of Borthik on the east, and a land of the late Thomas Swift on the west. Witnesses, Sir Robert Steill, John McMyllane, James Glendynnyn, John Lykprevyk, and High Wallas. John Mauchane is bailie.

28. 1528 Aug. 3. William Lauder, bailie, passed to the personal presence of Jonet Turing, relict of William Adamson, and there, in presence of the bailie, the said Jonet renounced her liferent of an annual-rent of 17 merks, out of a tenement of the said William Adamson, lying in the meal market, on the north side of the High Street, between a land of the late William Baroun on the east, and a tenement of Robert Haliburton on the west, and resigned the same in the bailie's hands, in favour of William Adamson, her son. Done in the dwelling-house of the said Jonet, in presence of Sir John Carkettil, George Henrison and John Charters.

29. 1528 Aug. 3. Sasine on resignation by Alexander Adamson, son of the late William Adamson, in favour of William Adamson, son and heir of the said deceased William Adamson of an annual-rent of 17 merks, out of a tenement of the said late William, on the north side of the High Street, between a land of the late William Baroun on the east, and a tenement of Robert Haliburton on the west. Witnesses, Sir David Young, curate, Master John Coldane and Sir Constantine Hannay, chaplains, John Coldane, John Anderson, William Thomson, David Purves and William Mow, serjeants. William Rynde is bailie.

30. 1528 Aug. 3. Sasine on resignation by William Adamson, in favour of Elizabeth Turing of an annual-rent of £10, out of a tenement of William Adamson, lying on the north side of the High Street and bounded as before described. Same bailie and witnesses as in the preceding sasine.

31. 1528 Aug. 3. William Rynde, bailie, passed to the foresaid tenement of William Adamson, lying on the north side of the High Street; and there the said William Adamson resigned an annual-rent of 2 merks upliftable from the said tenement, in the hands of the said bailie, who gave heritable sasine of the said annual-

rent to Sir David Young, curate of the collegiate church of Saint Giles in name and on behalf of the church, for an anniversary yearly to be done for the soul of the late William Adamson, according to the tenor of a charter to be made thereupon. Witnesses, Master John Coldane and Sir Constantine Hannay, chaplains, John Coldane, John Anderson, William Thomson, David Purves and William Mow, serjeants.

32. 1528 Aug. 4. Sasine on resignation by Alexander Rynde, in favour of James Rynde, his son and heir apparent, (1) of the said Alexander's land or mansion, in which he now dwells, lying on the north side of the High Street, between a land of Richard Litill on the south, and a certain waste land on the north, a tenement of Archibald Williamson on the east, and a tenement of the late John Cranston on the west. (2) An annual-rent of 2 merks, out of a land of the late Sir John Rynde, chaplain, lying in Buithraw, on the south side of the High Street, between a land of James Prestoun on the east, and a land of the late William Craik on the west. (3) An annual-rent of 3 merks, out of the lands of David Gillaspy, lying within the tenement of the said Alexander Rynde, on the south side of the High Street, between a tenement of the late William Cockburn on the east, and a tenement of the Laird of Borthik on the west; a land of the late William Fortoun on the south, and a land of the late Jasper Mayne on the north: Reserving the liferent of the said land and mansion and annual rents to the foresaid Alexander Rynde. Witnesses, Sir Philip Darling and Master Thomas Howy, chaplains, Master Thomas Majoribanks and John Coldane.

33. 1528 Aug. 4. Sasine on resignation by Alexander Rynde, in favour of James Rynde, his son and heir apparent, (1) of the foreland of the said Alexander's tenement, lying on the south side of the High Street, between the tenement of the late William Cokburne on the east, and the tenement of the Laird of Borthik on the west. (2) A ground-annual of 4 merks, out of the Land of the late Jasper Mayne, lying within the foresaid tenement, between the land of David Gillaspy on the south, and the back land of the said tenement on the north. And forthwith the said James Rynde resigned the foresaid foreland and ground-annual in the hands of William Rynde, bailie, who gave sasine and conjunct-infeftment of the same to the said James Rynde and Margret Forest, his affianced spouse: Reserving Alexander Rynde's liferent as before reserved. Same witnesses.

34. 1528 Aug 4. Sasine on resignation by James Rynde, in favour of himself and Margret Forest his affianced spouse in conjunct-fee of his lands lying contiguous in Nudriis Wynd, west side the trause thereof, between a land of the late Andrew Bertrame on the north, and a land of the late Master David Broune on the south. (2) An annual-rent of 20s, out of a land of the late William Nesbet, lying within a tenement of the late Robert Lauder, on the south side of the High Street, between a land of David Gray on the north, and a land of the late James Talzefeir on the south. Bailie and witnesses as before.

35. 1528 Aug. 5. Renunciation by Robert Gray, son and heir of the late Alexander Gray, in favour of Robert Huchesone, his heirs and assignees, of the liferent which the said Robert Gray has of the half of a waste land, lie workhouse, in the end of a tenement of the said late Alexander, beside the yard of the college of the Holy Trinity. And also the said Robert confesses himself well contented and fully paid by the said Robert Huchesone, of all sums of money promised by the said Robert to him for his lands, tenements and annual-rents whatsoever, alienated by the said late Alexander Gray to the foresaid Robert Huchesone; and likewise of all contracts, obligations and other writs whatsoever entered into between the said Robert Gray and Robert Huchesone, before the date of this present instrument. Done in the shop of William Lauder, bailie, in presence of these witnesses, the said William Lauder, bailie, Vincent Strathauchin, notary, and Thomas Arnot, serjeant of the burgh of Edinburgh.

36. 1528 Aug. 6. Sasine on resignation by Elizabeth Cranston, with consent of Edward Affleck her spouse, in favour of Mungo Tennent and Marion Harlaubankis his spouse, of an annual-rent of 6 merks, out of a tenement of the late John Twedy, lying on the north side of the High Street, between the land of the late John Dun, now pertaining to the heirs of the late Alexander Lauder of Blyth, knight, on the east, and a land of the late Alexander Bonkill on the west. With court and oath of the woman. Witnesses, James Bassendene, Robert Hall, Thomas Scotland, Andrew Henderson, Robert Haithwy and Patrick Lithqw.

37. 1528 Aug. 14. Sasine on resignation by David Tod, son and heir of the late Robert Tod, in favour of himself and Alesone Cokburne his spouse, in conjunct-fee, of his backland and mansion, in which the said David now dwells, lying within his tenement, beside the Nether Bow, on the south side of the High Street, between the fore land of the said tenement on the north, and a land of the late Alexander Anderson on the south; a land of John Purves on the east, and a land of James Bassenden on the west. Witnesses, Master Robert Galbraith, Master Thomas McCalzeane, Thomas Eldar, Alexander Mair, David Purves, and Thomas Arnot, serjeant. William Lauder is bailie.

38. 1528 Aug. 18. Sasine on resignation by Alexander Rynde, burgess, in favour of James Rynde, his son and heir apparent, of an annual-rent of 20s, out of a certain land lying on the south side of the High Street, in Liberton's Wynd, west side the trause thereof, between a land of Archibald Williamson on the north, and a land of James Blak on the south: Reserving the liferent thereof. Witnesses, Master Thomas Howy, John Coldane, Henry Lille and John Twedy.

39. 1528 Aug 20. Sasine to friar John Litill, on his cognition by William Rynde, bailie, as heir of the late Andrew Litill his father, of a certain waste land lying in Bestis Wynd, between a land of John Vaiche on the north, and a land of William Henderson on the south. And forthwith the said John Litill resigned the said waste land in the hands of the bailie, who gave sasine thereof to the said William Henderson and Agnes Forest, his

spouse. Witnesses, friar Patrick Pillane, John Vaiche, John Coldane, Richard Litill, Robert Coupland and David Purves, serjeant.

40. 1528 Aug. 31. John Mauchane, bailie, passed to a Land of James Darroche, lying beside the Over Bow, on the north side of the High Street, between a land of William Anderson on the west, and the said Bow on the east; and there John Turnour renounced all right and title of right which he had in and to an annual-rent of 2 merks, out of the said land: And forthwith Margaret Quhitheid resigned in the hands of the bailie her annual rent of 36s., leviable from the said land; and also her annual-rent of 6s., out of the foresaid land of William Anderson: which done the bailie gave sasine and conjunct-infeftment of the foresaid annual-rents to John Johnston and Alison Young his spouse. Witnesses, Sir Patrick Homyll, John Allane, John Hucheson, George Craik, John Anderson, and David Purves, serjeant.

41. 1528 Aug. 31. William Lauder, bailie, passed to a fore-land or tenement of the late John Napier, on the south side of the High Street, between a land of James Halkerston on the east, and a land of William Lauder on the west, a waste land of the said James Halkerston on the south, and the King's public street on the north; and there Master Robert Galbraith, procurator and in name of Margret Prestoun, sister of the order of Saint Katrine of the Senis, and relict of the said John Napier, renounced and dimitted as follows, in favour of William Adamson, burgess, and Jonet Nepar his spouse, (1) The said Margaret Preston's conjunct-fee of the fore-land and tenement above mentioned. (2) Her conjunct-fee of a waste land of the said James Halkerston, lying within the said tenement, east side the trause thereof, between the back land of said tenement on the north, and a land or yard of the late James Bertram on the south. And forthwith, without delay, the said William Lauder, bailie, cognosced and entered John Charteris attorney and in name of devout orators, viz., dames Elizabeth Napier, Margret Napier, Agnes Napier and Katrine Napier, sisters of the order of Saint Katrine of Senis, daughters and heirs of the late John Napier, burgess of Edinburgh, in and to their parts and portions, viz., each of them to a seventh part of the foresaid fore-land and back-land of the said tenement: Also each of them to a seventh part of the said annual-rent of 6 merks, by delivery to the said attorney, in name of the said ladies of the Senis, of hesp and staple, and of single pennies, etc., And forthwith Master Robert Galbraith, procurator and in name of the said sisters and ladies of Senis, resigned all and whole their respective parts and portions of the foresaid fore-land and tenement: Also of the said annual-rent of 6 merks, in the hands of the bailie, who thereupon gave heritable sasine and conjunct-infeftment of the foresaid parts of the said foreland and tenement; also of the annual-rent of 6 merks, to William Adamson, burgess, and Jonet Nepar his spouse, conform to the tenor of a charter of the said sisters to be made thereupon. Witnesses, Alexander Makneill, Alexander Adamson, Master Thomas McCalzeane, John Makneill, John Galbraith, Robert Morison, Robert Freland, and Patrick Lithqw, serjeant.

42. 1528 Aug. 31. William Lauder, bailie, passed to a certain land and yard of the late John Napier, lying on the south side of the High Street, in the lower end of a tenement of the late John Napier, east side the transe thereof, between a land or yard of the late James Bertrame on the north, and the king's public street of the Cowgate on the south; a land of Thomas Falcone on the east, and the transe of the said tenement on the west; which tenement lies on the south side of the High Street, between a land of James Halkerston on the east, and a land of William Lauder on the west; and there Elizabèth Dyksone, relict of the said John Napar, with consent of Alexander Prestoun her spouse, resigned the conjunct-fee which she had of the foresaid land and yard, in the hands of the bailie, in favour of William Adamson and Jonet Napier his spouse: Reserving the liferent thereof to the said Elizabeth Dyksone. And forthwith the said William Lauder, bailie, cognosced and entered John Charteris, attorney and in name of devout orators, viz., Dames Elizabeth, Margaret, Agnes and Katrine Napier, sisters of the order of Saint Katrine of the Senis, and heirs of the late John Napier, burgess, in and to their parts and portions, viz. each of them to a seventh part of the foresaid land and yard, by delivery to the said attorney of hesp and staple; and seised the said attorney, in name of the said sisters, in the foresaid land and yard, as is wont to be done to the heirs of burgesses in such cases within burgh. And forthwith Master Robert Galbraith, procurator and in name of the said sisters and ladies of the Senis, resigned their parts and portions of the foresaid land and yard in the hands of the bailie, who gave sasine of the same to William Adamson, burgess, and Jonet Napier his spouse. Witnesses as aforesaid.

43. 1528 Aug. 31. Sasine to Helen Napier, on her cognition by WillLauder, bailie, as daughter and one of the heirs of the late John Napier, of the following subjects, (1) Her part and portion viz., the seventh part of a fore-land and tenement of the said John Napier, lying on the south side of the High Street, between a land of James Halkerston on the east, and a land of William Lauder on the west, a waste land of the said James Halkerston on the south, and the king's public street on the north. (2) The seventh part of an annual-rent of 6 merks, out of a waste land of the said James Halkerston, lying within the said tenement, east side the transe thereof, between the back land thereof on the north, and the land or yard of the late James Bertrame on the south. (3) The bailie cognosced and entered the said Helen Napier, as sister and one of the heirs of late John Napier, in and to her part and portion, viz. the seventh part of the land and yard lying within the said tenement in the lower end thereof, between the land or yard of the late James Bertram on the north, and the king's public street of the Cowgate on the south, the land of Thomas Falcone on the east, and the transe of the said tenement on the west: Reserving the frank-tenement of the said land and yard to Elizabeth Dyksone during her lifetime. And forthwith the said Helen Napier, daughter and one of the heirs of the said late John Napier, and sister

and one of the heirs of the said late John Napier, her brother, of her own free will, as she affirmed, resigned her seventh part of the fore-land and tenement, annual-rent, land and yard above specified, in the hands of the bailie, who gave sasine of the said seventh part to William Adamson, burgess, and Jonet Napier his spouse: Reserving as above. Same witness as before.

44. 1528 Aug. 31. Sasine to Jonet Napier, on her cognition by William Lauder, bailie, as daughter and one of the heirs of the foresaid late John Napier, burgess, and as sister and one of the heirs of the foresaid late John Napier her brother, of her part and portion, viz. the seventh part of all and whole the foresaid fore-land and tenement, annual-rent of 6 merks, land and yard, lying and bounded as before described: which seventh parts the said Jonet Napier immediately resigned in the hands of the bailie, who gave sasine of the same to William Adamson, burgess, and Jonet Napier his spouse, in presence of the said witnesses. Reserving as before reserved.

45. 1528 Aug. 31. Sasine on resignation by William Adamson, with consent of Jonet Napier his spouse, in favour of Katrine Seytoun, prioress of the sisters of the order of Saint Katrine of Senis, and convent thereof, and her successors, sisters of the said place, of an annual-rent of £10, out of a foreland and tenement of the said William Adamson, on the south side of the High Street, between a land of James Halkerston on the east, a land of William Lauder on the west, a waste land of the said James Halkerston on the south, and the King's public street on the north; and out of another land and yard, lying within the said tenement in the lower end thereof, between a land and yard of the late James Bertrame on the north, the street of the Cowgate on the south, a land of Thomas Falcone on the east, and the trause of the said tenement on the west. With court and oath of the said Jonet not to revoke in time to come. Witnesses, Master Robert Galbraith, Alexander McNeill, Alexander Adamson, Master Thomas McCalzeane, John McNeill, John Galbraith, Robert Morison, Robert Freland, and Patrick Lithqw.

46. 1528 Sept. 4. Sasine on resignation by Elizabeth Scot, Lady Manerston, relict of James Wardlaw, in favour of Robert Wardlaw, son and heir of the said James, of her conjunct-fee of the subjects after specified; and on the said Robert's cognition by William Rynd, bailie, as heir foresaid, in and to (1) the lands of the said late James, lying within a tenement of the abbot and convent of the monastery of Cambuskenneth, on the south side of the High Street, between a land of Alexander Mauchane on the south, and the back mansions of the said tenement on the north, a tenement of the late James Aikman on the east, and a tenement of the said Elizabeth Scot, Lady Manerston, on the west. (2) These lands and stables contiguously adjacent, within the said tenement, between the land of the said Alexander Mauchane on the north, a waste land of the said tenement on the south, the transe thereof on the east, and the transe of the said Elizabeth Scot's tenement on the west. And forthwith the said Robert Wardlaw resigned the foresaid lands and stables

in the hands of the bailie, who gave heritable sasine and conjunct-infeftment of the same to the said Robert and Margaret Currour his spouse: Reserving the liferent to the said Elizabeth Scot. (3) An annual-rent of 40s, out of the lands of James Blak, lying contiguously adjacent on the south side of the High Street, in the vennel of Liberton's Wynd, west side the transe thereof, between a land of the late William Currour on the north, and the street of the Cowgate on the south. (4) The wester half of a land of the late John Eglintoun, lying below the castle wall, on the south side of the High Street, below the stair thereof, between a land of John Adamson on the east, a land of Lancelot Barcar on the west, a land of William Hamilton on the south, and the king's public street on the north, together with the loft of the said land; and an annual-rent of 8s., out of the easter booth of the foresaid land lying under the stair thereof: Reserving the liferent as aforesaid. Which annual-rent of 40s.,land,loft and annual-rent of 8s. the said Robert Wardlaw immediately resigned in the bailie's hands, in favour of himself and Margaret Currour, his spouse, who are thereupon seised in the same heritably and in conjunct-fee. Witnesses, John Ogilvy, William Raa, John Coldane, William Drumbrek and David Purves, serjeant.

47. 1528 Sept. 4, at the twelfth hour of the day, William Rynd, bailie, passed to a tenement of the late James Wardlaw, which formerly pertained to the late Hector Thomson, lying below the Nether Bow, on the south side of the High Street, between a tenement of the late John Ramsay on the east, and a land of the late John Nudry on the west, and there cognosced and entered Robert Wardlaw, son and heir of the late James Wardlaw, in and to the said tenement, which he immediately resigned in the hands of the bailie, who gave sasine and conjunct-infeftment thereof to the said Robert Wardlaw and Margaret Currour his spouse, in presence of the witnesses foresaid.

48. 1528 Sept. 4. Sasine on resignation by John Riddaill, with consent of Elizabeth Litstar his spouse, in favour of Alexander Mure, smith, and Jonet Flucar his spouse, of the said John's land lying in the vennel of the Blessed Virgin Mary of the Fields, west side the transe thereof, between a land of the late John Runsyman on the south, and a land of the late Andrew Cowane on the north. With court and oath of the woman not to revoke. Witnesses, Edward Litill, James Darroche, Andrew Brounehill, Thomas Turing, Richard Riddaill, and Thomas Arnot, serjeant. William Adamson is bailie.

49. 1528 Sept. 5. Sasine to Marion Napier, daughter and one of the heirs of the late John Napier, on her cognition by William Lauder, bailie, of (1) her part and portion, viz., the seventh part of a fore-land and tenement of her said father lying on the south side of the High Street, between a land of James Halkerston on the east, and a land of William Lauder on the west, a waste land of the said James Halkerston on the south, and the king's public street on the north. (2) The seventh part of an annual-rent of 6 merks, out of the fore-said waste land

of James Halkerston. Moreover, the bailie cognosced and entered the said Marion, as sister and one of the heirs of the late John Napier, her brother, in and to one seventh part of a certain land and yard, lying within the foresaid tenement, in the lower end thereof, between a land or yard of the late James Bertrame on the north, and the street of the Cowgate on the south, a land of Thomas Falcoun on the east, and the trause of the said tenement on the west. And forthwith the said Marion Napier, as daughter, sister, and heir foresaid, with consent of Richard Gray her spouse, resigned her parts and portions of the foreland and tenement, annual-rent, land and yard above specified, in the hands of the bailie, who thereupon gave sasine and conjunct infeftment of the said parts to William Adamson, burgess, and Jonet Napier his spouse: Reserving the liferent of the foresaid land and yard to Elizabeth Dyksone, spouse of Alexander Bartoun. With the said Marion's oath not to revoke. Witnesses, William Dick, notary, Patrick Carvour, John Charters, William Haw, Thomas Turing, Thomas Ramsay, Patrick Linlithqw and William Mow, serjeants.

50. 1528 Sept. 10. William Rynd, one of the bailies of Edinburgh, at the command of the other bailies, councillors and community of the said burgh, passed to the collegiate church of Field; and there the said bailie gave institution to Sir Bartholomew Hamyltoun, chaplain, at the service formed by the late ( ) Russall, at the high altar of the said collegiate (church), by delivery to him of a book, chalice and other vestments of the said altar, according to the tenor of a foundation made thereupon; and moreover, gave and delivered, as use is in such cases. The said Sir Bartholomew asked instruments. Done in the said collegiate church; witnesses, Sirs Alexander Couper Robert Lille and William Richartson, chaplains, Thomas Arnot and Robert Mortoun.

51. 1528 Sept. 12. William Adamson, bailie, passed to the lands of the late Alexander Anderson, lying on the south side of the High Street in "Sanct Mary wynd", west side the transe thereof, between a land of the late Robert Lamb on the north, a land of the late William Scheirsmyth on the south, and the lands of the hospital of the blessed Mary, Thomas Kemp and the said vennel, also the other lands contiguously adjacent, on the east, and the lands of Thomas Blyth and Alexander Young on the west; and there Elizabeth Borthik, with consent of Alexander Young her spouse, demitted her conjunct-fee of the foresaid lands in the hands of the bailie, in favour of Marion Anderson, Marjory Anderson and Margaret Anderson, daughter and heirs of the said late Alexander. And forthwith the bailie cognosced and entered the said Marion, Marjory and Margaret in and to their parts and portions, viz., to each of them respectively, a third part of the foresaid lands, with yard, etc. Also in and to a third part of another land of the said late Alexander Anderson, lying on the south side of the High Street, beside the Nether Bow, within a tenement of David Tod, between the lands of the said David on the south and north parts, a land

of the late Rolland Turnbull on the west, and a land of the said Alexander Young on the east, of which land also the said Elizabeth Borthik and her spouse renounced her conjunct-fee. This done, Marion, Marjory and Margaret Anderson resigned their portions above specified, of the foresaid lands and yard, in the hands of William Adamson, bailie, who gave sasine of the same to Alexander Young, notary, and the said Elizabeth Borthik his spouse in conjunct-fee. Witnesses, Sirs David Young, curate of Saint Giles Church, and John Carkettill, chaplains, Alexander Adamson, and William Mow, serjeant.

The said 12th day of Sept. 1528, Elizabeth Borthik, spouse of Alexander Young, with his consent, renounced her conjunct-fee of the half of land in Buithraw, south side of the High Street thereof, between a land of the late Robert Coksone on the east, and a land of the late David Macluill on the west, in favour of Marion Anderson and Margaret Anderson, daughters and heirs of the late Alexander Anderson, in presence of William Adamson, bailie, Alexander Anderson, Sir David Young, Sir John Carkettill and William Mow.

52. 1528 Sept. 12. Procuratory granted by Marion and Margaret Anderson to Sir David Young and Alexander Adamson, conjointly and severally, giving them power to take possession and sasine, in name of the said Marion and Margaret, of the third part of the half of the foresaid land in Buithraw, lying and bounded as above described; and after reception thereof to resign their said parts and portions of the said land in the hands of one of the bailies of Edinburgh, in favour of Alexander Young and Elizabeth Borthik his spouse, for sasine to be given to them conform to the tenor of a charter of the said ladies. Witnesses, William Adamson, bailie, Sir John Carkettill, Alexander Young, and William Mow, serjeant.

53. 1528 Sept. 12. Compared personally Marion Scot, daughter and heir of the late Marion Briggis, and, with consent of Henry Kirk, her spouse, renounced and delivered her stone or sepulchre, lying in Saint Giles church, on the south side of the altar of Saint James, in favour of Sir William Brown, chaplain, there present and accepting thereof: And John Marjoribanks, Dean of Guild, gave possession of the said stone or sepulchre to the said Sir William Browne, chaplain, as use is in such cases. Witnesses, Sir William Lyntoun, Master Alexander Levingston, Sir Mungo Spottiswode, and Simon Mason.

54. 1528 Sept. 15. Sasine in resignation by Alexander Bruse, burgess, in favour of Jonet Adamson, relict of John Bruse, burgess, her heirs and assignees, of a tenement of the said Alexander, lying on the south side of the High Street, between a land and tenement of the late Edward Bonkill on the east, and a land of the late Walter Blaklok on the west, a land sometime of Patrick Baroun, now pertaining to the heirs of the late William Ker on the south, and the King's public street on the north. Witnesses, Sirs John Kennedy and John Campbell, chaplains, Brice McCrekane, James Stanton, notary pulblic, and Thomas Arnot, serjeant.

JOHN FOULAR

The quhilk day Jonet Adamson the relict of Johne Bruse promittit to deliver ane reversioun to Alexander Bruse apone the redemption of the tenement of land befor and behind abone wryttin contenand the soume of iiijc. merkis of the quhilk soume the said Alexander Bruse has ressavit in hand bot jc. lib. and oblissis him that gif he pais nocht the said jc. lib. to the said Jonet within tua zeir eftir the dait heirof that he sall resaif the remanent of the said iiijc. merkis fra the said Jonet or hir airis and sall renunce the said reversioun and all rycht that he has to the said land fra him and his airis for evir to the said Jonet and her airis. And gif the said Alexander happenis to pay the said soume of jc. lib. to the said Jonet or hir airis within tua zeris as said is he to haif full regres and ingres in and to his haill tenement of land befor and behind syklyk and als fre as he now has the samyne befor the alienatioun thairof but ony impediment: Reservand allwayis to the said Jonet the lyfrent of the said tenement of land for all the dais of hir lyf as scho now had samyne. Attour the said Alexander in cais that he deces in his viage that he now is to pas in uther partis in merchandys and nane utherwayis he makis and constitutis James Bruse his brother his verray lauchfull cessionar and assignay in and to the remanent of the said soume of iiij merkis in cais he deces as said is and to the said reversioun for to lous and redeme the said tenement of land within the said ij zeris eftir the forme as is abone wryttin and gif he happin to cum hame saiflie this cessionarii nor assignay to be of nane avale force nor effect bot till use the said reversioun and soumes of money abone wryttin him self as said is without ony interruptioun or impediment. And all the partiis askit instrumentis. Witnesses Schir Johne Kennedy, Schir Johne Campbell, James Stantoun, Brys McCrekane and Thomas Arnot.

55. 1528 Sept. 24. Sasine on resignation by Thomas Borthik, procurator and in name of William Lord Borthik, in favour of David Gillaspy, baker, burgess of Edinburgh, and Elizabeth Gilleis, his spouse, of the waste land of the said Lord Borthik's tenement, on the south side of the High Street, between a tenement of Alexander Rynd on the east, and a land of the late John Carkettill on the west; which waste land lies in the lower end of the said tenement, and on each side the close thereof, between the lands of George Gude and John Glen on the north, the street of the Cowgate on the south, the lands of the said David Gillaspy on the east, and the lands of the late John Balfour and John Cattell on the west. Witnesses, Alexander Rynde, Andrew Myddilbie, John Stewart, George Blair, Thomas Ross, Robert Bolton, John Fynlaw and David Purves, serjeant.

56. 1528 Sept. 25. William Adamson, bailie, passed to a land of the late Elizabeth Wode, lying in Buithraw, on the south side of the High Street, between a land of the late Robert Coksone on the east, and a land of the David Mailuill on the west; and there cognosced and entered Alexander Adamson, procurator and in name of Marion Anderson, Marjorie Anderson and Mar-

garet Anderson, kinswoemen and heirs of the said late Elizabeth Wode, in and to their parts and portions, viz. each of them to a third part of the third part of the half of the foresaid land: which third parts the said Alexander Adamson, as procurator foresaid, resigned in the hands of the bailie, who thereupon gave sasine of the same to Alexander Young, notary public, and Elizabeth Borthik, his spouse. Witnesses, Sirs David Young and John Styrk, chaplains, and William Mow, serjeant.

57. 1528 Sept. 25. Sasine on resignation by Sir William Lethame, monk of the monastery of Paisley, and son of the deceased William Lethame, in favour of friar John Lethame; and proceeding also on cognition of the said John Lethame, by John Mauchane, one of the bailies of Edinburgh, as son and heir of the said late William Lethame, of a land of his said father, on the south side of the High Street, lying within a tenement of the late Thomas Butlar, west side the transe thereof, between a land of John Glen on the north, a land of John Con on the south, and a land of Alexander Rynd, now of David Gillaspy, on the west. Saving all rights. The said friar John asked instruments. Witnesses, friar John Touris, John Henderson, Vincent Strathauchin, notary, Patrick Lithqw and David Purves, serjeants.

58. 1528 Sept. 19. Sasine on resignation by Henry Young, with consent of Marion Wardlaw, his spouse, in favour of Mungo Tennent and Marion Harlaubanks his spouse, of an annual-rent of 10s., out of a fore-land of the late William Cranston of Rathobyris, now pertaining to Mungo Tennent, on the north side of the High Street, between a land of the late John Tyndaill, now pertaining to George Gude, on the east, and a land of the late Walter Young on the west, a land of the late Patrick Creichton of Cranston-Riddaill on the north, and the king's public street on the south. With court and oath of the woman not to revoke in time to come. Witnesses, Michael Makquhen, Richard Wardlaw, Sir John Young, Patrick Arnot, David Purves and Thomas Arnot, serjeants, with divers others. William Rynde, bailie, gave the sasine.

59. 1528 Sept. 30. Sasine on precept of chancery in favour of John Symson, as lawful and nearest heir of the late Michael Symson, burgess, his father, of a land lying on the south side of the High Street, in the vennel of Forstar's Wynd, east side the trause thereof, between a land of the late William Falcone on the south, and a land of the late John Falcone on the north: Reserving the liferent of the said land to Alison Haliburton. Witnesses, Robert Watson, Robert Elphinston, Thomas Williamson, John Richartson, John Symson and William Nesbet. William Adamson is bailie.

60. 1528 Oct. 2. John Mauchane, one of the bailies of Edinburgh, passed to the hospital and place of Saint Paul, near Trinity College; and there the said bailie, in name of the provost, bailies, council and community of the said burgh, patrons of the service and chaplaincy founded by the late Thomas bishop of Aberdeen, gave and delivered the said service and chaplaincy to Sir John Tyndale, chaplain, by delivery to him of a book, chalice and vestments of the high altar of the said place and

dignities thereof, and invested and instituted him in the said service and chaplaincy, with all its annual-rents, emoluments, fruits, profits and pertinents thereof, and this as freely as the same were possessed and enjoyed by his predecessors, according to the foundation made thereupon. Witnesses, Edward Litill, John Marjoribanks, Alexander Adamson, James Barbour, John Broune and William Adamson.

61. 1528 Oct. 2. Renunciation by John Symson, son and heir of the late Michael Symson, burgess, in favour of Robert Watson and his spouse, of a letter of reversion granted by the said Michael to the said Robert and his spouse, of and upon the redemption of an annual-rent of 10 merks out of his land in Forstar's Wynd lying and bounded as described in the said John Symson's sasine, folio 25. Done in the booth of the common clerk of Edinburgh, Sirs William Broune and Mathew Symson, chaplains, John Symson, William Symson, John Adamson younger, and James Sym, are witnesses.

62, 1528 Oct. 15. William Lyndesay, bailie, passed to a certain land of John Richartson, son and heir of the late Thomas Richartson, lying on the south side of the High Street, in the wynd of the Friars Preachers, west side the trause thereof, between a land of John Loch on the south, and a land (   ) on the north; and there the said John Richartson resigned his fee of the foresaid land in the hands of the bailie, who gave sasine thereof to Margaret Richartson, spouse of Alexander McNeill, notary public, and sister to the said John Richartson, her heirs and assignees: Reserving the liferent of the said land to the resigner. Witnesses, Master Henry Henrison and James Stanton, notaries public, Sirs Thomas Watson and and William Young, chaplains, and William Nesbet, serjeant.

The said 15th day of October 1528. The quhilk day Margret Richartson the spous of Alexander McNeill with the consent and assent of the said Alexander oblissis hir faithfully, and hir airis, and John Richartson, hir brother, that how sone or quhensoevir it sall happin the said John Richartson to cum hame in Scotland eftir his viage that he is now to mak in uthir partis beyond sey, and requyres hir to gif our hir fee of the land aboue wryttin liand in the Freir Wynd, etc., that incontinent scho sall renunce and gif ovir the samyne, with all rycht and titill that scho hes therintill, in favouris (sic.) to be gevin agane to the said Johne Richartson and to the airis lauchfully to be gottin of his body and nane utheris: ffalzeand of the airis of his body till cum agane till the said Margret and hir airis et Johannes petiit (sic.) Attour the said Johne Richartson for luif and favouris that he beris and hes to Alexander McNeill and Margret his spous he makis and constitutis the said Alexander McNeill and Margret his spous and thar airis his verray lauchfull and unrevocable cessionaris and assignais in and to all and sundry the byrun males and proffitis of his landis liand in Nudrys Wynd and Freir Wynd on the west syde of the samyne awand till him be Andro Mowbray be the space of ix yeris bygane and transferris all rycht thairof fra him and his airis in and to the said Alexander and his spous and thair airis eftir the form of the contract maid betwix the saidis Alexander and Johne wryttin and subscrivit with thair handis datit at Edinburgh the day of October the zeir of God jm. vc. xxviij zeris. And thereupon asked instruments. Done upon the ground of the said land. Witnesses aforesaid.

63. 1528 Oct. 21. James Johnston, bailie, passed to a tenement pertaining to William Anderson, on the south side of the High Street of the Cowgate, between a land of the late Master Alexander Inglis, archdeacon of St. Andrews, on the east, and a land of the late Robert Galloway on the west, and there Patrick Inglis, procurator and in the name of George Inglis, resigned an annual-rent of 10 merks, out of the foresaid tenement, in the hands of the said James Johnston, bailie, who gave sasine thereof to Sir Bartholomew Martyne, chaplain of the service and chaplaincy founded by the said George at the altar of Saint Salvator, situated in the church of Cambusmichell, and his successors, chaplains of the said service, according to the tenor of a charter of foundation made therupon. The said Sir Batholomew asked instruments. Done upon the ground of the said tenement; witnesses, John Wallas, Patrick Hamilton, Alexander Cummyn, Thomas Henry, James Blak, Master Alexander Levingston, John Johnston and Hugh Wallas, serjeants.

64. 1528 Oct. 22. William Elphistoun, bailie, passed to a certain land of Adam Mayne, with the bakehouse, lying on the south side of the High Street, in the vennel of Peebles Wynd, east side the trause thereof, between a land of Mary Magdalen on the north, and a land of John Glen on the south; and there the said Adam resigned his said land in the hands of the bailie. The bailie passed also to another land, on the north side of the High Street, in Halkerston's Wynd, on the west side of the transe thereof, between a land of the late George Halkerston on the south, and a land of the late Thomas Zar on the north; and there the said Adam Mayne resigned his part or half of the said land, containing a laich hall with two cellars under the same, in the hands of the bailie. Thereafter the bailie passed to a land lying in the street of the Cowgate, on the south side thereof, between a land of the late William Sinclar on the east, a land of the Friars Preachers on the west, and a waste land on the south; and there the said Adam Mayne resigned the foresaid land in the hands of the bailie: which resignations having been so made, the said bailie gave heritable sasine of all and whole the foresaid lands, as before specified, to Alison Rouche, mother to the said Adam, her heirs and assignees. Witnesses, Thomas Elphinston, John Tod, Thomas Greif, Andrew Peirson, Patrick Lithqw and Thomas Arnot, serjeants.
The quhilk day Alison Rouche oblissis hir faithfully, hir airis executouris and assignais that in cais scho deces or Adam Mayne hir sone be maid preist in that cais scho oblis hir and hir airis executouris and assignais till content and pay till the said Adam the haill avale of his said landis abone wryttin or ellis in the meyntyme to resigne the said landis in ane ballies handis and put the said Adam heretablie therintill as he

was obefor. And in this meyntyme to find the said Adam clething and all uthir necessar thingis and eftir he be preist syklyke for hir lyftyme. And this to be extendit in the best forme. The said Adam asked instruments. Witnesses, William Elphinston, bailie, and the others foresaid.

65. 1528 Oct. 24. Compeared personally Jonet Adamson, relict of John Bruse, on the one part, and Alexander Bruse, son and heir of the said John, on the other part, which parties contracted and made agreement as follows in the vernacular. At Edinburgh the xv day of September the zeir of God jm. vc. xxviij zeris. It is appoyntit betuix ane honorable woman Jonet Adamson, the relict of umquhile Johne Bruse, burgess of Edinburgh, on that ane part, and Alexander Bruse the son and air of the said umquhile Johne Bruse on that uthir part, as eftir followis. That forasmekle as the said Alexander Bruse has sauld heretablie be charter and sesing to the said Jonet Adamson hir airis, etc., all and haill his tenement of land undir and abone bak and fore liand within the burgh of Edinburgh on the south syde kingis street of the samyne in the quhilk the said Jonet inhabitis and has in conjunct-fee the day of the dait of thir presentis, undir ane reversioun contenand the soume of four hundreth merkis usuall money of Scotland as charter sesing and reversioun maid thairapone proportis. Neverthelles the said Jonet Adamson will and grantis and als lelely and treuly bindis and oblissis hir be the faith and treuth of hir body for hir and for hir airis and assignais That in cais the said Alexander Bruse his airis, etc., plesis or happynis within the space of tua zeris immediat followyng the dait heirof to redeme fra the said Jonet hir airis, etc., the forsaid land and tenement, etc., with the forsaid iiijc merkis eftir the forme of the reversioun maid thairapone that the said Jonet hir airis, sall allow and defalk till the said Alexander his airis, etc., the soume of ijc.xl merkis in to the said soume of iiijc merkis money forsaid as it war nominit and debursit money to the said Jonet hir airis or assignais be the said Alexander his airis,etc. Quhilk soume of ijc.xl merkis restis unpaiit to the said Alexander Bruse be the said Jonet Adamson nochtwithstanding the reversioun maid be the said Jonet to the said Alexander contains the soume of iiijc. merkis foirsaid money. Or ellis the said Jonet Adamson faithfully bindis and oblissis hir and als hir airis, etc., to content and pay to the said Alexander, his heirs, etc., the said soume of ijc.xl merkis quhat sumevir tyme it plaisis the said Alexander his airis, etc., within the space of the foirsaid tua zeris apone the premunition of xl dais obefor to desyre and ask the samyne fra the said Jonet, hir airis, etc., in compleit payment of the forsaid soume of iiijc merkis contenit in the said reversioun. Apone the quhilk soume of iiijc merkis the forsaidis Alexander and Jonet has convenit be thir presentis and maid price on the said land and tenement undir and abone bak and foir swa that it sall nocht be lefull to the said Alexander his airis, etc., to ask mair for the said land undir and above bak and for fra the said Jonet hir airis, etc., than the said soume of iiijc merkis. And in cais the said Alexander, his airis, etc.,

ressavis nocht the said soume of ijc.xl merkis and redemys
nocht the said land and tenement within the said space of tua
zeris eftir the dait of the reversioun viz. the xv day of September zeir of God jm.vc.xxviij zeris quharthrow the said reversioun will expyre and be of nane avale as the reversion beris
in the self in that cais the said Jonet faithfully bindis and
oblissis hir and als hir airis, etc., be the faith and treuth
in hir and thair bodys till content and pay thankfully without
ony demand question or pley the forsaid soume of ijc.xl merkis
usuall money of Scotland to the said Alexander his airis, etc.,
quhilk as zit restis unpaiit to the said Alexander of the soume
of iiijc merkis contenit in the said reversion. The quhilk soume
of ijc.xl merkis being paiit be the said Jonet hir airis, etc.,
to the said Alexander, his airis, etc., and the forsaid tua zeris
being outrynyn fra the xv. day of September zeir of God jm.vc.-
xxviij zeris it sall nocht be lesum to the said Alexander his
airis nor assignais to redeme the said land and tenement, under
and above, etc., fra the said Jonet hir airis, etc., bot the
said Alexander sall renunce quytclame and discharge the said
reversioun and be thir presentis dischargis the samyne for now
and evir in cais forsaid. And to the observyng of the premissis
baith the saidis partiis ar oblist and sworne the Holy Ewangellis tuichit. In witnes of the premissis baith the forsaidis partiis desyrit and askit instrumentis in the handis of Johne Foular
and James Stanton befor thir witnes Thomas Arnot, Thomas Purdy, with otheris divers. Both parties asked instruments. Done
in the dwellinghouse of the said Jonet.

66. 1528 Oct. 13. Renunciation by Jonet Leyis, with consent of Thomas Sinclar her spouse, in favour of Archibald Cutlar, indweller
in the town of Leith, of a letter of reversion made or promised
to be made by the said Archibald, of and upon the half part
of three acres of Temple lands, alienated by the said Jonet
and her spouse to the foresaid Archibald, lying in the wester
end of Greinsyde, between the lands of Robert Logane of Coitfeild on the east, west, south and north, in the barony of Lestalrig, and within the shire of Edinburgh. With the said Jonet's
oath not to revoke in time coming. Done in the house of the
notary. Witnesses Master Thomas Howy, James Henrison and John
Anderson.

67. 1528 Nov. 7. Sasine on resignation by Alexander Dunbar, with
consent of Katrine Scowgall his spouse, in favour of Gilbert
Knox, his heirs, etc., of the resigner's land lying within a
tenement of the late David Knox, on the north side of the High
Street, between a tenement of the late Symon Doweill on the
east, and a tenement of the late Archibald Preston on the west;
east side the transe of the said tenement, between a land of
the late John Blakstok on the south, and a land sometime of
John Broune on the north. Witnesses, William Broune, Robert
Gray, John Gray, William Hill and Thomas Arnot, serjeant. William Elphinston is bailie.
Moreover, the said Katrine Scowgall, in absence of the said
Alexander her husband, neither coerced nor compelled or forced,

as she affirmed, gave her consent to all and sundry the premises, and gave her bodily oath, the scriptures touched, not to revoke in time to come. Further, the said Gilbert promised to pay to the said Alexander and Katrine his spouse, for the said land, the sum of £30, betwixt this and the feast of St. Andrew next to come, viz. xx lib. 10s. to the foresaid Alexander Dunbar, and the remaining ten pounds to the foresaid Katrine.

68. 1528 Nov. 7. Compeared personally Master David Wauchop, parson of Pennycuk, asserting that he is personally conjunct with Katrine Scowgall, spouse of Alexander Dunbar, and nearest in kin to the said Katrine, which Master David passed to a land of the said Alexander and Katrine, lying as contained in the protocol above written; and there the said Master David, in name of the said Katrine, protested against the sasine given by William Elphinston, bailie, of the foresaid land, after resignation made by the said Alexander and Katrine, to Gilbert Knox and his heirs; and that because the said Katrine was forced and deceived into the giving of her consent to the resignation thereof. Therefore he broke the said sasine by the breaking of a dish upon the ground of the said land, and protested that it do not yield any prejudice to the said Katrine as to her conjunct-fee thereof in times coming, and for remeid of law, when and where it effeirs. Witnesses, James Johnston and William Elphinston, bailies, Thomas Elphinston, and William Mow, serjeant.

69. 1528 Nov. 6. Compeared personally Alexander Belsches in name and on behalf of Agnes Cant and Katherine Adamson her sister, and also Nicholas Cheyne in name and on behalf of Elizabeth Cant his spouse: Likewise compeared George Mayne in name of Jonet Turing his spouse and Elizabeth Turing her sister, and John Kyncaid, asserting themselves to be heirs of the late Alexander Barcar, and protested that whatsoever shall be done by Archibald Douglas and Elizabeth Hoppar his spouse, concerning the alienation of a certain land or tenement, lying within the burgh of Edinburgh, on the north side of the High Street, between a land of the late Henry Cant elder on the east, and a land of Gilbert Lauder on the west, to Master Francis Boithnell and his spouse, shall not injure them; and whatever the said Master Francis or his spouse may build upon the said tenement shall not turn out in prejudice to them nor to their heirs, and for remeid of law, when and where it effeirs. Witnesses, William Elphinston, bailie, Thomas Elphinston, Alexander Adamson, George Wilson and John Malcom.

70. 1528 Nov. 20. Alexander Adamson, bailie, passed to a land or yard of Anthony Brisset, lying on the south side of the High Street, in Peebles Wynd, west side the transe thereof, between a land of Robert Law on the north, and a land of the late Master David Vocat on the south; and there John Levingtoun, brother and heir of the late Charles Levingtoun, resigned an annualrent of 10s., out of the foresaid land or yard, in the hands of the bailie, who gave sasine thereof to the foresaid Anthony

Brisset, his heirs and assignees, before these witnesses, Thomas Coupland, Alexander Halkerston, Richard Mader, and David Purves, serjeant.

71. 1528 Nov. 30. Procuratory granted by a noble and potent lord, Hugh Lord Sommervell, to Michael Tullois and John Anderson, constituting them, conjointly and severally, his free and undoubted procurators, actors, factors, etc., giving and committing to his said procurators, conjointly and severally, his free, full and irrevocable power and mandate, for him and in his name, to resign, quitclaim and overgive, from him his heirs and assignees, that his land, built and waste, with the yard thereof, lying within the burgh of Edinburgh, in the street of the Cowgate, north side the High Street thereof, in the end of a tenement of the abbot and convent of Melrose, between a land sometime of Walter Lauder, now pertaining to George Gibson, on the east, a land of the late Henry Cant on the west, and a land or yard of the said abbot and convent of Melrose on the north, by delivery of earth and stone in the hands of one of the bailies of Edinburgh: which land and yard the said Hugh Lord Sommervell, led not by force or fear, but of his own free will, as he affirmed, by these presents, surrenders and purely and simply resigns, with all right, claim, property and possession which he has to the same, in the hands of one of the said bailies, in favour of Master Adam Ottirburne of Auldhame, his heirs and assignees, for his infeftment in the said land, and heritable sasine, thereof to be given to him according to the tenor of a charter of the said lord to be made thereupon. Moreover the said Lord Sommervell promises to hold firm and stable whatsoever his procurators should do in his name in the premises, and thereupon asked instrument. Done in the lodging of the said lord, within the burgh of Edinburgh, witnesses Mathew Kilpatrick, William Sommervell and Mathew Irland.

72. 1528 Dec. 5. Sasine on resignation by Thomas Prestoun, son and heir of the late Archibald Prestoun, in favour of Francis Aikman, his heirs and assignees, of a tenement of the said Thomas, lying on the north side of the High Street, between a tenement of Margaret Broune on the east, and a tenement of the late Richard Hoppar on the west, the yard of Trinity College on the north, and the king's public street on the south. Witnesses, Alexander Makneill, notary public, Thomas Smethberd, Patrick Ewin, William Hay, Gilbert Logane, Patrick Lithqw and Thomas Arnot, serjeants.

73. 1528 Dec. 7. Sasine on precept of chancery, in favour of Isobella Dee, as lawful and nearest heir of the late Richard Scot, her great-grandfather of a certain land lying within a tenement of William Vernour, west side the transe thereof, between a land of James Johnston on the south, and the "thorthour houss" of the tenement on the north; which tenement lies on the south side of the High Street, between a land of the late John Bell on the east, and a land of the late John Butlar on the west: also of a certain waste, containing 3 particates of land, lying within the easter tenement of the said John Butlar, east side

the transe thereof, between a land of the late David Henrison, dyer, on the south, and so ascending towards the north even to a waste land of the said John Butlar, reserved for a passage to the 'througang' of the said tenement and also for supporting annual-rents (*pro suis luminaris fiendis*), on the north, the land of the said James Johnston on the east, and the said throughgang on the west. Dated at Edinburgh the 26 November and sixteenth year of the king's reign. William Lyndesay as bailie gave the sasine, witnessed by John Vernour, James Henrison, Robert Urquhart, Thomas Purdy, John Anderson, Andrew Bruse and James Stanton, notary public, Andrew Wallas, and Thomas Arnot serjeant.

74. 1528 Dec. 7. Sasine to Isobella Dee, on her cognition by William Lyndesay, bailie, as heir of the late Alexander Dee, burgess, her father, of an annual-rent of 2 merks, out of a certain land lying within a tenement of the late William Vernour, on the south side of the High Street, west side the transe thereof, and bounded as before described. Same witnesses as above.

75. 1528 Dec. 7. Sasine on resignation by John Anderson, procurator and in name of Hugh Lord Somervell, in favour of Master Adam Otterburne of Auldhame, of a land of the said Lord Somervell lying in the Cowgate, on the north side thereof, in the end of a tenement of the abbot and convent of the monastery of Melrose, and bounded as described in the procuratory of resignation granted by the said Lord on 30th. Nov. 1528. James Hendirson is procurator for Mr. Adam Otterburne. Same witnesses as in the foregoing sasine to Isobella Dee.

76. 1528 Dec. 7. Compeared a prudent man, William Watson, in the presence of William Lyndesay, bailie, and there the said William, for himself and for Katherine Carmuir, his spouse, protested, that the sasine given by the said William Lyndesay, bailie, of the land of the late William Inglis, now pertaining to Hugh Lord Somervell, to James Hendirson, attorney of Master Adam Otterburne, lying as in the protocol immediately before written, shall not turn to his hurt, nor that of his spouse, as to their liferent of the said land, and for remeid of law, and asked instruments. Done within the tenement of the abbot of Melrose, near the said land, in presence of the witnesses foresaid.

77. 1528 Dec. 10. William Lyndesay, bailie, passed to a certain land lying in St. Mary Wynd, in which James Darroch now dwells, east side the transe thereof, between a land of Saint Severin on the south, and a land (   ) on the north; and there Helen Foular, spouse of Laurence Kilpatrick, in name of her spouse, asserting that she is heir of the late Sir Alexander Kynnew her brother, protested that the sasine given by the said bailie, of an annual-rent of 6s.8d., out of the said land, to Jonet Kilpatrick shall not turn to the prejudice of the said Laurence, and broke the same sasine by the breaking of a dish: And in like manner broke a sasine given to the said Jonet by the said bailie, of a land built and waste, lying on the north side of the High Street, within a tenement of the late (   ) Turing, and protested that the foresaid sasines of the foresaid annual-rents and lands, so delivered to the said Jonet by the

said bailie, hurt not the said Laurence as lawful heir of the
said late Sir Alexander, his brother, and for remeid of law
when and where it effeirs. The said Helen asked instruments.
Witnesses, Andrew Wallas, Thomas Chalmer, James Darroch, Sir
John Young, Sir Quintin Cadzo, and John Johnston, serjeant.

78. 1528 Dec. 16. Sasine on resignation by Jonet Scheirsmyth, kinswoman and heir of the late William Scheirsmyth, burgess, in
favour of John Mure, burgess, and Agnes Fairbarne his spouse,
and the longest liver of them, and the heirs lawfully procreated
or to be procreated between them, whom failing, the one half
of the lands after mentioned to go to the said John Mure, and
his heirs whomsoever; and the other half to the said Agnes
and her heirs whomsoever, viz. of the said Jonet's lands, lying
contiguous, built and waste, on the south side of the High Street beyond the Nether Bow, in St Mary Wynd, on the east side
of the trause thereof, between the lands of the late James Young
and the late Edward Bonkill on the north, the port of the said
vennel and the common vennel on the south, a waste land of
the late Edward Thomson on the east, and the king's common
street of the said vennel on the west. And forthwith the said
John Mure and Agnes resigned an annual-rent of 40s., out of
the foresaid lands, in the hands of James Johnston, bailie,
who gave sasine thereof to the said Jonet Schersmyth, heir heirs
etc. Witnesses, John Spethy, John Davidson, George Mayne, William Quhite, Walter Anderson, James Lauder, Thomas Arnot and
David Purves.

79. 1528 Dec. 22. Sasine on resignation by Duncan Wicht, in favour
of John Wicht his son, and the heirs lawfully to be procreated
of his body, whom failing to his heirs whomsoever, of the said
Duncan's back-land lying within his tenement, on the north
side of the High Street, between a land of the late James Baty
on the east, and a land of the late George Halkerston on the
west, a land of the said Duncan on the south, and the foreland
of the said tenement on the south: Reserving the liferent to
the said Duncan. Master Henry Lauder is attorney. Witnesses,
William Pettigreif, David Wicht, James Thomson, James Johnston,
and David Purves, serjeant.

80. 1528/9 Jan. 2. Sasine on resignation by John Dennunn, son and
heir of the late Patrick Dennunn, with consent of Agnes Merschell his spouse, in favour of James Johnston, smith, and Margret
Marlzone his spouse, of a land of the said John Dennunn, below
the castle wall, in the burgh of Edinburgh, west side the High
Street thereof, between a land of William Raa on the north,
a land of Robert Bruse on the south, a land of Thomas Kincaid
on the west, and the King's common way on the east. With court
and oath of the said Agnes not to revoke in time to come: Under
reversion of £16. That quhat tyme or how sone the said Johne
Dennunn or his airis pais the said soume of xvj lib. he to haif
redres to his land excepand the said James and his wif and
thair airis to haif vij zeris eftir the lousing the said land
pay and thairfor the annuell and iiij merkis of maill yeirlie
to the said Johne and his airis, and to uphald the said land
zeirlie. And apone all this thingis abone wryttin all pairtiis

askit instrumentis. Witnesses, James Makgill, William Stewart, John Peirson, James Broune, John Carnoquhen; James Wallas, John Johnston, and David Purves, serjeants.

81. 1528/9 Jan. 2. Sasine on resignation by Thomas Mureleyis, in favour of himself and Helen Haliday his spouse, of his land on the Cowgate, lying on the south side of the High Street, between a land of the late Thomas Swift on the east, a land of the late James Lamb on the west, a land of Sir Thomas Tod, knight, on the north, and the said street of the Cowgate on the south. Witnesses, David Douglas, George Lauson, William Bowy, Thomas Smyth, David Purves and John Johnston, serjeants. James Johnston is bailie.

82. 1528/9 Jan. 8. Sasine on resignation by Patrick Cockburne, son and heir of the late Edward Cockburne, with consent and authority of Arthur Panteir his curator, in favour of Jonet Hamilton, mother to the said Patrick, of the liferent of his tenement, lying on the south side of the High Street, between a land of James Preston on the east, and a tenement of Alexander Rynd on the west. Witnesses, Robert Smyth, John Purves, Master George Forstar, John Adamson, John Reid, John Marjoribanks, and Richard Lundy. Alexander Adamson is bailie.

83. 1528-9 Jan. 11. James Elphinston, bailie, passed to the lands and tenements of the late William Aldjoy, lying upon the castle hill, on the south side of the High Street thereof, between a land of the late Francis Towris on the east, a land of the late Mr. Richard Lauson on the west, the King's Wall on the south, and the King's common way on the north; and there Agnes Rynde, relict of the said William Aldjoy, resigned in the hands of the bailie her conjunct-fee of the said lands and tenements, with the yard and waste land thereof, in favour of George Aldjoy, son and heir of the said late William: Reserving the liferent of the said subjects to the said Agnes Rynde. Which done, the bailie cognosced and entered the said George Aldjoy in and to the foresaid lands and tenements, with yard, etc., as heirs of his said father. And forthwith the said George resigned the said lands, tenements, yard, etc., again in the hands of the bailie, who thereupon gave sasine of the same to the said George Aldjoy and Margaret Towris his affianced spouse: Reserving as aforesaid. Witnesses, John Mauchane, Master Henry Lauder, William Fairly, Sir John Aikman, chaplain, John Likprevik, William Aldjoy, and John Johnston, serjeant.
The quhilk day, Agnes Rynde, the relict of umquhile William Aldjoy, is content of hir awin fre will, and grantis, that George Aldjoy, and Margaret Towris his wif haif and bruke the dwelling place and yard that his fadir duelt in, for hir lyftyme, that thai may duell in, thai payand iiij merkis and viijc. zerlie to the annuellaris and to uphald the samyn, and thairapone askit instrumentis. Witnes above writtin.

84. 1528-9 Jan. 16. Sasine on resignation by John Harvy, burgess, with consent of Jonet Forsyth his spouse, in favour of Thomas Harvy, their son, and Jonet Richartson his affianced spouse, of the said John Harvy's upper land or chamber above the stair

a tenement of the late Margaret Quhitheid, on the south side of the High Street, between a land of William Adamson on the east, a tenement of the late David Bell on the west, and a land of Andrew Uddart on the south. With the said Cristina's oath not to revoke. Witnesses, Symon Fortoun, John Galbraith, William Aikinheid, Patrick Murray, and William Mow, serjeant.

85. 1528-9 Jan 16. Sasine on resignation by John Harvy, burgess, with consent of Jonet Forsyth his spouse, in favour of Thomas Harvy, their son, and Jonet Richartson his affianced spouse, of the said John Harvy's upper land or chamber above the stair of the foreland or tenement of the late John Rynde, and loft thereof with pertinents, lying on the north side of the High Street, between a tenement of Archibald Williamson on the east, a land of James Cranston on the west, a land of Richard Litill on the north, and the king's public street on the south. Witnesses, Sir Thomas Ewin, chaplain, Alexander McNeil, notary public, John McNeill, William Forsyth, William Mow, and Thomas Arnot, serjeant.

86. 1528-9 Jan. 28. Compeared Jonet Henrison, daughter of the late Master James Henrison of Fordale, and of her own free will, as she affirmed, confessed that she had received full payment from Helen Baty, her mother, of the sum of 100 merks; which sum the late Margaret Baty bequeathed to her in her latterwill and testament: On which account the said Jonet, of her own proper motive, exonered and quitclaimed the said Helen Baty her mother, and Master Adam Otterburne her cautioner, of the said sum for now and ever, and consented that all acts and writings made thereupon shall be deleted out of the Books of the Official of Lothian. And, moreover, the said Jonet constituted the said Helen Baty, her mother, her assignee, as in her own business, in and to the sum of £100, which sum the late Alan Stewart bequeathed to the said Jonet in his testament; and this for certain gifts and favours frequently bestowed by the said Helen her mother upon the said Jonet. Done in the booth of the common clerk, in presence of these witnesses, Sir Robert Stalker, John Dykson, George Arnot and John Adamson.

87. 1528-9 Feb 1. Procuratory granted by Master Adam Otterburne to Michael Tullois and John Williamson, conjunctly and severally, to resign an annual-rent of 40s., out of the foreland of the late James Baty, lying on the north side of the High Street, between a land of the late Richard Hoppar on the east, and a land of Duncan Wicht on the west, in favour of Walter Borthik, son and heir of the late Agnes Baty, for infeftment and heritable sasine to be given to him thereupon. George Henrison asked instruments. Done in the dwelling house of the said Master Adam; witnesses, Master William Cheyne, Michael Tullos and Walter Oliphant.

88. 1528-9 Feb. 1. William Lyndesay, bailie, passed to the foreland of the late James Baty, on the north side of the High Street and bounded as in the preceding procuratory; and there John Williamson, procurator and in name of Master Adam Otterburn, resigned an annual-rent of 3 merks out of the said fore-land

in favour of Walter Borthik, son and heir of the said late Agnes; which done the bailie cognosced and entered the said Walter Borthik, as heir of his said mother, in and to an annual-rent of 6 merks upliftaƀle furth of the said foreland: And forthwith, on being seised therein, the said Walter resigned the same in the hands of the bailie, who thereupon gave conjunct-infeftment of the said annual-rent of 6 merks to George Henrison, burgess, and Katrine Adamson his spouse with the oath of the said Walter, without a court, not to revoke. Witnesses, Alexander Adamson, John Vernour, Michael Tullois, John Johnston and William Mow, serjeants.

89. 1528–9 Feb. 1. Sasine on resignation by Andrew Edgar, with consent of Margaret Clerk, his spouse, in favour of John Hay and Margaret Wallas, his spouse, of the said Andrew's land, sometime pertaining to the altar of St. Ann and the confraternity of Tailors, lying on the south side of the High Street, in the lower end of a tenement of the late John Bell, west side the transe thereof, between a land of John Hay on the north, and a land of James Henrison on the south. Witnesses, Gilbert Gibson, William Forstar, John Smythe, Archibald Lauder, Sir James Dennyston, and John Johnston, serjeant.

90. 1528 Feb. 1. Robert Gray the sone and air of umquhile Alexander Gray and als brother and air to umquhile Johne Gray burgess of this burgh of Edinburgh grantis him till haif ressavit thankful payment in noumerit money be Robert Huchesone of all maner of soumes of money and uthir gudis promitit till him be the said Robert for all and sundry his landis quhilk he analiit till him liand within the tenement of umquhile Alexander Gray on baith the sydis the said tenement, viz. the great mansion and dwelling-place that was the said umquhile Alexanderis the corshous and gardin hous with the zardis and bark hous togither with the north sellar of the land of Adam Lyndesay and the hous on the est syde the transe of the said tenement baith analiit till the said Robert and to Andro Huchesone his sone and haldis him weill content thairof and dischargis the said Robert and Andro thair airis executouris and assignais now and for evir and grantis that he never maid alienation nor contract to na othir persone of the landis above wryttin privatlie nor in pairt and in speciale nocht till Adam Lyndesay. And gif he has maid ony as he grantis nocht now as than and than as now he revokis the samyn now presentlie and in all tymes tocum for evir. And this to be extendit in the best and largest form that can be maid or divisit. Exceptand the contractis maid betwix the saidis Robert Huchesone and Robert Gray anent the said Robert Grayis barnis. And heirapone all partiis askit instrumentis. Done in the house of the notary public; witnesses, Master William Ballingawy, William Lyndesay and Alexander Craig.

91. 1528–9 Feb. 5. Sasine on renunciation by Margaret Robisone, relict of David Quhite, burgess, of her conjunct-fee or liferent of a land of William Wilkesone, burgess, and Elizabeth Quhite his spouse; proceeding also on a resignation by the said spouses,

in favour of Michael Lochmyll, baker, burgess, of their foresaid land lying on the south side of the High Street, in the vennel of the Friars Preachers, east side the transe thereof, between a land of the said friars on the south, and a land of George Gibson on the north. Witnesses, George Gibsone, John Vernour, James Broune, Richard Henrison, James Caribberis, John Mader, Sir John Kers, chaplain, and Thomas Arnot, serjeant.

The same day, renunciation by William Wilkesone and Elizabeth Quhite, his spouse, in favour of Michael Lochmyll, of a letter of reversion, made or promised to be made to them by the said Michael, of and upon the redemption of an annual-rent of 4 merks, alienated to the said Michael out of their land, now pertaining to the said Michael Lochmyll.

92. 1528–9 Feb. 16. Sasine on resignation by Alison Rouche, relict of Jasper Mayne, in favour of Katrine Mayne her daughter, of the following subjects, (1) The said Alison's land or bake-house lying on the south side of the High Street, in Peebles Wynd, east side the trause thereof, between a land of Mary Magdalene on the north, and a land of John Glen on the south, (2) Her half part of a land lying on the north side of the High Street, in Halkerston's Wynd, west side the trause thereof, between a land of the late George Halkerston on the south, and a land of the late Thomas Zair on the north. (3) The said Alison's land in the Cowgate, south side thereof, between a land of the late William Sinclair on the east, a land of the Friars Preachers on the west, and a certain waste land on the south. (4) Her half part of the booth of the fore tenement of the late William Foular, in which Leonard Stevinson now dwells, lying on the north side of the High Street, between a land of Andrew Dyksone on the east, and the land of the late John Blakstok on the west: Reserving the liferent to Alison Rouche. Witnesses, Edward Litill, Robert Staithury, Leonard Stevinston, Sir Thomas Canny, Robert Law, Henry Dempster, Robert Home, William Watson, John Sydsarf, John Clerk, John Hoge, Hugh Wallas and Thomas Arnot serjeant, with divers others.

93. 1528–9 Feb. 23. William Lyndesay, bailie, passed to the lands respectively and successively after mentioned, and there, Alexander Forstar, burgess of Stirling, renounced and demitted in the hands of the bailie, his fee of the following subjects, in favour of Robert Fostar, his son and heir apparent, reserving the liferent of the same to himself, viz., (1) His fee of two booths, together with the loft above the same, of a land lying in Buithraw, on the south side of the High Street, between a land of Alexander Mauchane on the east, and a land of the late Francis Peblis on the west. (2) The fee of an annual-rent of 13s4d. out of a certain nether booth, lying immediately on the west side of the trause of the Stynkand Style, pertaining to Robert Dennun, between the said trause on the east, and another booth of the said Robert Dennun on the west. (3) His fee of an annual-rent of 6 merks, out of a land of John Berclay, on the south side of the High Street, between a land of the late John Murray on the east, a land of John Davidson on the

west, a waste land on the south, and a land of William Lyndesay on the north. (4) The fee of an annual-rent of 20s. out of a land of John Crummy, on the south side of the High Street, between a land of Cristina Cowane on the east, a land of John Purves on the west, and the lands of James Bassenden on the south and north: Which renunciations, as above set forth, having been so made, the said William Lyndesay, bailie, gave heritable sasine of the fee of the foresaid two booths with the loft above the same; and also of the fee of all and sundry the foresaid annual-rents, to the said Robert Forstar, son and apparent heir of the said Alexander, and son and heir of the late Elizabeth Dunsyair his mother, his heirs and assignees: Reserving the liferent of the said subjects to the said Alexander Forstar. Witnesses, James Young, Robert Dennun, Adam Wallas, James Mason, Francis Spottiswode, James Corsbe, Sir William Gothrasone, and Thomas Arnot, serjeant.

94. 1528–9 Feb. 23. Sasine to Robert Forstar, son of the late Elizabeth Dunsyar, on his cognition by William Lyndesay, bailie, as heir of his said mother, of the following subjects, viz. (1) The half of a back land and mansion *lie* corshouse, with the half of the close on the north side thereof, and half of the yard on the south side thereof, lying within a tenement of the late Jonet *alias* Dowy Linton, on the south side of the High Street, between a land of the late William Fawsyde on the east, a land of the late Archibald Todrik on the west, a waste land of John Berclay on the north, and the yard of the archbishop of St. Andrews on the south. (2) The tenement of the said late Elizabeth Dunsyre, lying on the north side of the High Street, between a land or tenement of the late Archibald Napier on the east, and a land or tenement of Margaret Broune on the west. (3) Another land, in which Elizabeth Mowbray now dwells, lying within the said tenement, between a land of the late William Dunsyar on the north and a land of the late David Mailuill on the south. And forthwith the said Robert Forstar resigned his foresaid lands, viz. the said corshouse with the yard and close thereof. Also the foresaid tenement with the land lying within the same, in the hands of the said bailie, who thereupon gave liferent sasine of the foresaid subjects to a prudent man, Alexander Forstar. Witnesses, Francis Spottiswode, Robert Brog, Adam Wallas, James Corsbe, Sir William Gothrasone, chaplain, and Thomas Arnot, serjeant.

95. 1528–9 Feb. 23. Sasine to Robert Forstar, on his cognition by William Lyndesay, bailie, as son and heir of the late Elizabeth Dunsyar, of an annual-rent of 13s4d., out of a land or tenement of William Lyndesay, on the south side of the High Street, between a land of the late Master John Murray on the east, a land of John Davidson on the west, a land of John Berclay on the south, and the King's public street on the north. Immediately thereafter, the said Robert Forstar, with consent of Alexander Forstar, his father, resigned in the hands of the bailie an annual-rent of 6s8d. out of the foresaid annual-rent of 13s4d., upliftable as aforesaid, who gave sasine and conjunct-infeftment of the same to the said William Lyndesay, burgess, and Kather-

ine Young, his spouse. Witnesses, James Jameson, Michael Lochmyll, and Hugh Wallas, serjeant.

96. 1528-9 March 3. William Tod walx maker burges of Edinburgh gaif full licens and tollerans till Thomas Mureleyis burges of the said burgh till big up the south gavill of the said Williamis land liand on the north pairt the said Thomas land at the fut of umquhile Sir Thomas Toddis Close fornent the merket cors of syklyke hicht as he plesis apone the said Thomas expens And the said Thomas to big up the said Williamis bosom of his chimnay foundit in the said gavill And in tyme tocum the said William grantis for him and his airis that the tane half of the said gavill till pertene till the said Thomas and his airis heritablie for evir And gif he may bruke ane chimnay in his umast loft in the said gavill he to haif the samyne, apone the quhilkis the said Thomas askit instrumentis. Done in the house of the notary public. Witnesses, John Dalmahoy, Nicholas Howison and Alexander Knycht.

97. 1528-9 March 3. Sasine to John Andirsone, on his cognition by James Johnston, bailie, of a certain land in which William Boyd sometime dwelt, lying within a tenement of the late Sir Thomas Tod, knight, now pertaining to William Anderson, on the south side of the High Street and the Market Cross, between a land of Archibald Williamson on the east, a land of John Adamson on the west, a land of Patrick Carvour and Jonet Reid his spouse on the north, and a land of the said late Sir Thomas Tod on the south, conform to a letter of apprising made thereupon, which land the said John Anderson resigned in the hands of the bailie, who gave sasine and conjunct-infeftment of said land to the said William Anderson and Helen Litill his spouse. Witnesses, William Lyndesay, bailie, John Broune, Sir Philip Quhitbrow, William Watson, Thomas Hamilton, and John Johnston, serjeant.
The quhilk day in presence of the James Johnston, ballie, William Tod, walx maker, declarit that he had iiij merkis of annuell of the said land that William Boyd duelt in and had chartour and instrument of sesing thairapone and was in possession thair of tharfor he protestit that the sesing of the said land gevin be James Johneston ballie till John Anderson and William Anderson and his spous that the samyne hurt nocht him nor his said annuell of iiij merkis nor na uthir richt that he has to the said land and for remeid of law quhen and quhar it efferit. And als in presens of the said ballie the said William Tod causit Johne Johnstone serjand till poynd for his said annuell, quhilk serjant poyndit for the samyne. And the said William Andirsone tuke the said poynd of the said serjandis hand and held the samyne with the charge and the said serjand brak his wand apone the said William quhairapone the said William Tod askit instrumentis. Witnesses above written.

98. 1528-9 March 11. Sasine on resignation by Robert Haliburton, grandson of the late David Hoppar, with consent of Jonet Henrison his spouse, in favour of Adam Hoppar, burgess, and Katrine Ballentyne his spouse, of an annual-rent of 40s., out of the

said Robert's booths and houses below the stair of the foreland of a tenement of the said late David Hoppar, grandfather to the said Robert Haliburton, lying on the north side of the High Street, between a tenement of the late William Adamson on the east, a tenement of the late Andrew Harvy on the west, a land of Adam Hoppar on the north, and the King's public street on the south. With the said Jonet's oath not to revoke. Witnesses, Archibald Ramsay, Maurice Coupland, John Johnston and Patrick Lithqw, serjeants.

99. 1528-9 March 11. Renunciation by John Thomson in favour of George Henrison, of the said John's liferent of his land lying on the north side of the High Street; within a tenement of the late Richard Hoppar, west side the transe thereof, between a land of the said Richard on the south, and the lands of the late Master John Lokart and John Howison on the north, to be possessed and enjoyed by the said George, conform to the tenor of his evidents made thereupon. Witnesses, Alexander Young, notary public, Thomas Michelsone, Andrew Dalmahoy, James Talzefeir, John Williamson and William Mow.

100. 1528-9 March 13. Sasine on precept of chancery in favour of John Scot, nephew and lawful and nearest heir of the late James Scot, his father's brother, of the following subjects, (1) A certain back-land lying at the Castle Hill on the south side of the High Street thereof, between a land of the late Master John Malison, now pertaining to Patrick Baron, on the east, a land of the late John Levington on the west, a certain fore land of the late James Cadzow on the north, and a waste land or yard of Thomas Smyth on the south. (2) An annual-rent of 8 merks, out of a tenement of the late Sir John Bigholme canon of Jedburgh, now pertaining to James Fenton and Euphame Adamson, his spouse, lying on the south side of the High Street, near to the collegiate church of Saint Giles, between the common transe and the land of the late Robert Vaus on the north, and the Cowgate on the south, a land of the late Henry Preston on the east, and the cemetery of St. Giles on the west. (3) An annual-rent of 2 merks, out of a land of the late George Micheson, now pertaining to John Scharp, baker, on the south side of the High Street, in the lower end of a tenement of the late George Bervyk, in the Cowgate, between a land of the late John Johnston on the east, and a land of the late William Godiskirk on the west and north, and the said street of the Cowgate on the south. (4) An annual-rent of 13s4d., out of a tenement of the late Hector Thomson, baker, on the south side of the High Street, below the Nether Bow, between a land of the late George Faulo on the east, a land of the late Alexander Bonkill, on the west, the Strand on the south, and the king's common way on the north. Dated at Edinburgh 12 March in the sixteenth year of His Majesty's reign. The sasine, given by William Lyndesay, bailie, is witnessed by William Preston, William Steill, Mathew Pynkerton, James Scot, James McGill younger, James Gilbert, David Michelson, Patrick Lithqw and David Purves, serjeants.

101. 1528-9 March 13. Sasine on resignation by John Scot, nephew

and heir of the late James Scot, in favour of Thomas Scot, indweller in the Canongate, and Elizabeth Logane his spouse, of the said John's waste back-land, lying in the burgh of Edinburgh, at the Castle Hill, on the south side of the High Street thereof, and bounded as in the preceding sasine: Also of an annual-rent of 8 merks, out of the tenement of the late Sir John Bigholme, canon of Jedburgh, now pertaining to James Fenton and Eufame Adamson his spouse, lying on the south side of the High Street, and bounded as before described. Witnesses aforesaid.

102. 1528-9 March 19. Sasine on resignation by John Scot, nephew and heir of the late James Scot his father's brother, in favour of Thomas Scot, indweller in the Cowgate, his heirs and assignees, of an annual-rent of 2 merks, out of the land of the late George Michelson, now pertaining to John Scharp, baker, in the lower end of a tenement of the late George Bervyk in the Cowgate: Also of an annual-rent of 13s4d., out of the tenement of the late Hector Thomson, baker, below the Nether Bow, and bounded as before described. Witnesses the same as aforesaid.

103. 1528-9 March 19. William Lyndesay, bailie, passed to a land of the late Thomas Wardlaw, lying on the south side of the High Street and Tolbooth, between a land of the late William Adamson on the north, and a land of the late John Falcoun on the south; and there Henry Young and Richard Wardlaw, burgesses, presented to the foresaid bailie certain letters of retour of an apprising, under the common seal of cause of the burgh of Edinburgh, and under the seals of those who passed upon the said apprising, written on parchment, bearing a mandate by deliverance of the Lords of Council, upon the back thereof, of which retour of apprising and mandate of the Lords the tenors follow, and are thus in the vulgar tongue:-
Till all and sundry quhais knawlege thir present Lettres sall to cum the Provest Baillies and Counsale of the burgh of Edinburgh Greting in God everlasting. Forasmikle as thir personis undir writtin, viz. Henry Young Richart Wardlaw cessionaris and assignais maid be umquhile Barbara Wardlaw to the soume of Four hundreth merkis comperit befor Ws in jugement and persewit Elizabeth Wardlaw and Cristiane Wardlaw for the said soume and produit befor Ws the said Lettre of Cessionarii and Assignarii with ane Decreit of the Lordis of Counsale and the Kingis Lettres direct therupon chargeand Ws to call the saidis Richart and Henrye on that ane pairt Elizabeth and Cristiane Wardlaw on that uthir pairt befor Ws and tak cognitioun in the said matter and gif it wer fundin that the said Hendry and Richart wer maid lauchfull cessionaris and assignais in and to the said soume eftir the forme of the said decreit of the lordis and gif the alienation of the land contained in the said decreit maid be the saidis Elizabeth and Cristiane was eftir the dait of the said decret, and gif sua wer fundyhe, that We suld put the secund pairt of the said decreit to execution at the instance of the said umquhile (Barbara Wardlaw)

That is to say to poynd and distrenze for the said soume of
Four hundreth merkis becaus the saidis Elizabeth and Cristiane
refusit to mak Warrandyce to the said umquhile Barbara and
to fulfill the first pairt of the said decret and thairfor that
we suld apprys the said Land and Tenement for the said soume
nochtwithstanding the said Alienation as at mair leuth is contenit in the said Decret and Lettres schawin and producit befor
Ws in jugement Thairapone We beand deligentlie avisit with
the saidis Lettres the richtis ressouns and allegationis of baith
the saidis pairtiis at lenth sene and understandin and therwith
beand ryple avisit at all poyntis and be verteu thairof Decernis
and ordanis that the ballies caus and compell certane famous
nychtbouris till ane sufficient nummer unsuspect till pas and
apprys the said land and tenement quhilk lyis within this burgh on the south syde the Tolbuith betwix the land of umquhile
John Falcoun on the south pairt and the land of umquhile William Adamsone on the north pairt for the said soume of Four
hundreth merkis safer as it is of availl or extendis to eftir
the forme of the said decreit and command of the kingis lettres
past thirapone And thaireftir the saidis ballies gart ordourlie
call the personis undir wryttin in jugement and causit thame
be sworne the Holy Evangellis tuchit that thai suld pas and
apprys the said land and tenement to the utter availl for payment of the said soume to the saidis Richart and Henry, that
is to say, Alexander Adamson ballie, Thomas Andersone, Alane
Mosman, Johne Wache, Robert Rymald, Johne Lytill, Symon Clerk,
Robert Mailuill, Thomas Baird and James Balcasky quhilk personis past to the ground of the said land and tenement and vesyit
the samyne within and without at all partys under and abone,
and eftir that, with consciens and knowlege sett and apprysit
the said haill land and tenement under and above to the soume
of ten pundis foreby the annuell of fourty schillingis awand
to the chaplane of Sanct Colms altar situated within the colleg
kirk of Sanct geill that is to say fyiftene merkis fre and apprysit ilk merkis thairof to sevintene merkis usuale money of
Scotland Reservand to Marione Falcoun the liferent of the said
haill land and tenement for all the dayis of hir lyfe eftir the
tennour of hir instrumentis and evidentis producit and schawin
thairapone in jugement. And this to all and sundri quham it
efferis or may effeir We mak it knawin be thir presentis. In
witnes of the quhilk thing we have to thir presentis gart append our common Seill of Caus togidder with the Seillis of them
that past apone the said apprysing at Edinburgh the ten day
of Februar the zeir of God ane thousand fyve hundreth and
twenty aucht zeiris.
Follows the tenor of the said deliverance or mandate of the
Lords of Council:-
At Edinburgh the first of March in the year of the Lord jm.vc.
xxviij. The Lordis ordanis the Provest and Ballies of Edinburgh to gif sasing of this Land eftir the forme of the apprysing.
After the reading of which apprising, and publication thereof
by me notary public under written, the foresaid William Lynde-

say, baillie, in virtue of his office, and also of the mandate of the said Lords of Council, gave state, corporal possession and sasine of the one half part of the foresaid land to Henry Young, burgess, his heirs and assignees; likewise of the other half part of the said land to Richard Wardlaw, his heirs and assignees. Witnesses, James Johnston, bailie, Alan Mosman, John Cuke, John Kyle, James Stevinsone, Thomas Murray, John Vaiche, James Coky and Patrick Lithqw.

104. 1528-9 March 19. Compeared Marion Falcone, relict of Thomas Wardlaw, in presence of William Lyndesay, bailie, and protested, that the sasine given by the said bailie, of the land in the protocol immediately preceding, to Henry Young and Richard Wardlaw, according to the tenor of the said protocol, hurt not her liferent thereof, and for remeid of law. Likewise protested, that the said sasine, so delivered to the said Henry and Richard, shall not result in any prejudice to Sir Andrew Harper, his right to the said land. Same witnesses.

105. 1528-9 March 20. Sasine on resignation by John Malcom, son and heir of the late William Malcom, in favour of Ninian Thomson, burgess, and Helen Myans, his spouse, of the said John's land lying on the north side of the High Street, within a tenement of the late Simon Doweill, west side the transe thereof, between a land of the late David Leche on the south and a land of the late Robert Scot on the north; which tenement lies on the north side of the High Street, between a tenement of Alexander Cant on the east and a tenement of the late David Knox on the west. Witnesses, Thomas Nory, John Geychane, John Bayne and Thomas Elphinstone. Thomas Arnot is attorney for the said Helen.

The said day hour and witnesses, the said Ninian Thomson resigned a ground-annual of 2 merks, upliftable from the foresaid land, in the hands of William Elphinston, bailie, who gave sasine thereof to the said John Malcom.

106. 1528-9 March 22. Renunciation by Robert Gray, son and heir of the late Alexander Gray in the hands of William Elphinston, bailie, of all right which he has in and to an annual-rent of 5 merks, leviable from a certain land lying on the south side of the Tolbooth, now pertaining to Marion Broune, at the head of Bestis Wynd; and likewise renounced his right to the said land, in favour of the said Marion Broune, her heirs and assignees. Witnesses, Thomas Wode, John Vaiche, and Thomas Arnot, serjeant.

107. 1528-9 March 22. William Lyndesay, bailie, passed to a land formerly pertaining to William Tod and Jonet Lowrestoun his spouse, now to Adam Mak and William Mak, lying on the south side of the High Street, in Forstaris Wynd, west side the transe thereof, between a land of Thomas Ramsay on the south, and a certain transe and land of the Lord of Corstorphin on the north, and a waste land of the said William Tod on the west; and there Adam Mak and William Mak, sons of the late William Mak,

in a full and open court, held before the said bailie, upon the ground of the said land, chose and desired Thomas Lowristoun to be given to them as their curator, for completing the matter under written; which curator the said bailie gave to the said pupils, and caused him to give his oath, *de fideli* for the faithful administration of the said office. After which the foresaid Adam and William Mak, with consent and authority of their curator, confessed the foresaid land to be now lawfully redeemed from them by the said Wm. Tod and Jonet Lowristoun, by payment of £140, under reversion of which sum the said land was alienated: Upon which the said bailie gave sasine to the said William Tod and Jonet Lowristoun his spouse, of the said land, to be possessed by them as freely as before the alienation thereof. Witnesses, William Blaklok, Walter Bruse, James Lowriston, Thomas Lowriston, William Lowriston, Patrick Dykson, Thomas Williamson, James Johnston, *alias* Edinburgh, Thomas Arnot, David Purves and Patrick Lithqw, serjeants.

108. 1528-9 March 22. Sasine on resignation by William Tod, with consent of Jonet Lowristoun his spouse, in favour of William Ogill, notary public, his heirs and assignees, of the said William's land lying in Forstar's Wynd and bounded as described in the foregoing sasine. With the said Jonet's oath not to revoke. Witnesses the same as aforesaid.

109. 1529 March 31. Assignation by Geills Cranston, sister and one of the heirs of the late Patrick Cranston, with consent of Edward Affleck her spouse, in favour of James Creichton of Cranstonriddell, of a certain letter of reversion, made or to be made, of and upon the redemption of the Four merk lands of Ugstoun, lying in the barony of Hartsyde and shire of Berwick; and that for certain sums of mony presently paid, and other favours done by the said James. Done in Saint Giles Church, in the aisle of the Holy Blood, in presence of these witnesses, Mungo Stevinsone, Sir Patrick Pollok, Martin Creichton, Alexander Lumly and James Stevinsone.

110. 1529 April 2. Sasine to David Chapman, son of the late Walter Chapman, on his cognition by William Elphinston, bailie, as heir of his said father, of a tenement of the said Walter lying in the Cowgate, on the south side thereof, between a tenement of Patrick Flemyng on the east, and a tenement of the late William Halkerston on the west. And forthwith in a full and open court held and fenced before the said bailie, upon the ground of the said tenement, the foresaid David Chapman chose and desired Michael Tullois to be given to him as his curator, to solely carry out the effect underwritten and to last for the space of the next 20 days; which curator the said bailie assigned and gave to the said David taking from him the oath of faithful administration in his said office: Upon which the said David Chapman, with consent of the said Michael Tullos his curator, resigned the foresaid tenement in the hands of the bailie, who thereupon gave liferent sasine thereof to Agnes Cokburne, mother to the said David, in presence of Master John Lethame and William Stevinsone, notaries public, Andrew Gibsone Michael Tullois,

and Thomas Arnot, serjeant.

111. 1529 April 2. Compeared personally, Agnes Cokburne, relict of Walter Chapman, in presence of William Elphinstone bailie; and there the said Agnes gave and delivered to David Chapman, son and heir of the said Walter, all and sundry the moveable goods heritably pertaining to the said David by reason of the decease of his said father; and in token of the delivery of the same, the said Agnes gave to the said David one silver coffer, one mirror, one spoon and one silver saltcellar. And there the said David Chapman confessed that he received in his hands all and sundry the foresaid heritable goods; which goods he with consent of Michael Tullois his curator, for certain reasonable causes, favours and good deeds done to him by the said Agnes his mother, gave back again to her, and in token thereof delivered to the said Agnes Cokburne the symbols above mentioned, in presence of the witnesses foresaid, with divers others.

112. 1529 April 5. Sasine to Sir John Ker, chaplain, son of the late John Ker, on his cognition by William Lyndesay, bailie, as heir of his said father, in and to a certain land lying within a tenement of the abbot and convent of the monastery of Melrose, on the south side of the High Street, west side the transe of the said tenement, between a land of the late Walter Chapman on the east, and a land of the late Henry Cant on the west, a land or great mansion of the said abbot and convent of the said monastery on the south, and a land of the late Sir Thomas Halkerston, provost of Creichtoun, on the north; Also in and to another land lying within the said tenement, east side the trause thereof, between a land of the said late Sir Thomas Halkerston on the north, and from thence extending and descending in breadth the same as the land of the said Sir Thomas, and in length by the whole space of the dwelling-house of the said late Walter Chapman, even to the land of the late Sir George Cottis, respectively. Sir John Ker asked instruments. Witnesses, Hector Alexanderson, John Quhite, Thomas Arnot and David Purves, serjeants.

113. 1529 April 7. Sasine to John Anderson, son of John Anderson, burgess, on his cognition by James Johnston, bailie, as heir of his said father, in and to an annual-rent of 20s., out of a tenement of John Symsone, lying below the Castlewall, beside the muse well, on the south side of the High Street, between a land of the late James Stury on the east, and a land of the late Thomas Broune on the west: Which annual-rent the said John Anderson resigned in the hands of the said bailie, who thereupon gave sasine thereof to John Symsone, son and heir apparent of the said John Symsone, in fee and heritage; and to Margaret Pettigreif, mother to the said John, in liferent. Witnesses, John Menzies, William Aitkin, Richard Huchesone, Patrick Bannatyne, and David Purves serjeant.

114. 1529 April 10. Sasine on resignation by Master Henry Henrison in favour of Marion Gawy, his affianced spouse, in liferent of the fore-land of his tenement lying on the south side of the

High Street, of the Cowgate, between a land of the late John Runsyman on the east, and a tenement of Patrick Flemyng on the west. Witnesses, Edward Craufurd, Andrew Wallas, James Dunbar, Robert Cottis, James Coluill, and Hugh Wallas, serjeant. William Lyndesay is bailie.

115. 1529 April 13. Sasine on Resignation by William Blakstok, procurator and in name of William Lord Sinclar, in favour of John Hay, burgess, and Margaret Wallas his spouse, of the said Lord Sinclair's land or tenement on the south side of the High Street, within the vennel of Bell's Wynd, west side the trause thereof, between a land of the late John Bell on the north, a land of John Purves on the south, and a land of the late William Vernour on the west. Witnesses, Master Andrew Foular, vicar of Arbroath, Alexander Reid, Patrick Lithqw, John Johnston, and David Purves, serjeant. William Elphinston is bailie.

116. 1529 April 15. Sasine to Agnes Liddaill, daughter and one of the heirs of the late Margaret Quhitheid, on her cogn. by William Elphinston, bailie, in and to her part, viz. the fourth part, of the tavern or wester vault of the fore-land or tenement of the said Margaret Quhitheid, lying on the south side of the High Street, between a land of William Adamson on the east, a tenement of the late David Bell on the west, a land of Andrew Uddart on the south, and the King's public street on the north. George Ker is attorney. Witnesses, Andrew Ker of Greynheid, William Ker, Gilbert Huntar, Master Thomas Ker, John Symson, Andrew Symson, Patrick and Thomas Arnot, serjeants.
And in like manner the said bailie cognosced and entered Jonet Liddaill, daughter and one of the heirs of the late Margaret Quhitheid, in and to her part, viz. a fourth part, of the said tavern and vault, as use is within burgh. Same attorney and witnesses.

117. 1529 April 17. Sasine on resignation by Archibald Litill, with consent of Jonet Lauder his spouse, in favour of William Dyk and Katherine Litill his spouse, of an annual-rent of 40s., out of a tenement of the late George Levingtone, now pertaining to the heirs of the late John Carkettill, lying on the south side of the High Street, between a tenement of the late Lord Borthik on the east, and a land of the late John Swift on the west: Under reversion of the sum of £36; that whenever it shall please the said Archibald or his spouse, or his heirs or assignees, to pay the foresaid sum to the said William or his heirs, then they shall have regress in and to the said annual-rent as they formerly had. Witnesses, David Tod, James Brys, Ninian Lauson, Alexander Foular, Sir Philip Quhitbrow, and John Johnston, serjeant. James Johnston is bailie.

118. 1529 April 28. William Elphinston, bailie, passed to a land of the late John Cowane, lying beside the Nether Bow, on the south side of the High Street, between the lands of James Bassenden on the west and north, a land of Andrew Mowbray on the south, and a certain vennel on the east; and there the said bailie cognosced and entered Sir Alexander Scot, chaplain, grandson and heir of the late John Cowane his grandfather, in and

to the foresaid land, and seised the said Sir Alexander in the same, by putting him in possession thereof as the manner is within burgh, in the case of heirs of burgesses: Reserving all rights. And forthwith the said Sir Alexander Scot resigned his said land in the hands of the bailie, who gave sasine thereof to William Scot, his heirs and assignees. Witnesses, John Marjoribanks, Patrick Flemyng, John Arnot, Gilbert Skeill, Rolland Donaldson, Master James Carmuir, and Thomas Arnot, serjeant.
The quhilk day in presens of the said ballie William Elphinstoun, Rolland Donaldson protestit the quhat wir war done be the ballie anent the entering of Sir Alexander Scot as heir to his gudsir to the land lying besyde the Netherboll and resignation maid thairof agane be the said Sir Alexander in the said ballies handis and sesing gevin agane of the said land to William Scot hurt nocht him anent the soume that he had optenit apone the said Sir Alexander contenit in the Kingis Lettres that the samyne hurt nocht the said Rolland and for remeid of law quen and quhar it efferit. Same witnesses.

119. 1529 April 28. Assignation by Walter Borthik, son and heir of the late Agnes Baty, sister and one of the heirs of the late James Baty, in favour of George Henrison his cousin, of two letters of reversion, viz. one made by John Broune to the said James Baty, of and upon the redemption of an annual-rent of 10 merks, out of a land lying in Halkerston's Wynd, east side the transe thereof; and the other of and upon the redemption of an annual-rent of 30s., viz. 20s. out of a land of the late William Halkerston, lying on the north side of the High Street, between a land of the late Peter Marshe on the east, and a land of the late George Halkerston on the west. Done in the chamber of Robert Stalkar in presence of these witnesses, Sir Robert Stalkar, chaplain, Andrew Richartsone, John Williamson and John Fair.

120. 1529 April 29. Sasine on resignation by Robert Mailuill, son and heir of the late David Mailuill, in favour of himself and Jonet Spittall his spouse, (1) Of the said Robert's land containing hall, chamber and cellar, lying within a tenement of the late William Dunsyare, on the north side of the High Street, between a tenement of the late Archibald Napier on the east, and a tenement of Margaret Broune on the west, and the lands of the said Robert on the south and north. (2) Of his house lying within a tenement of the said late David Mailuill, lying on the south side of the High Street, between a tenement of the late Archibald Todryk on the east, and a tenement of the late Thomas Ramsay on the west: Reserving to Adam Wallas the frank-tenement of the said last land, according to the manner of the courtesy of Scotland. Witnesses Master Henry Spittaill, William Watson, James Litiljohne, James Johnston, John Baron, Thomas Arnot and Patrick Lithqw.
Which day Thomas Quhithill declared that the foresaid land containing a hall, chamber and cellar, lying in Dunsyaris Close pertains to him by reason of the courtesy of Scotland, through the decease of Margret Mailuill his spouse: Therefore he protested, that the sasine given by William Elphinston, bailie,

of the foresaid land, after resignation, to the said Robert and Jonet Mailuill his spouse, hurt not him as to his life interest in the said land, and asked instruments in presence of the witnesses above written.

121. 1529 May 4. Sasine on renunciation by John Berclay in favour of William Nudry, (1) Of the half part of a back-land and mansion to wit the cors house, with the half of the close on the north side of the said mansion; together with the half of the yard on the south side thereof, lying within a tenement of Jonet *alias* Dowy Lyntoun, on the south side of the High Street, between a land of the late John Murray on the east, and a land of John Davidson on the west; all lying within the said tenement, between a land of the late William Fawsyde on the east, and a land of the late Archibald Todryk on the west, a waste land of the late Robert Coksone on the north, and another waste land of the said tenement on the south. (2) A certain tenement of land, lying on the south side of the High Street, in the vennel of the Blessed Virgin Mary of the Church of Fields, east side the transe thereof, between the lands of Andrew Auld, Thomas Vaiche, and a piece of the yard pertaining to the prebendaries of the said Church of the virgin Mary, on the south, a land of the late Stephen Law on the north, the common transe of the said vennel on the west, and a land of Patrick Inchecok on the east. Witnesses, Master Gawin Logy, Master Thomas Slewman, Sir Andrew Myll, Alexander Wode, David Purves and John Johnston, serjeants.

122. 1529 May 4. Sasine on resignation by William Nudry, cousin and heir of the late Thomas, abbot of the monastery of Culross, in favour of Master Gawin Logy, his heirs and assignees, of the foresaid half part of the back-land and mansion *lie* Cors House, half part of the close on the north side of the said mansion; together with the half of the yard on the south side thereof, pertaining to the said William Nudry, all lying within the tenement of the late Jonet *alias* Dowy Lyntoun, on the south side of the High Street: Also of the said William Nudry's tenement in the vennel of the Kirk o' Fields, and all bounded as before described. Witnesses, Sir Andrew Myll, chaplain, Master Thomas Slewman, Alexander Wode, David Purves and John Johnston, serjeants.

123. 1529 May 12. Sasine on resignation by Marion Alison, relict of Andrew Home, of her conjunct-fee in favour of Isobel Home, daughter and heir of the said late Andrew Home; and on cognition of the said Isobel as heir foresaid, in and to his land, with the yard thereof, lying below the Castle Wall, on the south side of the High Street, between a land of John Anderson on the east, and a land of the late James Stury on the west: Which land and yard the said Isobel instantly resigned in the hands of the bailie, who thereupon gave sasine thereof to the said Isobel Home and John Menzeis her spouse in conjunct-fee: Reserving to the said Marion Alison the liferent of the same. Witnesses, James McGill, William Raa, Patrick Bannatyne, William Richartson, John Lescheman, Robert Wilson,, and David Purves, serjeant.

124. 1529 May 28. Sasine on resignation by John Symson, son and heir of the late Michael Symson, burgess, in favour of Robert Watson, burgess, and Elizabeth Baroun, his spouse, of the said John's land lying on the south side of the High Street, in Forstar's Wynd, east side the trause thereof, between a land of the late William Falcoun on the south, and a land of the late John Falcoun on the north. Witnesses, John Rig, William Symson, Jasper Legat, and Patrick Lithqw, serjeant.

125. 1529 May 29. Sasine on resignation by Stephan Buchane, son and heir of the late Alan Buchane, in favour of himself and Jonet Symson, his affianced spouse, of the said Stephan's land lying within a tenement of the late George Halkerston, on the north side of the High Street, between a land of Dimean Wicht on the east, and a land of Robert Lyndesay on the west. Witnesses, William Coldane, Ninian Lauson, William Johnston, Sir Mathew Symson, chaplain, Thomas Dryburgh, Andrew Peirson, and David Purves, serjeant.

The same day, Stephen Buchane promised before the said witnesses, that, in case the said Jonet should decease within a year and day after the date of this present instrument, he would deliver and pay to the nearest friends of the said Jonet the sum of 20 merks; which sum he received in his hands for the marriage contracted between them; and thereupon the said woman asked instruments. James Johnston is bailie.

126. 1529 June 10. James Johnston, bailie, passed to a certain tenement sometime pertaining to the late Thomas Swift, burgess, commonly called the Stoiffis, with a certain waste land contiguously adjacent to the said tenement, on the south side thereof, within the burgh of Edinburgh, on the south side thereof, lying between a land of the late James Fairlie on the north, and the King's common way of the Cowgate on the south, a land sometime pertaining to the said late Thomas Swift on the east, and the trause of the vennel of the late Sir Thomas Tod, knight, on the west; and there the said bailie gave heritable sasine of the said tenement of land *lie* Stoiffis: Also of the said waste land, by delivery of the key of the door to Jonet Swift, sister and heir of the said late Thomas Swift: Which Jonet Swift, instantly after receiving the said sasine, of her own free will, personally surrendered and resigned the foresaid tenement of land *lie* Stoiffis, together with the foresaid waste land on the south side thereof, in the hands of the said bailie, in favour of James Meldrum, notary public, and Jonet Sleuchman, his spouse; which bailie receiving the said resignation gave sasine of the said tenement called the Stoiffis, together with the said waste land, by delivery of earth and stone of the ground thereof to the foresaid James Meldrum and Jonet Sleuchman his spouse: Reserving the frank-tenement of the dwelling-house in which the said Jonet Swift now dwells, together with the cellar immediately below the same to the said Jonet Swift during her lifetime, as, her liferent of the annual-rent of the said tenement. Witnesses, George Matheson, burgess of the said burgh, John Maxwell, John Sydsarf, and Hugh Wallas, serjeant.

JOHN FOULAR

127. 1529 June 26. Sasine to William Bell, son and heir of the late John Bell, on his cognition by William Elphinston, bailie, in and to the said John's tenement, on the south side of the High Street, between a tenement of the late Margaret Quhithead on the east, and a land of John Vernour on the west, a land of John Hay on the south, and the King's public street on the north. Witnesses, David Wode, Paul Kynloch, William Stevinson, John Bell, Patrick Lithqw and Thomas Arnot, serjeants.
The same day, before the said witnesses, William Stevinson, in name of the children of the said late John Bell, protested that the sasine given by William Elphinston, bailie to William Bell, as heir of the late John Bell, of his tenement of land lying in the protocol before written hurt not them as to their annual-rents which they have upliftable from the foresaid tenement, and for remeid of law where and when it effeirs.

128. 1529 June 26. Sasine on resignation by Andrew Mowbray, in favour of himself and Katrine Hoppar his affianced spouse, of the following subjects. (1) His fore-land or tenement lying on the north side of the High Street, between a land of the late William Lokkart on the east, a land of the late James Turing on the west, a land of Master James Foulis on the north, and the King's public Street on the south. (2) A land and yard of the said Andrew, on the south side of the High Street, between a land of the late William Scheirsmyth on the east, and a waste land and yard (   ) on the west, the lands of the said Andrew called the Galry or Stable and a land of James Basseildene and the late Philip Forstar on the north, and the King's public street of the Cowgate on the south. (3) Another land of the said Andrew Mowbray, in which Archibald Donaldson now dwells, on the south side of the High Street, between a land of the said Andrew on the south, a land of the late John Cowane on the north, a land of James Bassenden on the west, and the transe of the tenement on the east. Witnesses, Adam Stewart, John Jameson, Patrick Kincaid, Patrick Otterburn, Archibald Donaldson, Albert Smyth, and Thomas Arnot, serjeant. William Elphinston is bailie.

129. 1529 June 30. Sasine on resignation by Beatrix Anderson, relict of George Broune, in favour of Marion Broune, her heirs, etc., of an annual-rent of 2 merks, out of the said Marion's fore-land, which sometime pertained to Adam Suerde, lying on the south side of the High Street and Tolbooth, between a land of the said Marion on the east, and a land pertaining to the chaplain of the altar of Saint James, situated within the church of Saint Giles, on the west, a land of the late William Adamson on the south, and the King's public street on the north. Witnesses, William Libertoun elder, William Libertoun younger, Sir Philip Quhitbrow, chaplain, William Mow, and David Purves, serjeant. James Johnston is bailie.

130. 1529 July 10. James Johnston, bailie, passed to a tenement of Margaret Broune, lying on the north side of the High Street, between a tenement of the late William Dunsyar on the east, and a tenement sometime of Thomas Preston, now pertaining to

Francis Aikman, on the west; and there Sir Alexander Coupar, chaplain and one of the prebendaries of the collegiate Church of our Lady of the Fields, resigned his annual-rent of 2 merks, to be levied from the foresaid tenement, in the hands of the said bailie, who thereupon gave heritable sasine of the foresaid annual-rent of 2 merks to Sir Robert Lille, chaplain and one of the prebendaries of the said church, in his own name and of the other prebendaries of the foresaid collegiate church, and their successors, for an anniversary, and distribution to the poor, to be made yearly, conform to the tenor of a charter to be made thereupon. The said Sir Robert Lille asked instruments. Witnesses, William Lyndesay, bailie, William Wilson, William Watson, Master John Williamson, Nicholas Coupar, and Hugh Wallas, serjeant.

131. 1529 July 15. Sasine on renunciation by Agnes Litiljohn, relict of James Haw, in favour of James Harlabankis, of the liferent of the said Agnes Litiljohn's half part of a certain land of the said late James Haw, lying beside the Over Bow, on the east side of the High Street thereof, between a land pertaining to the altar of Saint James on the north, and a land of the said James Harlabankis on the south: The said Agnes gave her bodily oath, the Scriptures touched, not to revoke. Witnesses, Mungo Tennent, Andrew Quhite, James Fairly, Alexander Darling and Thomas Quhite.

132. 1529 July 31. Sasine on resignation by William Bailze, with consent of Katrine Wicht, his spouse, in favour of Sir Mathew Symson, chaplain of the altar of the Holy Blood, in name of the Church, and in name of the other brothers of the confraternity of the said most Holy Blood, of the said William's land, below the Castle Wall, on the south side of the High Street, between a land sometime of Laurence Barcar on the east, and a land of Alexander Chalmer on the west: Reserving the franktenement thereof to the said William Ballze and Katrine his spouse, the survivor of them. The said Katrine's oath not to revoke. Witnesses, William Lavy, John Forstar, John Law, William Clerk, Alexander Chesholme, David Jameson and Patrick Young. James Johnston is bailie.

133. 1529 Aug 2. Sasine to John Fresall, son of Jonet Broune, relict of Thomas Fressall, on renunciation by the said Jonet of her conjunct-fee, and cognition of the said John by William Lyndesay, bailie, in and to a waste land of the said Thomas Fressall, lying within a tenement of William Broune, west side the transe thereof, between a land and mansion of the said late Thomas on the south, and a land of Robert Bruse on the north: Which waste land the said John Fressall resigned in the hands of the bailie, who gave sasine thereof to Robert Bruse, his heirs and assignees, according to the tenor of the charter; with the half part of the north gable of the said mansion. Witnesses, Sir William Murray, chaplain, John Bruse, James Bruse, and Thomas Arnot.

134. 1529 Aug. 3. Sasine on resignation by John Broun in favour

of Katrine Aikman his spouse, in liferent of his land containing a hall, chamber and two cellars below the same, lying within a tenement of the late William Dunsyar, on the north side of the High Street, between a tenement of the late Archibald Napier of Merzemstoun on the east, and a tenement of Margaret Broun on the west, a land of the late David Maluill on the south, and a land of the late Elizabeth Dunsyar on the north. Witnesses James Aikman, Alexander Peblis, Sir William Cady, chaplain, William Smert, and David Purves, serjeant.

135. 1529 Aug. 9. Sasine on resignation by Thomas Falcone, with consent of Agnes Mathy his spouse, in favour of Sir David Young, chaplain, curate of Saint Giles church, in name of the Church, of an annual-rent of 18s., out of the resigner's land on the south side of the High Street, lying within a tenement of the late Thomas Tavernar, between a land of the late Thomas Richardson on the east, a land of the late John Napier on the west, a land of the deceased George Halkerston on the north, and the street of the Cowgate on the south, yearly to be distributed by the said curate and his successors, on the day of the decease of the said Thomas, when it shall happen, viz. for the souls of the said Thomas and his spouse, and their children, namely 15s. for a triginтal of masses to be celebrated on the said day at the altars, namely of the Ascension, of Saint Sebastian and Mary Magdalene, situated within the said church, 18 pennies in wax, bread and wine, and 18 pence to the said curate for his labours. Witnesses, Sir William Thomson, Richard Wardlaw, Thomas Arnot and Hugh Wallas, serjeants. William Lyndesay is bailie.

136. 1529 Aug. 13. Sasine to Jonet Kennedy, daughter and heir of the late Donald Kennedy, burgess, on her cognition by William Lyndesay, bailie, in and to a certain land, built and waste, lying within a tenement of the late James, bishop of Dunkeld, now pertaining to Robert Bertoun of Uvirbertoun, on the north side of the High Street, between a land of the late James Cameron on the east, and a tenement of the late William Selyman on the west, the land of David Flucar immediately on the south, and the North Loch on the north. Which land the said Jonet forthwith resigned in the hands of the bailie, who thereupon gave sasine thereof to the said Jonet Kennedy and David Bonar, her spouse. Witnesses, Sir David Farnlie, prior of Monymusk, Sir James Inglis, William Stevinson, notary public, Alexander Spens, Alexander Walkar, John Gardner, Thomas Fresall, and Thomas Arnot, serjeant.

137. 1529 Aug. 13. Another sasine to Jonet Kennedy on her cognition by William Lyndesay, bailie, as heir of the late Donald Kennedy her father, of another land within the said tenement of the late James, bishop of Dunkeld, between a land of the said Robert Bertoun on the south, and a land of the said Donald Kennedy on the north: Reserving the liferent of said land to Helene Flucar Which land also the said Jonet Kennedy resigned in the hands of the bailie, who gave sasine thereof to her and David Bonar her spouse, reserving as aforesaid. The same

witnesses.

138. 1529 Aug. 13. Sasine on resignation by Jonet Kennedy, in favour of herself and David Bonar her spouse, of her annual-rent of £10, out of the lands, tenements, and buildings of John Con, flesher, lying within a tenement of the late William Cokburne on the south side of the High Street, between a tenement of the late Henry Preston on the east, a tenement of Alexander Rynde on the west, a land of the late William Lethame on the north, and a land of the late Sir William Broune, chaplain on the south. Witnesses aforesaid.

139. 1529 Aug. 18. William Lyndesay, bailie, passed to lands and tenements lying contiguously adjacent on the north side of the High Street, at the Castlehill, between a tenement of the late John Wicht on the east, and a tenement of William Valange on the west, a land of George, bishop of Elphin, on the north, and the King's public street on the south; and there Katrine Forest, relict of John Young, with consent of Robert Henrison her affianced spouse, renounced and demitted in favour of John Young, son and heir of the said late John Young, her conjunct-fee of the foresaid lands and tenements: Reserving the liferent of the said Katrine: Also the said Katrine's conjunct-fee of an annual-rent of 8 shillings, out of a land of Archibald Wischart, lying in the end of the said tenements at the North Loch, between the waste land of the said bishop of Athens on the south, and the North Loch on the north. And forthwith the said bailie cognosced and entered the said John Young as heir of his said father, in and to the foresaid lands and tenements, lying contiguously adjacent, built and waste, etc., and to the said annual-rent of 8 sh. which lands and tenements, with the said annual-rent, the said John Young, with consent of Alexander Young his curator, resigned in the said bailie's hands, who thereupon gave heritable sasine and conjoint-infeftment of the same to the said John Young and Isobel Henrison, his affianced spouse: Reserving the liferent thereof to the said Katrine. Witnesses, Sir George Heslihop, Robert Henrison, John Hendirson, Peter Falconer, John Porro, Martin Carwode, Master John Bell, Thomas Arnot and David Purves, serjeants.

140. 1529 Aug. 18. Sasine to John Young, son and heir of the late John Young, on renunciation by Katrine Forest, relict of the said John, with consent of Robert Henrison, her affianced spouse, of her conjunct-fee; and on cognition of the said John by William Lyndesay, bailie, in and to a certain land lying within a tenement of John Fischar, on the north side of the High Street, between a tenement of the late Andrew Harvy on the east, and a tenement of the late Thomas Anderson on the west, a land of the said John Fischar on the south, and a land of the late John Young on the north: Reserving the liferent of the said Katrine Forest. And forthwith the said John Young, with consent and authority of Alexander Young his curator, resigned his foresaid land in the hands of the bailie, who gave conjoint-infeftment thereof to him and Isobel Henrison, his affianced spouse: Reserving as above. Witnesses, Sir George Heslihop and

Master John Bell, chaplains, and the others aforesaid.

141. 1529 Aug. 18. Another sasine to the said John Young on renunciation by Katrine Forest, with consent of Robert Henrison, her affianced spouse, of her conjunct-fee; and on his cognition as heir of his late father, of a certain land and mansion of the said late John Young, within the tenement of John Fischar, lying and bounded as before described, west side the transe thereof, between a land of the said late John Young on the south, and another waste land of Adam Hoppar, beside the North Loch, on the north. And immediately thereafter John Young resigned his said land and mansion in favour of himself and Isobel Henrison, his affianced spouse, who are thereupon seised therein by William Lyndesay, bailie, in conjunct-fee: Reserving Katrine Forest's liferent of the same. Same witnesses.

142. 1529 Aug. 18. Sasine to John Young above designed, on renunciation of her conjunct-fee by Katrine Forest, with consent of Robert Henrison, her affianced spouse; and on the said John's cognition as heir aforesaid, of an annual-rent of 8 merks, out of the fore-land of a tenement of the late John Mason, lying on the north side of the High Street, between a tenement of the late Andrew Archbukill on the east, and a tenement of Master Adam Otterburn on the west: which annual-rent the said John Young resigned also in the hands of William Lyndesay, bailie, who gave sasine thereof to him and Isobel Henrison his spouse in conjunct-fee. Witnesses as above.

143. 1529 Aug. 25. Sasine on resignation by David Gillaspy, in favour of John Blackwood, burgess of Lanerik, of the said David's land lying in the vennel of the Kirk o' Field, west side the transe thereof, between a land of Alexander Mure on the south, and a land (   ) on the north, and a land (   ) on the west. Witnesses, Sir Bartholomew Hamilton and Sir Alexander Coupar, chaplains, William Lyndesay, and Thomas Arnot, serjeant.

144. 1529 Aug. 26. Sasine on resignation by John Levington, brother and heirs of the late Charles Levington, in favour of Sir Robert Lille, chaplain, prebendary of the Kirk o' Field, his heirs and assignees, of an annual-rent of 13s.4d., out of a land of the late Mr. David Vocat, on the south side of the High Street, in the end of the vennel of Peebles Wynd, between the said vennel on the east, a land of the late John Ramsay on the west, a land of Anthony Brissait on the north, and the street of the south. Witnesses, James Forbes, John Hendirson, Thomas Arnot and Hugh Wallas, serjeants.

145. 1529 Sept. 3. Sasine on resignation by John Tennent, with consent of Christian Allane his spouse, in favour of Ninian Blakstok and Elizabeth Pinkerton his spouse, of the said John's land, lying on the north side of the High Street, in the vennel of Halkerston Wynd, east side the transe thereof, between a land of the late Robert Colyne on the south, a land of the late Thomas Halkerston on the north, and a waste land of the late Peter Marche on the east. Witnesses, John Gyrdwode, John Gray,

William Watson, Patrick Lithqw and Thomas Arnot, serjeants. William Elphinston is bailie.

146. 1529 Sept. 4. Sasine on resignation by George Paterson, son and heir of the late Luke Paterson, in favour of Thomas Uddart, burgess, and Barbara Ferry, his spouse, of the said George's land, on the south side of the High Street, in Nudry's Wynd, east side the transe thereof, between a land of the late David Melrose on the south, a land of the late Walter Bertram on the north, and a land of the late Walter Blaklok on the east. Witnesses, William Bertoun, John Burgane, Andrew Uddart, Alexander Levingtoun, and David Purves, serjeant: Under a reversion of £200, with a tack of 9 years after the redemption thereof, made by the said George to the said Thomas and his spouse, etc., to be extended in the surest form, with all clauses necessary; and thereupon the said George asked instruments. William Elphinston is bailie.

147. 1529 Sept. 6. Sasine to John Anderson, son and heir of the late John Anderson, burgess, on his cognition by James Johnston, bailie, in and to the lands lying contiguously adjacent, built and waste, lying within a tenement of the late Archibald Todryk, on the south side of the High Street, between a tenement of the late John Davidson on the east, and a tenement of the late David Mailuill on the west, a land of the said Archibald Todryk on the north, a land of James Ur on the south, the lands of the late Maurice Wardlaw on the west, and the trause of the said tenement on the east. Which lands the said John Anderson resigned in the hands of the bailie, who thereupon gave sasine of the same to the said James Ur, flesher, burgess, and Jonet Hart his spouse. Witnesses, James Johnston, John Currour, James Neilson, William Wichtman, Andrew Home, Robert Clerk, and Hugh Wallas, serjeant.

148. 1529 Sept. 22. Sasine to William Stallis, on his cognition by William Lyndesay, bailie, as heir of the deceased John Stallis his father, of a certain land of the said John, lying in Kirk of Field Wynd, east side the transe thereof, between a land sometime pertaining to the Abbot of Jedburgh on the south, and a land of the late Henry Scot on the east and north: which land the said William resigned in favour of himself and Elizabeth Brady his spouse, who are thereupon seised therein in conjunct fee by the said bailie. Witnesses, Nicholas Craufurd, Patrick Scot, James Anderson, John Rantoun, Henry Scot, Sir David Fresall, chaplain, David Purves and Patrick Lithqw, serjeants.

149. 1529 Sept. 22. Sasine on resignation by Elizabeth Brady, in favour of herself and William Stallis her spouse, of a land or tenement of the said Elizabeth, lying in the vennel of the Friars Preachers, east side the transe thereof, between a land of Alan Mosman on the south, a land of the late John Stewart on the north, and a land of the late Robert Stanelie on the east. Witnesses, Patrick Scot, James Anderson, John Rayntoun, Sir David Fresall, and the others foresaid.

150. 1529 Sept. 24. William Elphinston, bailie, passed to a land sometime of Gilbert Welsche, lying within a tenement of the late Thomas Bervyk, between a land of the late John Hainslie on the east, a waste land of the late Henry Liberton on the west, and a waste land of the late Ninian Goddiskirk, now pertaining to John Scharp, on the south, and a certain transe of the said tenement on the north; and there the said bailie, in virtue of his office, gave heritable sasine of the foresaid land to Andrew Uddart, burgess, conform to the tenor of a process of recognition led by the said Andrew Uddart, before the provost and bailies of Edinburgh. Witnesses, Alexander Levingtoun, Richard Bald, John Burgane, John Lyntoun, and Hugh Wallas, serjeant.

151. 1529 Sept. 25. Sasine on resignation by Master Andrew Bonar, chaplain, in favour of Alexander Rynd, his heirs and assignees, of an annual-rent of 4 merks, out of a land of the late Sir John Rynd, chaplain, lying in the Buithraw, on the south side of the High Street, between a land of the late George Fysche on the east, and a land of the late Philip Craik on the west: Which annual-rent the said Alexander Rynd immediately resigned in the hands of James Johnston, bailie, who gave sasine thereof to Master Thomas Marjoribanks, attorney, and in name of James Rynd and Margaret Forest his spouse: Reserving to Alexander Rynd the liferent of the said annual-rent. Witnesses, Nicholas Carncors, Master Thomas Hoy, George Mayne, William Davidson, George Wilson, Thomas Gibson and Patrick Lithqw.

152. 1529 Sept. 6. Sasine on precept from chancery in favour of Ninian Lord Ross, as lawful and nearest heir of the deceased John Lord Ross, his great grandfather, of a back-land and mansion in which the said John Lord Ross died last vest and seised, lying within a tenement of the late James Turing, between a land of the said James Turing on the south, and a land of the late John Mure on the north; which tenement lies on the north side of the High Street, between the lands of Andrew Mowbray and Master James Fowlis on the east, and a tenement of Archibald Napier on the west. The precept is dated at Edinburgh 4th. September in the 16th. year of the King's reign. The giving of the sasine is witnessed by George Mayne, Sir Robert Kyd, Thomas Railstoun of that Ilk, Alexander Park, Thomas Elphinston, and Thomas Arnot, serjeant.

153. 1529 Sept. 27. Sasine to John Grahame, on his cognition by William Elphinston, bailie as heir of the late Alexander Grahame his father, of an annual-rent of 30s., out of a certain land lying in Kirk-of-Field Wynd, east side the transe thereof, between a land of the late Sir Patrick Hamilton of Kincavill, Knight, on the south, a land of Francis Inchecok on the east, and a land of the late John Bullok on the north. Witnesses, Master Robert Galbraith, Master William Wichtman, John Cowtis, James Lauson, and David Purves, serjeant.

154. 1529 Sept. 27. William Elphinston, bailie, passed to a land of the late Andrew Horne, lying in the foresaid burgh, below the

Castle Wall, on the south side of the High Street, between a land of John Anderson on the east, and a land of the late James Stury on the west; and there cognosced and entered Master Robert Galbraith, attorney and in name of Agnes Liddaill, daughter and one of the heirs of the late Margaret Quhitheid in and to her fourth part of an annual-rent of 26s.8d. out of the foresaid land.

And in like manner the said bailie cognosced and entered the said Master Robert Galbraith, attorney and in name of Jonet Liddaill, daughter and one of the heirs of the late Margaret Quhitheid, in and to her fourth part of the said annual-rent of 26s.8d. Witnesses, Master William Wichtman, Henry Levingtoun, John Menzeis, John Lichtman, John Anderson, and David Purves, serjeant.

155. 1529 Sept. 30. Sasine on resignation by Isobel Forfar, daughter and heir of the late David Forfar, with consent of James Heleis her spouse, in favour of Patrick Flemyng and Jonet Doby his spouse, of an annual-rent of 20s., out of a certain land lying on the south side of the High Street, in Saint Mary Wynd, between a land of the late John Fausyde on the south, and a land of the late Henry Cant on the north. Witnesses, Thomas Liberton, John Grahame, George Craik, William Aitkin, John Will, and David Purves, serjeant. William Lyndesay is bailie.

156. 1529 Oct. 4. Sasine to James Cant, grandson and heir of the late Henry Cant, on his cognition by William Lyndesay, bailie, as heir foresaid, of a tenement of the said Henry Cant on the south side of the High Street, between a tenement of the late abbot and convent of the monastery of Melrose on the east, a tenement of the late Edward Bonkill on the west, the King's public street on the north, and the street of the Cowgate on the south. Witnesses, John Porro, James Liberton, Sir George Kynloch, Robert Purdy, Robert Urquhart, Fynlay Merschell, and Thomas Arnot, serjeant.

The which day Katherine Adamson, in her own name and in name of George Cant her son, protested that whatsoever may have been done by William Lyndesay, bailie, in the seising and entering of James Cant, as heir of the late Henry Cant his grandfather, shall not hurt her, and for remeid of law where and when it shall effeir.

157. 1529 October 4. Sasine to James Cant, grandson and heir of the late Henry Cant, on his cognition by William Lyndesay, bailie, in and to a land of the said Henry, lying in Saint Mary Wynd, east side of the transe thereof, between a land of Patrick Flemyng on the south, and a land of the late James Grahame on the north. Witnesses, James Liberton, Robert Urquhart, Sir George Kynloch, chaplain, Robert Johnston, William Johnston, James Craufurd, John Davidson, and Thomas Arnot, serjeant.

158. 1529 Oct. 4. William Lyndesay, bailie, passed to the land of the late Henry Cant, lying in Saint Mary Wynd, east side the transe thereof, between a land of Patrick Flemyng on the south, and a land of the late James Grahame on the north; and there,

in a full and open court held before the said bailie, James Cant, of his own free will, chose John Purro, whom he desired to be given to him as his curator; which curator the bailie gave to the said James, and took from him the oath de fideli as to the faithful administration of his said office. And forthwith the said James Cant, with consent of the said John Purro his curator, resigned his foresaid land in the hands of the bailie, who gave sasine thereof to Alexander Belsches and (   ) Cant his spouse. Witnesses aforesaid.

159. 1529 Oct.4. Sasine on resignation by Master Adam Ottirburne, in favour of himself and Eufame Mowbray his spouse, of a land of the said Adam, which formerly pertained to the late William Inglis, built and waste, with the yard thereof, lying in the street of the Cowgate, on the north side thereof, in the end of a tenement of the abbot and convent of the monastery of Melrose, between a land of George Gibson on the east, a land of the late Henry Cant on the west, and a land or yard of the said abbot and convent on the north. And forthwith the said Master Adam, with consent of his said spouse, resigned in the hands of the said bailie their conjunct-fee of the foresaid land, built and waste, with the yard thereof, who thereupon gave sasine of the fee of the said land and yard to Robert Ottirburne, son of the said Master Adam, his heirs and assignees. Witnesses, George Henrison, Richard Multray, Michael Tullois, Alexander Halkerston, Sir Bartholomew Hamilton, John Anderson, and Thomas Arnot, serjeant.
The same day and witnesses, William Watson, for himself and in name of his wife Katherine Carmuir, protested that the sasine given by William Lyndesay, bailie, of the foresaid land, after the resignation made by the said Master Adam Ottirburne, to the said Master Adam, Eufame Mowbray, and to Robert Ottirburne in fee, hurt not him nor his wife as to their liferent thereof, and for remeid of law, and asked instruments.

160. 1529 Oct. 8. Simon Preston, one of the bailies of Edinburgh, passed to a tenement of the late Henry Preston, lying on the south side of the High Street, between a tenement of John Vernour on the east, and a tenement of the late William Cokburne on the west; and there Gilbert Hunter, with consent of Jonet Moris his spouse, resigned an annual-rent of 33s.4d., out of that his annual-rent of 4 merks which he has, leviable from a certain land lying within the said tenement, between the foreland thereof on the north, and the land lie Corshouse pertaining to William Pacok on the south, in the hands of the bailie, who thereupon gave sasine thereof to Sir Robert Stalkar, chaplain, his heirs and assignees. And forthwith the said Sir Robert Stalkar resigned his said annual-rent of 33s.4d. in the hands of the said Simon Preston, bailie, who gave heritable sasine thereof to Sir George Litiljohne, chaplain, in name of the church and his successors. Witnesses, Mungo Tennent, Stephen Thomson, Sir James Huntar, chaplain, David Purves, Patrick Lithqw and Thomas Arnot, serjeant.

161. 1529 Oct.11. Patrick Baroun, one of the bailies of Edinburgh,

passed to the lands of the late Evangelist Passer, on the south side of the High Street, below the Nether Bow, between the lands and yard of Andrew Matheson on the east, and a land or yard of the late Robert Carmichael on the west, the lands of the late William Craik, Christian Edname and John Boiswall on the north, and the stream or strand descending towards the monastery of Holyrood on the south; and there the said Patrick Baroun cognosced and entered Evangelist Passer, son and heir of the said late Evangelist Passer, burgess of the said burgh, in and to the foresaid lands, built and waste, with yards, etc. The said Evangelist and Marjorie Bassenden in his name asked instruments. Witnesses, Alexander Baroun, James Baroun, John Gray, Andrew Meloun, John Werrok, Sir Thomas Gothrasone, chaplain, and Thomas Arnot, serjeant.

162. 1529 Oct. 16. Sasine on resignation by Sir Andrew Murray, chaplain, and one of the prebendaries of the Kirk-o'-Field founded by the late Master Clement Fairlie, with consent of Master Thomas Frank, procurator, as he affirmed, of the provost and other prebendaries of the said kirk, in augmentation of divine service and the profits of the said prebend, in favour of Robert Law, dyer, and Katherine Robison his spouse, of the wester part of the fore-land of a tenement of the said late Master Clement Fairlie, lying in the Cowgate, on the north side of the High Street thereof, beside the place of the Friars Minors, between a land of John Cant on the east, and a land of John Somer on the west: Also the back-land of the said tenement, built and waste, on either side of the close of the said tenement, with the yard thereof and all their pertinents belonging to the said prebend, lying in the Cowgate, north side thereof, between the easter part of the said fore-land and the lands of John Cant and Maurice Coupland on the east, the lands of John Somer and Andrew Wode on the west, the King's Wall on the north, and the said street of the Cowgate on the south: The said Robert Law and his spouse paying 12 merks yearly to the said Sir Andrew and his successors of the said prebend. Witnesses, Alexander Baroun, Peter Greirson, Alexander Anderson, William Blaklok, Sir Andrew Myll, Henry Seytoun, John Bervyk, David Purves and John Johnston, serjeants. Patrick Baroun is bailie.

163. 1529 Oct. 20. Sasine on resignation by Agnes Cattall, daughter and heir of the late Thomas Cattall, with consent of John Bulcraig her spouse, in favour of David Gillaspy, burgess, and Elizabeth Gilleis his spouse, of a waste land of the said Agnes, lying in the lower end of a tenement of the late Charles Levington, on the south side of the High Street, between a tenement of William Lord Borthik on the east, and a tenement of the late Thomas Swift on the west; lying within the said tenement, between a land of the late John Balfour on the north, the street of the Cowgate on the south, a land of David Gillaspy on the east, and the waste land or tranſe of the tenement of the said Thomas Swift on the west. Witnesses, Nicholas Prechour, Alexander Gylour, Robert Lauchlane, Robert Gray, David Sellar,

and Thomas Arnot, serjeant. Symon Preston is bailie.

164. 1529 Oct. 29. Mungo Tennent, one of the bailies of Edinburgh, passed to a tenement of Nicholas Broune, lying beyond the Over Bow, on the south side of the High Street thereof, between a land of the late John Mosman, now of the heirs of the late Alexander Reid, on the east, and a land of John Arres and John Quhite on the west, and the King's common way on the north, descending from thence, and containing in length seven particates of land and the fourth part of an ell, even to a land of the late William Levington, now of the heirs of the late John Wyndzettis, on the south; and there the said Nicholas Broun, with consent of Jonet Askirk his spouse, resigned an annual-rent of 4 merks, out of his foresaid tenement, in the hands of the bailie, who gave sasine thereof to Master John Chapman, burgess, his heirs, etc. Witnesses, William Ker, William Askirk, Master Thomas Keyne, notary public, Thomas Mabane, David Purves and Patrick Linlithqw, serjeants.

165. 1529 Oct. 29. Sasine on resignation by Nicholas Broune, with consent of Jonet Askirk his spouse, in favour of Marion Broune their daughter, of two halls or lower houses* of the back-land of a tenement of the said Nicholas, lying beyond the Over Bow, on the south side of the High Street, and bounded as before described, with the yard of the said tenement. Witnesses, Master John Chapman, William Ker, Master Thomas Keyne, and the other aforesaid. Mungo Tennent is bailie.
The said 29th day of October the said Marion promised that she would make a letter of reversion upon redemption of the said houses and yard, containing the sum of £40, to the foresaid Nicholas and William Broune his son only and to none others. The said Nicholas asked instruments in presence of the witnesses foresaid.

166. 1529 Nov. 4. Mungo Tennent, bailie, passed to these two tenements pertaining to the late Andrew Elphinston of Selmis, now of Mr. Henry Spittall, of which one lies beside the Nether Bow, on the north side of the High Street, between the vennel of Leith Wynd on the east, a land of the late William Adamson on the west, a land of Patrick Baroun on the north, and the said Nether Bow on the south; and the other tenement lies on the south side of the High Street, between a land of John Adamson on the east, the common passage that leads to Saint Giles Church on the west, a land of Robert Vaus on the south, and the king's public street on the north; and there Robert Leslie resigned an annual-rent of 7 merks 6 shillings, with an obol of Scots money, in the hands of the bailie, who gave sasine of the said annual, upliftable out of the foresaid two tenements, to Master John Dingwall, apostolic prothonotary, provost of Trinity College church near Edinburgh, his heirs and assignees. Witnesses, Master William Meldrum, Sir Andrew Harper and Sir David Reid, chaplains, Thomas Wode, James Roule, and David Purves, serjeant of the said burgh.
And forthwith the said Master John Dingwall, provost foresaid, resigned his annual-rent of 7 merks 6 shillings and 1 obol in the hands of Mungo Tennent, bailie, who gave sasine of the

same to Sir John Craufurd, chaplain, procurator, as he alleged, and in name of the Prioress and Sisters and place of the most devout Order of Saint Katrine of the Senis, and their successors sisters of the said place, according to the tenor of a charter of foundation to be made thereupon. Witnesses aforesaid.

167. 1529 Nov. 8. Patrick Baroun, bailie, passed to a tenement of John Preston, son and heir of the late Archibald Preston, lying on the north side of the High Street, between a tenement of the late Stephen Knox on the east, a land of the late James Touris on the west, the King's public street on the south, and the North Loch on the north; and there Alexander Young, procurator and in name of the said John Preston, resigned the foresaid tenement, back and fore, under and above, built and waste; together with all annual-rents due to the said John Preston out of the said tenement, in the hands of the said bailie, who thereupon gave heritable sasine and conjunct-infeftment of the foresaid tenement, and annual-rents out of the same pertaining to the said John Preston, to John Mauchane, burgess, and Jonet Richartson his spouse. Witnesses, Alexander Mauchane, Edward Kincaid, James Baroun, John Lekprevik, David Purves, and John Johnston, serjeants.

The quhilk day in presens of the saidis witnes Andro Uddart comperit and declarit that he had xij yeris tak of his merchant buith maid till him be Johne Preston yet to rin and tharfor he protestit that the sesing gevin of the haill tenement till Johne Mauchane and his wif hurt nocht him nor his xij yeris tak of his buith considdering he had paiit thairfor aforehand as he allegit; and for remeid of law and thairapoun askit instrumentis.

The quihilk day in presens of the saidis witnes and me notar comperit Richart Nicholson and his wif and declarit how that thai had conquest fra John Preston obefor in heretage ane hall chalmer and keching and had chartour and instrument thairapoun liand within his tenement: and als had the remanent of his tenement in claus of warandis to kep the uthir land fre of all anuell except iiij merkis. And inlykwis how that he had xls. of anuell of the litle chalmer of the backland and a merk of John Lowrisonis land liand within the said tenement and vjs.viijd. of the est pairt and half of the yard and waist land: And tharfor he protestit that the sesing gevin to Johne Mauchane and his spous of the haill landis and annuellis hurt nocht him and for remeid of law, and asked instrumentis in presence of the witnesses before written.

168. 1529 Nov. 16. Symon Preston, bailie, passed to a tenement of the late James Cameron, now pertaining to John Fischar and the heirs of the late William Lokkart, lying on the north side of the High Street, between a tenement of the late George Halkerston on the east, and a tenement of the late Margaret Levingtoun, now pertaining to Robert Bertoun of Uvirberntoun, on the west; and there Jonet Cameron, relict of William Strathauchin, renounced her conjunct-fee of an annual-rent of 4 merks out of that other annual-rent of 8 merks, upliftable from the

foresaid tenement, in the hands of the said bailie, in favour of Jonet Strathauchin, daughter and one of the heirs of the said late William Strathauchin, for sasine and entrance to be given to her thereof: Reserving the frank-tenement of the said annual to Jonet Cameron during her lifetime. Which done, Symon Preston, bailie, cognosced and entered the said Jonet Strauchin, as heir foresaid, in and to the said annual-rent of 4 merks. And forthwith the said Jonet resigned the said annual in favour of herself and John Wilson her affianced spouse, who were thereupon seised therein in conjunct-fee heritably: Reserving as aforesaid. Witnesses, John Achinsone, Sir James Baron, James Fenton, Robert Law, John Adamson, Vincent Strathauchin and David Purves.

169. 1529 Nov. 23. Procuratory granted by Beatrix Anderson to Sir William Broune, chaplain, to resign her annual-rents under written, viz. (1) An annual-rent of 20s., out of a land of the late William Halkerston, lying on the north side of the High Street, between a land of the late Peter Marche on the east, and a land of the late George Halkerston on the west. (2) An annual-rent of 10s., out of a land of the late John Carkettill, lying on the north side of the High Street, between a land of the late Margaret Levingtoun, now pertaining to Robert Berton, on the east, and a land of the late Sir Alexander Lauder on the west, in the hands of one of the bailies of Edinburgh, for heritable sasine of the said annual-rents to be given to the church for an anniversary yearly to be made, according to the tenor of a charter to be made thereupon by the said Beatrix. Done within the dwellinghouse of the constituter. Witnesses, Master Thomas Broune, Thomas Williamson and Stephen Riddaill.

170. 1529 Nov. 26. Sasine on resignation by Alexander Schaw in favour of himself and Jonet Merschell his spouse, of his land in the vennel of Kirk-o'-Field, west side the trause thereof, between a land of Patrick Flemyng on the west, the lands of Master Henry Henrison and David Vaiche on the north, and the king's common way that leads to the South Port of the burgh of Edinburgh, near the Kirk-o'-Field, on the south. Witnesses, Sir John Williamson, Sir William Murray and Sir William Merschell, chaplains, Alexander Borthik, Thomas Quhite and David Purves, serjeant.

171. 1529 Nov. 26. Sasine to William Bell, son and heir of the late John Bell, burgess, on his cognition by Mungo Tennent, bailie, as heir foresaid, of a land or tenement of the said John Bell lying below the Nether Bow, on the south side of the High Street, between a land of the late Stephen Borthik on the east, the lands of Gilbert Logan on the south and west, and the king's common street on the north. And forthwith the said William Bell chose and desired Sir George Heslihop to be given to him as his curator, which the said bailie accordingly did, and took from him the usual oath *de fideli*. This done, William Bell, with consent of the said Sir George Heslihop, his curator, resigned the foresaid land or tenement in the hands of Mungo Tennent, bailie, who gave sasine thereof to Gilbert Logane and

Helen Cowgas his spouse. Witnesses, Sir William Merschell, John Porro, Mathew Pynkertoun, Mathew Cottis, James Johnston, Thomas Arnot, Patrick Lithqw and David Purves, serjeants.

172. 1529 Dec. 6. Sasine on resignation by John Vaiche, in favour of himself and Margaret Strathauchin his spouse, of his lands and tenements lying in the vennel of Bestis Wynd, west side the transe thereof, between a land of the late Thomas Ottirburne on the north, and a land of William Henderson on the south: Also of those other lands of the said John Vaiche lying in the said vennel, east side the transe thereof, between a land of the late Thomas Bigholme on the north, and a land of John Wicht on the south. Witnesses, Sir William Broune, chaplain, William Raa, James Baroun, John Coldane, George Arnot, and John Johnston, serjeant.

173. 1529 Dec. 7. Mungo Tennent, bailie, passed to a certain land pertaining to the provost, bailies and community of Edinburgh, lying on the south side of the High Street, beside the Nether Bow, between a land of John Purves on the west, a land of Alexander Anderson on the south, the king's common way of Saint Mary Wynd on the east, and the said Bow on the north; and there the said bailie, in virtue of his office and the mandate of the said provost, bailies, council and community, gave heritable sasine of the foresaid land to Master Thomas Marjoribanks, his heirs and assignees. Witnesses, William Foular, William Wilkeson, Henry Tullas, Robert Spens, David Calder, Robert Henrison, Patrick Flemyng, Thomas Blyth and Hugh Wallas.

174. 1529 Dec. 14., at the eighth hour after mid-day, the third indiction, in the sixth year of the pontificate of Pope Clement the seventh. It is aggreit and finalie concordit betuix Alexander Halkerston on that ane pairt Eduard Thomson and Johne Wait on that uthir pairt in this maner as eftir follows: The said Alexander Halkerston of his awin fre and motif will makis constitutis and ordanis the saidis Eduard and Johne his verray lauchfull procuratouris factouris and intromettouris of his pairt of all and haill the teyndis of Wrichtishoussis and in and to the letter of tak of the samyne quhilk he haif of Thomas of Corry of Keldwode pertenand to the abbay and convent of Halyrudhous and transferris all rycht of the said letter of tak and teynd schavis fra him and his airis and assignais in and to the saidis Eduard and Johne and thair airis executouris and assignais durand all the termes and space contenit in the said lettir of tak: And this is done for certane soumes of money and gratitudes done be the saidis Eduard and Johne to the said Alexander to be extendit in the best forme that can be maid or divisit. The said Eduard and Johne askit instrumentis in presens of Andrew Afflek William Inglis and Alexander Ros witnesses.
Alexander Halkerston protestit that he be quyt and dischargit of all maner of expens or costis to be maid ony maner of way apoun the saidis teyndis of Wrichtishousis in tyme tocum, and thair apoun askit (instruments.)

175. 1529 Dec. 22. Mungo Tennent, bailie, passed to a tenement of the late Andrew Harvey, now pertaining to the heirs of the late Francis Towris, lying on the north side of the High Street, between a land or tenement of the late Adam Hoppar and Robert Haliburton on the east, and a land of John Fischar on the west; and there the said bailie, in virtue of a precept of Our Sovereign Lord the King directed thereupon, and in virtue of his office of bailiary, gave heritable sasine and conjunct-infeftment of an annual-rent of 12 merks, out of the foreland of the said tenement, between a land of Andrew Livingtoun on the south, and a waste land of the said tenement on the north, to John Murray, burgess, and Margaret Talzefeir his spouse. Witnesses, John Quhite, James Nisbet, William Stevinsone, notary public, Alexander Rynde, Andrew Baroun, George Nicholl, Andrew Quhite, and David Purves, serjeant.

176. 1529 Dec. 23. Sasine to Edward Bissait, son and heir of the late James Bissait, on his cognition by Symon Preston, bailie, as heir foresaid, of a land of the said James, lying on the south side of the High Street, in the vennel of the Friars Preachers, west side the transe thereof, between a land of the late George Dykson on the south, a land of the Earl of Morton on the north, and a land of the abbot and convent of the monastery of Melrose on the west. Witnesses, Robert Grahame, John Clerk, Patrick Robertson, Robert Hoge, Adam Clerk, David Purves and Thomas Arnot, serjeants.

177. 1529 Dec. 31. Sasine on resignation by John Towris, son and heir of the late Francis Towris, in favour of himself and Alison Uddart his affianced spouse, of the following annual-rents, (1) An annual-rent of 4 merks, out of a land of the late Henry Thomson, now pertaining to Master James Foulis, lying on the north side of the High Street, between a land of the late Andrew Harvy on the west, a land of the late Thomas Folkart on the east, the foreland of the late David Hoppar on the south, and a waste land of the said David on the north. (2) An annual-rent of 4 merks, out of the said foreland of David Hoppar. (3) An annual-rent of 7 merks, out of a land of the late William Bigholme, lying on the south side of the High Street, between a land of the late Alexander Gray on the north, a land of John Vaiche on the south, the cemetery of Saint Giles church on the east, and the transe of Bestis Wynd on the west. (4) An annual-rent of 6 merks, out of a land of the late Thomas Haithwy, now pertaining to William Lauder, lying on the south side of the High Street, between a land of the late John Napier on the east, and a land of Mary Magdalene on the west. (5) An annual-rent of 4 merks, out of a land of the late Thomas Levingtoun, lying in Nudry's Wynd, east side the transe thereof, between the lands of the late Walter Bertram on the south and north. (6) An annual-rent of 20s., out of a tenement of the late Hector Thomson, lying on the south side of the High Street, below the Nether Bow, between a land of the late Edward Bonkle on the west, and a land of the late John Broune on the east. (7) An annual-rent of 40s., out of a land of the late John Gray,

lying below the Nether Bow, on the south side of the High Street, between a land of the late Robert Merschell on the east, a land of Alan Borthik on the west, a land of the late John Broune on the north, and a certain waste land on the south: Reserving the frank-tenement of the said annual-rents, except that of the last 40s., to Jonet Richartson during her lifetime. Witnesses, James Uddart, William Uddart, Patrick Baroun, Master George Cuke, Robert Haliburton, Patrick Lithqw and James Johnston, serjeants.

178. 1529 Dec. 31. Sasine on renunciation by Jonet Richartson, relict of Francis Towris, in favour of John Towris, of her conjunct-fee, and cognition of the said John by Mungo Tennent, bailie, as heir of the said Francis his father, of an annual-rent of 6 merks, out of a land of the late Adam Johnston, lying on the north side of the High Street, within a tenement of the late James Baron, between a land of the late (   ) and William Hoppar on the south, and the North Loch on the north: Reserving the liferent of the said Jonet Richartson: Which annual-rent of 6 merks the said John Towris resigned in favour of himself and Alison Uddart his affianced spouse, who are thereupon seised in the same in conjunct-fee. Witnesses, William Uddart, James Uddart, James Young, Sir Mathew Symson, and Patrick Lithqw, serjeant of the said burgh.

179. 1529 Dec. 23. Mungo Tennent, bailie, passed to the lands now pertaining to Master Francis SpittaiH, James Hall and James Harlaubankis, lying beside the Over Bow, on the east side of the High Street, between a land of the late Bartholomew Karnis on the south, a land of the altar of Saint James on the north, a land of the late Thomas Smyth on the east, and the king's public street on the west; and there Sir Thomas Ewin, chaplain, resigned (1) An annual-rent of 20s. out of the foresaid lands. (2) An annual-rent of 13s.6d. out of the lands of the late John Barcar, lying below the Castle Wall, on the north side of the High Street, between a land of Thomas Kincaid on the east, and a land of James Layng on the west, viz. 7s. leviable from the easter part of the said land, which Andrew Moncur presently possesses, and 6s.6d. from the wester part thereof, now pertaining to Robert Watson. (3) a ground annual of 6 merks, out of a tenement of the late James Turing, lying on the north side of the High Street, between a land of Andrew Mowbray on the east, a land of the late Archibald Napier of Merzemstoun on the west, the king's public street on the south, and the yard of Trinity College on the north: Which resignations made, the said Mungo Tennent, bailie, gave heritable sasine of the foresaid annual-rents, and of each of them singly, to William Sym, master of the confraternity of the Most Holy Blood and altar thereof, situated in the church of Saint Giles, for an anniversary and 'le dale' yearly to be made for the soul of the said Sir Thomas Ewin, according to the tenor of a contract between the brethren of the said confraternity and the said Sir Thomas, and a charter of foundation to be made thereupon. Upon which the said William Sym, in name of the brethren of

the said confraternity of the Most Holy Blood asked instruments. Witnesses, Sir Mathew Symson, chaplain, James Branwode, Andrew Quhite, John Blakstok, William Blaklok, Thomas Quhite, James Farnle, and Thomas Arnot.
James Harlaubankis protestit that his land be nocht compellit till pay for the annuell to Schir Thomas Ewin na vjs.viijd. as he was wont till do, and for remeid, and asked instruments.

180. 1529-30 Jan.5. Sasine on resignation by Francis Aikman in favour of himself and Beatrix Blacater his affianced spouse, of a tenement of the said Francis, lying on the north side of the High Street, between a tenement of Margaret Broune on the east, a tenement of the late Richard Hoppar on the west, the yard of Trinity College on the north, and the king's public street on the south. Witnesses, John Pardovyne, Gilbert Fynlay, Robert Hector, Thomas Arnot and Patrick Lithqw, serjeants. Symon Preston is bailie.

181. 1529-30 Jan.10. Sasine on resignation by Gilbert Lauder, in favour of Isobel Mauchane his spouse in liferent, of the said Gilbert's tenement lying on the north side of the High Street, between a land of the late Alexander Barcar, now pertaining to Master Francis Boithuell, on the east, and a land of the late William Haliburton, now pertaining to George Gude on the west. Witnesses, John Mauchane, Henry Tullois, Sir John Aikman, James Donaldson, etc.

182. 1529-30 Jan.8. In presence, John Mauchane passed to a land of the late Adam Johnston, lying on the north side of the High Street, between a land, vc.; and there the said John Mauchane, in presence of Patrick Baroun, bailie, showed and declared that it had lately come to his knowledge, how that Jonet Richartson, his spouse, had renounced her conjunct-fee of a certain annual-rent of 6 merks, out of the foresaid land, in the hands of Mungo Tennent, bailie, without his consent and assent; and that the said bailie gave sasine thereof to John Touris and Alison Uddart his spouse; therefore the said John protested that the said sasine so given shall be null and of no effect, and in token thereof broke the said sasines by breaking of a cup upon the ground of the said land, protesting for remeid of law where and when it effeirs. Witnesses, Gilbert Lauder, John Coldane, William Schaw and John Bardun.

183. 1529-30 Jan.15. At the 11th hour in the 3rd indiction, witnesses, Nicholas Cheyne, Alexander McNeil, William Steill, John McNeill, David Michelson, James Scot, Thomas Softlaw, William Preston and Thomas Arnot.
The quhilk day Thomas Scot, litstar, promittis faithfully to Alexander Scot his guid sone and to Marioun Scot his dochter spous to the said Alexander and to thair airis and assignais and als giffis and grantis to thame the duellinghouse quhilk the said Alexander now occupiis with the sellar of the samyne liand within his tenement on the est syde Leith Wynd, for all the dais of the said Thomas Scottis lyf maile fre and at thai sall pay nathing thairfor during his lyftyme. Quharapoun the

said Alexander Scot asket instrumentis. Done in the dwelling-house of the said Thomas Scot.

184. 1529–30 Jan. 15. Mungo Tennent, bailie, passed to a tenement pertaining to Alexander Scot and Marion Scot, his spouse, in fee, and to Thomas Scot and Elizabeth Logane in liferent, lying on the south side of the High Street, between a land of Gilbert Logane on the east, and a land of Thomas Craufurd on the west; and there the said Alexander Scot, with consent of the said Marion Scot his spouse, resigned their fee of the foresaid tenement in the hands of the bailie, who gave heritable sasine and conjunct-infeftment of the foresaid fee of the said tenement to Jonet Scot, daughter of the said Thomas and Elizabeth, and to Henry Scot her affianced spouse: Reserving the liferent of said tenement to the foresaid Thomas Scot and Elizabeth Logane his spouse. Witnesses, Alexander McNeill, notary public, Sir James Watson, and the others foresaid.

185. 1529–30 Jan. 15. Sasine on resignation by Thomas Scot, with consent of Elizabeth Logane his spouse, in favour of Jonet Scot their daughter and Henry Scot her affianced spouse, (1) Of an annual-rent of 8 merks, out of a tenement of the late John Bigholme, canon of Jedburgh, now pertaining to James Fenton and Euphame Adamson his spouse, lying on the south side of the High Street, near the church of Saint Giles, between the common transe and a land of the late Henry Vaus on the north, the street of the Cowgate on the south, a land of the late Henry Preston on the east, and the cemetery of St. Giles Church on the west. (2) Of the back-land (or waste-land) of the said Thomas, lying at the Castlehill, on the south side of the High Street, between a land of Master John Malison, now pertaining to Patrick Baroun, on the east, a land of the late John Levingtoun on the west, the fore land of the late James Cadzow on the north, and a waste land or yard on the south: Reserving the franktenement of the said annual-rent and land to the foresaid Thomas Scot and Elizabeth Logane his spouse. Witnesses, Alexander McNeill, notary public, Sir James Watson, chaplain, William Steill, William Prestoun, James Scot, Michael Logane, William Stallis, David Pomfrason, Thomas Scot, Thomas Smyth, and Thomas Arnot, serjeant.

186. 1529–30 Jan. 15. Mungo Tennent, bailie, passed to a tenement of the late Richard Scot, lying in the street of the Cowgate, on the south side of the High Street thereof, between a land of James Johnston on the east, the vennel of the Virgin Mary of the Field on the west, a land formerly pertaining to the Abbot of Jedburgh on the south, and the king's public street on the north; and there Margaret Forous, relict of the said late Richard Scot, with consent of John Fresall now her spouse, renounced her fee or conjunct-infeftment which she had of the foresaid tenement in the hands of the said bailie, in favour of Henry Scot, son and heir of the said late Richard: Reserving the liferent thereof to the said Margaret: which done the said Mungo Tenent, bailie, cognosced and entered the said Henry Scot, as heir of his said father, in and to the said tenement,

and seised him therein as the manner is within burgh in the case of heirs of burgesses: Reserving as aforesaid. And forthwith the said Henry Scot resigned his said tenement in the hands of the bailie, who gave heritable sasine and conjunctinfeftment thereof to the said Henry Scot and Jonet Scot his affianced spouse. Witnesses, Thomas Softlaw, Sir James Watson, William Stawis, David Pomfrason, and the others foresaid.

The quhilk day in presens of me, notar, and thir witness abone wryttin, Henry Scot promittit faithfully, in presens of Mongo Tennent, ballie, that quhen evir he happinit to optene the land quhilk Marioun Liddaill, the spous now of Robert Hectour, has in conjunct fe be hir umquhile spous, Robert Forous, and gat sesing thairof, or ony part of the samyne, that he sall put the said Jonet Scot his wuddit wif in coniunct fee thairof, and to the airis gottin or to be gottin betuix thame. And this to be extendit in the surest form. The woman asked instruments. Done upon the ground of the above written tenement.

187. 1529–30 Jan. 19. Sasine to Robert Blak, on his cognition by Mungo Tennent, bailie, as heir of the late William Blak his father, of an annual-rent of 46s.8d. out of a land of Master Thomas Marjoribanks, on the south side of the High Street, near the Netherbow, between a land of John Purves on the west, a land of the late Alexander Anderson on the south, the king's common way of the vennel of the Virgin Mary on the east, and the said Bow on the north. Which annual-rent the said Robert Blak resigned in the hands of the bailie, who gave sasine thereof to Master Thomas Marjoribanks, his heirs and assignees. Witnesses, John Huchesone, Robert Cady, Thomas Blythe, Gawin Wallas, Robert Lauson and Patrick Lithqw, serjeant.

188. 1529–30 Jan. 15. Sasine on resignation by Master Thomas Marjoribanks, in favour of himself and Jonet Purves his spouse, of his land on the south side of the High Street, beside the Netherbow, and bounded as before described. Witnesses aforesaid. Mungo Tennent is bailie.

189. 1529–30 Jan. 26. Sasine on resignation by David Campbell, in favour of Michael Campbell, his heirs, etc., of an annual-rent of 2 merks, out of a land of the said Michael, lying within a tenement of the late William Foular, west side the transe thereof, between a land of the said William Foular on the south, and a land of the late William Fleschour on the north; which tenement lies on the north side of the High Street, between a tenement of the late Donald Kyle on the east, and a tenement of Andrew Dyksone on the west. Moreover, the said David Campbell, in presence of Mungo Tennent, bailie, and affirmed that he did all and sundry above written of his own free will, and gave his bodily oath, the Scriptures touched, not to revoke in time coming. Witnesses, Sir James Dennystoun, Thomas Arthour, Walter Summervell, Archibald Wilson, Peter Pacok, William Bowman, James Bennet, Mathew Strathern, and David Purves, serjeant.

190. 1529–30 Jan. 26. Sasine on resignation by Michael Campbell,

burgess, with consent of Margaret Tait his spouse, in favour of Thomas Arthour, burgess, of the said Michael's land lying within the tenement of the late William Foular, on the north side of the High Street, and bounded as before described. Witnesses, Sir James Dennystoun, chaplain, Mathew Strathern, and the others before named.

191. 1529-30 Jan. 28. Sasine on resignation by George Mathesone in favour of himself, and Isobel Cleghorne, his affianced spouse, (1) Of the said George's land lying within a tenement of the late Sir Thomas Tod, knight, east side the trause thereof, between a land of Archibald Williamson on the north, and a land of the late Walter Kyle on the south; which tenement lies on the south side of the High Street, between a land of the said Archibald Williamson on the east, and a land of John Adamson on the west. (2) Of the said George's upper land or loft of the foreland of a tenement of the late David Knox, lying on the north side of the High Street, between a tenement of the late Symon Doweill on the east, and a tenement of the late Archibald Preston on the west. Witnesses, Alexander Young, notary public, Archibald Williamson, James Kincaid, Ronald Donaldson, John Cleghorne, Henry Tullois, William Cleghorne, Sir John Thomson and Sir William Adamson, chaplains, and John Johnston, serjèant.

192. 1529-30 Feb. 1. Renunciation by Marion Menzeis, with consent of Robert Gray her spouse, in favour of Robert Huchesone, his heirs, etc., of her liferent of a certain small house lying in the Corshouse, upon the river bank, and piece of yard lying in the end of a tenement of the late Alexander Gray; and this for a certain sum of money paid to the said Marion and Robert her spouse by the said Robert Huchesone. Moreover, in an open court held before Symon Preston, bailie, the said Marion, in the absence of her husband, affirmed that she did all and sundry above written of her own free will; and gave her bodily oath, the Scriptures touched not to revoke in time to come. Done in the booth of the Common Clerk of Edinburgh; witnesses, Sir William Hannay, Edward Thomson, William Adamson, George Arnot and Patrick Linlithqw, George Ur and Peter Greir.

193. 1529-30 Feb. 3. Sasine on resignation by Andrew Stury, in favour of Jonet Richartson his affianced spouse, of his back-land, built and waste, of a tenement of the late James Stury, below the Castle Wall, on the south side of the High Street, between a tenement of the late Andrew Home on the east, and a land of the late James Symsone on the west; with the yard thereof and its pertinents, lying between the foreland of the said tenement on the east, and the lands of Hieriggis on the south; together with the easter cellar of the said foreland. Witnesses, John Anderson, John Menzeis, Patrick Bannatyne, Peter Robisone, Laurence Laverok, and David Purves, serjeant.

194. 1529-30 Jan. 31. Assignation by Alexander Bruse, son and heir of the late John Bruse, burgess, in favour of Marion Baroun his spouse, of a letter of reversion made to the said Alexander

by Jonet Adamson, relict of the said John Bruse, upon the redemption of a certain land or tenement lying on the south side of the High Street, between a tenement of the late Edward Bonkill on the east, a land of the late Walter Blaklok on the west, a land of the late William Ker on the south, and the king's common way on the north; and for payment to the said Jonet of the sum contained in the said letter of reversion and contract made and entered into between the said Alexander and Jonet, viz., the sum of £100. And after redemption of the foresaid tenement, to receive the same from the said Jonet, by resignation as use is, with all charters, instruments and evidents made thereupon, conform to the tenor of the said letter of reversion and contract. And immediately after the redemption and loosing of the said tenement, and payment to the said Jonet of the foresaid sum, now as then and then as now, the said Alexander made and constituted John Mauchane and Alexander Baroun, conjunctly and severally, his procurator, etc., giving to them his very lawful and irrevocable power and special mandate, for him, and in his name, to resign the foresaid tenement in the hands of one of the bailies of Edinburgh, for heritable sasine thereof to be given to the said Alexander or his certain attorney, and to the foresaid Marion Baroun his spouse, and the survivor of them, and to the heirs lawfully procreated or to be procreated between them, whom failing, to the heirs of the said Marion, always and until the sum of 200 merks shall have been paid to her, her heirs, executors and assignees; and that the said Marion shall make a letter of reversion to the said Alexander, his heirs or assignees, upon redemption of the said tenement, containing the said sum of 200 merks. Moreover the said Alexander promised to hold firm and stable all and whatsoever his said procurators behoved to do in the premises, and gave bodily oath, the Scriptures touched, not to revoke in time to come; and thereupon Patrick Baroun, father to the said Marion, asked instruments. Done in the booth of the Common Clerk; witnesses, Patrick Baroun of Spittalfield, John Mauchane, Alexander Baroun, John Cranston, William Anderson, Sir Robert Baroun, Vincent Strathauchin and George Arnot.

195. 1529-30 Feb. 7. Sasine on resignation by Jonet Broune, relict of Thomas Fresall, in favour of John Fresall her son, of her conjunct-fee, and on cognition of the said John as heir of the said late John Fresall his father, of the third part, viz., the wester part of a certain fore-land, lying on the north side of the High Street, between a land of the late John Broune on the east, a land of the late James Baroun on the west, a land of Robert Bruse on the north, and the King's public street on the south: Reserving the liferent thereof to the said Jonet Broune. Witnesses, Sir Thomas Kanny, Master Francis Boithuell, William Guild, James Anderson, John Johnston and Patrick Lithqw, serjeants. Symon Preston is bailie.

196. 1529-30 Feb. 7. Sasine on resignation by John Fresall, son and heir of the late Thomas Fresall, with consent of his beloved mother Jonet Broune, frank-tenement of the third part of the

land under written, in favour of Richard Hoppar, son and heir of the late Adam Hoppar, burgess, in fee heritably, and of Katherine Ballentyne, mother to the said Richard and relict of the said Adam, in liferent, of 4 merks, out of a certain foreland lying on the north side of the High Street, between a land of the late John Broune on the east, and a land of the late James Baron on the west: With the said John Fresall's oath in an open court held before Symon Preston, bailie, not to revoke in time to come. Witnesses, as in the preceding sasine.

197. 1529–30 Feb. 15. Sasine on precept from Chancery in favour of John Cannon, as lawful and nearest heir of the late Gilbert Cannon his uncle, of a certain land lying on the north side of the High Street, within a tenement of the late Sir Alexander Lauder of Blyth, knight, between a land of the late James Ross on the south, a waste land of the said late Alexander Lauder on the north; a land of the late Sir Thomas Tod, knight, on the east, and a land pertaining to the abbot and convent of the monastery of Newbottle on the west. The precept is dated at Ayr the third day of February in the seventeenth year of the King's reign. Immediately thereafter the said John Cannon resigned his foresaid land in the hands of Edward Kincaid, bailie, who thereupon gave heritable sasine thereof to a prudent man, James Ur, flesher, burgess of Edinburgh, his heirs, etc. Moreover, the said James Cannon constituted the said James Ur his assignees, in and to all fermes and profits due to him out of the foresaid land by James Gilry, and others whomsoever. Witnesses, William Adamson, John Marjoribanks, John Hammyltoun, George Ur, James Stevinsone, Thomas Arnot and Hugh Wallas.

198. 1529–30 Feb. 19. Sasine on resignation by Master Francis Boithuell, in favour of himself and Katherine Ballentyne his spouse, the survivor of them, and after their decease to the lawful and nearest heirs of the said Master Francis whomsoever, of his tenement lying on the north side of the High Street, between a tenement of the late Henry Cant elder on the east, and a tenement of Gilbert Lauder on the west, the North Loch on the north, and the king's public street on the south. Witnesses, Sir Thomas Richartson, James Anderson, Sir Patrick Ballentyne, and James Johnston *alias* Edinburgh, serjeant. Mungo Tennent is bailie.

199. 1529–30 Feb. 18. Sasine to Walter Borthik, son and heir of the late Agnes Baty, on his cognition by Mungo Tennent, bailie, as heir of his said mother, of her land or tenement lying on the north side of the High Street, in the vennel called Halkerston's Wynd, east side the transe thereof, between a land of the late Robert Colyne on the north, and a land of the late William Halkerston on the south. And forthwith the said Walter Borthik resigned his foresaid land or tenement in the hands of the said bailie, who thereupon gave heritable sasine thereof to George Henrison, burgess, his heirs and assignees. Moreover the said Walker, in presence of the bailie, gave his bodily oath, the Scriptures touched, not to revoke in time to come. Witnesses, William Adamson, Alexander Adamson, James Kynnard,

William Forsyth, William Wilkesone, John Anderson, Sir Patrick Muir, chaplain, and Thomas Arnot, serjeant.

200. 1529-30 Feb. 23. Sasine on resignation by James Chalmer, kinsman and heir of the late Sir David Forstar, chaplain, in favour of John Lyntoun, burgess, of an annual-rent of 20 shillings, out of a waste land of the late Andrew Hainslie, lying on the south side of the High Street, within a tenement of the late Thomas Bervyk, between a land of Alexander Pennycuke on the south, a land of Gilbert Welsche on the west, and the common transe of the said tenement on the east and north parts. Witnesses, Vincent Strathauchin, notary public, John Huchesone, Mathew Carryk. Richard Stewart and Thomas Lyndesay.

201. 1529-30 Feb. 23. Patrick Baroun, bailie, passed to a tenement of John Preston, son and heir of the deceased Archibald Preston, lying on the north side of the High Street, between a tenement of the late Stephen Knox on the east, a land of the late James Towris on the west, the king's public street on the south, and the North Loch on the north; and there Alexander Young, procurator and in name of the said John Preston, resigned his ground-annual of 4 merks in the hands of the bailie, upliftable from a land of Richard Nicholson, containing hall, chamber, and kitchen, lying within the said tenement, between the fore land thereof on the south, and a land of John Lowristone on the north, who gave heritable sasine and conjunct-infeftment of the said ground-annual to John Mauchane, burgess, and Jonet Richartson his spouse. Witnesses, Nicholas Carncors, Vincent Strathauchin, John Coldane, John Anderson, Sir Cuthbert Craig, chaplain, and David Purves, serjeant, with divers others. James Meldrum is notary to the procuratory.

202. 1529-30 Mar. 9., at the ninth hour in the forenoon, in the third indiction, in the seventh year of the pontificate of Pope Clement the seventh, Mungo Tennent, bailie, passed to a chapel or land lying upon the Castlehill, on the south side of the High Street therof, between the lands of John Sprot and his wife and of James Scot on the east, the lands of Andrew Haithwy and the late Mathew Harvy on the south, the waste lands and the vennel of the castle on the west, and the king's public street on the north; and there Evangelist Passer, son of the late Evangelist Passer, burgess of Edinburgh, presented a certain precept, directed to the said bailie after retour to his Majesty's Chancery, of which the tenor follows:— James by the grace of God King of Scots to the provost and baillies of our burgh of Edinburgh, greeting, because with advice and consent of our treasurer we have given and granted heritably to our beloved Evangelist Passer, son of the late Evangelist Passer, burgess of our burgh of Edinburgh, for the good, faithful and grateful service done to us by the foresaid late Evangelist, all and whole the chapel and houses with pertinents, lying upon our Castlehill of Edinburgh, on the south side of the High Street thereof, between the lands of John Sprot and his wife and of James Scot on the east, the lands of Andrew Haithwe and the late Mathew Harvy on the south, the waste lands and vennel

of the Castle on the west, and our public street on the north: which lands, chapel and houses pertained to the late George bishop of Elphin *alias* of Greece, and now through his decease pertain to us as ultimate heir by the laws of our Kingdom and the privileges of our crown, as in our charter made to him thereupon is more fully contained. We therefore charge you and command, that incontinent without delay, ye give sasine to the said Evangelist, or to his certain attorney, bearer of these presents, of the said chapel and houses with pertinents, conform to the tenor of our charter which he has justly thereof thence of us. And this ye in nowise omitt. Given under testimonial of our Great Seal, at Edinburgh the twenty seventh day of December in the seventeenth year of our reign. After the reading of which precept, and publication thereof by the notary, the foresaid Mungo Tennent, bailie, in virtue of his office and of the mandate of the said precept, gave state, corporal possession and heritable sasine of the said chapel and houses, by delivery of earth and stone to the said Evangelist Passer; and thereupon the said Evangelist and Marjory Bassendean his mother asked instruments. Witnesses, Andrew Moncur, John Gray, John Smyth, Walter Ramsay, and David Purves, serjeant.

203. 1529–30 Mar. 9. Sasine to Walter Borthik, son and heir of the late Agnes Baty, on his cognition by Patrick Baroun, bailie, as heir of his said mother, (1) Of an annual-rent of 40d., out of a land of the late Thomas Ottirburne, lying on the south side of the Tolbooth, in Bestis Wynd, east side the transe thereof, between a land of John Vaiche on the south, and a land of Marion Broune on the north. (2) An annual-rent of 6s.8d., out of a land of James Johnston *alias* Edinburgh, serjeant, lying in the Cowgate, on the south side of the High Street thereof, between a tenement of Francis Inchecok on the east, and a tenement of the late Patrick Scot on the west. (3) An annual-rent of 8 shillings and eight pence, out of a land of the late James Talzefeir, lying within a tenement of William Lauder, west side the transe thereof, between a land of the late William Nisbet on the north, and a land of the late Walter Merlzon on the south: Which annual-rents the said Walter Borthik resigned in the hands of the bailie, who thereupon gave sasine of the same to John Broune, burgess. With the oath of the said Walter, without a court, as use is. Witnesses, John Dyksone, Alexander Dalrumpill, John Coldane, Alexander Napier, John Symsone, Robert Sinclar, David Purves, John Johnston.

204. 1529–30 March 10. Symon Preston, bailie, passed to the Altar of our Lady of Pity, situated within the church of Saint Giles; and there the said Symon Preston, bailie, in name and by mandate of the provost, bailies, and council of Edinburgh, patrons of the chaplaincy or service founded by the late James Towris at the said altar, gave and delivered possession and institution of the said chaplaincy and service of the said altar to Sir William McDowell, chaplain, by delivery to him of a chalice book and other ornaments of the said altar, as is wont to be done in such cases, conform to the charter of foundation, for

his lifetime. The said Sir William asked instruments. Done beside the said altar; witnesses, Sirs James Moffat, John Smythe, John Stewart, chaplains, John Blakstok and Master David Ireland.

205. 1529–30 March 11. Sasine on resignation by Jonet Forsyth, daughter and one of the heirs of the late William Forsyth, in favour of herself and Robert Staithwy her spouse, the heirs lawfully procreate or to be procreated between them, etc., of her south part or half of a land of the said late William Forsyth, lying in Saint Mary Wynd, west side the transe thereof, between a land of the late William Scheirsmyth on the south, and a land of the said late William on the north. Witnesses James McLellane, Robert Bell, John Speithy, Thomas Arnot, David Purves and Patrick Lithqw, serjeants.

206. 1529–30 Mar. 13. Robert Grahame, procurator and in name of Thomas Scot and Elizabeth Logane his spouse, passed to the personal presence of a noble Lord, George Lord Saint John, Preceptor of Corstorphine at Edinburgh, and there, upon bended knees reverently as became, surrendered and simply resigned, by delivery of earth and stone, staff and baton, in the hands of the said Lord Saint John, as in the hands of the lord superior thereof, all and whole his land or tenement of Temple land, lying within the burgh of Edinburgh, beside the Friars Minor, on the north side of the High Street, between a land now pertaining to Patrick Ur on the east, a land of Robert Lyne on the north, and the king's public street on the west and south, in favour of Marion Scot and Alexander Scot, her spouse: Reserving the liferent of the said Thomas and his spouse: Which resignation having been so made, and by the said Lord received, he as lord superior gave and delivered all and whole the said land or tenement of Temple land, back and fore with the pertinents, by delivery of the said earth and stone, staff and baton, as use is, to the foresaid Alexander Scot, for himself and Marion his spouse, and their heirs and assignees, conform to the tenor of a charter to be made thereupon: Done in the collegiate church of Saint Giles, before these witnesses, Master Adam Ottirburne, George Home of Spot, Alexander Weddaill, Michael Tullos and Henry Scot.

207. 1529–30 Mar. 15 Sasine to Henry Hoppar, grandson and heir of the late Richard Hoppar, and brother and heir of the late George Hoppar, on his cognition by Patrick Baroun, bailie, as heir of the said late Richard his grandfather, and of the said late George his brother, (1) Of a certain land lying within a tenement of the late Michael Frog, now pertaining to Master Adam Ottirburne of Auldhame, lying on the north side of the High Street, between a tenement of the late John Mason on the east, and a tenement of Henry Young on the west; east side the transe of the said tenement, between another back land of the said Henry Hoppar on the south, and another land of the said late Richard Hoppar on the north. (2) Of a certain other land lying within the said tenement, between the said first land now pertaining to the said Henry on the south, and the North Loch on the north. Witnesses, Robert Henrison, John

PROTOCOL BOOK

Garland, John Russall, John Coldane, William Kay, and David Purves.

208. 1529-30 Mar. 17. Sasine on resignation by William Liberton, in favour of William Liberton his son, of the fore-land sometime of Thomas Haliday, now pertaining to the said William Liberton, lying in the Cowgate, on the south side thereof, between the trause of a tenement of the late Thomas Butlar on the east, and a land of the late (   ) on the west, and another land of the said Thomas Haliday on the north. Reserving the liferent thereof to the foresaid William Liberton elder. Witnesses, William Liberton younger, Alexander Muire, Robert Liberton, and David Purves. Symon Preston is bailie.

209. 1529-30 Mar. 18. Compeared personally an honourable man, Alexander Weddaill, templar bailie of a noble lord, George Lord Saint John, Preceptor of Torfichyne, within the shire of Edinburgh, generally constituted, at a land or Temple tenement, lying within the burgh of Edinburgh, in the Cowgate, on the north side thereof, near the church of the Friars Minor, between a land of Patrick Vrry on the east, and the king's common way on the west, a land of Robert Lyne on the north, and the said street of the Cowgate on the south; and there the said Alexander Weddaill, bailie, in virtue of his office and of the mandate of the said Lord Saint John, gave heritable sasine and conjunct-infeftment of all and whole the foresaid land or tenement of temple land to Alexander Scot, burgess, and Marion Scot his spouse: Reserving the liferent thereof to Thomas Scot and Elizabeth Logane his spouse. Witnesses, William Tod, Robert Grahame, William Dundas, John Johnston, David Pomfray, Henry Scot, and Thomas Arnot.

210. 1529-30 Mar. 18., at the twelfth hour of the day, the third indiction, the pontificate of pope Clement the seventh year. The quhilk day in presens of me notar publict and thir witnes under wryttin comperit honest men, that is to say, William Johnston, duelland in Arnfillane, apone ij merk land and ane half, pertenand to the provestry of Linclowden, and Andro Makelarsay in the Suffok, pertenand to the said provestry, liand within the barony of Corsmichell, within the Stewartry of Kirkcuthbricht, and thar of thair awin fre will uncompellit renuncis and dischargis frelie thair takkis of the said landis, and all rycht that thai had ony maner of way of the saidis landis be richt or entres of the bishop of Galloway, elder or younger, or ony utheris, in favouris of Maister William Stewart, provost of Linclowden, till be disponit at his plesour; and puttis thame, thair takkis and richt of the saidis landis, alluterly in the said provostis will. And thereupon the said Master William asked instruments. Done within the burgh of Edinburgh, in the booth of the common clerk; witnesses thereto, John Lokart, Peter Huchesone and George Arnot, with divers other witnesses specially called and required to the premises.

211. 1529-20 Mar. 21. Sasine to John Fausyde, on his cognition by Patrick Baroun, bailie, as son and heir of the late John Fau-

syde, burgess, of the two part of a certain land or tenement lying in the Cowgate, north side thereof, between the vennel of Forstaris Wynd on the east, and a land of the late George Michelsone, now pertaining to John Scharp, on the west, and a land of the late John Home on the north. Witnesses, James Meill, John Hoip, John Young, John Coldane, and John Johnston, serjeant.

212. 1529-30 Mar. 21. Sasine on resignation by Archibald Nairne, with consent of Cristina Broune his spouse, in favour of John Fawsyde, his heirs and assignees, of the said Archibald's third part of a certain land or tenement lying in the Cowgate, on the north side thereof, between the vennel of Forstaris Wynd on the east, and a land of the late George Michelson, now pertaining to John Scharp, on the west, and a land of the late John Home on the north. Witnesses, James Meill, John Hoip, John Young, John Coldane, and John Johnston, serjeant. Patrick Baroun is bailie.

213. 1529-30 Mar. 22. Renunciation by Sir Andrew Stevinson, canon of the monastery of Quhithorne, in favour of John Mauchane, assignee of John Preston, son and heir of the late Archibald Preston, of a land and dwelling-house, containing hall, chamber, kitchen, and loft immediately above the same, with the gallery thereof, of the back-land of a tenement of the said late Archibald Preston, lying in the burgh of Edinburgh, between the fore land of the said tenement on the south, and a land of John Louriston on the north: Also of the south cellar lying in the ground of the foresaid land, with their pertinents, now lawfully redeemed by the said John Mauchane, by payment to the foresaid Sir Andrew Stevinson of the sum of £46, conform to the tenor of a letter of reversion made thereupon. Witnesses, Thomas Gibson, John Russall, Henry Tullos, Ronnald Donaldson and David Purves.

214. 1529-30 Mar. 24. Sasine on resignation by Master William Blakstok, procurator and in name of a religious man, friar Adam Ireland, novice of the Order of the Friars Minor of Saint Francis of the Observance, in favour of Master David Ireland, burgess of Edinburgh, of a certain back-land of the late John Ireland, which formerly pertained to the Earl of Cassillis, lying in the Cowgate, on the south side thereof, between a land of the late Sir Thomas Tod, knight, now pertaining to Thomas Laverok on the west, a land of the late James Earl of Buchane, now pertaining to William Doby on the east, the croft of the late Adam Layng, now pertaining to the Sisters of Saint Katrine of Senis, on the south, and the fore land pertaining to Lady Jonet Kennedy on the north: Reserving the frank-tenement of the foresaid back-land to Cristina Blakstok, mother to the said Master Adam Ireland, during her lifetime. Witnesses, Robert Ramsay, Master Thomas Slewman, Thomas Cumyn, James Murray, Peter Murray, and Patrick Lithqw, serjeant. Symon Preston is bailie, and the procuratory is subscribed by Master Thomas Slewchman, notary public.

215. 1530 Mar. 28. Symon Preston, bailie, passed to the back house or upper mansion of a tenement of Lord Borthuik, which Robert Paule last occupied, lying on the west side of the transe of the vennel of Borthik's Wynd, immediately above the mansion now occupied by Robert Borthuik, between the side wall of the fore land of the said tenement on the north, and the side wall of the mansion of the said William Lord Borthuik, now occupied by the said Lord, on the south, the trause of the said vennel on the east, and a land of the late John Carkettill on the west; and there Thomas Borthuik, procurator and in name of the said William Lord Borthuik, resigned the foresaid house or upper mansion, with the pertinents, in the hands of the said bailie, who thereupon gave heritable sasine thereof to William Sym, burgess, his heirs and assignees. Witnesses, Michael Blythe, John Merlzone, Adam Dyksone, and Patrick Lithqw.

216. 1530 April 1. Compeared personally a discreet man, Master Richard Cutlar, vicar of Rarig, son and heir of the late Henry Cutlar, burgess of Haddington, and constituted his procurators, viz. John Cutlar, George Robisone, Thomas Dykson and John Anderson, conjointly and severally to take possession and sasine of a certain land or tenement pertaining to him heritably by reason of the decease of the said late Henry his father, lying within the burgh of Haddington, on the north side of the king's highway of the same (   ) And after receiving sasine of the foresaid land or tenement, to resign the same in the hands of one of the bailies of the said burgh, for sasine and infeftment thereof to be given to Archibald Cutlar, brother to the said Master Richard, conform to the tenor of a charter to be made thereupon: Reserving the frank-tenement thereof to the said constitutor during his lifetime. Done within the burgh of Edinburgh, in the booth of the Common Clerk. Witnesses, Sir William Dyksone, vicar of Kirkcuthbrycht, Sir Alexander Boutstar, monk of Dundranen, David Forstar, John Inglis, Vincent Strathauchin, notary public, and George Arnot.

217. 1530 April 1. Procuratory granted by Master Richard Cutlar, vicar of Rarig, son and heir of the late Henry Cutlar, burgess, in favour of John Cutlar, George Robisone, Thomas Dyksone and John Anderson, conjointly and severally, to resign his tenement or temple land lying in the foresaid burgh, in the South Street, between a land of Alexander Achinsone on the south, and a land of Jonet Hoip on the north, a land of the late John Reidpethe on the west, and the king's street on the east, in the hands of Lord Saint John, Preceptor of Torphichen, as in the hands of the lord superior thereof, in favour of Archibald Cutlar and his heirs, for sasine thereof to be given to the said Archibald by the said lord superior: Reserving the frank-tenement thereof to tne constituter. Witnesses as aforesaid.

218. 1530 April 4. Sasine to John Hay, burgess, on resignation by James Henrison, of his waste land lying within a tenement of John Vernour, on the south side of the High Street, between a land of the late John Bell on the east, and a land of James Preston on the west; a land of the said James on the south,

and a land of James Johnston on the north: Also the residue of the said tenement in security thereof, lying between a land of the late Alexander Dee on the south, and the King's public street on the north. Witnesses, Robert Henrison, Andrew Baron, John Donaldson, James Brounleis, Thomas Rynde and James Johnston. Patrick Baron is bailie.

219. 1530 April 8. Sasine in favour of John Berclay, burgess, and Elizabeth Nudry his spouse, on resignation by Robert Forstar, fiar, with consent of Alexander Forstar his father, freeholder of the said Robert's half of a backland and mansion lie Corshouse, together with the half of the close on the north of the said mansion, with the half of the yard on the south side thereof lying within a tenement of the late Jonet alias Dowe Lintoun, on the south side of the High Street, between a land of the late William Fausyde on the east, and a land of the late Archibald Todryk, on the west; a waste land of the late Robert Cokson on the north, and a land or yard of the Archbishop of Saint Andrews on the south; and which tenement lies as aforesaid between a land of the late Master John Murray on the east, and a land of the late John Davidson on the west. Witnesses, William Watson, Alexander Wardlaw, David Orrok, John Ramsay, Patrick Linlithqw and Thomas Arnot, serjeants. Edward Kincaid is bailie.

220. 1530 April 8. Sasine on resignation by John Berclay, with consent of Elizabeth Nudry his spouse, in favour of Robert Forstar in fee, and of Alexander Forstar his father in liferent, of an annual-rent of 9 merks out of the said John's land or mansion lie Thortourhouse, within the tenement of the late Jonet alias Dowe Lyntoun, lying and bounded as before described. Same witnesses and bailie.

221. 1530 April 12. xij April in the year of our Lord jm.vc.xxx, at the sixth hour after midday, in the 3rd. indiction, of the pontificate of pope Clement the seventh the seventh year, Symon Preston, one of the bailies of Edinburgh, passed to a land or tenement of the late Andrew Hume, lying below the Castle Wall, on the south side of the High Street thereof, between the lands of John Anderson on the east, and the lands of the late James Towris on the west; and there James Murray, attorney and in name of our Sovereign Lady, Margaret Queen of Scotland, presented to the said bailie, a certain precept of sasine of our Sovereign Lord's Chancery, of which the tenor follows:- James by the grace of God King of Scots, to the provost and bailies of the burgh of Edinburgh, greeting, forasmuch as we have given and granted to our most beloved Queen, her heirs and assignees, all and whole the wester arch or vault, fore and back with pertinents, situated within the tenement and foreland of the late Margaret Quhitheid, lying on the south side of our burgh of Edinburgh, between the lands of William Adamson on the east, the lands of the late John Bell on the west, the lands of Andrew Uddart on the south, and the public street of our foresaid burgh on the north: Also 2 merks annual-rent upliftable yearly from the lands and tenement of the late Andrew Hume, lying within

our burgh of Edinburgh foresaid below the Castle Wall thereof, on the south side of our public street, between the lands of John Anderson on the east, the lands of the late James Towris on the west: Which pertained heritably to Margaret Liddaill, Jonet Liddaill, Katherine Liddaill and Agnes Liddaill, daughters and heirs of the said late Margaret Quhitheid: Held by them immediately of us in free burgage. And were duly apprised for the sum of 200 merks recovered upon them by our said most beloved Mother; and in default of moveable goods of the said Margaret, Jonet and Agnes, distrainable for the said sum, were sold and assigned to our said most beloved Mother according to the tenor of an Act of our Parliament and of our letters directed thereupon, as in our charter made thereupon to our said most beloved mother is more fully contained. We charge and command you that incontinent and without delay ye give sasine to our foresaid most beloved mother the Queen, or to her certain attorney bearer of these presents, of the said wester arch or vault, and annual-rent above written, conform to the tenor of our said charter. And this ye in no wise omit. Given under testimonial of our Great Seal at Edinburgh on the 24th. December and of our reign the seventeenth year. After the reading of which precept, and publication thereof by me notary public under written, the foresaid Symon Preston, bailie, in virtue of his office and command of the said precept, gave state, corporal possession and heritable sasine of the foresaid wester arch or vault, and annual-rent of 2 merks, with all their pertinents, by delivery of earth and stone and one penny to the foresaid James Murray, attorney and in name of the said Margaret Murray, attorney and in name of the said Margaret our Queen, according to the tenor of the said precept: Reserving all rights. And forthwith without delay a prudent man Master David Ireland, procurator and in name of the said Margaret our Queen of Scotland, with consent of Henry Stewart, Lord Methven, her spouse, resigned the said annual-rent of 2 merks and wester arch or vault in the hands of the said Symon Preston, bailie, who thereupon gave sasine of the said subjects to Master Robert Galbraith, his heirs and assignees. Witnesses, Master Thomas Kincraig, Sir John Lithqw and Sir William McDowell, chaplains, Master Thomas Wichtman, John Menzeis and Patrick Linlithqw, serjeant.

222. 1530 April 16. Sasine in favour of James Stantoun, notary public, his heirs, etc., on resignation by Francis Inchecok, with consent of Cristina Dee his spouse, of the fee of their tenement lying in the Cowgate, on the south side thereof, between the vennel called Reparlawis Wynd on the east, and the land of James Robison on the west, the yard or land of the Virgin Mary founded by Master John Dingwall on the south, and the King's public street on the north: Reserving the liferent thereof to the resigners; with the said Cristina's oath not to revoke. Witnesses, Stephen Thomson, Thomas Glendynnyng, John Caribberis, James Paterson, and Patrick Linlithqw, serjeant. Symon Preston is bailie.

223. 1530 April 22. Renunciation by Alexander Towris, son and heir of the late William Towris of Moshouscheilis, and brother and heir to the late Andrew Towris, in favour of James Uddart, burgess of Edinburgh, and Cristina Towris his spouse, of a letter of reversion made by the said James and his spouse to him the said Alexander Towris, of and upon three husband lands of the Temple lands of Estirelbotill, formerly alienated by the said Alexander to the foresaid James and his spouse, lying within the shire of Edinburgh; and that for certain sums of money and other favours paid and delivered to the said Alexander. Also the said Alexander renounced and over gave other two reversions made by the said James and his spouse, viz. one of and upon the redemption of an annual-rent of 2 merks upliftable from a land of the late Sir John Rynd, chaplain; lying in Buithraw; and the other upon redemption of an annual-rent of 2 merks leviable from a land of the late William Ferry, lying in the end of the vennel of Peebles Wynd, in favour of the said James Uddart, and his spouse Cristina, for certain favours and sums of money paid for the said Alexander. Witnesses, James McCalzeane, notary public, Thomas Cuke, James Balcasky and John Litill.

224. 1530 April 23. Sasine to Isobel Bog, daughter and heir of the late Andrew Bog, burgess, on her cognition by Mungo Tennent, bailie, of these houses under written, viz. of the tavern of a tenement lying on the south side of the High Street, between a land of the late George Robison on the east, and a land of the late William Adamson on the west; a land of George Talzefeir on the south, and the King's public street on the north: Also of two booths, one above the said tavern, and the other above the said booth and upon the middle stair of the said tenement. Witnesses, Henry Levington, William Guild, Alexander Elphinstoun, James Balcasky, Laurence Kilpatrick, Thomas Arnot and David Purves, serjeants.

225. 1530 April 26. William Towris of Elwodsyde passed to certain lands lying beyond the West Bow of the burgh of Edinburgh, on the south side of the High Street, between the lands of the late Alexander Nichol, now pertaining to Robert Gray on the east, the lands of the late James Wallas, now pertaining to James McGauchane on the west; the lands of Hieriggis on the south, and the King's public street on the north, and within the shire of Edinburgh; and there the said William Towris of Elwodsyde, lord superior of the said lands gave sasine of the same, built and waste, to John Pady, kinsman and heir of the late Isobel Cristeson, according to the tenor of a letter of retour and the ancient infeftment made thereupon. The one half of which lands John Pady forthwith resigned in the hands of William Towris of Elwodsyde, as superior foresaid, who thereupon gave sasine thereof to William Maxwell, his heirs and assignees. Witnesses, Ur, John Smyth, Alexander Towris, William Schelis, John Broune, David Bayne, James Zaloleyis and John Broune, with divers others.

226. 1530 April 28. Sasine on resignation by John Quhite, in favour of James Bannatyne, burgess, of a tiled backland lying on the south side of the High Street, in the end of the said John's tenement, between a waste land of Master Adam Ottirburne on the north, and a land of Patrick Urry on the south; a land of Robert Lyne on the west, and the transe of the said tenement on the east: Under reversion of £20, promised by the said James to the resigner. Witnesses, John Hamilton, Edward Hoppringill, William Mure, James Reid, and John Johnston, serjeant.

227. 1530 May 2. Sasine on renunciation of the liferent by Jonet Barcar, relict of Thomas Neilson, with consent of John Rammage her spouse, and resignation of the fee by John Neilson, son and heir of the said Thomas, in favour of the said John Neilson and Elizabeth Thomson his affianced spouse, of a tenement of the foresaid Thomas, containing hall, chamber and kitchen, and 3 cellars below the same; together with the loft above and 'le prenteis' on the south side thereof, lying in the lower end of Nudryis Wynd, east side the transe thereof, between a land (　　　　) on the north, and another land (　　　　) on the south. Witnesses, John Adamson, Adam Wricht, David Trumbull, Andrew Bynnyng, James Lithqw and Hugh Wallas. Mungo Tennent is bailie.

228. 1530 May 13. Sasine on resignation by Margaret Quhite, with consent of John Quhite her father, in favour of herself and George Achinson her affianced spouse, the said John's tenement beyond the Over Bow, on the south side of the High Street thereof, between a land of Nichol Broune on the east, and a land of John Blakstok on the west, the foreland of John Arres on the north, and a waste land or yard of the said John Quhite on the south: Reserving the liferent of the half part of said tenement to John Quhite. Witnesses, Sir Philip Darling, Alexander Darling, Adam Wricht, William Smyth, John Anderson, and David Purves, serjeant. Edward Kincaid is bailie.

229. 1530 May 25. Edward Kincaid, bailie, passed to lands and tenements lying contiguous on the north side of the High Street, at the Castlehill, between a tenement of the late John Wicht on the east, and a tenement of William Wallange on the west, a certain waste land on the north, and the King's public street on the south; and there Archibald Williamson, son and heir of the late John Williamson, with consent of Jonet Adamson his spouse, confessed that an annual-rent of 40s., leviable from the foresaid lands and tenements, was now lawfully redeemed from them by Alexander Levington, son and heir of the late John Levington, by payment of £20, under reversion of which the said annual-rent was alienated by the said late John Levington to the said late John Williamson; and which annual-rent the said spouses therefore renounced in favour of Alexander Levington. And forthwith Edward Kincaid, bailie, cognosced and entered Alexander Levington, as son and heir of the late John Levington, in and to the said annual-rent. Thereafter the said Alexander resigned the same in the hands of the bailie who gave sasine of the fee thereof to John Young, and to Sir

George Heslihop, chaplain, in name and on behalf of Isobel Henrison affianced spouse to the said John Young: Reserving the liferent of the said annual-rent of 40s. to Katherine Forestar, mother to the said John. Witnesses, Sir William Adamson, John Porro, Archibald Blair, John Anderson, John Forman, John Henderson, and Thomas Arnot, serjeant.

The quhilk day in presens of the said bailie and witnes, Johne Young, the son and air of umquhile Johne Young, oblist him faithfully, his airis and assignais, till Robert Henrison, his airis executouris and assignais, that gif it sall happin, as God forbaid, the contract and mariage maid betuix the said Johne and Issobell Henrison, dochter to the said Robert, cum nocht till effect, nor beis nocht compleitit solemplie in the face of halikirk, in that cais to content and pay till the said Robert, his airis executouris and assignais, the soume of xxx lib. usual money of Scotland, quhilk the said Robert had laid doune for the bying in of the 40s. of annuell abone wryttin till the said John's behuif. And thair apoune the said Robert askit instrumentis. Witnes forsaid.

The quhilk day, in presens of the said bailie, Archibald Williamson deliverit to the said Alexander Levington ane instrument of sesing, quhar his fader got entres to the said 40s. of annuell, be resignation of umquhile John Levington, and declarit in presens forsaid that he had na uthir kynd of evidentis concernyng the said annual-rent. And thair apone the said Archibald askit instrumentis. Done upon the ground in presence of the witnesses foresaid.

230. 1530 May 30. Sasine on resignation by Margaret Broune, with consent of William Achinson her son and heir apparent, in favour of Francis Aikman and Beatrix Blacater his spouse, of an annual-rent of 2 merks, out of the said Margaret's backland lying within her tenement, west side the transe thereof, between the foreland on the south, and another land or mansion on the north: Also out of her other backland lying within her said tenement, between the land of Patrick Flemyng on the north: Which tenement lies on the north side of the High Street, between a land of the late William Dunsyar, burgess, on the east, and the land of Francis Aikman on the west. Witnesses, John Cannoch, Peter Marche, James Schort, James Sym, Robert Donaldson, Thomas Arnot and Hugh Wallas, serjeants.

The quhilk day in presens of Edward Kincaid ballie and witnes abone wryttin, Margret Broune, with the consent and assent of William Achinson hir son and appiarand air, for certane gratitudis and thankis done till hir gaif and grantit till Frances Aikman, his airis and assignais, all and haill the tane half of the west syde wall of hir bakland liand within hir tenement, on the west side the trans of that ilk, fornent the said Frances bakland, betuix the forland of hir tenement on the south pairt, and ane uther land and mansion of hirs on the north pairt: With full power, licens and faculte till the said Frances and his airis till tak doune the said haill wall, and big up the samyne again sufficientlie, that the samyne may serf and suffice to be syde wall baith to the said Frances land and to the said Margrettis bakland, and sua that baith thair cupillis may stand and rest apone the samyne. And the said Francis till haif and bruke all esiamentis that may be had or gottin thairintill, and to put his gestis therintill, and sett his cupill seyt apone the said wall. And that to be done apone the said Frances expens. And to reserve and keip to the said Margrettis bakland hir lichtis and conductis and segis siklyke as thai ar now. And als the said Margrett nor hir airis or assignais sall not stop the lichtis of the said Frances bakland in na tymes to cum. And thereupon the said Frances asked instrument. Done upon the ground of the said bakland. Witnesses foresaid.

231. 1530 June 25. Sasine to George Henrison, on his cognition by Mungo Tennent, bailie, as heir of the late James Henrison his brother, of the said James' land lying on the north side of the High Street, between a tenement of the late Robert Lyndesay on the east, and a tenement of the Archbishop of Glasgow on the west, a land of the Laird of Bass on the north, and the King's public street on the south. And forthwith the said George Henrison resigned his said land in favour of himself and Katherine Adamson his spouse, who are thereupon seised therein in conjunct-fee. Thereafter George Henrison, with consent of his said spouse, resigned an annual-rent of 11 merks, upliftable from the foresaid land, in the hands of the bailie who gave heritable sasine thereof to Jonet Turing, her heirs and assignees. Moreover the said Jonet Turing resigned the fee of the said annual-rent of 11 merks in the said bailie's hands who thereupon gave sasine thereof to Katherine Adamson, spouse of the said George Henrison: Reserving the liferent to the resigner. Besides, the said Jonet and Katherine promised to make a letter of reversion to the said George Henrison, upon the redemption of the said annual-rent, containing the sum of £88. Witnesses, Andrew Robison, William Adamson, Sir Robert Stalkar, John Wilson, Sir John Watson, Andrew Borthik and Patrick Lithqw.

232. 1530 July 9. Sasine on resignation by Alexander Chalmer in favour of John Grahame, son and heir of the late Alexander Grahame, of an annual-rent of 2 merks out of the resigner's land and yard, lying upon the Castlehill, south side the High Street thereof, between a land of William Loch on the north, and the King's Wall on the south; a land of the late David Pynchenot on the east, and a land of Patrick Baron on the west: And this in excambionand for relief of a land and tenement of the said Alexander, lying within the town of Leith, of an annual-rent of 2 merks pertaining to the said Alexander and his heirs. And the said John Grahame gave his annual-rent of 2 merks in excambion for the foresaid annual-rent of 2 merks resigned in his favour out of the said Alexander Chalmer's land lying upon the Castlehill. Witnesses, Adam Grahame, Archibald Leiche, David Young, Robert Gray, Andrew Moncur, and David Purves, serjeant. Symon Preston is bailie.

233. 1530 July 18. Edward Kincaid, bailie, passed to a tenement of Thomas Rynd, son and heir apparent of William Rynd, on the

south side of the High Street, in the vennel of the Friars Preachers, east side the transe thereof, between a land of the late John Stewart, now pertaining to John Vernour, on the south, and a land of the late Archibald Preston on the north; and there the said Thomas Rynd, in a full and open court held before the said bailie, upon the ground of the said land, chose and desired William Rynd his father to be given to him as his curator, to wit for the purpose under written; which the said bailie did, and took the said William's oath *de fideli* as to his administration of the said office, as the manner is. And forthwith the said Thomas Rynd, with consent of his said father and curator, resigned his foresaid tenement in the hands of the bailie, who thereupon gave sasine thereof to William Uddart, burgess, and Katrine Fischar his spouse. Witnesses, Nicholas Carncors, William Wilkesone, Edward Bissat, Robert Rynd, Henry Tullos, John Harkes, John Anderson, Thomas Arnot and David Purves, serjeants.

The said 18th. day of July 1530, the said William Uddart, with consent of Katrine Fischar his spouse, resigned an annual-rent of 8 merks, out of his tenement in the vennel of the Friars Preachers above described, in the hands of Edward Kincaid, bailie, who gave sasine thereof to Thomas Rynd, his heirs, etc., under reversion of £80. Same witnesses.

234. 1530 July 18. Sasine on his cognition by Edward Kincaid, bailie, in favour of William Uddart as heir of the late Andrew Uddart his father, of certain lands lying contiguous, within a tenement of the late David Dalrumpill on the south side of the High Street, between a land of William Adamson on the east, and a land of John Bell on the west; on either side of the said tenement, between the foreland thereof on the north, and a land of the late Rodger Murray on the south: which lands the said William Uddart resigned in favour of himself and Katrine Fischar his spouse, who are thereupon seised in the same by Edward Kincaid bailie. Witnesses, Nicholas Carncors, Thomas Uddart, William Rynd, John Cuming, Henry Tullois, and the serjeants foresaid.

235. 1530 July 19. Compeared personally Beatrix Anderson, relict of George Broun, and constituted Sir John Gylour, chaplain, her procurator, to resign in the hands of the bailies of Edinburgh, (1) An annual-rent of 20s., out of a land of the late William Halkerston, lying on the north side of the High Street, between a land of the late Peter Marche on the east, and a land of the late George Halkerston on the west, (2) Another annual-rent of 10s., out of a land of John Carkettill, lying on the north side of the High Street, between a land of the late Margaret Levingston, now pertaining to Robert Barton on the east, and a land of the late Alexander Lauder of Blyth, knight, on the west; and that for sasine to be given to one chaplain in name of the church, for an anniversary to be made yearly for the soul of the said Beatrix, conform to the charter to be made thereupon. Done within the dwelling house of the constituter; witnesses, James Uddart, Thomas Heriot, and Master Thomas Brown.

236. 1530 July 19. Sasine on resignation by Sir John Gylour, procurator and in name of Beatrix Anderson, in favour of Mr. Thomas Broune, in name of the Church of the two annual-rents mentioned in the foregoing procuratory of resignation, for an anniversary to be made for the soul of the said Beatrix. Witnesses, William Watson, Thomas Heriot, William Harvy, Hugh Wallas, and Patrick Lithqw. Edward Kincaid is bailie.

237. 1530 July 20. John Broune, son and heir of the late John Broune, declared that it lately came to his ears that Beatrix Anderson, by her procurator, resigned annual-rents, viz. 20s. out of the land of the late William Halkerston, and 10s. out of the land of the late John Carkettill, lying as contained in the protocol before written; and in prejudice of the said John, sasine thereupon was given to Master Thomas Broune, in name of the church. On which account the said John protested, that the said sasines of these annual-rents shall not hurt him nor his heirs, and broke the same by the breaking of a dish, and for remeid of law, and asked instruments. Witnesses, Robert Sinklar, Alexander Tennent, Archibald Wallas, Thomas Tullos and David Purves.

238. 1530 July 27. Sasine on resignation by Sir Thomas Kanny, chaplain, in favour of John Kanny his brother's son, of the fee of the back-land of the said Thomas's tenement, lying in the burgh of Edinburgh, below the Netherbow, on the south side of the High Street, between a land of David Dronar on the east, and a land of the late David Balfour of Cauldstoun on west: Reserving the liferent thereof to the said Thomas. Witnesses, Sir George Raa, Master William Ayton, John Coldane, Alexander Bruse, John Ayton, Thomas Ayton, Robert Monypenny, and John Johnston, serjeant. Patrick Baron is bailie.

239. 1530 Aug. 8. Renunciation by Margaret Blacater, with consent of Alexander Hamilton of Bathket her spouse, in favour of Peter Hamilton their son and apparent heir, and Elizabeth Cochrane his spouse, of the said Margaret's conjunct infeftment which she has of the 10 merkland of Quhitelaw, lying in the barony of Bathket within the shire of Renfrew: With her bodily oath, the Scriptures touched, neither to revoke nor contradict in time to come. Witnesses, George Cochrane of Bawbachlaw, Edward Cranfurd, William Cunynghame, David Purves and John Anderson. Done in the Tolbooth of Edinburgh.

240. 13th August 1530 at the 3rd. hour in the house of Gilbert Lauder. Gilbert Lauder, with consent of Isobel Mauchane his spouse, grantis till Master Henry Lauder, that the said Henry haif, bruke and joise the under house of his back land nixt the Loch, quhilk James Douglas occupys with the sellaris under the samyne, eftir the said Gilbertis deces, gif it happin him to deces befor the said Issobell, for all the dais of hir lyftyme, maill fre and annuell fre. Witnes, James Wallas and Thomas Dikson.

241. 1530 Aug. 9. Sasine on resignation by Agnes Tweedy, with consent of Alexander Elphinston, her spouse, and of John Elphinston, their son and heir apparent, of and annual-rent of 20s., out of their tenement lying on the

south side of the High Street, between a tenement of John Cant on the east, and a tenement of Edward Litill on the west, in favour of Sir David Young, curate of the collegiate church of St. Giles, in his own name and of the other prebendaries of the said church, and their successors, for an anniversary to be made yearly for the souls of the said Agnes, Alexander and John, their ancestors and successors, and of all the faithful departed: With the said Agnes Tuedy's bodily oath, the Scriptures touched, not to revoke. Witnesses, Sir John Keyne, Master Patrick Clerk, William Blaklok, James Baron, John Quhite, John Harkes, and John Johnston, serjeant. Patrick Baron is bailie.

242. 1530 Aug. 17. Sasine on precept from chancery, in favour of Andrew Dykson, as lawful and nearest heir of the late Andrew Dykson his father, of a back land lying within a tenement of the said late Andrew, on the north side of the High Street, between the tenement of the late William Foular on the east and west parts the foreland of the said tenement on the south, and another land or mansion of the foresaid Andrew on the north: Also of an annual-rent of 5 merks, out of the said foreland, between the back land of the said late Andrew Dykson on the north, and the King's public street on the south. Precept is dated at Linlithgow 11th. Aug. in the 17th. year of the King's reign. Witnesses to the sasine, John Foular, Andrew Edgar, Thomas Rynd, Andrew Tod, Robert Mar, John Johnston, and Patrick Linlithqw, serjeant. Symon Preston is bailie.

243. 1530 Aug. 23. Sasine on resignation by Peter Marche in favour of himself and Cristina Scrymgeour his spouse, of the foreland or tenement of the said Peter Marche, lying on the north side of the High Street, between a land of the Archbishop of Glasgow on the east, and a land of William Halkerston on the west. Witnesses, William Kynnynmont, Robert Grahame, Thomas Foular, Robert Smart, John Anderson, William Steill, and Hugh Wallas, serjeant.

244. 1530 Aug. 26. Renunciation by Jonet Adamson, relict of John Bruse, in favour of Alexander Bruse, son and heir of the said John, of his tenement on the south side of the High Street, between a tenement of the late Edward Bonkle on the east, and a tenement of the late Walter Blaklok on the west, a land of the late William Ker on the south, and the King's public street on the north: Which tenement the said Jonet Adamson confesses is now redeemed by the said Alexander: Reserving the liferent thereof to herself. Witnesses, Sir John Styrk, chaplain, John Mulikin, Andrew Baroun, Thomas Purdy, John Baroun, Vincent Strathauchin, and Thomas Arnot, serjeant. In token of which renunciation Jonet Adamson, in presence of Patrick Baroun, bailie, upon the ground of the said tenement, delivers to Alexander Bruse all the charters and evidents made thereupon.

245. 1530 Aug. 26. Patrick Baroun, merchand, contentit and payit till Jonet Adamson, the relict of umquhile Johne Bruse, in the name and behalf of Alexander Bruse and Marion Baroun his spouse, eftir the forme of ane contract maid betuix the said

Alexander and Marion, the soume of jc. pundis, for redemption of the said Alexander's land, as is contenit in the said contract; and has fulfillit the said contract in all poyntis: And thairfor requyrit the said Alexander for his pairt to fulfill the samyne, and thairapoun askit instrumentis. Same witnesses.

246. 1530 Aug. 26. Sasine on precept from chancery in favour of John Wardlaw, as lawful and nearest heir of the late James Wardlaw, his grandfather, of (1) the easter part or half of a certain tenement, together with the yard thereof, lying on the south side of the High Street, between the lands of the abbot and convent of the monastery of Cambuskynneth on the east and west parts of the said tenement, and a land of Margaret Lany on the west, the street of the Cowgate on the south, and the King's public street on the north. (2) The two easter booths lying below and above the stair of the foreland of the late Patrick Scot and the late James Towris, on the north side of the High Street, between the other booths of the said foreland, pertaining to the heirs of the said James Towris, on the west, and a land of the late John Preston on the east. The precept is dated at Linlithgow 25 Aug. in the 17th. year of the King's reign. Witnesses, John Coldane, Alexander Bruse, James Forstar, John Carmuir, Mark Coupland, James Johnston *alias* Edinburgh, Vincent Strathauchin, notary, David Purves and Thomas Arnot, serjeants. Patrick Baroun is bailie and Edward Craufurd is attorney.

The same day hour and witnesses, William Ra in his own name, and that of Jonet Rynd his spouse, protested that the said sasine of the said easter part of the foresaid tenement, and of the two booths so given to John Wardlaw, shall not turn out to the prejudice of him nor his spouse in the right which they have to their annual-rents upliftable therefrom, and for remeid of law, and asked instruments.

247. 1530 Sept. 9. John Young, the son and air of umquhile Johne Young, burgess of Edinburgh, grantis him till haif ressavit fra Robert Henrison his guidfadir and Katrine Forest his modir, all and sindry his movable gudis of airschip, pertenand till him throw deces of his said umquhile fadir, viz. a masser of silver ourgilt, a peis of silver, a silver spune, ane chargeour, ane plait, ane pot, ane quart stoup, ane pynt stoup, ane compter, a furnist bed, and almory, ane chymnay, ane waistaw, a schryne, ane chyiar, a form; and all uthir his gudis of airschip quhatsumevir pertenand till him; quhilk gudis of airschip the said John Young hes deliverit and laid in wad to Sir George Heslihop, chaplane, apone, the soume of xl lib. usuall money of Scotland. And quhatever tyme that evir it sall happin the said Johne or his airis till pay the said soume of xl lib. agane to the said Schir George, his airis executouris or assignais, the said Johne till haif full fre regres and ingres in and to all and sindry his said airschip gudis frely to be deliverit to him, but obstakle or impediment, als fre as he had the said airschip gudis or he laid the samyne in wod of the said soume. Apone the quhilk bayth parteis askit instrumentis. Done in the

dwelling-house of Robert Henrison; Witnesses, Robert Haliburton and Thomas Mosman.

248. 1530 Sept. 12. Sasine to Alexander Halkerston on renunciation by Jonet Balfour, relict of John Halkerston, with consent of John Flucar now her spouse, of her conjunct-fee, in favour of the said Alexander Halkerston and on his cognition by Mungo Tennent, bailie, as heir of the late John Halkerston his brother, of the said John's land lying on the north side of the High Street, in the vennel of Halkerston Wynd, east side the trause thereof, between a land of the late William Halkerston on the south, and a land of Duncan Forstar on the north: Which land the said Alexander Halkerston resigned in the hands of the bailie, who thereupon gave sasine thereof to the foresaid John Flucar, cutler, and the said Jonet Balfour his spouse in conjunct-fee. Witnesses, William Watson, Gilbert Anderson, John Kyle, John Softlaw, and David Purves, serjeant.

249. 1530 Aug. 31. Sasine to Alexander Bruse, son and heir of the late John Bruse, on redemption by him from Jonet Adamson, of a tenement of the said John Bruse, lying and bounded as described in the renunciation thereof to the said Alexander by Jonet Adamson on 26 August instant. (See fol. 88) Which tenement the said Alexander Bruse by his procurator resigned in the hands of Patrick Baron, bailie, in favour of himself and Marion Baron his spouse, who are thereupon seised therein in conjunct-fee, and the heirs lawfully procreated or to be procreated between them; whom failing to the heirs of the said Marion, always and until the sum of 200 merks shall be paid to her and her heirs. Witnesses, Master Henry Lauder, William Lauder, Alexander Baron, John Baron and Thomas Arnot, serjeants.

250. 1530 Sept. 24. John Crummy, burges of Lithqw, declarit how that he had analiit obefor to Archibald Cutler, induellar in Leith, be chartour and sesing, all and haill his akyr of land liand in the croftis of Hadington, etc., under ane reversion contenand the soume of xxiiij lib. And now had tane a mair soume fra the said Archibald in full contentation for the said akyr of land. And thairfor he renunsis and dischargis the said reversion for evir. And transferris and giffis to the said Archibald all rycht and titill that he or his airis may haif ony maner of way to the said akyr of land or reversion maid thairapone, dischargeand the said reversion, and all utheris reversionis maid or to be maid ony maner of way apone the redemption of the said akyr of land now and for evir. And in tokin thereof deliverit the said reversion to the said Archibald Cutlar in the bak. And als the said John Crummy grantis him award to the said Archibald ane chalder of bere, gude and sufficient stuf, and ane laid of aittis for money that he had ressavit fra the said Archibald for the samyn. And thairfor oblissis him faithfully till pay, or caus his tennentis in Hadington till pay and deliver the said chalder of bere and laid of aittis to the said Archibald, sufficient stuf and merkat met, betuix the dait heirof and Sanct Mertimes day next tocum. To be extended in more ample form. And thereupon the said Archibald

asked an instrument. Done in the house of the notary; witnesses, John Johnston, William Bowok and George Cunynghame.

251. 1530 Oct. 1. Patrick Baron, bailie, passed to a tenement of the late Andrew Kynpont, on the south side of the High Street, between a land of the late Richard Leithe on the west, and a land of Master John Murray on the east; and there Robert Glen presented to the foresaid bailie, a certain letter of gift of our Sovereign Lord the late King James the Fourth, of which the tenor follows in the common tongue:- James be the grace of God King of Scottis to all and sindry oure legis and subditis quham it efferis quhais knawlege thir oure lettres salcum and in speciale to the provest and ballies of oure burgh of Edinburgh, greting, Wit ye Ws to have gevin and grantis, and be thir oure lettres gevis and grantis, to oure lovit Robert Glene, burges of our said burgh of Edinburgh, for his gud and thankfull service done to Ws, ane annuel rent of xls. usuale money of our realme, aucht and pertenyng to umquhile Elizabeth Glene, sister to the said Robert, and now pertenyng to Ws as oure eschete be the lawis of oure realme, throw the deces of the said umquhile Elizabeth quhilk wes born bastard and deit but lauchfull are of hir body gottin; to be lyftit and takin up zeirly of ane land and tenement of umquhile Andro Kynpont, lyand in the said burgh of Edinburgh, upon the south side of oure street thairof, betuix the land of umquhile Richard Leich on the west pairt, and the land of Master Johne of Murray on the est pairt: To be haldin and to be had, the said annuell rent of 40s., to the said Robert and his airis, of Ws and our successouris in fee and heritage for ever; witht all and sindry comoditeis, fredoms, proffittis esementis and rychtues pertinentis quhatsumevir pertening or rychtuisly may pertene, to the samyne. Quhairfor we charge stratelie and command you all and sindry oure legis and subditis foresaidis, that name of you tak apone hand to mak ony impediment let or distrublance to the said Robert in the paciable bruking joising intrometting and disponyng apone the said annuell rent of xls., and that ye the said provest and baillies of our foresaid burgh of Edinburgh gyfe heretable stait and sesing of the said annuell to the said Robert, as efferis of the tenor of thir our lettres, under all pane and charge that eftir may fallow. Gevin under our Privie Sale at Edinburgh the vj day of August the yere of God jm.vc. and nyne yeris, and of our Regne the xxij yere. After the reading of which letter of gift and publication thereof by the notary public, the foresaid Patrick Baron, bailie, gave sasine of the said annual-rent of 40s. to the said Robert Glen.
And forthwith Robert Glen resigned his said annuell-rent of xls. in the hands of the bailie, who thereupon gave sasine thereof to Sir John Lauson, chaplain, and his successors, to pray for the souls of the late John Glen and Jonet (   ) his spouse, and mother to the said Robert, and for the souls of their ancestors and successors, conform to the tenor of a foundation made and to be made thereupon by the said Robert Glen. Witnesses, William Rynd, Alexander Baron, John Coldane, John Blak, John Ferguson, and David Purves, serjeant.

252. 1530 Oct. 6. Sasine given by William Sym, one of the bailies of Edinburgh, to friar Alexander Lauson, prior of the place of the Order of the Friars Preachers, in his own name and of the other friars preachers of the said place, conform to the tenor of a process of recognition led before the provost and bailies of the said burgh, of a land of the late William Richartson, lying in the foresaid burgh, below the Netherbow, on the south side of the High Street thereof, between a land of the late Robert Merschell on the east, a land of Alan Borthik on the west, a land of the late John Brown on the north, and a certain waste land on the south.
And forthwith the said friar Alexander Lauson, with consent of the convent of the Friars Preachers of the said place, after mature deliberation, in augmentation of the rental of the said place, resigned his foresaid land in the hands of the bailie, who gave heritable sasine and conjunct-infeftment thereof to William Elphinston, burgess, and Katrine Curll his spouse: They paying yearly therefor to the saids friars and their successors of the place thereof, an annual-rent of 35s. Witnesses, Master Henry Lauder, George Gude, Vincent Strathauchin, James Kynnaird, Thomas Craufurd, John Pardovan, Thomas Baird, John Mudy, William Wilkieson, and Patrick Lithqw, serjeant.

253. 1530 Oct. 8. Margret Broune confessit and grantit hir till haif sauld and analiit till Francis Aikman, and his airis, all and haill hir west half and part of hir waste land of hir tenement liand fra the Lord Seton's land till the college yaird, for iiij lib. and half ane ell of veluos; and thairapone tuke a crowne of xxs. in payment. And oblist hir and hir airis till gif him stait and sesing thairof, be resignation in ane of the ballies handis, annuell free; and sall seill him ane chartour thairapone, and till bind all the laif of hir tenement till keep him scaithies of annuell. Upon which the said Francis asked instrument. Done in the house of the notary, in presence of James Dundas, Alexander Johnston and Thomas Achinson.

254. 1530 Oct. 12. Sasine on resignation by John Smyth, son and heir of the late William Smyth, in favour of himself and Margaret Harper his affianced spouse, of (1) his land lying upon the Castlehill, on the north side of the High Street thereof, between a land of John Adamson on the east, and a land of Andrew Moncur on the west. (2) The land sometime of Alexander Chalmer, now of the said John Smyth, lying below the Castle Wall, on the south side of the High Street, between a land sometime of William Balze, now of the brethren of the Most Holy Blood, on the east, a land of Alexander Wilkesoun on the west, the lands of Hieriggis on the south, and the King's public street on the north. Witnesses, Henry Cranston, William Aikinheid, Walter Ramsay, Laurence Howy, William McTeir, William Richemant, Sir Andrew Harper, chaplain, and David Purves, serjeant. William Adamson is bailie.

255. 1530 Oct. 12. Hew Moncreif for him self on that ane pairt, and Maister Adam Ottirburne for David Wemys of that Ilk on that uthir pairt, continewis and prorogatis the compromitt maid

betuix the saidis pairtiis, in the samyne strenthe force and effect as it now is, quhill the thrid day of Februar next tocum. Both parties asked instruments. Done in the tolbooth of the burgh of Edinburgh, witnesses, Nicholas Carncors, George Gude, William Sym, William Raa, and Symon Prestoun.

256. 1530 Oct. 20. Sasine to Alexander Bruse, on his cognition by John Mauchane, bailie, as heir of the deceased John Bruse his father, of a tenement of the said John on the south side of the High Street, between a tenement of the late Edward Bonkill on the east, and a tenement of the late Walter Blaklok on the west; a land of the late William Ker on the south, and the King's public street on the north; to be possessed by him as freely as he had the same before the alienation and resignation thereof made by him to Jonet Adamson; which tenement the said Jonet confessed was lawfully redeemed from her by the said Alexander. And forthwith Alexander Bruse resigned the said tenement in the hands of the bailie, who gave heritable sasine and conjunct-infeftment thereof to the said Alexander and Marion Baron his spouse, the surviver of them, and the heirs lawfully procreated or to be procreated between them, whom failing to the said Marion and her heirs, always and until the sum of 200 merks shall be paid to her and her heirs, conform to the contract and charter made thereupon. Witnesses, Robert Urquhart, Patrick Baron, William Reid, Thomas Arnot and William Watson, serjeants. On which day Jonet Adamson, in presence of the said bailie, protested that the said sasine given by John Mauchane, bailie, to Alexander Bruse and Marion Baron his spouse, shall not prejudice her liferent, which she has of the foresaid tenement, and for remeid of law.

257. 1530 Oct. 26. Sasine on resignation by Alexander Bruse, son and heir of the late William Bruse, with consent of Marion Baron his spouse; also with consent of Alexander Young, notary public, his uncle, in favour of Jonet Adamson, of an annualrent of 10 merks, out of the said Alexander's tenement on the south side of the High Street and bounded as before described: With the said Marion's bodily oath, the Scriptures touched, not to revoke. Witnesses, John Adamson, William Uddart, Thomas Uddart, William Lyndesay, Master James Scot, John Forman, Thomas Purdy, and David Purves, serjeant.
The quhilk day, in presens of the ballie William Adamson, and witnes abone wryttin, Marion Baron, the spous of Alexander Bruse, protestit the howbeit she consentit to the alienation of x merks of annuell, of the tenement of land pertenand till the said Alexander and hir, that it hurt not hir rycht that scho has of the said tenement. And the said Alexander Bruse promist, that gif evir God fortunat him till conques ony land or annuell rent, to the avale of the said x merkis that he had analiit till Jonet Adamson, of his tenement of land, that he suld infeft and put Marion Baron his spous in the samyn; and to the airis to be gottin betuix thame. Quharapone the said Marion askit instrumentis. Witnes aboue wryttin.

258. 1530 Oct. 26. William Towris of Elwansyde passed to a tenement of John Pady and William Maxwell lying beyond the West Bow of the burgh of Edinburgh, on the south side of the High Street thereof, between a land of the late Alexander Nicholas on the east, the lands of the late James Wallas now pertaining to James Makgauchane, on the west, the lands of Hieriggis on the south, and the King's public street on the north, in the barony of Dalry and shire of Edinburgh; and there John Pady and William Maxwell, with one consent and assent, resigned the foresaid tenement, with the yard thereof, in the hands of the said William Towris, of Elwansyde, as in the hands of the lord superior thereof; which resignation so made and by the said lord superior received, the said William Towris, lord superior foresaid, gave sasine of the said tenement to Alexander Ur, son of George Ur, in fee, and to the said George his father in liferent. Witnesses, Alexander Mauchane, John Mauchane, Alexander Towris, William Blaklok, Connall Small, David Scot, William Johnston, Adam Wrycht and William Watson.

259. 1530 Oct. 27. Sasine to Lancelot Barcar on his cognition by Alexander Belsches, bailie, as son and heir of the late James Barcar, of the backlands and yard of the said James, lying below the Castle Wall, on the south side of the High Street, within his tenement, between a land or yard sometime of William Hamilton, now pertaining to Master Francis Bothuell, on the east, a land or yard sometime of William Bailze, now pertaining to the brethren of the Holy Blood, on the west, the lands of Hieriggis on the south, and the lands of John Adamson on the north: Which backlands the said Lancelot Barcar resigned in the hands of the bailie, who thereupon gave sasine of the same to William Adamson, burgess. Witnesses, Henry Cranston, John Charteris, Richard Gray, William Aikinheid, Richard Wardlaw, John Loch, George Henrison, Duncan Donaldson and Hugh Wallas, serjeant.

260. 1530 Oct. 27. Sasine on resignation by Robert Glen, son and heir of the late John Glen, burgess, with consent of Marion Cokburn his spouse, in favour of Thomas Cuke, burgess, and Isobella Ramsay his spouse, of the said Robert's built land within a tenement of William Lord Borthik, on the south side of the High Street, between a tenement of Alexander Rynd on the east, and a tenement of the late John Carkettill on the west; west side the transe of the said tenement, between a land of the late David Linlithqw on the north, and a waste land thereof, now pertaining to David Gillaspy on the south: With the said Marion's oath not to revoke. Witnesses, Sir John Craufurd, Richard Wardlaw, Patrick Linlithqw and Thomas Arnot, serjeants. The same day, etc., Thomas Cuke and his wif promittis thame and thair airis till mak ane reversion till Robert Glen and his airis, apone the redemption of the said land quhilk he analiit to thame, liand as is abone writtin, contenand the soume of twa hundreth merkis; with ane zeir eftir the lowsing for xvij merkis of maill, and to pay the annuell; and that to be extendit in the more ample form. Robert Glen asked an instrument. Alexander Belsches is bailie.

261. 1530 Oct. 29. Sasine on resignation of her liferent by Margaret Brown, of the waste land of her tenement on the north side of the High Street, between a tenement of the late William Dunsyar on the east, and a tenement now of Francis Aikman on the west; which waste land lies on the east side as well as on the west side of the said tenement, viz. that on the west side, between a waste land of Lord Seyton on the south, and the yard of Trinity College on the north; and that on the east, equal with the north gable of a land of the late James Fyndgude on the south, and the said College yard on the north. The sasine proceeds also on resignation of the said waste land by William Achinson, son and heir of the late George Achinson, and son and heir apparent of the said Margaret Brown, in favour of Francis Aikman, burgess. Witnesses, Andrew Mowbray, James Henrison, William Stevinson, Rolland Donaldson, William Williamson, Thomas justice, William Stanton, Thomas Carmichell, Thomas Bryson, and Patrick Linlithqw, serjeant. William Sym is bailie.

The said day, etc., the said Margaret Broune renounced her liferent of an annual-rent of 2 merks, out of a land of Patrick Flemyng, lying within her said tenement, east side the transe thereof, in favour of William Achinson her son and apparent heir. Moreover the said William promised and obliged himself to his said Mother to receive Thomas Achinson his brother from her, and to sustain him in meat, drink, clothes and other necessaries as is becoming, during the space of 5 years next immediately thereafter; and that for the singular favour and love, and certain other favours often done by her to him.

262. 1530 Oct. 29. Sasine to Katrine Hoppar, on her cognition by William Sym, bailie, as daughter and one of the heirs of the late William Hoppar, of the half of the said William's land on the south side of the High Street, in St. Mary Wynd, west side the transe thereof, between a land (   ) on the south, and a land (   ) on the north: Which half of the said land Katrine Hoppar resigned in favour of herself and Andrew Mowbray her spouse, who are thereupon seised therein in conjunct-fee. Witnesses, David Kincaid, Francis Aikman, James Henrison, Andrew Galloway, Rolland Donaldson, William Williamson, and Patrick Lithqw, serjeant.

263. 1530 Nov. 4. Sasine on precept under testimonial of the Great Seal, in favour of Elizabeth Broun *alias* Smyth, of the half of a tenement of the late Thomas Brown *alias* Smyth, on the south side of the High Street, between a land of the late Connal Young on the east, and a land of the altar of St. James, situated in St. Giles Kirk, on the west; and a land of the late Bartholomew Karnis on the south, and the King's public street on the north: Also of the half of a foreland lying below the Castle Wall, on the north side of the High Street, between a land of the late James Hill on the east, and a land (   ) on the west. Witnesses, Master John Chapman, Thomas Foular, Andrew Paterson, Thomas Gibson, John Bayne, William Wilkieson, Edward Thomson and Thomas Arnot.

Beatrix Paterson protested that the said sasine of the foresaid

tenement so given hurt her not nor Katrine her daughter; and
for remeid of law. To be extended in more ample form.

264. 1530 Nov. 17. Sasine on resignation by John Arres, with consent
of Cristina Reidpeth his spouse, in favour of Elizabeth Silver,
of an annual-rent of 10 merks, out of the resigner's land on
the south side of the High Street, between a land of the late
James Homyll on the west and a land of Nicholas Broune on
the east. Witnesses, Sir James Duncanson, William Blaklok, William Johnston, Patrick Young, Nicholas Howison, and William
Watson, serjeant: With promise by the said Elizabeth to give
to John Arres, and his heirs, a letter of reversion, upon
redemption of the said annual-rent, containing the sum of £80,
to be extended in more ample form.

265. 1530 Nov. 17. Sasine on resignation by James Coky, son and
heir of the late John Coky, in favour of John Arres, elder, in
liferent, and John Arres his son in fee, of the said James
Coky's tenement on the south side of the High Street, between
a land of the late Henry Liberton on the east, the lands of
the late James Aikman and Henry Wilson on the west, a land
of the late James Fairly on the south, and the King's public
street on the north. Witnesses, Sirs James Duncanson, Andrew
Harper and George Litiljohne, chaplains, John Anderson, Symone
Cunynghame, David Robertson, and William Watson, serjeant.
John Mauchane is bailie.
Which day, in presence of the bailie and witnesses, James Coky
protested, that the resignation of his tenement by him in the
hands of John Mauchane, bailie, and the sasine thereof by him
to John Arres and his son, hurt not Jonet Barcar his mother,
as to her liferent thereof.

266. 1530 Nov. 24. The which day, Alexander Belsches, bailie, passed
to a tenement of John Vernour, lying on the south side of the
High Street, between a land of the late John Bell on the east,
and a land of John Preston on the west; and there the said
bailie, in virtue of his office and of a mandate of the provost,
bailies, and council, directed to him by the acts of the court
of the said burgh, gave state, possession and heritable sasine
of a certain waste land, lying within the foresaid tenement,
between a land of James Johnston on the north, and a land
of James Henrison on the south, to a prudent man James Henrison,
his heirs and assignees. Witnesses, George Henrison, Master
David Irland, John Foular, Francis Aikman, William Bruse and
James Johnston, Edinburgh.

267. 1530 Nov. 29. Sasine on resignation by Robert Glen in favour
of Isobel Levingston, Lady Roslyne, her heirs and assignees,
of the said Robert's land lying in Peebles Wynd, east side thereof, between a land (   ) on the north, and a waste land
on the south; and this in special warrandice of a certain land
of her tenement and annual-rent thereof lying in Nudry's Wynd,
east side the transe thereof, between a land of the late George
Achinson on the north, and St. Mary's chapel on the south,
formerly alienated by the said Robert Glen to the said Isobel

Lady Roslyne in warrandice, conform to a contract, charter and infeftment made by the said Robert to the said Lady thereupon. Witnesses, Patrick Baron, Richard Wardlaw, John Coldane, James Baron, Sir James Duncanson, and William Watson, serjeant. Mr. Alexander Levingston, attorney for the said Lady Roslyne.

268. 1530 Dec. 2. Sasine given by Alexander Belsches, bailie, to Sir Alexander Harpar, chaplain of the altar of St. Michael, situated within the church of St. Giles, of a certain land of the late James Ross, lying on the north side of the High Street, within a tenement of the late Sir Alexander Lauder of Blyth, knight, between the fore land and the back land of the said tenement on the south, and a land of the late Gilbert Canon on the north, conform to a process of recognition led before the provost and bailies of the burgh. Witnesses, William Lauder, William Tod, James Johnston and Thomas Arnot, serjeants.

269. 1530 Dec. 6. Resignation by Alison Haliburton, relict of Michael Symson, in favour of Robert Watson and his spouse, of the said Alison's liferent of a land of the said Michael now pertaining to the said Robert, on the south side of the High Street, in Forstar's Wynd, east side the transe thereof, between a land of the late John Falcon on the north, and a land of the late William Falcon on the south. Witnesses, Robert Bruse, Mungo Tennent, John Anderson, George Paterson and George Arnot. William Adamson is bailie.

270. 1530 Dec. 9. John Mauchane, bailie, passed to a tenement of the late Thomas Brown *alias* Smyth, lying on the south side of the High Street, between a land of the late Connal Young on the east, and a land pertaining to the chaplain of the altar of St. James on the west, a land of the Bartholomew Kairus on the south and the King's public street on the north; and there Beatrix Paterson, relict of the said Thomas Brown *alias* Smyth, with consent of John Dykson her spouse, resigned their conjunct-fee of the foresaid tenement in the hands of the bailie, in favour of Katrine Brown *alias* Smyth her daughter, and of Isobel Brown *alias* Smyth, daughters and heirs of the said late Thomas Brown *alias* Smyth, for sasine of the said tenement to be given to them: Reserving the liferent thereof to the said Beatrix. And forthwith the said bailie cognosced and entered Katrine Brown *alias* Smyth in and to the half of the foresaid tenement. And in like manner the bailie cognosced and entered Isobella Brown *alias* Smyth in and to the half of the said tenement, each of them as heir foresaid: And which half the said Isobella resigned in the hands of the bailie who gave sasine thereof to Katrine Brown *alias* Smyth her sister. Witnesses, Alexander Belsches, Master Thomas Brown, William Thomson, Thomas Foular, Edward Hoppringill, John Richartson, William Clerkson, Alexander Schaw, Henry Cranston, David Quhite, Adam Wilson, David Purves and William Watson.

271. 1530 Dec. 9. Sasine to Isobella and Katrine Brown *alias* Smyth (fo.97)on renunciation of her conjunct-fee by Beatrix Paterson, relict of Thomas Brown *alias* Smyth, with consent of John Dykson her

spouse, in favour of the said Katrine her daughter, and of the said Isobella, daughters and heirs of the said Thomas; and on cognotion of the said Isobella and Katrine by John Mauchane, bailie, as heirs foresaid, in and to a certain foreland or tenement of the said Thomas Brown lying below the Castle Wall, on the north side of the High Street, between a land of James Hill on the east, and a land of the late Mathew Harvey on the west: Also of an annual-rent of 30s. out of the back-land of the said tenement, between the said fore land on the south, and the King's Wall on the north; each of the said sisters in her own respective half of said fore land and annual-rent.
And forthwith Katrine Brown, in an open Court held and fenced before the bailie, upon the ground of the said fore-land, chose and desired John Dykson to be given to her as her curator, which curator the bailie gave to her accordingly, and took his oath *de fideli* Upon which the said Katrine, with consent and authority of her curator, resigned her half of the foreland and annual-rent aforesaid in the hands of John Mauchane, bailie, who gave sasine thereof to Isobella Brown *alias* Smyth her sister, her heirs and assignees, in presence of Andrew Quhite and the witnesses before mentioned.

272. 1530 Dec. 9. Sasine on resignation by Issobella Brown *alias* Smyth, daughter and one of the heirs of the late Thomas Brown *alias* Smyth, in favour of Michael Makquhen, burgess, of the foreland or tenement of the said Thomas, now pertaining to the said Issobella, lying below the Castle Wall, on the north side of the High Street, and bounded as before described: Also of an annual-rent of 30s. out of the back-land of the said tenement. Same witnesses.

273. 1530 Dec. 9. Compeared personally Isobella Brown *alias* Smyth, daughter and one of the heirs of the late Thomas Brown *alias* Smyth, and sister and apparent heir of Katrine Brown *alias* Smyth, and of her own free will constituted John Dykson and Beatrix Paterson his spouse, David Purves, Thomas Arnot, Hugh Wallas, Patrick Lithqw, William Watson, Master Robert Galbrayth, Master James Foulis, Master Henry Lauder, and William Thomson, conjointly and severally, her procurators. And also constitutes the said John and Beatrix Paterson, for the love and fervent aftection she has and bears towards them, in and to all and sundry lands, annual-rents and possessions, and all heritable goods, and other goods moveable and immoveable whatsoever, that shall happen to fall to her by decease of Katrine Brown *alias* Smyth her sister. Moreover the said Isobell grants to her said assignees license and power to intromit with all her said lands, annual-rents and goods, dispone to their own utility, and apply the same to their own use; also to impetrate and execute breves from Chancery upon the said lands and annual-rents, and to take and receive instruments thereupon. And after receiving sasine and possession, to resign all and sundry the foresaid lands and annual-rents in the hands of one of the bailies of the burgh of Edinburgh, in favour of the said Beatrix Paterson and John Dykson her spouse, the survivor

of them, and the heirs to be procreated between them, etc. for infeftment and sasine to be made thereupon: With the said Isobella's oath not to revoke. Done within the burgh of Edinburgh, beside the dwelling-house of the said Beatrix Paterson, in presence of Alexander Belsches, Michael Makquhen, Master Thomas Brown, William Thomson, Thomas Foular, Edward Hoppringill, John Richartson, William Clarkson, Alexander Schaw, Henry Cranston, David Quhite, Adam Wilson, David Purves and William Watson.

274. 1530 Dec. 10. Isobella Broune *alias* Smyth the dochter and ane of the airis of umquhile Thomas Broune *alias* Smyth burges of Edinburgh uncoakkit or compellit bot of hir awin fre and motif will grantis hir till haif ressavit thankfull payment be the handis of Beatrix Paterson the relict of the said umquhile Thomas Broune *alias* Smyth and Johne Dykson now hir spous, of all maner of gudis of airschip pertenand till hir throw the deces of hir said umquhile fadir: And als of all maner of soumes of money dettis or gudis awand till ony maner of way be legacy of hir gudsir or gudame or ony uther person quhatsumevir; and thairof for hir, hir airis executouris and assignais quytclamys and dischargis the saidis Beatrix Paterson and John hir spous thair airis executouris and assignais now and for evir be thir presentis; and promittis faithfully nevir till persen follow ask nor desyre nathir be hir self nor nane utheris in hir name ony forther payment or satisfaction fra the saidis Beatrix nor hir spous thair airis executouris and assignais for the saidis airschip gudis soumes of money dettis or legaciis forsaid in na tyme tocum under the pain of perjurie and maneswering. And thereupon the said John Dykson for himself and his said spouse asked an instrument. Done in the booth of the Common Clerk. Witnesses, John Mauchane, bailie, Vincent Strathaucin, notary public, Michael McQuhen, William Thomson, Thomas Laverok, Sir James Duncanson, chaplain, George Arnot, and David Purves, serjeant.

The quhilk day, in presens of the said witnes, Isobel Broune *alias* Smyth, dochter and ane of the airis of umquhile Thomas Broune *alias* Smyth, deliverit hir propir seill till Johne Mauchane, ballie, in keping, and gaif him command till seill hir charter to be maid till Michael McQuhen, of the land under the wall, quhilk scho had analiit to him; and als to seill all uther maner of uther evidentis wryttingis procuratouris chartouris acquittans, or uther documentis that may do steid or plesour to Beatrix Paterson, or Johne Dykson hir spous, or till Katrine Broune *alias* Smyth hir sister, ony maner of way, for thair securite to be maid to thame and consentis thairto als weill and syklyke as scho war present hir self in propir person. Upon which the said Michael Makquhan asked an instrument. Done in the booth of the Common Clerk.

275. 1530 Dec. 12. Sasine on resignation by William Anderson, burgess, with consent of Jonet Merschell his spouse, in favour of Master John Dingwall, apostolic protonotary, and Provost of Trinity College Church, his heirs and assignees, of an annualrent of 40s., out of a land of the said William Anderson on

the north side of the High Street, beyond the Over Bow, between a land of James Darroche on the east, and a land of the late John Mosman on the west, a land of the Laird of Ruthven on the north, and the King's public street on the south. With the said Jonet's oath in a full and open court, held before Alexander Belsches, bailie, the Scriptures touched, not to revoke.
And forthwith Master John Dingwall, Provost foresaid, resigned the said annual-rent of 40s. in the hands of the said Alexander Belsches, bailie, who thereupon gave heritable sasine thereof to Sir John Craufurd, chaplain, procurator as he affirmed, and in name of the Prioress and sisters of the place of the Order of Saint Dominic, now called Saint Katrine of the Senis, and her successors, sisters of the said Order, conform to the tenor of a charter of foundation to be made thereupon. Upon which the said Master John and the said Sir John Craufurd asked instruments. Witnesses, Master William Meldrum, Sir William Gibson and Sir James Wode, chaplains, Thomas Wode, Thomas Coupar and Patrick Linlithqw, serjeant.

276. 1530 Dec. 14. Renunciation by Robert Mailuill, son and heir of the late David Mailuill, burgess, in favour of Walter Scot and his spouse, of a certain letter of reversion made to him by the said Walter and Margaret his spouse, of and upon the redemption of an annual-rent of 5 merks alienated by the said Robert to them, upliftable from a tenement of the late William Fausyde, lying on the south side of the High Street, between a land of the late William Young on the east, a land of the late (   ) on the west, a land of the late Andrew Robison *alias* Sclater on the south, and the King's public street on the north. Moreover the said Robert Mailuill, with consent of Jonet Spittall his spouse, resigned another annual-rent of 40s. out of the foresaid tenement, in the hands of Alexander Belsches, bailie, who thereupon gave sasine thereof to the said Walter Scot and Margaret Bischop his spouse. Witnesses, Robert Grahame, James Balcasky, John Mayne, William Grahame, Thomas Arnot and William Watson, serjeants.

277. 1530 Dec. 15. Sasine on resignation by Robert Bruse, in favour of Robert Watson, burgess, and Elizabeth Baron his spouse, of the resigner's land, built and waste, lying on the south side of the High Street, below the Castle Wall, between a land of the late John Symson on the east, the lands of Robert Watson on the west and south, and the King's public street on the north. Witnesses, Alexander Young, notary public, Alexander Gylour, John Symson, Richard Wardlaw, William Brown, and Thomas Arnot, serjeant. Andrew Baron is attorney, and John Mauchane is bailie.

278. 1530 Dec. 20. Sasine on resignation by William Brown, son and heir of the late John Brown, burgess, with consent of his spouse Isobella Bruse, in favour of Thomas Tarbat, burgess, and Marjorie Brown his spouse, of the said William's land and mansion, lying within a tenement of the late Thomas Preston of Bynning, now pertaining to the said William Brown, on the north side of the High Street, between a land of John Brown

on the east, and a land of Andrew Baron on the west. Witnesses, Master Thomas Brown, Sir John Gylour, Sir John Stewart and Sir James Duncanson, chaplains, Adam Douglas, John Kyle, Patrick Linlithqw and William Watson, serjeants. John Mauchane is bailie.

279. 1530 Dec. 21. Sasine to Isobella Balfour on her cognition by William Adamson, bailie, as daughter and heir of the late John Balfour, of a land of her said late father, lying within a tenement of the late Charles Levington, between a waste land of the late Thomas Cattall, now pertaining to David Gillaspy, on the south, and a land of Henry Dumbartane on the north; which tenement lies on the south side of the High Street, between a tenement of William Lord Borthik on the east, and a tenement of the late Thomas Swift on the west. Witnesses, William Brown, James Styrk, John Williamson, George Weir, William Bowy, William Homyll and David Purves.

280. 1530 Dec. 21. William Adamson, bailie, passed to a tenement of the late Charles Levington, lying on the south side of the High Street, between a tenement of William Lord Borthik on the east, and a tenement of the late Thomas Swift on the west, and there David Gillaspy, burgess, with consent of Elizabeth Gilleis his spouse, resigned his waste land containing 12 ells, descending towards the south, from the south gable of a land of the late John Balfour, between the said land of John Balfour on the north, and another waste land of the said David on the south, the transe of the said tenement on the east, and the transe of a tenement of the late Thomas Swift on the west. With the said Elizabeth's oath not to revoke. Witnesses, William Brown, James Styrk, John Williamson, George Weir, William Bowy, William Homyll and David Purves, serjeant of the burgh.

281. 1530 Dec. 22. Sasine to Henry Hoppar on his cognition by Williamson, bailie, as grandson and heir of the late Richard Hoppar, burgess, of that land under and above lying within a tenement of Master Adam Otterburne of Auldhame, west side the transe thereof, on the north side of the High Street, between a tenement of the late John Mason on the east, and a tenement of the late Henry Young on the west, another built land of the said Henry Hoppar on the north, and the said Master Adam Otterburn's foreland on the south: Which foresaid land the said Henry Hoppar resigned in the hands of the bailie, who gave sasine thereof to John Hoip, burgess, and Elizabeth Edmond his spouse. Witnesses, John Somervell, John Fausyde, George Johnston, James Smyth, and David Purves, serjeant. Moreover, in presence of the said bailie and witnesses, the said John Hoip and his spouse promised to give to the said Henry, and his heirs, a letter of reversion upon redemption of the said lands containing the sum of £60.

282. 1530-1 Jan. 9. Sasine on renunciation by Jonet Brown relict of Francis Borthik, with consent of Alexander Spens her spouse, of her conjunct-fee in favour of Andrew Borthik, and upon cognition of the said Andrew by William Sym, bailie, as son and heir of the deceased Francis Borthik, of the backland and yard

JOHN FOULAR

of the tenement of the late Stephen Borthik, lying on the south side of the High Street, between a tenement of George Ur on the east, and a tenement of the late Francis Towris on the west; the King's Wall on the south, and the fore land of the said tenement on the north. And forthwith Andrew Borthik, in an open court held before the said bailie, chose and desired John Pardovyne to be given to him as curator, which the bailie accordingly did, and took from him the oath *de fideli*. This done, Andrew Borthik, with consent and authority of nis curator, resigned his backland foresaid, with the yard thereof, etc., in the hands of the bailie, who thereupon gave heritable sasine and conjunct infeftment of the same to Thomas Rynde, burgess, and Cristiane Ireland his spouse. Moreover, Andrew Borthik, in presence of the bailie, gave his oath, the scriptures touched, not to revoke in time to come. Witnesses, Masters William Blakstok and David Ireland, John Towris, William Rynde, John Wardlaw, John Fairlie, John Wyle, Alexander Mason, and David Purves, serjeant, and Alexander Pery.

283. 1530–1 Jan. 9. Andro Borthik the son and air of umquhile Frances Borthik declarit how that he had analiit his backland and yaird liand within this burgh, on the south syde the gait besyde the Castellhill, till Thomas Rynde and Cristiane his spous; heirfor he oblissis him faithfully that gif ony interdiction be fundin apone him maid be ony juge he suld caus annull the samyn; and oblissis him and his airis till enter of new again the said Thomas and his spous in and to the said backland and yaird with the pertinentis in the sikerest maner that can be maid or divisit. Apone the quhilk Thomas Rynde askit instrumentis. Done upon the ground of the said land: Witnesses the same as to the preceding sasine.
The quhilk day in presens of the ballie William Sym, Alexander Spens oblist him and promittis faithfully till underly and defend the pley betuix Sir Andro Chatto and the said Andro Borthik, apone his expens, and never to charge the said Andro with ony expens thairof, and to releif the said Andro of all danger that may cum thairthrow in tyme tocum as accordis apone the law. And thereupon the said Andrew asked an instrument.
On the which day John Pardovyne, in name of his spous Helen Forbes, protested that the sasine given by William Sym, bailie, to Thomas Rynde, and his spouse, hurt not her conjunct-fee which she has of the foreland and backland lying on the north side of the land alienated to the said Thomas Rynd, and for remeid of law when and where it effeirs. Witnesses *ut supra*.

284. 1530–1 Jan. 9. William Sym, bailie, passed to a certain land lying in the Buithraw, on the south side of the High Street, between a land of the late David Mailuill on the west, and a land of the late Michael Frog, now pertaining to Master Adam Otterburne, James McCalzeane and the late Elizabeth Dunsyar on the east; and there Andrew Borthik, son and heir of the late Francis Borthik, with consent and authority of John Pardovyne his curator, resigned his two part of the foresaid land, under and above, in the hands of the bailie: Also the said Andrew Borthik, son and heir *ut supra*, renounced and dimitted his

right and title of the patronage of the service founded by the
late Elizabeth Wode, at the altar of St. Eligius, situated within
the Kirk of St. Giles, in favour of John Spens his brother:
Which resignation and renunciation so made, as said is, the
bailie gave heritable sasine of the said two part of the said
land, with pertinents, to the said John Spens, brother to the
said Andrew Borthik, his heirs and assignees; together with the
right of patronage of the said service and altar of St. Eligius,
conform to the tenor of a charter to be made thereupon: Reserving, however, the frank-tenement of the said two part of the
foresaid land to the said Andrew Borthik during his lifetime,
after the decease of Jonet Brown his mother: Also reserving to
the said Andrew the disposition and donation of the said service
and altar of St. Eligius during his lifetime, when it shall happen the same to become vacant. Witnesses, John Towris, Masters
David Ireland and William Blakstok, William Rynde, John Wardlaw, Alexander Mason, Thomas Rynde, Alexander Spens, Alexander Pery, and David Purves, serjeant.
The quhilk day, in presens of the ballie William Sym, Maister
William Blakstok, in name of Clement Litill, protested that the
sasine given by the said bailie, of the two part of the land
above written, to John Spens, after resignation thereof made by
Andrew Borthik, hurt not the said Clement nor his spouse as
to the merchant booth lying within the said land, previously
alienated to them by the said Andrew by charter and sasine,
and for remeid of law when and where it effeirs. Same witnesses.
1530-1 Jan. 9. Assignation by Andrew Borthik, son and heir of
the late Francis Borthik, in favour of John Spens his brother,
of a letter of reversion made by Clement Litill and his spouse,
of and upon the redemption of the merchant booth, lying within
the land of the said late Francis, between a land of the late
David Mailuill on the east, and a land of Master Adam Otterburne on the west. Witnesses aforesaid.

285. 1530-1 Jan. 18. Sasine on resignation by John Barclay, with consent of Elizabeth Nudry his spouse, in favour of Symon Preston,
burgess, and Cristiane Blakstok his spouse, of the said John
Barclay's tenement lying on the south side of the High Street,
in the vennel of Mary of the Fields, east side the trause thereof, between the lands of Andrew Auld, Thomas Vaiche and the
piece of yard pertaining to the prebendaries of the Kirk-of-Field
on the south, a land of the late Stephen Law on the north, and
a land of Francis Inchecok on the east. With the said Elizabeth
Nudry's oath, the scriptures touched, not to revoke. Witnesses,
Sir George Kelle, John Werrok, Stephen Elder, and Patrick Linlithqw, serjeant. Alexander Belsches is bailie.

286. 1530-1 Jan. 19. Sasine on precept from chancery in favour of
Marjory Brown, as one of the lawful and nearest heirs of the
late Elizabeth Scot, Lady Manerston, her uncle's daughter, of
the wester part of a tenement of the said late Elizabeth Scot,
lying on the south side of the High Street, between the transe
of the said tenement and the easter part thereof on the east,
the lands of the late Patrick Richartson, Clement Litill, James
Home and Maurice Coupland on the west, the yard of the said

tenement on the south, and the King's public street on the north. The precept is dated at Perth 29 November in the 18th. year of the King's reign, (1530). Witnesses, Thomas Dyksone, Cuthbert Dyk, William Chamblet, William Blaklok, James Darroche, Alexander Elphinstone, Thomas Quhite, John Weddaill, and David Purves, serjeant. John Luf is attorney for the said Marjory, and John Mauchan is bailie.

287. 1530-1 Jan. 19. Sasine on resignation by Marjory Brown, cousin and one of the heirs of the late Elizabeth Scot, Lady Manerston, in favour of Sir James Ker, chaplain, son of the said Marjory, his heirs and assignees, of the half of the wester part of the said Lady Manerston's tenement, lying on the south side of the High Street, and bounded as before described. Same witnesses. David Purves is attorney, and John Mauchane is bailie.

288. 1530-1 Jan. 27. Sasine to John Michelson, on his cognition by Alexander Belsches, bailie, as heir of the late Cristiane Scallis, his mother, daughter and heir of the late Patrick Scallis, mason, of the said Cristiane's land on the south side of the High Street, in the end of a tenement of the late Robert Lauder, between another land of the said late Patrick on the south, and a land of the late John Lethame on the north. Witnesses, Laurence Montgumry, Thomas Greg, John Staill, Thomas Michelson, David Purves and Thomas Arnot, serjeants.

289. 1530-1 Jan. 28. Sasine on resignation by Margaret Forsyth, daughter and one of the heirs of the late William Forsyth, with consent of John Gray her spouse, in favour of Robert Grahame, burgess, and Margaret Aldjoy his spouse, of an annual-rent of 4 merks 6s.8d. out of the north part and one half of a land of the said William Forsyth, lying in St. Mary Wynd, west side the transe thereof, between the lands of the late William Scheirsmyth on the south and north parts: Under reversion of £30. Which reversion the said Robert promised to make and deliver to the said Margaret and her spouse, upon redemption of the said annual-rent. Witnesses, Walter Scot, Thomas Michelson, William Cristeson, Mungo Wauchop and Thomas Arnot. Alexander Belsches is bailie.

290. 1530-1 Jan. 30. Sasine on resignation by David Stratoun, with consent of Agnes Pollok his spouse, in favour of Margaret Henrison in fee, and Robert Henrison her father in liferent, of the lands and houses of the said David, lying contiguous, beyond the West Port of the burgh of Edinburgh, beside and opposite the lands of Hieriggis, between the common transe on the east, and the land or gable of the late John Paterson on the west; the king's common way on the north, and the said lands of Hieriggis on the south. Also of one yard of the lands of Hieriggis lying between a land of James Thomson on the east, the said common transe on the west; a land of the late Laurence Lille on the north, and the said lands of Hieriggis on the south. These lands and houses were resigned in the hands of William Towris of Elwandsyde, superior thereof, who also gave sasine of the same to Margaret Henrison and her father. Sir George Heslihop, chaplain, is attorney for the said Margaret. Witnesses,

Alexander Towris, David Douglas, John Henrison, John Weilfed and William Richeman.

291. 1530-1 Feb. 1. Sasine on resignation by George Towris, son of the late Francis Towris, burgess, in favour of John Towris, his brother, and Alisone Udward his spouse, of an annual-rent of 12 merks, out of the foreland of a tenement of the late Francis Towris, on the north side of the High Street, between the lands of the late Robert Halyburton and the heirs of the late Adam Hoppar on the east, and a land of John Fischar on the west; the High Street on the south, and a land of the late Cristiane Harvy, now pertaining to Henry Levingstone on the north: Also out of another land and mansion lying within the said tenement, between the said land of Henry Levingston on the south, and the North Loch on the north. Witnesses, Edward Henrison, John Chancellar, John King, Patrick Urry, William Aikinheid, Cuthbert Dik, John Scot and Patrick Linlithqw, with divers others, specially called and required to the premises. William Sym is bailie.

292. 1530-1 Feb. 3. Renunciation by James Johnston in favour of William Raa, assignee of John Dennun, of a land lying below the Castle Wall, on the west side of the High Street thereof, between a land of William Raa on the nortn, a land of Robert Bruse on the south, a land of Thomas Kincaid on the west, and the King's common way on the east: Which land, alienated by John Dennun to the said James Johnston, is now lawfully redeemed from him by William Raa, assignee foresaid, by payment of the sum of £19 reserving to the said James Johnston a tack of the said land for the space of 7 years after the redemption thereof. Done in the booth of the common clerk of Edinburgh, in presence of Vincent Strathauchin, Sir John Smyth, chaplain, notaries public, Henrie Cranston, William Aikinheid, William Coldane, George Arnot and George Allane.

293. 1530-1 Feb. 3. Sasine on resignation by Stephen Buchane, son and heir of the late Alan Buchane, with consent of Jonet Symson his spouse, in favour of William Coldane, burgess, of the said Stephen's land on the north side of the High Street, within a tenement of the late George Halkerston, west side the transe thereof, between a land of Robert Hucheson on the north, and a land of Thomas Ambrose on the south; the land of Duncan Wicnt on the east, and the land of the late Robert Lyndsay on the west. Witnesses, Sir Robert Abernethy, Alexander Blaky, James Anderson, Patrick Lithqw and Thomas Arnot, serjeants. William Adamson is bailie.

294. 1530-1 Feb. 13. Sasine on resignation by Thomas Cameron in favour of Sir John Dykson, chaplain, for celebrating divine service at the altar of Saint Katrine during his lifetime, and in name and behalf of his successors for the perpetual celebration of divine service at the said altar, of a tenement of the said Thomas Cameron lying in the Cowgate, south side the High Street thereof, between a land of the bishop of Dunkeld on the east, a land of the late William Raperlaw on the west, the King's common way on the north, and the way that leads to the Kirk of Field on the south; in pure and perpetual alms, conform

to the charter made thereupon: Reserving the liferent of the said tenement to the said Thomas Cameron. Both parties asked instruments. Witnesses, Robert Law, James Gray, David Brown, Robert Elphinston, Sir Alexander Cunynghame and Patrick Lithqw, serjeant.

295. 1530-1 Feb. 16. Sasine in favour of James Fairlie, son of the late James Fairlie, on renunciation of her conjunct-fee by Marion Harlawbanks, relict of the said James, with consent of Mungo Tennent her spouse, and on cognition of the said James as heir of his father by William Adamson, bailie, of a land on the south side of the High Street, within a tenement of the late James Aikman, east side the transe thereof, between a land of the late John Coky on the north, and a land (   ) on the south. Which land the said James forthwith resigned in the hands of the bailie, in favour of himself and Margaret Cant his spouse, who are thereupon seised therein: Reserving the liferent thereof to the said Marion Harlawbanks. Witnesses, Sir George Kinloch, chaplain, Alexander Belsches; Thomas Arnot, William Watson and David Purves, serjeants.

296. 1530-1 Feb. 16. Sasine on resignation by Margaret Cant, in favour of herself and James Fairlie her spouse, of her land, built and waste, lying within a tenement of the late James Barcar, on the north side of the High Street, between a land of the late John Bissait on the south, and (   ) on the north. Witnesses, Mungo Tennent,Sir George Kinloch,Thomas Arnot,Patrick Linlithqw,David Purves and William Watson, serjeants.

297. 1530-1 Feb. 27. Compeared personally Sir David Rannyk, chaplain, and constituted Sir David Young, vicar and collector of St. Giles church, his procurator, for him and in his name to receive sasine of an annual-rent of 2 merks, to be levied at two terms in the year from a land of the late Dougal Sturay, now pertaining to David Kincaid, lying below the Nether Bow, on the south side of the High Street, between a land (   ) on the east, and a land (   ) on the west; and after reception thereof to resign the same in the hands of one of the Bailies of Edinburgh, for sasine of the said annual-rent to be given to a chaplain, in name of the church, for an anniversary yearly to be made for the soul of the said Sir David Rannyk, conform to the tenor of a charter of foundation to be made thereupon: Reserving to the said Sir David his liferent of said annual-rent. Done in his own proper chamber, within the burgh of Edinburgh, in presence of Vincent Strathauchin, Sir John Geddes and Edward Kincaid.

298. 1530-1 Feb. 15. Sasine on process of recognition in favour of Master Hugh Congilton, chaplain of the service founded at the high altar in the Kirk-of-Field, and his successors, chaplains of the said service, of a certain waste land of the late Nicholas Goldsmyth, lying within a tenement of the late Charles Levingston, on the south side of the High Street, between a land of Lord Borthik on the east, and a land of the late James Gibson on the west; a land of the late David Chalmer on the south, and a land of the late John Scot on the north: Which process

of recognition was led by the said Master Hugh before the Provost and Bailies of the burgh of Edinburgh. Witnesses, William Anderson, Andrew Thomson, John Dumbertane, Thomas Dumbertane, and Thomas Arnot, serjeant.

299. 1530-1 Feb. 25. Sasine on resignation by Andrew Moncur, with consent of Jonet Cant his spouse, in favour of John Smyth, deacon or kirkmaster of the hammermen, in name of the brethren and masters of the said craft, and their successors, of an annual-rent of 26s.8d., out of the tenements of the said Andrew Moncur, lying at the Castle Hill, on the north side of the High Street thereof, between a land of the late William Smyth on the east, and a land lie Castle Bank on the west: Under reversion of £20, with consent of parties. Witnesses, Sir James Duncanson, Sir John Smyth, Walter Ramsay, John Dykson, Mungo Portuis, Andrew Cathkin, William Smeithberd, and David Purves, serjeant.

300. 1530-1 Mar. 6. Sasine to Elizabeth Dykson, on process of recognition led by her before the provost and bailies of Edinburgh, of the one half of a land of the late John Craik, on the north side of the High Street, lying within a tenement of the late John Knox, in the lower end thereof, between a land of the late James Harlaw on the east, and a land of the late Alexander Gray on the west: which half of the said land Elizabeth Dykson forthwith resigned in the hands of William Adamson, bailie, who thereupon gave sasine thereof to the said Elizabeth and Alexander Bartoun, her spouse, and the survivor of them, and the heirs lawfully procreated or to be procreated between them, whom failing to the heirs of the said Elizabeth whomsoever. Witnesses, Alexander Adamson, George Cant, Andrew Walker, James Costy, David Craufurd, and David Purves, serjeant.

301. 1530-1 March 6. Sasine to Jonet Dykson, on process of recognition led by the said Jonet before the provost and bailies of Edinburgh, of the one half of a land of the late John Craik, on the north side of the High Street, within a tenement of the late John Knox, in the lower end thereof, between a land of the late James Harlaw on the east, and a land of the late Alexander Gray on the west: which half of the said land Jonet Dykson resigned in the hands of the bailie, William Adamson, in favour of herself and George Cant her spouse, who are thereupon seised in the same, the longest liver of them, their heirs, etc. Witnesses aforesaid.

302. 1530-1 Mar. 7. Alexander Belsches, one of the bailies of Edinburgh, by command of the provost, bailies, councillors and community of the foresaid burgh, passed to the chapel of the hospital of the Virgin Mary, in the vennel of St. Mary Wynd; and there the said Alexander Belsches, in virtue of the said mandate gave institution and possession of the foresaid chapel and service of the said hospital of our Lady, by delivery of a mass book, vestments and other ornaments of the said chapel, to Sir John Kers, chaplain, for his lifetime, conform to the tenor of the letter to be made to him by the provost, bailies and community of the said burgh thereupon. Done in the said chapel in presence of Edward Henrison, David Dronar, John Huchesone and Thomas Arnot, witnesses.

303. 1530-1 Mar. 15. Sasine on resignation of her liferent by Jonet Henrison, relict of Edward Davidson, and of the fee by William Davidson, son and heir of the said Edward, with consent of Helen Wishert his spouse, of a certain waste land lying beyond the Overbow, in Battall Yairds, between a land of Andrew Wood on the east, and a land of the late John Currour on the west; a land of John Somer on the south, and the lands of Thomas Tunno and John Brown on the north, in favour of the said Thomas Tunno and Geils Davidson his spouse: With court and the oath of the said Helen Wishert not to revoke in time to come. Witnesses, William Wyndezettis, Henry Bartilmo, Henry Symson, Thomas Coupar, and David Purves, serjeant. William Adamson is bailie.
The said day and witnesses, Helen Wischart, spouse of William Davidson, protested that her consent given to the alienation of the waste land, as above, shall not yield any prejudice to her right to the residue of her land which she has in conjunct-fee, and for remeid of law.

304. 1530-1 March 23. Sasine on precept from chancery in favour of Elizabeth Cranston, as lawful and nearest heir of the late John Cranston her uncle, of the nether booth, with pertinents, lying in the fore land of a tenement of the late John Cranston, grandfather to the said John; which tenement lies on the north side of the High Street, between a land of the late Adam Strathauchin on the west, and a land of the late Richard Littill on the east; the King's public street on the south, and a land of the said Richard Littill on the north. The precept is dated at Edinburgh the 22nd day of March and eighteenth year of the King's reign. Witnesses to the sasine, Sir Thomas Barnard, Andrew Ferguson, Thomas Murray, John Brown, Patrick Aitkin, and Hugh Wallas, serjeant. William Adamson is bailie.

305. 1531 April 6. Sasine on resignation by Robert Freland, procurator and in name of Andrew Murray, son and heir of the late Master John Murray, in favour of Master John Chepman, burgess, of an annual-rent of 6s.8d., out of a piece of waste land lying on the south side of the High Street, on the west side of the house of the said Master John Chepman, now inhabited by him, between the lands of John Berclay on the south and north parts, and a dwelling house of the said John Berclay on the west, and the foresaid land or dwelling house of Master John Chepman on the east. Witnesses, William Lauder, John Berclay, James Curll, Thomas Keyne, Fynlay Gray, William Wilkeson, Thomas Arnot and Patrick Linlithqw, serjeants. Alexander Belsches is bailie.

306. 1531 April 7. Alexander Belsches, one of the bailies of the burgh of Edinburgh, passed to a land of the late Sir Alexander Scot, rector of Myddilbe, lying in the said burgh, on the south side of the High Street thereof, beside the Netherbow, between a land of James Bassenden on the north, and a land of Andrew Mowbray on the south; and there Rolland Donaldson presented to the foresaid bailie a certain letter of apprising upon the said land lawfully led, under the common seal of cause of the said burgh, of which letter the tenor follows and is thus:— Till

all and sindry quhais knawlege thir present lettres sall com, The provest ballies and counsall of the burgh of Edinburgh, greeting in God evirlasting, Wit your universiteis, forsamekill as our Soverane Lordis lettres, be decreit of the Lordis of his Counsall, war direct till us, chargeand us to pass and appryse ane land and tenement liand within this burgh, apone the south syde the Kingis Streit of the samyn, beside the Nethir Bow, betuix the land of James Bassandyne on the north pairt, and the land of Andrew Mowbray on the south pairt, for ane soume of ane hundreth pundis usuall mony of Scotland, awine be umquhile Sir Alexander Scot, persone of Myddilburgh (sic.), till Rolland Donaldsone, burges of the said burgh: Whilk land and tenement was the said umquhile Schir Alexander Scottis, persone of Myddilbe, and gevin be him to William Scot his sone in defraude of the said Rolland Donaldson his creditur, as at mair lenth is specifiit and contenit in our said Soverane Lordis lettres direct till us therapoun; and be vertu of the saidis lettres we gart ane officiar of our said burgh warne and charge the said William Scot, be ane act of our court, to compeir befor us, or ony of our ballies, apone the ground of the said land and tenement, the auchtene day of Marche instant, till here and see the said land and tenement apprisit to the said Rolland Donaldsone, for the said soume of ane hundreth pundis. At the quhilk day Alexander Belsches, ane of the ballies of the said burgh, past at the command of our Soverane Lordis lettres, and actis of our court, direct conforme to the samyne, to the ground of the said land and tenement, and thar, in ane plane court fensit and haldin be the said ballie apone the said ground, Thomas Arnot, serjand of the said burgh, previt, be himself and his witnes sworne thairto, that he warnit the said William Scot, personalie apprehendit, till compeir this day apone the ground of the said land and tenement, and here the samyn apprysit lanchfullie to the said William Donaldsone, for the said soume of ane hundreth pundis, eftir the forme of the saidis lettres, oft tymes callit and nocht comperand, the said Alexander Belsches, bailie, gart call thir famous nichbouris undir writtin, till pas and apprise the said land and tenement, for the soume of ane hundreth pundis awand to the said Rolland, that is to say, Edward Kincaid, David Tod, Patrik Flemyng, younger, Matho Penkyrtoune, Johne Garland, George Mathesone, David Creich, Robert Gilquhammyte, James Barbour, Thomas Blyth, Albert Strathauchyne and Gawin Wallace. The quhilk personis being sworne, the haly ewangellis tuichit, and deligentlie avisit with the said land and tenement and vesiit the samyne at all pairtis, undir and abone, fand at the said land was awand furth of the samyn, four merkis of annuall. And by that annuall thay apprisit the said haill land and tenement, undir and abone, with the pertinentis, to the soume of ane hundreth pundis usuall mony, that was awand to the said Rolland Donaldsone, and thaireftir offerit the said land to ony persone that wald giff ony mair soume for the samyn na it was apprisit to, or giff ony persone wald giff the said soume of ane hundreth pundis for the said land. And because na persone wald by the said land and tenement, nor giff sameikile for it as was prysit to, thay assignit the samyn land and tenement, undir and aboue, with the pertinentis, to the said Rolland Donaldsone, for the said soume of ane hundreth pundis awand till him. And fand that the said land and tenement was haldin of our souerane lord the King be service of burgh, usit and wount, and ordanit sesing thairof to be gevin to the said Rolland and his airis heretablie, to be brukit and joysit be thame in tyme tocum, eftir the forme of the act of parliament maid apone prysit landis: The said Rolland, his airis and assignais, payand furth yeirlie of the said land and tenement to the annuallaris thairof, the said four merkis of annuall, usuall mony of Scotland, at twa usuall terms in the yeir, Witsonday and Mertymes in wynter, be evin proportionis allanerlie. And this till (all) and sindry quham it efferis, or may effeir, we mak at knawin be thir presentis. In witnes of the quhilk thing we haif to thir presentis gart append our common seil of cause of the said burgh, togidder with the said ballie seil, and ane pairt of the personis selis that past apone the said apprysing, at Edinburgh the xviii day of Marche the yeir of God ane thousand vc and xxx yeiris. After the reading of which letter and publishing thereof by me, notary public under written, the foresaid Alexander Belsches, bailie, in virtue of his office, and according to the tenor of the said letter of apprising, gave state, corporal possession and heritable sasine of all and whole the foresaid land, under and above, with pertinents, by delivery of earth and stone to the said Rolland Donaldson, his heirs and assignees, conform to the tenor of the said letter of apprising. Reserving all rights. Whereupon the said Rolland asked an instrument. Witnesses, Andrew Mowbray, Edward Bissait, Archibald Donaldson, Walter Donaldson, John Hucheson, David Purves and Thomas Arnot, serjeants.

307. 1531 Apr. 15. Sasine on resignation by John Malcome, son and heir of the late William Malcome, in favour of himself and Elizabeth Yelloleyis his spouse, of the following subjects: (1) The said John's half of the fore land of a tenement of the late John Swift, lying on the south side of the High Street, between a land of the late John Carkettill on the east, and a land of Archibald Williamson on the west, a land of Hugh earl of Eglintoun on the south, and the king's public street on the north; which half part contains a tavern and back vault, together with the merchant booth above the said tavern. (2) The upper house and loft in the top of the said foreland, in which James Meldrum now dwells. (3) An annual-rent of 8 merks, out of a land of the late Robert Mite, lying on the south side of the High Street, between a land of the late George Fysche on the north, and the transe that leads to St. Giles church on the south and west, and the knig's common way on the east. Witnesses, James Johnston, Thomas Craig, John Purro, John Litill, Robert Frew, Thomas Tarbot, Thomas Duncane, Vincent Strathauchyn, notary public, and Patrick Linlithqw, serjeant.

308. 1531 Apr. 22. Sasine on resignation by Archibald Williamson,

son and heir of the late John Williamson, in favour of Nicholas Craufurd of Oxingangis, justice clerk of our sovereign lord the King, and Margaret Knollis his spouse, of the said Archibald's tenement, lying on the south side of the High Street, in Liberton's Wynd, west side the transe thereof, between a land or great building of James Johnston on the north, another land of the said Archibald on the south, and a land of James Aikman on the west. Witnesses, Henry Wardlaw of Kilbalbirtoun, George Richartson, John Currour, James Craufurd, Archibald Wardlaw, James Belsches, and John Raynton, notary public, with divers others. Alexander Belsches is bailie.

309. 1531 April 22. Sasine on resignation by Archibald Williamson above designed in favour of the foresaid Nicholas Craufurd and Margaret Knollis his spouse, of a land of the said Archibald in Liberton's Wynd, west side the transe thereof, between another land or great building of the said Archibald on the north, a land of the late William Currour on the south, and a land of James Aikman on the west. Same bailie and witnesses as aforesaid.

310. 1531 April 27. Sasine on resignation by Master James Knollis, rector of Roskeyne, in favour of Robert Leslie, burgess of Edinburgh, and Cristina Wardlaw his spouse, of a land of the late James Ross, now pertaining to the said Master James Knollis, lying on the north side of the High Street, within a tenement of the late Sir Alexander Lauder of Blyth, Knight, between a land of the late Thomas Selyman on the east, and a land of the late John Twedy on the west; the foreland and backland of the said tenement on the south, and a land of the late Gilbert Canon, now pertaining to James Ur, on the north. Witnesses, Master Patrick Knollis, Patrick Knollis, Robert Merser, John Campbell, Henry Nory, William Foularton, William Smert, and Hugh Wallas, serjeant.

311. 1531 Apr. 28. Sasine on resignation by James Henrison in favour of Francis Aikman, his heirs and assignees, of the fee of the resigner's lands and tenements lying on the south side of the High Street, between Bell's Wynd on the east, the lands of the late Henry Henrison on the west, the lands of John Hay on the north, and the king's public street of the Cowgate on the south. Witnesses, John Hendirson, John Nicholson, Thomas Smyth, William Stevinson, notary public, and Patrick Linlithqw, serjeant.

312. The quhilk day in presens of Alexander Belsches, ballie, and witnes undir wryttin, Frances Aikman oblissis him faithfully, be the faith and treuth in his body, his 'airis and assignais, to James Henrison, burges of Edinburgh, that quhat tyme that evir the said James Henrison personally him self requyris the said Frances Aikman, his airis or assignais, till renunce and gif ovir frelie to the said James, all and haill the fee of his landis and tenementis, befor and behind, with the pertinentis, quhilk he had put him in obefor liand within this burgh, on the south syde the Kingis streit of the samyne, betuix the transe of Bellis Wynd on the est pairt and the land of umquhile

Lourens Hendirson on the west pairt and the landis of John Hay on the north pairt, and the common kingis streit of the Cowgate on the south pairt, that he and his airis and assignais sall renunce and frelie gif our the saidis landis and tenementis, befor and behind, with the pertinentis be resignation in ane of the ballies handis of the said burgh, and put the said James therintill, als frelie to be bruikit be him as evir he had the samyne obefor ony tyme undir the pain of jm.lib. to be paiit be the said Frances to the said James, but ony maner of pley, obstakle or impediment to be maid therintill, but fraude or gyle. Witnesses aforesaid.

313. 1531 May 6. Sasine on resignation by Robert Gray, with consent of Helen Keith his spouse, in favour of William Rowat, burgess, and Marjorie Cunynghame his spouse, of the said Robert's tenement, with the barns, kill and yard thereof, lying beyond the west Bow, on the south side of the High Street, between a land of the late John Nicholson, now pertaining to George Ur, and the lands of Hieriggis on the west, the lands of the said Robert Gray and a waste land of the burgh of Edinburgh on the east, the said lands of Hieriggis on the south, and the king's common street on the north. Witnesses, William Lauder, Robert Gray, Robert Purdy, Robert Rowat and Patrick Linlithqw, serjeant. Alexander Belsches is bailie.
Moreover the said Robert Gray, with consent of his spouse, renounced all letters of reversion, and other letters whatsoever promised to him by the said William, upon the redemption of all annual-rents previously alienated by the said Robert, out of the foresaid tenement.

314. 1531 May 8. Sasine on resignation by Adam Fausyde, with consent of Elizabeth Lyndesay his spouse, in favour of John Jacob *alias* Stevinson and Agnes Henrison his spouse, of an annual-rent of 3 merks 5s.4d., out of a land of the said John James *alias* Stevinson, lying within a tenement of the said Adam, on the south side of the High Street, between a tenement of the late Luke Young on the east, and a tenement of the late Master John Murray on the west; the foreland of the said tenement on the north, and a land of Master James Chapman on the south. Witnesses, Edward Henrison, Patrick Gowanlock, William Hendirson, John Atkinson, John Gardner, and Thomas Arnot. William Sym is bailie.
Under reversion of 60 merks. Attour the said Adam promist and oblist to the said John, that gif he analiit the tother iij merkis that he had of the said John's land, that he suld analy the samyn to the said Johne befor ony uthir, he giffand thar for that utheris wald gif; and thereupon the said John asket instruments.

315. 1531 May 26. Sasine on resignation by David Kincaid of Cottis, with consent of Helen Mowbray his spouse, in favour of Edward Kincaid, burgess, and Jonet Mauchane his spouse, of an annual-rent of 6 merks, out of the said David's land lying within a tenement of the late Alexander Harlaw, now pertaining to Duncan Wicht, on the north side of the High Street, between a land of

the late James Baty on the east, and a land of the late George Halkerston on the west, and the lands of the said Duncan Wicht on the south and north. Witnesses, John Achinson, William Blaklok, John Anderson, Alexander Paterson, Charles Wilson, and Patrick Linlithqw, serjeant. John Mauchane is bailie.

316. 1531 May 26. Sasine on resignation by Michael Gilbert, goldsmith, in favour of himself and Elizabeth Currour his spouse, of his back lands lying below the Castle Wall, on the south side of the High Street, between a land pertaining to the laird of Innerleith on the east, a land of James Makgill on the west, the dyke of the yard on the south, and the fore land of the late John Burgane on the north. Witnesses, James McCalzeane, James Johnston, Thomas Currour, Alexander Boyd, John Caddell. Sir John Kers, chaplain, William Watson, and Patrick Linlithqw, serjeant. Alexander Belsches is bailie.

317. 1531 May 27. Sasine on resignation by Alexander Boyd in favour of James Gray, flesher, of an annual-rent of 20s., out of a tenement of the late William Baroun, lying on the north side of the High Street, between a land of the late James Towris, now pertaining to Master Robert Galbraith, on the east, and a land of the late Gilbert Fische, now pertaining to William Adamson, on the west. Witnesses, Robert Symson, John Young, John Wyle, Thomas Gibson, Alexander Gourlaw, Thomas Harvy, Thomas Arnot and Hugh Wallas. William Sym is bailie.

318. 1531 June 1. Sasine to John Dougall, on his cognition by John Mauchane, bailie, as heir of the late John Dougall, burgess, his father of the following subjects: (1) A built land lying within a tenement of the late Nicholas Spethy, on the north side of the High Street, between a tenement of the late John Levington on the west, and the waste lands of the said late Nicol Spethy on the south and north. (2) Another land of the said late John Dougall lying in Leith Wynd, west side the transe thereof, between the waste lands or walls of the burgh of Edinburgh on the south and north. And forthwith the said John Dougall resigned the two lands foresaid in the hands of the said baillie who thereupon gave sasine of the same to the said John Dougall and Margaret Wicht his affianced spouse in conjunct-fee. Witnesses, Sir Thomas Barnet, chaplain, John Wicht, John Somervell, Symone Clerk, William Thomson, Robert Gray, and William Watson, serjeant.

319. 1531 June 1. Sasine to John Lowrison on his cognition, by John Mauchan, bailie, as heir of the late Andrew Lowrison his father, of a certain land, under and above, lying within a tenement of the late Archibald Preston, on the north side of the High Street, now pertaining to the said John Mauchane, between a tenement of the late David Knox on the east, and a land of the late James Towris on the west; a land of Andrew Uddart on the north, and the back land of the said tenement, pertaining to the said John Mauchane on the south: Which land the said John Lowrison resigned in the hands of the bailie who gave sasine thereof to John Dougall and Margaret Wicht his spouse

in conjunct-fee: Reserving the liferent of the loft above the kitchen of the said land to the resigner. Witnesses, Sir John Kers and Sir Thomas Barnet, chaplains, John Wicht, John Somervell, William Thomson and William Watson.

320. 1531 June 1. Sasine on resignation by friar John Greirson, professor of theology, and provincial of the whole order of the Friars Preachers within the kingdom of Scotland, with consent of the subprior and convent of the place of the Friars Preachers of the burgh of Edinburgh, in favour of Robert Grahame, burgess, and Margaret Aldjoy his spouse, of his built land, with pertinents, lying within a tenement of the late Nicholas Spethy, on the north side of the High Street, between a tenement of the late Master James Henrison on the east, and a tenement of the late John Levington on the west. Witnesses, William Uddart, friar John Mure, Sir John Portuis, chaplain, William Grahame, Vincent Strathauchin and Alexander McNeil, notaries public, and David Purves, serjeant.

321. 1531 June 2. John Mauchane, bailie, passed to a great building of James Johnston, lying on the south side of the High Street, in Liberton's Wynd, west side the transe thereof, between a land of the late Henry Liberton on the north, and a land of the late John Williamson on the south, and there Agnes Goddiskirk, with consent of Thomas Clerkson her spouse, renounced her liferent which she had of two halls, and chambers thereof, lying contiguous on the north side of the said great building, in the hands of the bailie, in favour of Edward Litill her son. And forthwith the said Edward, son and heir of the late Cuthbert Litill, resigned her foresaid two halls and chambers thereof in the hands of the said John Mauchane, bailie, who thereupon gave sasine of the same to Thomas Clerkson, burgess, and the said Agnes Goddiskirk his spouse, in conjunct-fee, the survivor of them, etc. Witnesses, Sir James Duncanson, chaplain, William Raa, William Makteir, John Wallas and David Purves, serjeant.

322. 1531 June 3. William Sym, bailie, passed to a certain land or tenement of the late Thomas Wardlaw, now pertaining to Sir Andrew Harpar, chaplain, lying on the south side of the High Street and of the Tolbooth, between a land of the late William Adamson on the north, and a land of the late John Falcoun on the south; and there the said Sir Andrew Harpar resigned the foresaid land or tenement in the hands of the bailie, who gave sasine thereof as follows: (1) Of the one half of the said land or tenement to Elizabeth Wardlaw, daughter of the said Thomas Wardlaw, her heirs and assignees. (2) Of the other half of the said land or tenement to Cristina Wardlaw, also daughter of the said late Thomas Wardlaw, her heirs and assignees. And afterwards Marion Falcoun, relict of the said Thomas, renounced her liferent, which she had of the foresaid land or tenement, in the hands of the bailie, in favour of the said Elizabeth and Cristina her daughters; which Elizabeth and Cristina forthwith resigned, each of them respectively, her half part of the said tenement in the hands of the bailie, who gave sasine and

conjunct-infeftment of the foresaid land or tenement to Symon Marjoribanks, burgess, and Jonet Grahame his spouse. Witnesses, Master James Symson, rector of Forfar, Master Thomas Marjoribanks, John Wicht, John Tait, Robert Brown, John Kyle, John Anderson, and William Watson, serjeant.

The quhilk day in presens of the ballie and witnes aboue writtin, Marion Symson allegit and said that scho had takkis of the said land for v yeris to ryn; and tharfor scho protestit that the sesing gevin of the said land to Symon Marjoribank suld nocht hurt hir takkis and for remeid of law; and tharapone askit instrument.

323. 1531 June 9. Sasine on resignation by Thomas Clerkson, with consent of Agnes Goddiskirk his spouse, in favour of William Clerkson, burgess, and Jonet Sommervell his spouse, of the said Thomas's two halls, and chamber thereof, on the north side of a great building of James Johnston in Liberon's Wynd, as described in his sasine of 2 June instant. Witnesses, Edward Craufurd, Walter Somervell, William Raa, merchant, William Ra, cutler, William Muirheid, Sir James Duncanson, chaplain, David Purves and Patrick Lithqw.

324. 1531 June 12. Sasine on resignation by Adam Bell in favour of Robert Ramsay, his heirs and assignees, of the said Adam's land lying beyond the Overbow, on the north side of the High Street, between a land of the late Master Richard Lauson on the east, and a land of Patrick Richartson on the west; the King's Wall on the north, and the king's common street on the south. Witnesses, Henry Wardlaw of Kilbaberton, Sir William Sprot, chaplain, William Blaklok, John Bell, Andrew Brys, Thomas Arnot and David Purves, serjeants.

The said Robert promised to give the said Adam a reversion upon the redemption of the said land, containing the sum of iiij scoir merkis, attour quhat resonable expens necessar that he makis, to be paiit als weill as the principall soum.

325. 1531 June 15. Sasine on resignation by Robert Stratoun in favour of William Stratoun his son, of an annual-rent of 6 merks, out of a tenement of Master Henry Hendirson lying on the south side of the Cowgate, between a land of the late John Runsyman on the east, and a tenement of Patrick Flemyng on the west, the yard of the late William Schaw on the south, and the king's common street on the north. Witnesses, Robert Ross, son and heir of the late Ninian Lord Ross, etc., David Straton, David Millar, Walter Gordon, Alexander Gibson, and Thomas Arnot, serjeant. Alexander Belsches is bailie.

The quhilk day, in presens of the said baillie and witnesses, David Straton, son and apperand air to the said Robert Straton, allegit and said that his said faddir had gevin his annuell of vj merkis till William Straton, in defraude of him that wes his air, becaus it succedit be heretage; tharfor he protestit that it hurt him nocht, and for remeid of law quhen and quhar it efferit. And thereupon David asked instrument. Done upon the ground.

326. 1531 June 13. Sasine on resignation by William Craik, son and

heir of the late William Craik, in favour of himself and Jonet Flemyng his affianced spouse, of his land lying in the Boothraw, on the south side of the High Street, between a land of the late Sir John Rynd, chaplain, on the east, and a land of Alexander Mauchane on the west. Witnesses, Patrick Flemyng, elder, Patrick Flemyng, younger, John Burgane, William Scallis, John Ayton, Thomas Brown, John Craik, Thomas Arnot and Hugh Wallas, serjeants. Alexander Belsches is bailie.

327. 1531 june 17. Sasine to William Craik, on his cognition by Alexander Belsches, bailie, as heir of the late William Craik, burgess, his father, of a tenement of the said late William, lying below the Netherbow, at the Lople Stane, on the south side of the High Street, between a land (   ) on the east, and a land of Christian Edname on the west: Which tenement the said William Craik instantly resigned in the hands of the bailie, in favour of himself and of Jonet Flemyng his affianced spouse, who are thereupon seised therein in conjunct-fee. Witnesses, Patrick Flemyng, William Lyndesay, William Watson, Patrick Flemyng, younger, John Busby, James Belsches, Thomas Arnot and David Purves, serjeants.

328. 1531 July 4. Sasine on resignation by John Levingtoun, with consent of Cristina Lamb his spouse, in favour of John Carnoquhen, of an annual-rent of 9s. out of a land of the said John Carnoquhen on the south side of the High Street, in Peebles Wynd, west side the transe thereof, between a land of Robert Law on the south and a waste land of John Levingtoun on the south. With court and the woman's oath not to revoke. Witnesses, Vincent Strathauchin, notary public, John Murray, Sir John Mailuill, chaplain, Archibald Weddell, John Johnston and David Purves.
Moreover the said John Levingtoun obliged himself and his heirs to warrant the foresaid land from payment of whatsoever annual-rents are due to the heirs of the late Master James Haliburton, heir of law to the late laird of Fenton, in time to come.

329. 1531 July 12. Sasine to Jonet Strathauchin on renunciation by Jonet Cameron, relict of William Strathauchin, of her conjunct-fee, and on cognition of the said Jonet as one of the heirs of the said late William Strathauchin her father by William Sym, bailie, of an annual-rent of 4 merks out of a tenement of the late James Cameron, now pertaining to John Fischar and the heirs of the late William Lokkart, lying on the north side of the High Street, between a tenement of the late George Halkerston on the east, and a tenement of the late Margaret Levington, now pertaining to Robert Bertoun of Over Berntoun on the west: Which annual-rent of 4 merks the said Jonet Strathauchin resigned in favour of herself and William Court her spouse, who are thereupon seised therein in conjunct-fee: Reserving, however, the liferent thereof to the foresaid Jonet Cameron. Witnesses, William Tod, Alexander Litill, John Richartson, James Brog, James Johnston, Sir James Baron, Edward Davidson and Hugh Wallas.

330. 1531 July 17. Sasine on precept from chancery in favour of

Margaret Martyne, as kinswoman and one of the lawful and nearest heirs of the late Elizabeth Scot, Lady Manerston, who was daughter of the said Elizabeth's good dame's brother, of the half of the wester part of a tenement of the said Elizabeth Scot, lying on the south side of the High Street, between the transe of the said tenement on the east side thereof on the east, and the lands of the late Patrick Richartson, Clement Litill, James Horne and Maurice Coupland on the west; the yard of the said tenement on the south, and the King's common street on the north. Dated at Edinburgh 19 January in the eighteenth year of His Majesty's reign. The sasine is witnessed by John Blak, George Aldjoy, Thomas Eldar, Walter Bruse and David Purves, serjeant. John Mauchane is bailie.

331. 1531 July 17. Sasine on resignation by Margaret Martyne, kinswoman and one of the heirs of the late Elizabeth Scot, Lady Manerston, in favour of herself and John Mayne her spouse, of her half of the wester part of the tenement of the said Lady Manerston, lying on the south side of the High Street, and bounded as before described. Same bailie and witnesses.

332. 1531 Aug. 12. At the seventh hour after mid-day, compeared personally Alexander Levingtoun, sone and air of umquhile Johne Levingtoun, burgess of Edinburgh, and of his awin fre motif will giffis and grantis full faculte, licence and tollerance till Robert Grahame, burges of the said burgh, till mak ane squair wynde in the south pairt of his nether hall, quhar the round Oo is now of his land, liand within this burgh, within the tenement of umquhile Nichol Spethy, on the est syde the umquhile Johne Levingtonis land, als hiche and wyde, and of the samyne kynd and mesour that the tother wynde is on the north pairt in the samyne hall; and that for certane gratitudis done be the said Robert till the said Alexander. And thereupon the said Robert Grahame askit instrumentis. Done within the burgh of Edinburgh, in the shop of William Uddart: present there, George Lauson, William Tod, John Park and John Anderson.

333. 1531 Aug. 16. Sasine on resignation by John Anderson, son and heir of the late John Anderson, burgess, with consent of Elizabeth Watson his spouse, in favour of John Young, burgess, and Elizabeth Bothwell his spouse, of the upper hall, chamber, kitchen, and loft above the same, of his land or building, which John Young now occupies; together with 3 cellars in the lower part thereof, with all their pertinents, lying within a tenement of the late James Towris, on the north side of the High Street, between a tenement of the late Archibald Preston, now pertaining to John Mauchane, on the east, and a tenement of the late William Carkettill on the west; east side the transe of the said tenement, between a land of the said late James Towris, now pertaining to John Burgane, on the south, and a land formerly pertaining to Thomas Coupland, now to Thomas Paterson, on the north. Also of the one half of a waste land or yard lying within the said tenement, on the said east side of the transe thereof, descending immediately from a waste land or garden of the late William Malcome on the south, to another

waste land on the north. Witnesses, Sir James Duncanson, chaplain, George Audjoy, Andrew Bryss, James Blaklo, and William Watson, serjeant.
Under reversion of vj scoir x lib. and ij yeris eftir the lousing for xij merkis of maill in the yeir.

334. 1531 Aug. 25, at the twelfth hour of the day, in the fourth indiction, of the pontificate of pope Clement the seventh the eighth year, passed personally an honourable man, Alexander Belsches, one of the bailies of Edinburgh, to a land of Robert Glen . . . . . . (Partial entry only)

335. 1531 Aug. 27. Compeared personally John Young, burgess, and constituted Sir Thomas Richartson, chaplain, and John Anderson, conjunctly and severally, his procurators, granting to them his irrevocable power and mandate, for him and in his name to resign all and whole his lands of Howiston, with their pertinents, lying in the barony of (   ) and within the shire of (   ) in the hands of James Sandilands of Calder, lord superior thereof, for heritable sasine and conjunct-infeftment of the same to be given to the said John Young and Elizabeth Bothuell his spouse: Promising to hold firm and stable whatsoever should be done by his said procurators in the premises. Done in the collegiate church of St. Giles in presence of Archibald Ramsay, Stephen Bell, John Layng and John Anderson.

336. 1531 Sept. 11. Sasine on resignation by Nichol Howison and Margaret Lany his spouse, in favour of Richard Nicholson, cordiner, burgess, and Elizabeth Henrison his spouse, of the resigner's land or tenement in the Cowgate, on the north side thereof, between a land and yard of the late Elizabeth Scot Lady Manerston on the east, a land of John Cant on the west, and a land of Maurice Coupland on the north; with the Barkhouse and yard thereof, Lime Pots and their pertinents: Reserving the liferent of the said subjects, now occupied by Richard Nicholson, to the said Margaret Lany and Nichol Howison her spouse. Witnesses, Alexander Willesone, Robert Dyksone, Robert Hog, Robert Weir, George Richartson, Alexander Scot and William Watson.
The said day hour and witnesses, Nichol Howison and Margaret Lany oblist thame, and the langer levar of thame twa, yeirlie till uphald the said land and tenement, befor and behind, in all necessar thingis, as it now is, apone thair expens during thair lyftymes.

337. 1531 Sept. 12. Sasine on resignation by Gilbert Lauder, with consent of Isobell Mauchane, his spouse, in favour of James Wallas, mason, and Christian Marlzeon his spouse, of the said Gilbert's land lying on the north side of the High Street in the vennel of the late Thomas Malcome, between a land of the late Sir David Flucar on the east, and the lands of the late Andrew Sclater on the west, south and north. Witnesses, Allan Lauder, William Smert, Thomas Lyn, Hugh Wallas, and David Purves, serjeant.
And forthwith the said James Wallas, with consent of Christian Marlzeon his spouse, resigned an annual-rent of 6 merks, out

of his foresaid land with pertinents, in the hands of the bailie, who thereupon gave heritable sasine thereof to Gilbert Lauder, burgess, and Isobel Mauchane his spouse, in presence of the witnesses foresaid.

338. 1531 Sept. 12. Sasine on resignation by David Lauson, with consent of Isobel Balfour his spouse, in favour of John Lauson his son, of the upper hall and chamber and cellar of a land of the said David, newly built, lying on the south side of the High Street, within a tenement of the late Charles Levington, between the transe of the said tenement on the east, and the transe of a tenement of the late Thomas Swift on the west, a land of the late John Balfour on the north, and a waste land of David Gillaspy on the south: Reserving the liferent of the foresaid subjects to the resigners. Witnesses, Sir Richard Lauson, chaplain, John Swan, Thomas Johnston, Alexander Gylour, John Wrycht, John Tait, and David Purves, serjeant. William Sym, bailie.

339. 1531 Sept. 12. Sasine on resignation by David Lauson, with consent of Isobel Balfour his spouse, in favour of Richard Lauson, son of the said David, of the lower hall, with chamber and cellar of his land newly built, on the south side of the High Street, lying and bounded as above described: Reserving as aforesaid. Same bailie and witnesses.

340. 1531 Sept. 12. Sasine on resignation by David Lauson, with consent of Isobel Balfour his spouse, in favour of William Lauson, son of the foresaid David, of the two south cellars of his land, newly built, lying within a tenement of the late Charles Levington, and bounded as before mentioned. Reserving as aforesaid. Bailie and witnesses *ut supra*.

341. 1531 Sept. 13. Alexander Belsches, bailie, passed to a certain foreland lying on the north side of the High Street, between a land of the late John Brown on the east, a land of the late James Baron on the west; a land of Robert Bruse on the north, and the king's common street on the south; and there Jonet Broune, relict of Thomas Fresall, renounced her liferent of the third part of the said foreland, containing three booths, with pertinents, in favour of John Fresall her son, lord fiar thereof. And forthwith the said John Fresall, son and heir of the said late Thomas, resigned the foresaid third part of the said foreland, containing as above, in the hands of the bailie, who gave sasine of the same to Richard Hoppar, son and heir of the late Adam Hoppar, burgess, his heirs and assignees, in fee and heritage, and to Katherine Ballantyne, mother to the said Richard, now spouse of Master Frances Bothuell, in liferent. Moreover, in a full court, held before the bailie upon the ground of the said foreland, Jonet Broune and John Fresall gave their bodily oath, the scriptures touched, not to revoke in time to come. Upon which the said Richard Hoppar and Katherine Ballantyne asked instruments. Witnesses, Nichol Scheyne, Master Richard Bothuell, younger, Sir Thomas Richartson, John Cruke, Vincent Strathauchin, and David Purves, serjeant.

342. 1531 Sept. 16. William Litill deliverit till (   ), clerk of Thom Mortonis schip, the haill process in the mater betuix him and Robert Monchell, that is to say, the commission and artiklis that was send fra Deip, with the depositionis of the witnes sworne and examynat in this toune, be vertu of the said commission, all closit undir the seill of canis: And thairfor the said William protestit, that considdering he had done his diligens in that mater, that quhat danger cum tnerto throw the schip or other wayis hurt nocht him nor turn him to na scayth, and thereupon asked an instrument. Done in the booth of the common clerk; witnesses, the provost of the burgh, Sir John Tyndaill, George Arnot and Hugh Wallas.

343. 1531 Sept. 27. Sasine on resignation by Mungo Tennent, with consent of Marion Harlawbankis his spouse, in favour of Alexander Tennent their son, of: (1) Two merchant booths of that foreland pertaining to the said Mungo, lying on the north side of the High Street, between a land of the late John Tyndaill, now pertaining to George Gude, on the east, and a land of the late Walter Young on the west, the land of Patrick Creichton of Kinglassy on the north, and the king's public street on the north (sic.) (2) An annual-rent of 6 merks out of a tenement of the late John Tweedy on the north side of the High Street, between a land of the late John Dun, now pertaining to the heirs of the late Sir Alexander Lauder of Blyth, knight, on the east, and a land of the late Alexander Bonkill on the west: Reserving to the said spouses their liferent of the foresaid subjects. Witnesses, William Grahame, John Caddell, William Symson, James Adamson, William Gulde, John Smyth, Archibald Smyth, William Smert, William Smethberd, David Purves and William Watson, serjeants. Alexander Belsches is bailie.

344. 1531 Oct. 2. Sasine on resignation by Archibald Williamson, son and heir of the late John Williamson, in favour of Master William Blakstok and Marion Sinclar his spouse, of a land or building, with loft and houses thereof, lying on the north side of the High Street, between the foreland pertaining to the chaplain of the altar of the Holy Cross, situated within the parish church of Dalkeith, on the south, and another land of the said Archibald on the north, a certain transe on the east, and another trause of a tenement of the said Archibald on the west. Witnesses, Thomas Rynde, John Blakstok, Master David Irland, Master Thomas Slewman, Sir William Makdoweill and Sir William Adamson, chaplains, Thomas Arnot, William Watson and Patrick Linlithqw, serjeants. John Mauchane is bailie.
The quhilk day, in presens of the said ballie, Archibald Williamson promist faithfully till deliver till Maister William Blakstok and his spous, all maner of evidentis that he has or mycht get concernyng the land that he analiit till thame; and thairapon the said Maister William askit instrumentis.
Alsua the said Archibald Williamson declarit to the said Maister William Blakstok and his spous, that he wald on na wys gif licens till enter throw his forland to the bak loft of the said Maister Williamis in tyme to cum. Witnesses above written.

345. 1531 Oct. 5. Sasine on renunciation by Thomas Cameron in the hands of Symon Preston, bailie, of his liferent of the wester part of the said Thomas's tenement lying in the Cowgate, south side thereof, between a land of the lord bishop of Dunkeld on the east, a land of the late William Rapperlaw on the west, and the common way which leads to Kirk of Field on the south, with the whole yard thereof: Excepting the garden: which part, with the yard, the bailie gave in liferent sasine to Sir John Dykson, chaplain, his heirs and assignees, during the lifetime of the said Thomas Cameron; and after his decease to the said Sir John his successors, chaplains of the service of the altar of St. Katherine, situated within the church of St. Giles, conform to the tenor of a mortification made thereupon. Witnesses, Robert Knox, Patrick Bykkerton, Sir Alexander Cunynghame, Patrick Lithqw, Hugh Wallas and William Watson.

346. 1531 Oct. 27. Sasine on resignation by Robert Lyne, with consent of Katrine Dalrumpill his spouse, in favour of Marion Lyne their daughter, of the said Robert's land lying beside the place of the Friars Minor of the Observance, on the east side of the High Street of the burgh, between the land of David Ferry on the east, a land of Alexander Dalrumpill on the south, and the king's common ways on the west and north: Reserving the liferent of the said land to the resigners. Witnesses, John Loksmyth, George Arnot, Alexander Baron, Robert Law, John Coldane, John Auld, James Abernethy, John Laverok, Henry Seton and David Purves, serjeant. Patrick Baron is bailie.
The quhilk day in presens of Patrick Baroun, ballie, Marion Lyn oblist hir faithfully till hir sister Elizabeth Lyn, that because hir fadir Robert Lyn had put hir in the fee of the land and tenement quhilk he duellis in, lyand on the eist syde the Gray Freris, that in cais hir said fadir deceis or he put the said Elizabeth his dochter in the tempill land that lyis on the north syde the Gait, within the Lord Sanct Johnis fredome and privilege, that scho sall nevir clame or desyre ony rycht to the said tempill land; bot now as than scho renuncis and dischargis all rycht and titill of rycht that scho may haif therto ony maner of way, in favouris of the said Elizabeth, hir sister, because hir said fadir had stakit hir and put hir in the fee of his said uthir land. And gif mister be scho oblissis hir eftir hir fadiris deceis gif sa happinnis till entir to hir pairt of the said tempill land, and thereftir resigne the samyne, and infeft the said Elizabeth in the haill tempill land, to be brukit and joysit be hir and hir airis peciably for evir: And swore the holy ewangellis tuichit nevir tocum in the contrar heirof in tyme tocum. And thereupon the said Elizabeth asked an instrument. Done in the dwelling house of the said Robert Lyne; witnesses, John Locksmyth, George Arnot, Alexander Baron, Robert Law, John Coldane, John Auld, James Abirnethy, John Laverok, Henry Seytoun, and David Purves, serjeant.

347. 1531 Nov. 4. Sasine on resignation by Jonet Kennedy, daughter and heir of the late Donald Kennedy, with consent of David Bonar her spouse, in favour of Friar John Greirson, professor of theology and provincial of the whole order of the Friars

Preachers within the kingdom of Scotland, and convent of the
place of the Friars Preachers of the burgh of Edinburgh, and
their successors forever, conform to the tenor of a contract made
between the said David his spouse and the said Friars Preachers of the said place, of an annual-rent of 8 merks out of the
said Jonet's lands lying contiguous within the tenement of Robert
Berton of Over Berntoun, on the north side of the High Street,
between a land of the late James Cameron on the east, and a
tenement of the late William Selyman on the west, a land of the
said Robert Berton on the south, and the North Loch of the said
burgh on the north: Always and until the said David and his
spouse, by themselves or their procurators, shall infeft the said
friars and their successors, by charter and sasine, in 12 acres
and 17 particates of arable land in Newhaven; and after
receiving the said infeftment and sasine of the said acres and
lands in Newhaven by the said friars, as said is, then the said
annual-rent of 8 merks shall remain with the said friars of the
said place, and their successors, in special warrandice of the
said 12 acres and 17 particates of land in Newhaven, according
to the tenor of the said contract. With court and oath of the
said Jonet Kennedy, in absence of the said David her husband,
not to revoke in time to come. Witnesses, William Sym, Andrew
Bonar, John Martyne, Adam Erskin, Malice Malloch, Lewis Gude,
Hugh Wallas, Thomas Arnot and Patrick Linlithqw, serjeant.
Edward Kincaid is bailie.

348. 1531 Nov. 4. Sasine on resignation by Jonet Kennedy, with
consent of David Bonar her spouse, in favour of William Sym,
burgess, of an annual-rent of £10, out of the lands, tenements
and buildings of John Con, flesher, lying within a tenement of
the late William Cockburn, on the south side of the High Street,
west side the transe thereof, between a tenement of the late
Henry Preston on the east, and a tenement of Alexander Rynde
on the west; a land of the late William Lethame on the north,
and a land of the late Sir William Broun, chaplain, on the
south. Witnesses, John Smyth, William Wischart, Malice Malloch,
Thomas Arnot, Hugh Wallas and Patrick Linlithqw, serjeant. Edward Kincaid is bailie.
The quhilk day, in presens of the said ballie and witnes aboue
writtin, the said David Bonar and Jonet Kennedy his spous
oblist thame, and thair airis, till warrand and defend the said
annuell-rent of x lib. till the said William Sym, his airis and
assignais, except the reversion that Johne Con has to redeme
the said annuell. And gif the said reversion contene mair in
it na xj scoir merkis, the said David and his spous obliss
thame and thair airis till refound the samyne to the said
William and his airis, samekle as it is mair na the said
xj^{xx} merkis; and gif it contene les na the said xj^{xx} merkis,
in that cais the said David and his spous obliss thame and
thair airis to fulfill the said soume, and mak the samyne xi
scoir of merkis and na mair. Apon the quhilkis promittis the
said William askit actis. Done upon the ground of the saidis
lands.

349. 1531 Nov. 14. Sasine on precept from chancery in favour of

Marjorie Sclater *alias* Robison, as nearest lawful heir of the late Andrew Sclater *alias* Robison her father, of a certain land or building of the said Andrew, lying on the north side of the High Street, between a land of John Pennycuke on the south, a land of Gilbert Lauder on the north; a land of the late William Selyman on the west, and the trause of a tenement in which the said land lies on the east. At Dunbertane 6 November in the 19th year of the King's reign. And forthwith George Elphinston, attorney and in name of the said Marjorie Robison and his spouse, resigned the said land or building in the hand of Mungo Tennent, bailie, who thereupon gave sasine thereof to Alexander Tennent, burgess, and Jonet Bell his spouse, the longest liver of them, and the heirs lawfully procreated or to be procreated between them. Witnesses, Adam Lyndesay, Lewis Gude, James Powis, Henry Tyndaill and David Purves.

350. 1531 Nov. 17. Sasine on resignation by Alexander Tennent, with consent of Jonet Bell his spouse, in favour of Mr. Thomas Broune, in name of the church, for an anniversary or distribution to the poor to be made yearly for the souls of the late George Broune and Beatrix Anderson his spouse, conform to the tenor of a charter to be made thereupon, of an annual-rent of 26s.8d., out of a land of the said Alexander Tennent, on the north side of the High Street, between a land of John Pennycuke on the south, a land of Gilbert Lauder on the north; and a land of the late William Selyman on the west, and the transe of the tenement in which the said land lies on the east. Witnesses, Sir John Stewart, chaplain, Stephan Riddaill, and David Purves, serjeant. Mungo Tennent is bailie.

351. 1531 Nov. 22. Sasine on resignation by Archibald Williamson, son and heir of the late John Williamson, in favour of John Paterson, burgess, and Isobel MacKewyn his spouse, of the said Archibald's tenement on the north side of the High Street, beside the Castlehill, between a land of William Wallange on the east, a land of the late Mr. Richard Lauson on the west; the North Loch on the north, and the King's public street on the south. Witnesses, John Huntar, Thomas Penny, Thomas Home, John Archibald, James Currour and Patrick Lithqw. Mungo Tennent is bailie.

352. 1531 Nov. 28. Sasine on resignation by Robert Glen, son and heir of the late John Glen, burgess, with consent of Marion Cockburn his spouse, in favour of James Gray, flesher and burgess, and Geilis Elphinston his spouse, of the said Robert's land lying within a tenement of the late John Butlar, on the south side of the High Street, between a land of Alexander Rynd on the west, a land of Henry Preston on the east, a land of the late William Lethame, now pertaining to John Marlzone, on the south, and a certain waste land of the said tenement on the north. Witnesses, William Elphinston, Mathew Michelson, Thomas Scowgall, Thomas Galloway, John Glen and Thomas Arnot, serjeant.

353. **1531 Dec. 9.** Sasine on resignation by Alexander Cant in favour of himself and Katrine Mayne his affianced spouse in conjunct-fee, of the following subjects: (1) His land and mansion in which he now dwells, lying within his wester tenement on the north side of the High Street, between his easter tenement on the east, and a tenement of the late Symon Doweill on the west. (2) His foreland of the said tenement between his land or chamber newly built on the north, and the king's public street on the south. (3) The foreland of his said easter tenement lying between a land of the late John Blakstok on the east, and the said wester tenement on the west; a land of the late Thomas Haithwy on the north, and the king's public street on the south. Witnesses, Sir George Litiljohne and Sir John Portuis, chaplains, John Burrowman, William Cunynghame, and Thomas Arnot, serjeants. Mungo Tennent is bailie.

354. **1531 Dec. 9.** Sasine on resignation by Katrine Mayne in favour of herself and Alexander Cant her affianced spouse, of the following subject: (1) Her half part of the booth of the foreland of a tenement of the late William Foular, lying on the north side of the High Street, between a land of the late Andrew Dykson on the east, and a land of the late John Blakstok on the west. (2) Land or bakehouse of the said Katrine, in Peebles Wynd, east side the trause thereof, between a land of St. Mary Magdalene on the north, and a land of John Glen on the south. (3) Her half part of a land, containing lower hall and two cellars, lying on the north side of the High Street, in Halkerston's Wynd, west side the transe thereof, between a land of the deceased George Halkerston on the south, and a land of Thomas Zare on the north. (4) Land of the said Katrine lying in the Cowgate, south side thereof, between a land of the late William Sinclair on the east, a land of the Friars Preachers on the west, a waste land on the south: Reserving the liferent of the lands and booth foresaid to Alison Rouche, mother to the said Katrine. Witnesses, Sir George Litiljohne, Sir John Portuis, chaplains, and the others foresaid. Mungo Tennent is bailie.

354a. Later insert.
Information for Mr. Alexander Guthrie in the particularis following.
In the first to remember to caus extract the Sasingis followiing, Viz.
Ane Sasing quhair Alexander Cant, guidsir to Mr. Jhone Paip, younger, is enterit to all his landis and annuelrentis in Edinburgh, the 15 day of Apryll 1522.
Lib. 4 Joannis Fouller
Ane Sasing quhair Alexander Cant and Katharene Mayne his spous ar infeft, in the eister and vester fore tenementis on the north syde of the gait, daitit the 9 of December 1531, in John Fowlaris bukis. Ane sasing quhair Eduart Bassindyne, guidsir to Mr. John Paip, younger, is infeft in certane landis. This is to be fund in Alexander Guthreis 4 buik fo. 3.

355. **1531 Dec. 13.** Sasine on resignation by Marion Carkettill, spouse of Robert Logane of Coitfeild, with his consent, in favour of

John Purves, burgess, and Elizabeth Logane his affianced spouse, the longest liver of them, and the heirs lawfully to be procreated between them, etc., for the marriage contracted and solemnly to be performed between them in face of holy kirk, of the said Marion and Robert's land and great building, lying within a tenement of Andrew Mowbray, on the north side of the High Street, west side the transe thereof, between a land of the late William Lokart on the east, and a tenement of the late Adam Turing on the west, a land of James Foulis on the south, and the yard of Trinity College on the north. Witnesses, Patrick Kincaid, John Cranstoun, James Logane, Mathew Michelson and William Watson. Edward Kincaid is bailie.

356. 1531 Dec. 14. Sasine in favour of Margaret Robison *alias* Sclater, on her cognition by Edward Kincaid, bailie, as daughter and one of the heirs of the late Robert Sclater *alias* Robison, in and to the fourth part of the said Robert's land, lying on the *south* (sic.) side of the High Street, in Sclataris Close, west side the transe thereof, between a land of Master John Chapman on the north, and a land of Walter Scot on the south: Which fourth part the said Margaret resigned in the hands of the said bailie, in favour of herself and John Cleghorn her spouse, who are thereupon seised in the same. Witnesses, Sir George Litiljohn, David Carny, Henry Tullois, Thomas Askill, David Kinloch, James King and David Purves.

357. 1531 Dec. 14. Sasine in favour of Cristina Robison on her cognition by Edward Kincaid, bailie, as daughter and one of the heirs of the late Robert Robison *alias* Sclater, in and to a fourth part of the foresaid land lying in Sclataris Close, west side the transe thereof: Which fourth part the said Cristina resigned in the hands of the bailie who gave liferent sasine thereof to Isobella Wardlaw her mother. Same witnesses.

358. 1531 Dec. 14. Sasine in favour of Helen Robison, daughter and one of the heirs of the late Robert Robison *alias* Sclater, on her cognition by Edward Kincaid, bailie, in and to the fourth part of the land of the said Robert, lying in Sclataris Close, west side the transe thereof, between a land of Mr. John Chepman on the north, and the land of Walter Scot on the south: Which fourth part the said Helen resigned in the hands of the bailie, who thereupon gave liferent sasine thereof to Isobell Wardlaw mother to the said Helen. Witnesses aforesaid.

359. 1531 Dec. 20. Sasine in favour of Marjorie Broune, kinswoman and one of the heirs of the late Elizabeth Scot, Lady Manerston, on her cognition by Mungo Tennent, bailie, in and to the half part of an annual-rent of 40 shillings, out of a land of Mathew Loch, lying within the tenement of the said Lady Manerston, on the south side of the High Street, between the easter part of the said tenement on the east, and a land of the late Patrick Richardson on the west; west side the transe thereof, between the foreland of said tenement on the north, and another land thereof on the south. And forthwith David Purves, procurator and in name of the said Marjorie, resigned the foresaid half annual-rent, extending to 20s. Scots, in the hands of the bailie,

who gave sasine thereof to Sir James Ker, chaplain; who instantly resigned the same in favour of Mathew Loch and Jonet Bell his spouse; and they are thereupon seised therein, the longest liver of them, and their heirs therein specified. Witnesses, John Blak, Thomas Barcar, Maurice Coupland, John King, David Robison, and David Purves, serjeant.

360. 1531 Dec. 20. Sasine in favour of Margaret Martyne, on her cognition by Mungo Tennent, bailie, as kinswoman and one of the heirs of the late Elizabeth Scot, Lady Manerston, of the half of an annual-rent of 40s., upliftable from the land of Mathew Loch, lying and bounded as before described. Same witnesses.

361. 1531 Dec. 22. Sasine on resignation by Margaret Robison, with consent of John Cleghorne her spouse, in favour of Isobella Wardlaw her mother in liferent, of her fourth part of a land of the late Robert Robison *alias* Sclater, lying on the south side of the High Street, in the close called Sclataris Close, west side the transe thereof, between a land of Master John Chepman on the north, and a land of Walter Scot on the south. Witnesses, Walter Scot, George Gibson, John Aldinstoun, John Howison, Thomas Horne, and Thomas Arnot, serjeant.

362. 1531-2 Jan. 1. Adam Stewart, burgess, procurator and in name of Sir David Stewart, chaplain of the altar or service of St. Nicholas, situated within the collegiate church of St. Giles, passed to the personal presence of our supreme Lord the King; and there the said Adam, procurator and in name of the said Sir David, surrendered and simply resigned in His Majesty's hands, as undoubted patron thereof, all and whole his foresaid chaplainry and service of the said altar, with all lands, fermes, annual-rents and profits thereof, with their pertinents. And forthwith His Majesty, of his own certain knowledge, gave and delivered the said chaplainry or service of the altar of St. Nicholas, with all lands, fermes, annual-rents, oblations, emoluments, and other profits whatsoever, by delivery of a paper schedule, to Sir John Stewart, chaplain, during his lifetime. Upon which the said Sir John asked this present public instrument to be made to him thereupon. Done within the palace of our sovereign Lord the King, beside the Monastery of Holyrood. Henry bishop of Whithorn and of the Chapel Royal, the lord earl of Argyle, the Lord Flemyng, William Wode, John Pardovyne, and Andrew Purves, are witnesses.

363. 1531-2 Jan. 10. Renunciation by Robert Bruce of Bynning, burgess of Edinburgh, in favour of Archibald Fairnlie, lord fiar of the lands and barony of Braid, of the superiority of all and whole the lands of Plewlands; and also of the superiority of the lands of Brighouse, lying in the barony of Braid and within the shire of Edinburgh: Which superiorities Robert Bruce hereby declares are now lawfully redeemed from him by the said Archibald: Reserving to the said Robert, his heirs and assignees, an annual-rent of 40 shillings, leviable forth of the lands of Brighouse: To hold of our sovereign Lord the King, conform to the tenor of a charter made thereupon. Done beside the

merchant booth of the said Robert Bruse. Witnesses, Master Adam Otterburne of Auldhame, provost of Edinburgh, John Fischar, Thomas Paterson, Michael Tullois, Thomas Arnot, John Chancellar and Richard Hereis.

364. 1531-2 Jan. 12. Sasine in favour of Alexander Levingston on his cognition by Edward Kincaid, bailie, as heir of the late John Levingston, burgess, his father, of an annual-rent of 2 merks, out of a waste land and chapel, of old pertaining to George bishop of Elphin, lying upon the Castle Hill, on the south side of the High Street, between a land of the late James Scot on the east, the Castle Wynd on the west, the lands of the late Mathew Harvy and Thomas Haithwy on the south, and the said Castlehill on the north. Witnesses, John Gibson, George Heslihop, John Smyth, Patrick Kincaid, James Anderson, Walter Ramsay, Alexander Vaiche, and David Purves, serjeant.

365. 1531-2 Jan. 18. Patrick Baron, bailie, passed to a tenement of the late John Currour, lying on the south side of the High Street, beside the Castlehill, between a land of the late William Adamson on the east, and a land of the late John Dee on the west; and there the said bailie cognosced and entered Marion, Isobella, Elizabeth, Jonet, Margaret, Agnes and Cristina Currours, as sisters and heirs of the late George Currour, each of them respectively in and to her part of the foresaid tenement. And forthwith David Tod, procurator and in name of the said Cristina Currour resigned her part of the foresaid tenement in the hands of the bailie, who gave sasine of the said seventh part to Marion Currour, in her own name and of her other sisters, to be equally divided between them, conform to the tenor of a division made between the foresaid sisters. Witnesses, Mr. James Murray, William Craik, Alexander Peebles, John Coldane, Alexander Baron, Vincent Strathauchin, notary public, and William Watson.

366. 1531-2 Jan. 18. Sasine in favour of Marion Currour, on her cognition by Patrick Baron, bailie, as one of the heirs of the late George Currour her brother, in and to the foreland of a tenement of the late John Currour, lying on the south side of the High Street, beside the Castlehill, and bounded as before described; paying thence yearly an annual-rent of 2 merks, or ground-annual, to whatsoever persons the same may be lawfully due. And forthwith the said Marion Currour, of her own free will, as she affirmed, resigned her said foreland containing chamber, loft, and cellar below the stair thereof, in the hands of the bailie, who thereupon gave heritable sasine and conjunctinfeftment of the same to the said Marion Currour and Alexander Rynd her spouse, conform to the letter of division made thereupon. Witnesses aforesaid.

367. 1531-2 Jan. 18. Sasine to Agnes Currour, on her cognition by Patrick Baron, bailie, as one of the heirs of the late George Currour, in and to the back hall of the back land of the foresaid tenement of the late John Currour, beside the Castlehill, with the cellar thereof, now occupied by John Litill, conform to the letter of division made between the said Agnes and her

other sisters: Which back hall and cellar Agnes Currour resigned in the bailie's hands, who thereupon gave sasine of the same to the said Agnes and Henry Tyndaill her spouse. Same witnesses.

368. 1531-2 Jan. 18. Patrick Baron, bailie, passed to the tenement of the late John Currour, on the south side of the High Street, beside the Castlehill; and there cognosced and entered Isobel Currour, sister and one of the heirs of the late George Currour her brother, in and to the other back house of said tenement, with the two cellars presently occupied by James Aikman; and to an annual-rent of 13s.4d. leviable furth of the lower hall and three cellars, with pertinents, pertaining to Jonet Currour and John Litill her spouse, conform to division. And forthwith Isobel Currour resigned the foresaid back house, 2 cellars and annual-rent in the hands of Patrick Barron, bailie, who instantly gave sasine of the said subjects to Isobell Currour and James Aikman her spouse.

369. 1531-2 Feb. 18. Sasine in favour of Jonet Currour, on her cognition by Patrick Baron, bailie, as sister and one of the heirs of the late George Currour, in and to the nether hall of the back land of a tenement of the late John Currour, beside the Castle Hill; with the waste land adjacent thereto, and three cellars thereof, conform to the division of the said tenement between her and her sisters: Paying yearly therefrom a ground-annual of 13s.4d.; and also an annual-rent of 13s.4d. to Isobell Currour and James Aikman her spouse. After which the said Jonet resigned the foresaid hall, with 3 cellars and waste land thereof in the hands of the bailie, who thereupon gave sasine of the said subjects to Jonet Currour and John Litill her spouse.

370. 1531-2 Jan. 19. Sasine on resignation by William Sym in favour of himself and Marion Kyle his spouse, of the back house or upper mansion of a tenement of Lord Borthick now pertaining to the said William Sym, lying on the west side of the transe of Borthick's Wynd, in which the late Robert Borthick dwelt, between the side wall of the fore land of the said tenement on the north, and the side wall of the mansion of the said Lord Borthick presently occupied by him, on the south, the transe of the said vennel on the east, and a land of John Carkettill on the west. Witnesses, George Leiche, John Pardovyne, James Kyle, John Kyle, James Johnston and John Coldane.
The same day hour and witnesses, the said Marion Kyle promised to the said William Sym her spouse, in presence of the bailie, that if it shall happen the said William Sym to pre-decease the said Marion, and she to marry another husband, in that case she obliges herself to renounce and over give the said house and mansion in favour of the children procreate between the said William and the said Marion.

371. 1531-2 Jan. 23. Mungo Tennent, bailie, passed to a tenement of the late Stephen Knox, lying on the north side of the High Street, between a tenement of the late Symon Doweill on the east, and a tenement of the late Archibald Preston on the west,

the North Loch on the north, and the King's public street on the south; and there Jonet Lambe, relict of the said Stephen Knox, renounced in favour of Gilbert Knox, son and heir of the said deceased Stephen, the following subjects: (1) Her conjunct-fee of the foresaid tenement. (2) An annual-rent of 2 merks out of (a Land) of John Blakstok lying within the said tenement. (3) Item an annual-rent of 4 merks out of a land of the late Thomas Broune, lying within the said tenement. (4) Another annual-rent of 4 merks out of a land of the late John Adamson, lying within the said tenement. (5) An annual-rent of 3 merks out of a land of William Johnston and his spouse, lying within the said tenement. (6) An annual-rent of 20 shillings out of a land of the late Thomas Broun, lying in the lower end of the said tenement. (7) And an annual-rent of 8 shillings, out of a certain merchant booth occupied by the relict of William Lokart, below the stair of the foreland of the said tenement. And forthwith the bailie cognosced and entered Gilbert Knox, as son and heir of the said late Stephen Knox his father, in and to the said tenement; and likewise in and to all and sundry the foresaid annual-rents, by delivery to the said Gilbert of hesp and staple, earth and stone, as use is: Reserving the liferent of the said mansion, booths and annual-rents to Jonet Lambe. Which tenement (excepting the merchant booth occupied by Jonet Lambe, of old pertaining to (   ) Lundors; as also all and sundry the foresaid annual-rents) the said Gilbert Knox resigns in the hands of the bailie who thereupon gives heritable sasine and conjunct-infeftment thereof to the said Gilbert Knox and Elizabeth Lauson his affianced spouse. Witnesses, Master James Lauson, Master James Broune, Rector of Fiddirisso, proto-notary apostolic, Archibald Scowgall, John Swayne, Andrew Broun, Adam Heston and Thomas Arnot, serjeant.

372. 1531-2 Feb. 1. Sasine on resignation by John Melros, son and heir of the late David Melros, with consent of his beloved spouse Margaret Wauchoip, in favour of Master Richard Boithuell, provost of the Kirk-of-Field, his heirs and assignees, of an annual-rent of 40 shillings, out of a land of the said John Melros, lying on the south side of the High Street, in Nudries Wynd, west side the trause thereof, between a land of the late Thomas Karnis on the south, and a land of the late Luke Paterson, now pertaining to Thomas Uddart, on the north: With the said Margaret Wauchope's oath, in a full and open court held before Patrick Baron, bailie, upon the ground of the said land, in absence of John Melrose her husband, not to revoke in time to come. And forthwith Master Richard Bothwell, provost of the said collegiate church, resigned the foresaid annual-rent of 40 shillings in the hands of the bailie, who thereupon gave sasine thereof to Sir Bartholomew Hammyltoun, chaplain, in name of the said collegiate church. Witnesses, Sir Richard Lauson, Sir John Bowok and Sir John Jakson, chaplains, John Hucheson, John Coldane, Hugh Wallas, William Watson and David Purves, serjeants. Under reversion of £21, without instrument.

373. 1531-2 Feb. 14. Sasine to David Boiswell of Afflek, as heir of the late Master John Boiswell his uncle, on his cognition by

Edward Kincaid, bailie, of a land of Master John Boiswell, built and waste, lying below the Netherbow, on the south side of the High Street, within a tenement of the late Martin Huntar, between a land of the said Martin Huntar on the north, and the strand on the south; which tenement lyes in the burgh of Edinburgh, on the south side of the High Street, between a land of the late Patrick Richardson on the east, and a land of the late John Craik, now pertaining to William Craik, on the west. Which land David Boiswell resigned in the hands of the bailie, who gave sasine thereof to Patrick Boiswell, his heirs and assignees. Witnesses, Adam Stewart, Patrick Makquhen, John Carnoch, John Gourlaw, Thomas Mathew, William Thomson, and William Watson.

374. 1531-2 Feb. 23. Sasine on resignation by Andrew Tod, as procurator for and in name of George Bell, son of the late John Bell, in favour of William Bell his brother, his heirs, etc., of an annual-rent of 10 merks, out of the fore land of the said John Bell's tenement, on the south side of the High Street, between a land of the late David Dalrumpill on the east, and a tenement of the late William Vernour on the west, and the back land of the said tenement on the south. Witnesses, Sir Andrew Murray, chaplain, John Scharp, Patrick McQuhen, David Blantyre, James Rynd, Patrick Lithqw and William Watson, serjeants.

375. 1531-2 Feb. 24. Sasine on resignation by Alexander Bruse, son and heir of the late John Bruse, burgess, with consent of Marion Baroun his spouse; and also with consent of Alexander Young, notary, his friend, in favour of Jonet Adamson, her heirs and assignees, of an annual-rent of 10 merks out of the said Alexander's tenement, lying on the south side of the High Street, between a tenement of the late Edward Bonkill on the east, a tenement of the late Walter Blaklok on the west; a land of the late William Ker on the south, and the king's public street on the north: With the said Marion's oath not to revoke. Witnesses, Master James Scot, William Uddart, Robert Urquhart, Patrick McQuhen, Thomas Purdy, Sir John Styrk, chaplain, and David Purves, serjeant.

376. 1531-2 Feb. 27. Sasine on renunciation by Margaret Symson, relict of Adam Johnston, of her conjunct-fee, in favour of John Johnston, son and heir of the said Adam, and on the said John's cognition by Mungo Tennent, bailie, in and to a waste land lying within a tenement of Robert Haliburton, on the north side of the High Street, between a tenement of the late William Adamson on the east, and a tenement of the late Francis Touris on the west; lying on the east side of the trause of the said tenement, between the north gable of a stable of the said Adam on the south, and the North Loch on the north. And forthwith the said John Johnston, with consent of his mother, resigned his foresaid waste land in the hands of the bailie, who gave sasine thereof to Adam Small and Katrine Trumbill his spouse. Afterwards the said Adam Small, with consent of the said Katrine his spouse resigned an annual-rent of 16 shillings,

out of the said waste land, in the hands of the bailie, in favour the foresaid Margaret Symson, who is thereupon seised therein in liferent, and the said John Johnston in fee. Witnesses, Master James Foulis and Master George Cuke, Robert Dennune, Mathew Roger, William Foulis, Richard Curre and David Purves, serjeant.

377. 1531-2 Feb. 28. Assignation granted by Thomas Cameron, burgess, in favour of Sir John Dykson, chaplain, during his lifetime, whom failing to William Dykson, whom failing to Master Richard Boithuell, younger, whom he constitutes his cessioners and assignees in and to all and sundry the fermes and profits of a certain tenement of land lying in the Cowgate, on the south side thereof, between a land of the lord bishop of Dunkeld on the east, and a land or transe of the late William Raperlaw on the west, the King's common way on the north, and the common way that leads to the Kirk of Field on the south: And in case the said Thomas Cameron shall die before the said Sir John, then the said Sir John Dykson shall have the said fermes and profits at his disposal, as chaplain of the altar of Saint Katrine, situated within St. Giles kirk, during his lifetime; and after his decease, his successors, chaplains of the said altar and service thereof, to be nominated by the patrons of the said service, as in the foundation thereof is more fully contained. With full power to the said Sir John and Master Richard to intromit with the said tenement and profits thereof, dispone and set to feuferm, levy the fermes and profits, and if necessary to distrenzie the tenants therefor according to order of law: Under hypothec and obligation of all their goods present and to come. Witnesses, Mungo Tennent, bailie, Sir John Portuis and Sir Alexander Cunninghame, chaplains, Robert Knox, Thomas Arnot, Patrick Linlithqw and William Watson, serjeants. Done upon the ground of the said tenement.

The quhilk day in presens of the witnes aboue wryttin and me notar publict, Thomas Cameron protestit that quhatever he did anent the making of Sir Johne Dykson his assignay to the malis and proffittis of his tenement of land hurt nocht the fundation that is maid thairapon at Sanct Katrinis altar. And thereupon the said Thomas asked instruments. Done upon the ground of the said tenement. Witnesses foresaid.

378. 1531-2 Mar. 13. In presens of me notar publict and witnes undir wryttin, Jonet Scheirsmyth (   ) and air of umquhile William Scheirsmyth, burges of Edinburgh, grantis hir weill contentit assithit and paiit be the handis and deliverans of Maister Adam Ottirburn of Auldhame, provost of Edinburgh, of all maner of airschip guids and soumes of money that evir pertenit till hir ony maner of way, throw the deces of the said umquhile William Scheirsmyth, or throw the deces of ony of his bairns, or ony uther wayes. And syklyk grantit hir fullelly contenit and assithit be the said Maister Adam, for the landis of Carlowry, and money that was gottin tharfor. Of the quhilkis airship guidis and soumes of money pertenand till hir ony maner of way, throw the deces of the said umquhile William, his barnis, or utherwayis, for the landis of Carlowry, scho held hir weill

contentit assithit and paiit be the said Maister Adam; and tharof, for hir, hir airis executouris and assignais, quytclamys and dischargis the said Maister Adam Otterburn, his airis and assignais, now and for evir, baith befor God and man. And thereupon the said Master Adam asked an instrument. Done in the collegiate church of St. Giles, before these witnesses, Sir David Young, curate of the said kirk, Sir Bartholomew Hammylton, Michael Tullois and William Watson.

379. 1531-2 Mar. 13. Sasine on resignation by Andrew Lichton, son and heir of the late John Lichton, in favour of Anthony Brussait, burgess, of an annual-rent of 10 merks, out of the said Andrew's land lying within a tenement of the late Thomas Haithwy, now pertaining to William Lauder, on the west side of the transe thereof, between a land of the said William Lauder on the north, and a land of Anthony Brussait on the south; which tenement lies on the south side of the High Street, between a tenement of the late John Napier on the east, and a land of St Mary Magdalen and her altar situated in St.Giles church on the west. Witnesses, Sir James Goldsmith, James Aikman, Gilbert Hunter and Thomas Arnot, serjeant. Under reversion, the sum not named but general.

380. 1531-2 Mar. 21. Sasine on resignation by John Brown in favour of Thomas Tunno and Geils Davidson his spouse of the said John's land, built and waste lying beyond the Overbow, on the south side of the High Street thereof, within a tenement of the late Edward Davidson, between the transe and land of Andrew Wode on the east, and a land of the said Edward Davidson on the north, and the lands of Thomas Tunno on the south and west. Witnesses, Jasper Legait, Henry Bartilmo, William Wyndezettis, John Wilson, Adam Wricht, and David Purves, serjeant. The said John Brown oblissis him till mak the said land fre of all annuell at the terme of Whitsonday nixt to come.

381. 1532 Mar. 26. Sasine on resignation by Thomas Cuke, with consent of Isobella Ramsay his spouse, in favour of John Cuke, their son and apparent heir, and Elizabeth Matheson his affianced spouse, of the following subjects: (1) Their part of the foreland of a tenement pertaining to the said Thomas Cuke and John Malcome, lying on the south side of the High Street, between a land of the late John Carkettill on the east, and a land of Archibald Williamson on the west; a land of the earl of Eglinton on the south, and the king's public street on the north, containing 4 booths, viz. 2 easter merchant booths below the stair of the said foreland; and 2 booths immediately above the stair thereof. (2) Their land, under and above, lying within a tenement of William Lord Borthik, on the south side of the High Street, between a tenement of Alexander Rynd on the east, and a tenement of the late John Carkettill on the west; west side the transe of the said tenement, between a land of the late David Lithqw on the north, and a waste land of the said tenement, pertaining to David Gillaspy on the south. (3) An annual-rent of 4 merks 6 shillings and 8 pence, out of a land of Henry Dumbartane, lying within a tenement of the late Charles Leving-

ton, between the trause thereof on the east, and the trause of a tenement of the late Thomas Swift on the west; a land of the late John Balfour on the south, and a land of the late Nicholas Goldsmyth on the north. Witnesses, John Matheson, Sir David Wardlaw and Sir Alexander Romannos, John Fische, John Matheson, younger, and David Purves, serjeant. Reserving the liferent of the foresaid booths, land and annual-rent to the resigners.

382. 1532 Mar. 29. Compeared personally James Halkerston, burgess of Edinburgh, on the one part, and John Fischar, burgess of the said burgh, on the other part; which parties appointed and agreed as follows in the common tongue. At Edinburgh the 21 day of Merche the yeir of God jm.vc.xxxj. yeris. It is appoyntit and fynaly aggreit betuix honorable men, James Halkerston, burges of Edinburgh, nevoy and air to umquhile Adam Halkerston his grantsir, on that ane pairt, and John Fishar, burges of the said burgh, on the tother pairt, anent all materis debatable betuix thame in this maner. That is to say, the said James, for him and his airis, sall discharge the said John and his airis, of the by-run annuellis of ane merk of annuell, quherof and of uthir thre merkis of annuell to be uptakin of all Cameronis land, now pertenand to the said John and to Mars Inglis, and to the airis of umquhile William Lokkart, in the best forme the said Johne Fischar can devise: And als sall gif heretabill stait and sesing of the said merk of annuell to the said Johne, Elizabeth Wyndezettis his spouse, and to thar airis, be resignation in the ballies handis of the said burgh of Edinburgh, be erd and stane, or be delivering of ane penny in the best forme according to the consuetude of burgh. And syklyke the said James, for him and his airis, sall discharge, and be thir presentis dischargis, the said Johne his said spous and thar airis, of the remanent of the said annuell, extending to 3 merkis annuell; and sall never perseu nor follow thame, nor na pairt of thar landis nor tennentis of the samyn, quhilk was Cameronis land, safer as pertenis now to the said John Fischar tharfor, in jugement nor outouth jugement ony maner of way, nor molest nor truble thame be poynding, or utherwayis, in all tymes cummyng. For the quhilk the said Johne and his spous sall content and pay to the said James, eftir the geving of the said sesing, and making of the said securiteis, the soume of xvj usuall money of Scotland. And attour sall nevir persew be hirself nor be nane utheris that he may lett ane summons of errour rasit apon the jugis and inquest that servit the said James of the said four merk annuell, bot sal stop the samyne safer as he may. And to that effect sall deliver the said summons in the handis of John Achinston to be observit fra calling att his uttir power. And baith the saidis pairtiis dischargis and extingis all pleyis movit or to be movit be the occasioun forsaid, and oblissis thame faithfully tharto. In witnes heirof baith the saidis pairtiis has subscrvit this present contract and apponctuament, the said Johne with his hand at the pen: and will and consentis the samyne be insert and maid in forme of instrument, befor thir witnes, worschipful men, Sir

Alexander Scot, Provost of Corstorphin, Henry Wardlaw of Kilbabertoun, and Johne Achinson, with otheris divers. And attour the said Johne Fischar sall with deligens keip the said James Halkerstoun scathles of the guttar lyand betuix thar saidis tenementis conform to resoun and gude nychtbourheid to him tharapon. Upon which both parties asked instruments. Done upon the ground of the said tenement, in the booth of the said John Achinson, in presence of Sir Alexander Scot, provost of Corstorphin, Clement Litill, Master James Scot, John Scot, Thomas Wauchop, John Achinson, notary public, Sir John Achinson, chaplain, and Patrick Lithqw, serjeant.

383. 1532 Mar. 29. Sasine on resignation by James Halkerston in favour of John Fischar, of an annual-rent of 13s.4d., out of the said John Fischar's land lying on the north side of the High Street, between a tenement of the said James Halkerston on the east, and the trause of a tenement of the late James Cameron and a land of the late William Lockhart on the west, a waste land on the north, and the king's public street on the south. Moreover James Halkerston obliges him and his heirs to warrant the said John Fishar concerning an annual-rent of 3 merks, leviable out of a tenement of the late James Cameron, at the hands of all and sundry, conform to the tenor of a contract between them. Symon Preston is bailie. Same witnesses as aforesaid.

384. 1532 Apr. 19. Symon Preston, bailie, passed to a land of the late Sir Mathew Doweill, chaplain, lying on the south side of the High Street, within a tenement of the late Master Richard Robertson, between the lands of the said late Master Richard on the north, and a land of the late Thomas Wallas on the south, and a land of the late Henry Preston on the east, and the common transe between the said land and the cemetery of St. Giles church on the west; and there the said bailie gave heritable sasine of the foresaid land to James Fentoun and Eufame Adamson his spouse, conform to the tenor of a process of recognition led by the said James and his spouse, before the bailies of Edinburgh, upon the said land. Witnesses, Thomas Mureleyis, William Raa, William Hammyltoun, Alexander Straton, Patrick Ireland, Maurice Coupland, David Bayne, Patrick Lithqw and William Watson, serjeants.

385. 1532 Apr. 19. Sasine on resignation by James Fentoun and Eupham Adamson his spouse, in favour of Andrew Wode and Katrine Allane his spouse, of the resigner's land, built and waste, of old pertaining to the late Sir Mathew Doweill, chaplain, lying within the tenement of the late Master Richard Robertson and bounded as before described. Witnesses aforesaid.

386. 1532 Apr. 22. Sasine on resignation by Alexander Cant, in favour of Alexander Josse, burgess, and Elizabeth Cant his affianced spouse, the survivor of them, and the heirs to be lawfully procreated between them, whom failing, to the lawful and nearest heirs and assignees of the said Alexander whomsoever, in name of date, in default of other moveable goods and chattels, for the marriage to be solemnly contracted between

them in the face of holy kirk, of the foreland of the said Alexander Cant, lying on the north side of the High Street, beside the Netherbow, between a land of the late William Adamson on the east, and a land of the late John Davidson on the west. Witnesses, William Elphinston, John Marjoribanks, Robert Ector, Alexander Baroun, John Coldane, Thomas Baron, Patrick Urre, Vincent Strathauchin, notary public, and Thomas Arnot, serjeant.

387. 1532 Apr. 25. Sasine in favour of William Lord Sinclair, of an annual-rent of 3 merks, out of a land of the late John Bell, newly built, lying within a tenement of the late Andrew Bell, on the south side of the High Street, between a land of the late John Dalrumpill on the east, and a land of the late William Vernour on the west; the foreland thereof on the north, and another land of the said late Adam Bell on the south: And this on redemption by the said Lord Sinclair of the said annual-rent from John McGauchan, by payment of £23.6s.8d., contained in a certain reversion made thereupon. Sir Thomas Maluill is procurator for the said Lord Sinclair. Symon Preston is bailie. Witnesses, Sir Patrick Ballentyne and Sir George Kinloch, chaplains, Master Thomas Marjoribanks, William Watson, and Patrick Linlithqw, serjeants.

388. 1532 May 7. Sasine on precept from chancery, under testimonial of the great seal, in favour of James Lauson, son and heir of the late Robert Lauson of Hieriggis, of: (1) A land and tenement lying in the vennel called Forrester's Wynd, on the east side thereof, between a land of the late John Ramsay, knight, on the north, and the lands of John Foular on the south. (2) Another land and tenement lying in the vennel of the Friars Preachers, on the east side thereof, between the lands of George Gibson on the south, and the lands of William Scawis on the north: And which lands and tenements formerly pertained heritably to Alan Mosman, burges; held immediately him of the Crown in free burgage; and were apprised from him by James Lauson, conform to a decreet of the Lords of Council, for the sum of £540, in part payment of the sum of £567.9s.4d. Dated at Edinburgh 27 April in the 19th year of His Majesty's reign. Witnesses, Sir Gilbert Robisone, chaplain, George Gibson, John Swan, Thomas Lauson, Andrew Watson, Thomas Arnot and Hugh Wallas.
The quhilk day in presens of the bailie abou wryttin comperit Alane Mosman and declarit, that his land was wrangously optenit fra him be ane pretendit apprising therof; and that Margret Borthik his spous was in the conjunct-fee of baith his landis, ane liand in the Freir Wynd and ane uther in Forstaris Wynd. And therfor he protestit that the sesin gevin of his said landis to James Lauson, eftir the form of the said pretendit aprising, hurt nocht him nor his said spous, nor thar airis; and broke the sesing be ane dische; and for remeid of law quhen and quhar it efferit. And therapon the said Allane and his spous askit instrument. Done upon the ground of the said land in Forstaris Wynd. Witnesses above written.

389. 1532 May 8. Sasine on resignation by John Blakwode in favour of Thomas Dalgleish and Jonet Penman his spouse, of the said John's land lying in the vennel of the Virgin Mary of the Fields, west side the trause thereof, between a land of the late Master Mathew Ker on the north, and a land of the late Andrew Cowane on the south. Witnesses, Henry Cranston, John Morison, Gilbert Williamson, David Anderson, John Wauche, Alexander Mure, and David Purves, serjeant. Symon Preston is bailie.

390. 1532 May 10. Sasine on resignation by Robert Glen, with consent of Marion Cokburne his spouse, in favour of Elizabeth Levingston, her heirs and assignees, of the lands and back houses of the said Robert Glen's tenement, lying on the south side of the High Street, in Nudries Wynd, east side the transe thereof, between a land of the late George Achinson, now pertaining to George Cranston, on the north, and the land or chapel of the Virgin Mary on the south, and a land of the late Walter Blaklok on the east: Which lands and back houses of the said tenement lie one either side of the close thereof; with the lofts and galleries of the same, and a small house on the east side of the trause of the said close: Also all and whole these two lower houses of the foreland of the said tenement, below the great hall and stair thereof; together with the loft above the said great hall, and all other houses and pendicles of the said tenement in which an honourable Lady Elizabeth Levingston was infeft. Witnesses, Master Robert Galbraith, Master Henry Sinclair, Master Alexander Levingston, Alexander Baron, John Young, James Levingston, and William Watson, serjeant.
The quhilk day the said Elizabeth promised to deliver and mak ane reversion to the said Robert and his airis, apon the redemption of the saidis landis and houses, contenand iiii merkis, in the best forme. And therapon the said Robert askit instrumentis.

391. 1532 May 13. Sasine on precept from chancery in favour of Thomas Dykson, as lawful and nearest heir of the late George Dykson his father, of a piece of waste land lying on the south side of the High Street, in the back part of a tenement of the late James Lamb, between a land of the late Master Richard Robertson on the south and a land of the late John Robertson on the north. At Edinburgh 1st.May in the 19th year of His Majesty's reign. Witnesses, Nicholas Carncors, Alexander Berton, George Cant, Sir William Makdowell, Sir John Tyndaill, William Watson and Thomas Arnot, serjeant.

392. 1532 May 15. Sasine on resignation by James Cant, son and heir of the late George Cant, in favour of himself and Margaret Makgill his spouse, of the foreland and back mansion of his tenement lying on the south side of the High Street, between a tenement of the late Sir Thomas Halkerston, provost of Crichton on the east, and a tenement of the late Edward Bonkill on the west; the back land in which Alexander Blyth now dwells on the south, and the king's public street on the north. Witnesses, Sir David Young, vicar of St. Giles church, Alexander Belses, George Gibson, Fynla Merschell, Thomas Arnot, serjeants. Symon Preston is bailie.

393. 1532 May 17. Compeared personally Robert Esdaill, cousin and heir of the late Sir Robert Huntrodis, and constituted Sir William Cady, chaplain, Thomas Mosman and John Young his procurator, conjunctly and severally, to impetrate and raise a brief or brieves from chancery, for serving of the said Robert as heir to his said cousin; and present the same to the bailies of Edinburgh to be duly and lawfully executed for serving the said Robert, as heir foresaid, in the lands within the burgh of Edinburgh in which the said Sir Robert Huntroddis died last vest and seised; and upon receiving sasine of the said lands in his name to resign the same in the hands of one of the bailies of the said burgh, in favour of William Henrison and his spouse, for sasine and infeftment to be given to them of the said lands, conform to a charter to be made thereupon by the said constituents: Protesting that whatsoever shall be done in the premises, for his interest, he shall hold as firm and stable as if done by himself. Witnesses, Vincent Strathauchin, notary public, Symone Preston, bailie, Archibald Williamson, Francis Wode.

394. 1532 May 17. Symon Preston, bailie, passed to a certain waste land lying on the south side of the High Street, in the back part of a tenement of the late James Lamb, between a land of the late Master Richard Robertson on the south, and a land of John Robertson on the north; and there Archibald Williamson declared that it had recently come to his notice, how that Mungo Tennent, bailie, delivered sasine of the said waste land to Thomas Dykson, as son and heir of the late George Dykson, and that the said land pertained heritably to him, as heir of the late Isobel Williamson: Therefore he protested, that the said sasine of the said land shall not hurt him in his right, and broke the said sasine by the breaking of a dish upon the ground thereof; and for remeid of law when and where it effeirs, and asked an instrument. Done upon the ground in presence of Master James Murray, prebendary of Dunglas, John Adamson and Laurence Broun.

395. 1532 May 18. Sasine on precept from chancery in favour of Robert Glen, as lawful and nearest heir of the late John Glen his brother, of a land or tenement lying on the south side of the High Street in Peebles Wynd, east side the transe thereof, between a land of the late William Ferry, now pertaining to William Lauder, on the south, and a land of the late John Quhiteheid on the north. Dated at Edinburgh 17 May and 19th. year of the King's reign. Witnesses, Master Thomas Marjoribanks, John Hay, Robert Balkasky, Alexander Heriot, Sir John Mekill, chaplain, and Patrick Lithqw, serjeant. Kentigern Tennent is bailie.

396. 1532 May 18. Sasine on resignation by Robert Glen, brother and heir of the late John Glen, in favour of Nicholas Carncors, Dean of Guild of the burgh of Edinburgh, and (   ) Dykson his spouse, of the said Robert's land or tenement lying in Peebles Wynd, east side the transe thereof, between a land of the late William Ferry, now pertaining to William Lauder, on the south,

and a land of the late John Quhiteheid on the north. Witnesses, Master Thomas Marjoribanks, John Hay, James Balcasky, Alexander Heriot, Sir John Mekle, chaplain, and Patrick Linlithqw, serjeant. Same bailie.

The quhilk day the said Nichol and his spouse promist ane reversion till the said Robert, apon the redeemyng of the said land, contenand iijc. merkis; and nocht to be redemit quhill v zeris war gane: The reversion to be maid in more ample form. And thereupon the said Robert asked an instrument. Witnesses foresaid.

397. 1532 May 31. Sasine on resignation by James Dornwyk, son and heir of the late John Dornwyk, in favour of Robert Reynald, burgess, and Agnes Davidson his spouse, of an annual-rent of 20s., out of the said James's land, lying in the burgh of Edinburgh, beyond the Nether Bow, in the vennel of St. Mary Wynd, east side the trause thereof, between a land pertaining to the weaver craft and the altar of Saint Severin, situated within the collegiate kirk of St. Giles, on the south, and a land of the late Edward Bonkill on the north. Witnesses, John Reynald, John Dykson, Thomas Huntar, John Kennedy, Alexander Burn, Robert Lun, John Hucheson and Hugh Wallas, serjeant. Under reversion of £10, which reversion the said Robert promised to give to the said James containing the said sum, upon redemption of the said annual-rent. The said James Dornwyk oblissis (him) till redeem the samyne with his awin propir gudis. And gif he happinis till analy the said land, or ony pairt thairof, he oblissis him till offir the samyne to the said Robert befor ony utheris xls. better chaip. Edward Kincaid is bailie.

398. 1532 May 25. Sasine on resignation by William Adamson, son and heir of the late William Adamson, with consent of Jonet Napier his spouse, in favour of Jonet Turing, mother to the said William, of an annual-rent of 20 merks, out of a tenement of the said late William Adamson, lying on the south side of the High Street, between a land of the deceased Richard Gamyll on the east, and a land of the late William Quhitheid on the west; to wit out of the said resigner's land newly built, lying within the said tenement, between a land of the late Sir Adam Creichton of Feldy, knight, on the east, the lands of Andrew Uddart and the late Roger Murray on the west, the lands of Robert Bishop and the late John Levingston on the south, and the lands of the said late William Adamson and the late Stephen Law on the north: Also out of another tenement of the said William and Jonet, lying on the south side of the High Street, between a land of James Halkerston on the east, a land of William Lauder on the west, a waste land of the said James Halkerston on the south, and the king's public street on the north: With the said Jonet Napier's oath in absence of her said spouse, the holy Scriptures touched, not to revoke in time to come. Witnesses, Sir David Young, curate, Alexander Young, notary public, John Charteris, John Thomson, Thomas Mosman, John Broun, and William Watson, serjeant. Symon Preston is bailie.

399. 1532 June 8. Sasine on renunciation by Alison Young, relict of

John Johnston, of her conjunct-fee, in favour of Thomas Johnston, and on cognition of the said Thomas by Patrick Baron, bailie, as heir of the said late John Johnston his father, of an annual-rent of 36 shillings, viz. xxxvj shillings out of a land of James Darroch, lying near the Overbow, on the north side of the High Street thereof, between a land of William Anderson on the west, and the said Bow on the east; and vj shillings out of the land of the said William Anderson: Which annual-rents of 36 shillings and 6 shillings the said Thomas Johnston resigned in the hands of the said bailie who gave sasine thereof to Elizabeth Brown in fee, and to the said Alison Young her mother in liferent. Witnesses, James Young, Andrew Baron, John Coldane, Thomas Todryk, Robert Gray, William Smith and William Anderson.

400. 1532 June 8. Compeared personally Alison Young, relict of John Johnston, on the one part, and Thomas Johnston, brother and heir of the said late John, on the other part; which Thomas Johnston confessed that he had received from the said Alison Young full satisfaction and payment, of all and sundry goods heritably pertaining to him by reason of the decease of the said late John his brother; and of all other goods and sums of money due and pertaining to him; and especially of the sum of £3, which the said Thomas sued for before the Official of Lothian against the said Alison; of which he held himself content and fully and wholly satisfied and paid; and of all which sums of money and goods foresaid the said Thomas hereby exoners and quitclaims the said Alison, her heirs, executors and assignees, forever. Done in the booth of Edward Kincaid. Witnesses, Patrick Baron, bailie, William Elphinston, John Young, Thomas Todryk, John Fausyde, John Anderson, and Vincent Strathauchin, notary.

401. 1532 June 14. Sasine in favour of William Wishert, on his cognition by Mungo Tennent, bailie, as grandson and one of the heirs of the late George Wishert, in and to his part of the lands of the late Archibald Wishert, lying on the south side of the High Street, in Forstar's Wynd, west side the transe thereof, between a land of the late William Clerk, now pertaining to Thomas Ramsay, on the south, a land of the laird of Corstorphyn on the north, a land of George Nicholson on the east, and a land of Alexander Mauchane on the west.
In like manner the said bailie cognosced and entered Thomas Wishert, grandson and another of the heirs of the said late Archibald, in and to his part of the said lands with their pertinents, and seised the said Thomas therein as use is within the burgh in such cases. Witnesses, Sir Thomas Ewin, chaplain, and Sir George Rogere, chaplain, John Gibson, Stephen Bell, William Aikinheid, Thomas Thomson, and David Purves.

402. 1532 June 14. Sasine in favour of Jonet Wishert, on her cognition by Mungo Tennent, bailie, as daughter and heir of the late Archibald Wishert, of her part of the said Archibald's lands lying in Forstar's Wynd, and bounded as before described: Which land the said Jonet resigned in the hands of the said bailie who thereupon gave sasine thereof, heritably and in

conjunct-fee, to John Hucheson and the said Jonet Wishert his spouse. Witnesses aforesaid.

403. 1532 June 14. Sasine on resignation by William Wischert, grandson and heir of the late Archibald Wischert, in favour of Thomas Wischert and John Hucheson, equally between them, of the said William's part, as one of the heirs of his said grandfather, of his the said Archibald's lands lying on the south side of the High Street, in Forstars Wynd, west side the transe thereof, between a land of the late William Clerk, now pertaining to Thomas Ramsay, on the south, and a land of the laird of Corstorphin on the north. Witnesses, Sir Thomas Ewin and Sir George Roger, chaplains, John Gibson, Stephen Bell, Ronald Aikinheid, Henry Thomson, and David Purves, serjeant.

404. 1532 June 14. Sasine on resignation by William Wishert, Thomas Wishert, and John Hucheson, with consent of Jonet Wishert his spouse, in favour of Henry Lille, deacon of the skinners, and Sir Thomas Stewart, chaplain of the said craft, in name of the altar of Saint Christopher, and his successors, of an annualrent of 4 merks out of the lands of the late Archibald Wishert, now pertaining to the said resigners, lying in Forstar's Wynd and bounded as before described. Witnesses aforesaid. Mungo Tennent is bailie.

405. 1532 June 15. Sasine to William Wishert, on his cognition by Mungo Tennent, bailie, as grandson and heir of the late Archibald Wishert, in and to the said Archibald's land and Barkhouse, with yard and waste land thereof, lying on the north side of the High Street, beside the North Loch, between a land of the late John Young on the south, and the North Loch on the north, a land (   ) on the east, and a land of William Vallange on the west. Witnesses, Stephen Bell, Patrick Aitkin, Henry Thomson, Henry Bartilmo, David Purves and Thomas Arnot, serjeants.

406. 1532 June 15. Sasine on renunciation by Margaret Huntroddis of her conjunct-fee, in favour of Alexander Evat and Robert Esdaill, and on cognition of the said Alexander Evat as one of the heirs of the late Sir Robert Huntroddis; and on cognition of the said Robert Esdail as kinsman and the other heir of the said Sir Robert Huntroddis, each of them in and to one half of the said late Sir Robert's land, lying on the south side of the High Street, in the lower end of Forstar's Wynd, east side the transe thereof, between a land of the late William Josse, now pertaining to Thomas Wode, on the north, the street of the Cowgate on the south, and a land of William Henrison on the east. And forthwith the said Robert Esdaill, and George Kairns, procurator and in name of the foresaid Alexander Evat, resigned their foresaid land, with pertinents, in the hands of Symon Preston, bailie, who gave heritable sasine and conjunct-infeftment of the same to William Henrison and Agnes Forest his spouse. And which land the said William and Agnes his spouse instantly resigned in the hands of Simon Preston, bailie, in favour of Michael Henrison their son, who is thereupon seised therein: Reserving the liferent thereof to the said spouses. Witnesses,

Thomas Laverok, Robert Abernethy, David Richartson, Thomas Henderson, John Anderson and Thomas Arnot.

The same day, etc., the said Michael Henrison obleist him faithfully, that quhat tyme or howsone that evir he enteris to the proffitt or males of the said land, that he sall content and pay till his youngest brother John Henrison the soume of xx lib., and, falzeing the said Johne by deces, to the secund brother eftir him, and failzeand of the secund brother, to the thrid and ferd, and sua furth. Apon the quhilkis the said William Henrison elder askit instrumentis. Done upon the ground.

407. 1532 June 18. Sasine to Marion Cowane, on her cognition by Mungo Tennent, bailie, as daughter and heir of the late Andrew Cowane, in and to the said Andrew's land, lying in the vennel of Mary of Field, west side the transe thereof, between a land sometime of David Vaiche, now pertaining to Thomas Dalgleiss, on the north, and a land sometime of John Riddaill, now pertaining to Alexander Mure, on the south. Which land the said Marion Cowane resigned in the hands of the said bailie, who thereupon gave heritable sasine thereof to Sir Robert Lille, chaplain, of the collegiate kirk of Mary of the Fields, his heirs and assignees. Witnesses, John Tait, John Tennent, Andrew Brounehill, John Robison, Sir George Kellie, chaplain, John Grob, David Purves and Hugh Wallas, serjeants.

408. 1532 June 18. Sasine on renunciation by Marion Broun, daughter of Nichol Broun, of her conjunct-fee, of two halls or lower houses of the backland of the said Nichol's tenement lying beyond the Overbow, with the whole yard thereof, and all their pertinents, on the south side of the High Street thereof, between a land of the late Alexander Reid on the east, and the lands of John Arres and John Quhite, and the king's common way on the north, and from thence descending towards the south, containing in length 7 particates of land and the fourth part of one ell, even to the land of John Windzettis on the south parts; and proceeding also on resignation by the said Nichol Broun, with consent of Jonet Erskirk his spouse, of the half part of his said tenement, with all its pertinents, in favour of the foresaid Marion Broun his daughter, her heirs and assignees, who are thereupon seised therein: Reserving the liferent of the said half to the saids Nichol and Jonet his spouse. Witnesses, John Murray, William Smyth, John Busbe, Adam Wilson, David Purves and Thomas Arnot. Mungo Tennent is bailie.

409. 1532 June 19. Sasine on resignation by David Tod, son and heir of the late Robert Tod, in favour of himself and Elizabeth Young his spouse, of his land or tenement lying on the south side of the High Street, beside the Netherbow, between a land of John Purves on the east, and the late James Bassinden on the west; a land of Alexander Young on the south, and the king's public street on the north. The said Elizabeth asked instruments. Witnesses, William Rutherford, Alexander Young, notary, Andrew Dalmahoy, William Lyndsay, Alexander Dykson, Thomas Arnot, serjeant.

410. 1532 June 25. Sasine in favour of John Adamson, on his cognition by Mungo Tennent, bailie, as heir of the late Alexander Adamson his brother, in and to the following subjects, viz. (1) An annual-rent of 20 shillings, out of a land of Archibald Williamson on the south side of the High Street and the Market Cross thereof, between a land of Thomas Cuke and John Malcolme on the east, and a land of William Anderson on the west. (2) An annual-rent of 8 shillings, out of a land of the late William Aldjoy, on the south side of the High Street upon the Castlehill, between a land of the late Francis Towris on the east, and a land (   ) on the west. (3) An annual-rent of 13s.4d. out of the foresaid land of Francis Towris on the south side of the High Street, between a land of the late Stephen Borthik on the east, and the said land of William Aldjoy on the west. (4) An annual-rent of 2 merks, out of a land of the late Richard Hardgrip, now pertaining to John Arres, lying beyond the Overbow, on the south side of the High Street, between a land of (   ) on the east, and a land of George Gude on the west. (5) An annual-rent of 20s., out of a backland, and the 2 south cellars hereof, of William Adamson, lying below the Castle Wall, on the south side of the High Street, within a tenement of the late Lancelot Barcar, between the fore land of the said tenement on the north, and the lands of Hieriggis on the south; the yard of Mr. Francis Bothwell on the east, and a waste land of the late William Balze on the west. Witnesses, Alexander Adamson, William Litill, Thomas Cuke, Richard Wardlaw, Thomas Paterson, John Litill, Sir John Clerk, George Talzefer, Sir John Tyndaill, Patrick Lithqw, David Purves and Thomas Arnot, serjeants.

411. 1532 June 25. Sasine to John Adamson, on his cognition by Mungo Tennent, bailie, as heir of the late Alexander Adamson his brother, of the following subjects: (1) An annual-rent of 5 merks, out of a tenement of the late Stephen Knox, lying on the north side of the High Street, between a tenement of the late Simon Doweill on the east, and a tenement of the late Archibald Preston on the west. (2) Land within the said tenement, west side the transe thereof, between a land of the said Stephen Knox on the south and a land of the late Symon Fynlaw on the north. (3) Land or tenement below the Castle Wall, on the south side of the High Street, between a land of the late James Wardlaw on the east, and a land of the late William Balze, now pertaining to the Holy Blood, on the west, and the land of William Adamson on the south. And forthwith the said John Adamson resigned the foresaid annual-rent of 5 merks, and lands or tenement, with houses and cellars thereof, in the hands of the bailie, who thereupon gave sasine thereof to Alexander Adamson his son, and the heirs of his body, whom failing to the lawful and nearest heirs of the said John freely reverting. Witnesses, Alexander Adamson and the others before named.

412. 1532 June 25. Sasine on resignation by John Adamson in favour of William Adamson his son, and the lawful heirs of his body, whom failing to revert freely to the lawful and nearest heirs

of the said John Adamson, of: (1) A land lying on the north side of the High Street, in Malcomes Close, west side the trause thereof, between a land of the late James Baron on the south, and a land of Thomas Coupland on the north; (2) A merchant booth, in which Thomas Marjoribanks now dwells, on the north side of the Tolbooth, and on the west side of the window called the Boiss Wyndo; (3) A land below the Castle Wall, on the south side of the High Street, between a land (   ) on the east, and a land of the late James Wardlaw on the west. Witnesses aforesaid.

413. 1532 July 5. Sasine to John Frissell, on his cognition by Mungo Tennent, bailie, as heir of the late Thomas Fressal his father, of a small land and chamber, with the north gable thereof, lying in a tenement of Thomas Preston of Bynning on the north side of the High Street, between a land of John Brown on the east, and a land of the late James Baron on the west; a land sometime pertaining to William Brown, now to Thomas Tarbot, on the south, and another land of the said Thomas Fressall on the north. Which subjects the said John Fressall forthwith resigned in the hands of the bailie in favour of the foresaid Thomas Tarbot and Marjorie Brown his spouse in conjunct fee, and who are thereupon seised therein. Witnesses, Thomas Kyle, William Wan, John Blak, Thomas Broune and David Purves.

414. 1532 July 10. Sasine on resignation by William Cunningham of Craggans in favour of Thomas Mosman, goldsmith, burgess of Edinburgh and Margaret Forest his spouse of the said William's land lying on the south side of the Tolbooth, in the vennel called Bestis Wynd, east side the transe thereof, between a land of the late William Malcolme on the north, and a land of William Rutherfurd on the south: Paying yearly to the said William Cunningham an annual-rent of 40s. out of the foresaid land. Witnesses, Thomas Mosman, James Curll, Gabriel Cunyngham, Thomas Campbell, William Blak, Thomas Arnot and David Purves, serjeants.

415. 1532 July 10. Sasine on resignation by Thomas Mosman, with consent of Margaret Forest his spouse, in favour of William Cunyngham of Cragans, of an annual-rent of 40s., out of the said William's land, now pertaining to the said Thomas, and for which the said land was granted to the said spouses in fee, lying in Bestis Wynd, and bounded as before described. Same witnesses, and Mungo Tennent is bailie.

416. 1532 July 12. Sasine on resignation by William Broune, with consent of Isobella Bruse his spouse, in favour of Richard Hoppar, son and heir of the late Adam Hoppar, his heirs and assignees, heritably in fee, and to Katherine Ballentyne, mother to the said Richard, now spouse of Mr. Francis Boithuell, in liferent, of a certain foreland lying on the north side of the High Street, between a land of John Broune on the east, a land of the late James Baron on the west, and a land of Robert Bruse on the north. With court and the said Isobella's oath not to revoke. Witnesses, William Guld, Master Richard Boithuell, William Craike, Archibald Ramsay, William Young and Patrick

Lithqw. Symon Preston is bailie.

417. 12 July 1532, at the third hour after mid-day, Master Francis Boithuell pait and deliverit to William Broune and Isobella Bruse his spous, the soume of xv lib., in compleit payment of lx lib., promitit till him for the third pairt of the land aboue wryttin, quhilk thai had analiit to Richard Hoppar and his modder. And the said William and his spous grantit thame weill paiit of the said soume of lx lib., for the said third of the said land, and quytclamys the said Master Francis and his spous, their airis executouris and assignais, therof now and for evir. And the said William promist to seill his charter to be made therapon. The said Mr. Francis asked an instrument. Done upon the ground. Witnesses, William Young, James Anderson and William Hoppar.

418. 1532 July 18. Sasine on resignation by William Bog, son and heir of the late Andrew Bog, burgess, with consent of his spouse Margaret Lyndesay, in favour of Marion Adamson, relict of Edward Litill, burgess, of an annual-rent of 5 merks, out of a tenement of the late John Bonkill, now pertaining to the heirs of the said John and of the late James Baty, lying on the north side of the High Street, between a land of the late John Barcar on the east, a land of the late Alexander Harlaw, now pertaining to Duncan Wycht, on the west, the North Loch on the north, and the High Street on the south. With the said Margaret Lyndesay's oath not to revoke in time to come. Witnesses, William Litill, Alexander Kay, John Adamson, Cuthbert Fresall, William Watson, Thomas Arnot and Patrick Linlithqw, serjeants.

419. 1532 July 20. Sasine on resignation by Alexander Litill, with consent of Margaret Makcalzeane his spouse, in favour of Clement Litill, burgess, and Elizabeth Fischar his spouse, of an annual-rent of 10 merks, out of a land of James Makcalzeane, lying on the north side of the High Street, between a tenement of the late Walter Young on the east, and a tenement of the late John Ireland on the west. Witnesses, John Achinson, William Ogill, Thomas Gray, Thomas Arnot and David Purves. Under reversion of £100. Symon Preston is bailie.

420. 1532 July 24. Renunciation by Marion Baroun, spouse of Alexander Bruse and with his consent, of her conjunct-fee which she has of a tenement of land, with pertinents, lying in the burgh of Edinburgh, on the south side of the High Street thereof, between a tenement of the late Edward Bonkill on the east, a tenement of the late Walter Blaklok on the west, a land of the late William Ker on the south, and the King's public street on the north, by delivery in the hands of Mungo Tennent, bailie, in favour of Jonet Adamson, her heirs and assignees, for heritable sasine thereof to be made and given to the said Jonet. Moreover in a full and open court held before the said bailie, the foresaid Marion Baron, with consent of Alexander Bruse her spouse foresaid, constituted, as by the tenor of these presents she constitutes, Patrick Linlithqw, William Watson and Sir John Styrk, chaplain, her procurators with full power and liberty for her and in her name to resign the

foresaid tenement in the hands of one of the bailies of the said burgh, in favour of the said Jonet Adamson, her heirs and assignees for her infeftment in the same; with power to them to do all other things necessary in the premises, promising to hold the same as firm and stable as if done by the said Marion herself: With oath in court not to revoke in time to come. Upon which both parties asked instruments. Done within the burgh of Edinburgh, in the dwellinghouse of the said Alexander. Witnesses, Master James Scot, Thomas Purdy, Alexander Sinclair and David Purves.

421. 1532 July 24. Sasine on resignation by Alexander Bruse, son and heir of the late John Bruse, burgess of Edinburgh, with consent of Patrick Linlithqw, procurator and in name of Marion Baron, spouse of the said Alexander Bruse; also with consent and authority of Alexander Young, notary public, her friend, in favour of Jonet Adamson, relict of said John Bruse, her heirs and assignees, of the tenement of land described in the foregoing renunciation. Witnesses, William Adamson, Master James Scot, Sir John Styrk, chaplain, Robert Lokart, Thomas Purdy, William Watson and David Purves, serjeants.

422. The said 24 day of July 1532, Alexander Bruse oblist him faithfully, his airis, etc., till Jonet Adamson the relict of umquhile John Bruse, that notwithstanding that he had analiit his land and tenement, liand within this burgh, on the south side the gait, to the said Jonet Adamson, and had tane for the samyne the soume of iiijc merkis; nevertheless the said Alexander oblissis him faithfully, his airis, etc., that gif he happinis to deces within xl dayis efter his resignation of the samyne, or and the said Jonet be vexit or troublit be the law ony maner of way, or gif the said tenement be won fra hir; sua that scho may nocht bruike the samyne peciablie, efter the form of hir charter and alienatioun maid thairapon, that he sall content and pay agane till the said Jonet, hir airis, etc., the said soume of iiiic merkis that he resavit for the said tenement of land; togidder with jc merkis for costis staithis dammage and entress, gif scho sustenis ony thairintill. Apoune the quhilk the said Jonet askit instruments. Done upon the ground of the said tenement, in presence of the witnesses aforesaid.

423. 1532 July 27. Sasine on resignation by William Wilkeson in favour of John Quhite, notary public, of a small house or stable, with the loft above the same, in the north part of his land lying within the tenement of the late Luke Young, on the south side of the High Street, between a land of John Purves on the east, and the lands of Walter Scot and William Tod on the west, a land of the late John Bell on the south, and a land of John Cunninghame on the north. Witnesses, Master Robert Lauson, vicar of Egilsgreg, Patrick McQuhen, John Ramsay, James Cragmylie and Alexander Foular. Under reversion of £20. The said William asked an instrument upon the reversion. Mungo Tennent is bailie.

424. 1532 July 29. Robert Grahame, burgess of Edinburgh, procurator and in name of Master James Sutherland, Rector of Killerne,

assignee of Gilbert Grahame of Knokdoliane, passed to the personal presence of Archibald Colquhoun, and there forewarned the said Archibald to compear in the parish church of Dumbarton, on the 10th day of November, and there to receive the sum of xiij score and x merks, with a letter of tack of and upon the redemption of the lands of Wallaston and Ardochmore, with the pertinents lying in the Lordship of Levenax and shire of Dumbarton, conform to the tenor of a letter of reversion made upon the redemption of the said lands. Done in the burgh of Edinburgh, in the booth of Alexander Forstar; witnesses, the said Alexander Forstar, James Curry, Charles Murray and William Wallas.

425. 1532 July 30. Sasine to James Anderson on his cognition by Mungo Tennent, bailie, as heir of the deceased Lancelot *alias* Laurence Anderson his father, burgess, of Edinburgh, of an annual-rent of 40 shillings, out of a land of the late William Anderson, now pertaining to Alexander Young, lying on the south side of the High Street, within a tenement of the late Patrick Balbirny, now truly the tenement of David Tod, west side the trause thereof, between the lands of the late Thomas Edname and the said late Patrick, now the lands of the said David Tod, on the south and north: Which annual-rent of 40s. the said James Anderson resigned forthwith in the hands of the bailie, who thereupon gave sasine thereof to Alexander Young, notary public, burgess of Edinburgh, and Elizabeth Borthuik his spouse: With court and oath of the said James Anderson not to revoke in time to come. Witnesses, James Bassenden, Alexander Spens in Auldliston, Hugh Curry, Robert Lokkart, and Thomas Arnot, serjeant.

426. 1532 August 2. Sasine to Elizabeth Hoppar on her cognition by Symon Preston, bailie, as sister and heir of the late Alexander Hoppar, son and heir of the late Agnes Broune, of (1) the said Alexander's land lying on the south side of the High Street, between a land or tenement of the late Elizabeth Scot, Lady Manerston, on the east, a tenement of John Cant on the west, a land of Clement Litill on the south, and the foreland of the late Patrick Richartson on the north; (2) another land of the said late Alexander Hoppar, lying on the north side of the High Street, within a tenement of the late Richard Hoppar, his grandfather, between a land of the late James Baty on the north, and a land or mansion of the said late Richard Hoppar on the south. Witnesses, Edward Kincaid, Vincent Strathauchin, notary public, Clement Litill, William Stallis, John Arkittis, Alan Flemyng, William Edname and William Watsone, serjeant.

427. 1532 August 2. Sasine to Elizabeth Hoppar, on her cognition by Symon Preston, bailie, as daughter and heir of the late Master Henry Hoppar, of the foreland of the said late Master Henry, lying on the north side of the High Street, between a tenement of the late James Baty on the west, a land of Master Adam Otterburn on the north, and the king's public street on the south. The same witnesses as aforesaid.

428. 1532 August 5. Compeared personally a prudent woman, Elizabeth Carkettill, spouse of Adam Stewart, burgess of Edinburgh, who, with consent of the said Adam her spouse, constituted Sir John Stewart, chaplain, her procurator, to resign her annual-rent of 6 merks, out of a tenement of land of John Cokburne, lying on the south side of the High Street, between a land of James Preston on the east, and a land of Alexander Rynd on the west, in the hands of one of the bailies of the burgh of Edinburgh, in favour of Alexander Adamson and Jonet Cant his spouse, for sasine thereof to be given to them. Done in the dwelling house of the said Elizabeth, who asked and instrument. Witnesses, John Blacater, Patrick Keyne, and David Purves.

429. 1532 August 5. Sasine on resignation by Adam Stewart, burgess, with consent of Sir John Stewart, chaplain, procurator and in name of Elizabeth Carkettill, spouse of the said Adam, in favour of Alexander Adamson, burgess, and Jonet Cant his spouse, of an annual-rent of 6 merks, out of the foresaid tenement of John Cockburn son and heir of the late William Cockburn, lying and bounded as described in the foregoing procuratory of resignation. Witnesses, John Blacater, Patrick Keyne, William Liberton, Sir William Merschell and David Purves, serjeant.

430. 1532 August 5. Compeared personally Francis Inchecok, notary public, who confessed that he had received from William Liberton, elder, grateful payment of the sum of 10 merks, in part payment of £10 promised to him by the said William, for alienation and renunciation of his tenement of land, lying in the Cowgate, south side the High Street thereof, between the vennel called Raperlawis Wynd on the east, the lands of James Johnston on the west, the yard or land of the prebendaries of the collegiate Kirk o' Field on the south, and the King's public street on the north, in favour of the said William Liberton, his heirs and assignees. Moreover the said Francis and his spouse obliged them, their heirs, ptc., to refund to the said William Liberton and his heirs the said sum of 10 merks, in the event of the said William or his heirs being disturbed or molested in the peacable possession of the said tenement or any part thereof within 15 days after such molestation, without any impediment or obstacle whatsoever. Done upon the ground of the said tenement: Witnesses, John Murray, James Cuke, Master Robert Lauson, vicar of Eglisgreg, William Liberton, junior, Alexander Levington, David Purves, William Watson, and Patrick Linlithqw.

431. 1532 August 12. Which day, at 3 o'clock in the afternoon, Symon Preston, bailie, passed to the foresaid tenement of Francis Inchecok, lying in the Cowgate, between the vennel called Raperlawis Wynd on the east, and the lands of James Johnston on the west; and there gave heritable sasine of the said tenement to the said Francis Inchecok, his heirs and assignees; to be enjoyed by him as freely and peceably as the fee thereof was possessed by the late Robert Stanton: Which tenement the said Francis Inchecok resigned in the hands of the said bailie, who thereupon gave heritable state and sasine of the said tenement to William Liberton, elder, in Nether Liberton, his

heirs and assignees: Reserving the liferent thereof to the said Francis Inchecok, and Christian Dee his spouse, who also consents to the resignation of the fee in favour of William Liberton. Witnesses, John Ballentyne, Sir Alexander Cunynghame, chaplain, Alexander Levington, Francis Hardy and William Watson.

432. 1532 August 20. Sasine on resignation by John Michelson, son and heir of the late Christian Stallis, in favour of Thomas Michelson, burgess, and Jonet Anderson his spouse, of an annual-rent of 4 merks 6 shillings and 8 pence, out of the said John's lands lying contiguous on the south side of the High Street, in the end of a tenement of the late Robert Lauder, west side the trause thereof, between a land of the late John Lethame on the north, and the street of the Cowgate on the south. Witnesses, Alexander Baron, John Bell, John Anderson, Master Thomas Brown and John Coldon. Under reversion of £23. Patrick Baron is bailie.

433. 1532 August 29. Which day compeared personally Agnes Tweedy and Alexander Elphinston her spouse, who with one consent ratified and approved the alienation of an annual-rent of 6 merks, leviable yearly out of a land or tenement lying on the north side of the High Street, between a land of the late Sir Alexander Lauder of Blyth, knight, on the east, and a land of the late Alexander Bonkill on the west, made by Elizabeth Cranston and Geills Cranston, sisters and heirs of the late William Cranston of Rathobyres to Mungo Tennent and his spouse, conform to the tenor of their letters made thereupon. Moreover the said Agnes and Alexander her spouse renounced an annual-rent of 13s.4d. out of those six merks foresaid which they have: Reserving as in a certain instrument under the sign and subscription of Thomas Unthank, notary public, of date the 25 March 1466 is more fully contained. The said Agnes and Alexander renounced likewise a certain letter of reversion made by the late John Cranston to Alexander Twedy his predecessor, of and upon the redemption of the said annual-rent of 6 merks, in favour of the said Mungo Tennent, his heirs and assignees, for certain sums of money and other favours delivered to and bestowed upon them by the said Mungo. And in token of the said renunciation delivered the said instrument and letter of reversion to the foresaid Mungo. Moreover the said Agnes gave her bodily oath, the scriptures touched, not to revoke in time to come. Done in the booth of the common clerk: Witnesses, Symon Preston, Henry Levington, James McGill, James Adamson and Francis Wode.

434. 1532 Sept. 3. Sasine on resignation by Francis Aikman, lord fiar of the lands and tenements underwritten, in favour of James Henrison, of the fee of the said Francis Aikman's lands and tenements, lying on the south side of the High Street, between the trause of Peebles Wynd on the east, and the lands of the late Laurence Henrison on the west; the lands of John Hay on the north, and the king's public street of the Cowgate on the south. And forthwith James Henrison resigned his wester tenement

lying between his easter tenement and the common trause on
the east, and the lands of the late Laurence Henrison on the
west; the land of John Hay on the north, and the Cowgate on
the south, in the hands of Edward Kincaid, bailie, who gave
sasine thereof to Henry Lille, burgess, and Marion Forous his
spouse. The said bailie passed likewise to the easter tenement
of the said James, lying between the vennel of Bell's Wynd on
the east, and the said wester tenement on the west; the land
of John Hay on the north, and the Cowgate on the south; and
there the said James Henrison resigned his said easter tenement
in the hands of the bailie, who thereupon gave heirtable sasine
and conjunct-infeftment of the same to the foresaid Henry Lille
and Marion Forous his spouse, in special warrandice of his foresaid wester tenement. Witnesses, Sir Henry Lille, Stephen Bell,
Patrick McQuhen, Thomas Smyth, John Henrison, Patrick Lithqw,
Thomas Arnot and William Watson.
Moreover it was agreed between the said Henry and James Henrison, that it shall be lawful for the said James, his heirs and
assignees, to redeem the said tenement within 3 years, by
payment of the sum of 17 score merks to the said Henry, and
his heirs; and in the event of the non-redemption thereof within
3 years, the said Henry and his heirs shall possess and enjoy
the said tenement heritably for ever.

435. 1532 Sept. 5. Sasine on resignation by Thomas Borthik,
procurator and in name of William Lord Borthik, in favour of
William Sym, burgess, of the following subjects: (1) Small house
with vault thereof and loft above, lying within a tenement of
William Lord Borthik, on the south side of the High Street, between a tenement of Alexander Rynd on the east, and a tenement
of the late John Carkettill on the west; a land of the said Lord
Borthik lie Corshouse on the north, and a land of George Gude
on the south; (2) An annual-rent of 46 shillings and 8 pence,
out of the said land of George Gude lying within the said tenement, east side the transe thereof, between the said small house
on the north, and a waste land of the said tenement, now pertaining to David Gillaspy, on the south. (3) An annual-rent of
46 shillings and 8 pence, out of a land of the late David
Lithqw lying within the foresaid tenement of William Lord
Borthik, west side the trause thereof, between the Corshouse on
the north, and a land of the late John Glen, now pertaining
to Thomas Cuke on the south. Witnesses, Andrew Peirson, James
Arbuthnat, Alexander Levington, Thomas Arnot and William
Watson.

436. 1532 Sept. 6. Sasine on resignation by James Makcalzeane,
burgess, with consent of Marion Umphrason his spouse, in favour
of John Fyschar, burgess, and Isobella Wyndezettis his spouse,
of an annual-rent of 20 merks, out of the lands and buildings
of the late Robert Gray, now pertaining to Master Alexander
Dyk, lying contiguous on the south side of the Tolbooth, between
the cemetery of St. Giles church on the east, and the transe
of the vennel of Bestis Wynd on the west; a land of the late
William Bigholme on the south, the common land of the burgh
and a land of Marion Brown on the north: With the said Marion

Umfrason's oath not to revoke in time to come. Witnesses, Sir Alexander Scot, provost of Corstorphin, Master Thomas Makcalzeane, John Achinson, John Symson, Richard Young, Alexander Litill, Robert Meyne, Thomas Arnot, William Watson and David Purves. Symon Preston is bailie.

437. 1532 Sept. 6. Sasine on resignation by James Makcalzeane, in favour of himself and Marion Umfrason his spouse in conjunctfee, of an annual-rent of 8 merks, out of a land of James Preston, on the south side of the High Street, within a tenement of the late John Adamson, west side the transe thereof, between a land of the late Robert Vaus on the north, and a certain waste land on the south; the said transe on the east, and a land of the late Master Richard Robeson on the west. Witnesses, Master Thomas Makcalzeane, Alexander Litill, William Liberton, Thomas Arnot, William Watson and David Purves, serjeants. Symon Preston is bailie.

438. 1532 Sept. 9. Sasine on resignation by John Levington, brother and heir of the late James Levington, with consent of Christian Lamb his spouse, in favour of Sir John Kers, chaplain of the chapel of the hospital of our Lady in St. Mary Wynd, his heirs and assignees, of an annual-rent of 13 shillings and 4 pence, out of a land of the late William Ramsay, lying in the Cowgate, on the north side of the king's street thereof, between a land of the late Master David Vocat on the east, a land of the late Patrick Richartson on the west, and a certain waste land on the south, conform to the tenor of a charter to be made thereupon: With the oath of the said Cristina Lamb not to revoke in time to come. And forthwith the said Sir John Kers resigned the said annual-rent in the hands of Symon Preston, bailie, who thereupon gave sasine of the same to Cristina Haitly in her own name and of the other widows or beddrallis of the said hospital of our Lady, situated in St. Mary Wynd, and their successors, for the upkeep of one lamp burning yearly and mightly before the most holy Virgin Mary in the said chapel, and at the altar thereof in time of winter. Witnesses, Sirs Thomas Paterson, William Cady and David Purdy, chaplains, William Lowis, Martin Johnston, William Cunynghame, and Thomas Arnot.

439. 1532 Sept. 13. Resignation by Margaret Karnis, of her liferent which she has of a land or tenement of the late John Karnis, lying at the Over Bow, east side of the High Street thereof, between a land of James Harlaubankis on the north, and a land of the late David Laverok, now pertaining to David Purves, on the south; and this in favour of Alexander Auchinleck her son, lord fiar of the said land of tenement. Upon which the said Alexander asked an instrument. Witnesses, Andrew Wode, Thomas Tunno, John Anderson, Gawin Inglis and Thomas Arnot, serjeants. Resigned in the hands of Symon Preston, bailie.
The said Alexander Auchinlek promist till pay yeirly till Margaret Karnis his modir x merkis for the renuncing of hir lyfrent of the said land and tenement without instrument.
The quhilk day, in presens of the said baillie, Symon Preston, Andrew Wode declarit, that he and his wyf had tak and

assedation of all the bakland, with ane foirboth, a loft, and chalmer on the stair, maid till him be Margret Karnis, for all the dais of hir lyf; quhilk tak the said Alexander Auchinlek grantit of verite, and ratifiit and apprevit the samyne; and grantit faithfully till fulfill and keip the said tak till the said Andro and his spous, indurand his moderis lyftyme. And thereupon the said Andrew asked an instrument. Witnesses, the said Bailie, Thomas Tunno, John Anderson, Gawin Inglis and Thomas Arnot.

440. 1582 Sept. 17. Sasine on resignation by Marion Broune, in favour of herself and Hugh Douglas her spouse, of her land lying on the north side of the High Street, in the close of the late William Cathkin, east side the trause thereof, between a land ( ) on the south, and a waste land ( ) on the north: With court and oath of the said Marion not to revoke in time to come. Witnesses, John Henrison, elder, John Douglas, John Henrison, younger, William Bois, John Fairly and Thomas Arnot, serjeant.

441. 1532 Sept. 19. Compeared personally Thomas Litill, burgess, and of his own certain knowledge and free will, faithfully promised to make and deliver to Alexander Litill, a letter of reversion upon the redemption of an annual-rent of 10 merks; which annual-rent the said Alexander had previously alienated to the said Clement, yearly upliftable out of a land of James McCalzean, containing the sum of £100; to be made in the surest form. Done in the booth of the common clerk; Witnesses, Vincent Strathauchin, Alexander Anderson and Francis Wode.

442. 1532 Sept. 20. Compeared personally William Kynnard and constituted John Maine and James Kynnard, conjointly and severally, his procurators, with power of substitution in all his actions, causes and complaints; and particularly to prosecute Robert Broune, John Kennedy and James Tait, before whatsoever lords justices, as well secular as spiritual, for the sums due by them to the said William; and to grant acquittances upon receipts, etc., and all other things necessary to be done in the premises, promising to hold the same as firm and stable as if done by himself. Done in the dwellinghouse of the notary, in presence of Sirs John Kers and William Cady, chaplains, John Mayne and James Kynnard.

443. 1532 Sept. 20. James Henrison, of his awin fre motif will, gevis and grantis to Frances Aikman and his airis, his thre aikeris of land of the Burrowmuir, frelie to be disponit be the said Frances, and brukait be him as he mycht haif done him self; the said Frances biggand a barn and kill, efter the forme of the actis of the toune: And transferis all rycht that he has or may haif of the said thre aikeris of land, with thair pertinentis, fra him, and all utheris his airis or assignais, to the said Frances, his airis and assignais for evir. And attour the said James Henrison makis and constitutis the said Francęs his cessionar and assignay, in and to all and sundry his movable gudis quhatsumevir, beand within the realme of Scotland; and to all and sundry his malis and profittis and

dewiteis of his landis liand within this burgh, on the west syde Bestis Wynd; and gevis frelie to the said Frances all his landis eftir his deces, in cais he deces without airis of his body gottin; and transferis all rycht therof fra him and all utheris his airis or assignais in and to the said Francis, and his airis, for evir: And that for certain soumes of money that he had ressavit fra the said Frances, and was awand till him in tymes bygane. And this to be extendit in the best and largest form that can be maid or devisit. Upon which the said Frances asked an instrument. Done in the dwellinghouse of the notary, in presence of Sirs John Kers, William Cady and Henry Balfour, chaplains.

444. 1532 Sept. 27. Renunciation by Jonet Giffart, relict of William Kirkcaldie of Grange, in favour of Andrew Murray, son and heir of the late Master John Murray of Blakbarony, of her conjunct-fee, which she has of the lands called The Bruse's Lands, lying within the burgh of Kinghorn, with all right, claim of right, property and possession, which she has or can in anywise claim thereto forever. Moreover the said Jonet gave her bodily oath, the scriptures touched, not to revoke in time to come. Done in the booth of the common clerk of Edinburgh, in presence of Sir James Dennyston, chaplain, Thomas Stanhouse, William Edname, Walter Ramsay, John Craig, Francis Wode and Vincent Strathauchin, notary public.

445. 1532 Sept. 27. Sasine on resignation by John Scharp, with consent of Agnes Ewin his spouse, in favour of David Carnegy, burgess of Dundee, his heirs and assignees, of the said John Scharp's land or tenement, in which he now dwells, lying on the south side of the High Street, between a land of Alexander Pennycuke on the east, and a land of James Blak on the west; a land of Gilbert Welsche on the north, and the king's public street of the Cowgate and another land of the said John Scharp on the south. Witnesses, Master William Scot, Alexander Baron, Walter Scot, James Fairly, Stephen Bell, John Coldane, Alexander Scot, and William Watson, serjeant: With the said Agnes Ewin's oath not to revoke in time to come. And the said David Carnegy promised to make a reversion to the said John and his spouse, their heirs, etc., upon the redemption of the said land or tenement, containing the sum of £94. Patrick Baron is bailie.
The said hour and witnesses James Fairlie, in name of Henry Merschell protested, that whatever shall be done by John Scharp in the alienation of his land to David Carnegy, shall not be to the prejudice of the said Henry, as to the sum of £60, in which sum the said John Scharp is obliged to the said Henry, as in the Act of Court is more fully contained; and for remeid of law when and where it effeirs.

446. 1532 Sept. 28. Johne Scharp, baxter, burgess of Edinburgh, oblist him faithfully till ane honest man David Carnegy, burgess of Dundee, till content and pay till the said David xij merkis of maill for his land, quhilk he dwells in, in the year, gif it happinis that he redeme nocht the samyne betuix this and Witsonday nixt to come. Witnesses, Master William Scot, Vincent

Strathauchin, notary public and George Forster.

447. 1532 Oct. 11. Sasine to Issobella Bog, daughter and heir of the late Andrew Bog, burgess, on her cognition by William Lauder, bailie, in and to an annual-rent of 6 shillings and 8 pence, out of the easter half of a tenement of William Dawson, lying on the south side of the High Street, between a tenement of the late George Robison on the east, and a tenement of the late William Adamson on the west; a land of George Talzefeir on the south, and the king's public street on the north. And forthwith the said Isobella Bog resigned in the hands of the bailie the following subjects, namely a tavern and two booths of the foresaid tenement; together with the foresaid annual-rent of 6s.8d.: Which done the said William Lauder, bailie, gave heritable sasine and conjoint-infeftment of the said subjects to William Tod, wax maker, burgess of Edinburgh, and Margaret Lesly his spouse: With the said Isobella's oath, the scriptures touched, not to revoke in time to come. Witnesses, Sir David Dalglesche, Adam Hepburne, Sir Bartholomew Robison, James Gray, John Wode, Patrick Lithqw and James Johnston *alias* Edinburgh, serjeants.

448. 1532 Oct. 14. Sasine on resignation by John Scharp, with consent of Agnes Ewin his spouse, in favour of Peter Ramsay, his heirs and assignees, of an annual-rent of £10., out of the said John Scharp, baker, his lands lying on the south side of the High Street, between a land of John Fausyde on the east, and a certain waste land on the west; the waste land of Alexander Pennycuke and a built land of the said John Scharp on the north, and the street of the Cowgate on the south. Under reversion of £114.0.4d. whensoever the said John Scharp, his heirs or assignees shall pay to the said Peter, his heirs or assignees, then they shall have regress in and to the said annual-rent of £10 without impediment. Witnesses, Thomas Ramsay, John Rayntoun, Alexander Heriot, Robert Gray, John Dykson, Stephen Bell, James Johnston *alias* Edinburgh and Patrick Lithqw, serjeants. William Lauder is bailie. Under reversion of £113. Henry Marschell protested.

449. 1532 Oct. 25. Sasine on resignation by Robert Forstar, son and heir of the late Elizabeth Dunsyar, with consent of his beloved father Alexander Forstar, burgess of Striviling, in favour of Sir Thomas Mailuill, chaplain, his heirs and assignees of an annual-rent of £10, out of the foreland of a tenement of the said Robert Forstar, lying on the north side of the High Street, between a land or tenement of the late Archibald Napier of Merzenistoun on the east, and a tenement of the late Margaret Broune on the west: Also out of his other land lying within his said tenement, between a land of the late William Dunsyar on the north, and a land of the late David Mailuill on the south. Which annual-rent of £10, the said Sir Thomas Mailuill resigned in the hands of William Rynd, bailie, who thereupon gave sasine thereof to Sir George Kynloch, chaplain, in name of the church, conform to the tenor of a foundation to be made thereupon. Witnesses, William Watson, Thomas Rynd, Robert

Mailuill, James Eklis, Walter Lokart, Robert Forsyth, John Spittall, and David Purves, serjeant. The said Sir Thomas promised to give to the said Robert Forstar a letter of reversion upon the redemption of the said annual-rent of £10, containing the sum of 210 merks. William Rynd is bailie.

450. 1532 Oct. 26. Sasine on resignation by Robert Forstar, with consent of Alexander Forstar, burgess of Stirling, in favour of Thomas Ramsay and Marion Ramsay his spouse, of the said Robert's merchant booth, in which Thomas Ramsay now dwells, lying within a certain land in the Buithraw, on the south side of the High Street, between a land of Alexander Mauchane on the east, and a land of the late Francis Peebles on the west. Witnesses, John Achinson, notary public, Clement Litill, Sir John Clerk, chaplain; William Watson, Thomas Arnot, David Purves, and Patrick Lithqw, serjeants. Moreover the said Thomas and his spouse promised to the said Robert to make a letter of reversion to him and his heirs, etc., upon the redemption of the said booth, containing the sum of 100 merks. William Rynd is bailie.

451. 1532 Oct. 26. Sasine on resignation by Robert Forstar above designed, with consent of Alexander Forstar, burgess of Stirling, his father, in favour of Clement Litill, burgess, and Elizabeth Fischar his spouse, of the merchant booth in which Alexander Litill now dwells: Also the over loft thereof, lying in Buithraw, between the land of Alexander Mauchane on the east, and the land of the late Francis Peebles on the west: Under reversion of 100 merks. Same bailie and witness as aforesaid.

452. 1532 Oct. 31. Sasine on renunciation by Marion Adamson, relict of Edward Litill, of her conjunct-fee of the following subjects, in favour of William Litill, son of the said Edward, and on cognition of him as heir of his said father by William Anderson, bailie, in and to (1) the said Edward Litill's tenement lying on the south side of the High Street, between a tenement of Alexander Elphinston and his spouse on the east, and a land of the late Connall Young on the west: reserving the liferent of the said Marion. And forthwith the said William Litill resigned the same tenement in the hands of the bailie in favour of himself and of Margaret Murray his affianced spouse, who are thereupon seised therein heritably in conjunct-fee: Reserving as aforesaid; (2) a certain land or building lying within a tenement of John Blakstok on the north side of the High Street, between a tenement of the late William Foular on the east, and a tenement of Alexander Cant on the west: which land the said William Litill also resigned in favour of himself and of Margaret Murray his affianced spouse, in the hands of William Anderson, bailie, who forthwith gave heritable sasine and conjunct-infeftment thereof to the said William and his affianced spouse: Reserving thereof the liferent to Marion Adamson. Witnesses, Andrew Murray, James Hoppar, Cuthbert Fresall, William Grahame, John Anderson, Hugh Wallas and David Purves.

453. 1532 Oct. 31. Sasine on resignation by Robert Forstar, son of

the late Elizabeth Dunsyre, with consent of Alexander Forstar, burgess of Stirling, his father, in favour of John Barclay and Elizabeth Mudy his spouse, of (1) An annual-rent of 9 merks out of a land or mansion of the said John Barclay called the Corshouse, lying within a tenement of the late Jonet alias Dowy Lyntoun, on the south side of the High Street, between a land of the late Master John Murray on the east, and a land of the late John Davidson on the west, lying in the said tenement between a land of the late William Fausyde on the east, and a land of the late Archibald Todryk on the west; a waste land of the late Robert Cokson on the north, and a land or yard of James Archbishop of St. Andrews on the south; (2) an annual-rent of 6 merks out of another land of the said John Barclay, lying within the said tenement, west side the transe thereof, between a land of William Lyndesay on the north, and a waste land of the said Robert Cokson on the south. Witnesses, William Watson, Robert Henrison, John Anderson, John Greinhill, Robert Forsyth, Walter Coupar; Thomas Arnot, David Purves and William Watson, serjeants. Under reversion of the sum of 207 merks 6s. and 8d. William Anderson is bailie.

454. 1532 Nov. 4. Sasine to John Loch, son and heir of the late John Loch, burgess, on his cognition by William Anderson, bailie, as heir foresaid, of the said deceased John's land, lying on the south side of the High Street, in the vennel of the Friars Preachers, west side the transe thereof, between a land of the late Thomas Richartson on the north, and another land of the said John Loch on the south. Which land the said John Loch forthwith resigned in the hands of the bailie, who thereupon gave sasine thereof to James Hill, burgess, and Jonet Flemyn his spouse in conjunct-fee, the survivor of them, etc. Witnesses, John Vchiltrie of Canach, William Richartson, Edward Bissait, and Patrick Lithqw.
Under reversion of jc. lib. viz. iiijxx. unicornis and xl crownis of the sun, price of the pece xxs. And quhat expenssis that the said James makis necessar on the said house salbe allowit with the principal soume.

455. 1532 Nov. 5. Sasine on resignation by Maurice Coupland, burgess, with consent of Margaret Haliburton his spouse, in favour of Sir John Mekill, chaplain, in name of the altar of Sts. Bartholomew and Severin pertaining to the weaver craft, in name and for the part of the deacon and other brethren of the said craft, and his successors in office, of an annual-rent of 26s.8d., out of a land of the said Maurice lying within a tenement of the late Patrick Ritchartson on the south side of the High Street, between a tenement of the late Elizabeth Scot, Lady Manerston on the east, and a tenement of John Cant on the west; west side the trause thereof, between a land of Clement Litill on the north, and a land of James Home on the south. With the oath of the said Margaret not to revoke in time coming. Witnesses, Thomas Rynd, John Matheson, William Hill, John Scot, Andrew Mekill, George Mekill, James Eklis, and James Johnston alias Edinburgh, serjeant. Under reversion of £20. William Rynd is bailie.

456. 1532 Nov. 7. Sasine to George Forstar on his cognition by William Rynd, bailie, as heir of the late (   ) Thomas Forstar of Strathenry his father, of a certain land on the north side of the High Street, in Halkerston's Wynd, west side the transe thereof, between a land of the late William Currour on the south, and a land of the late William Bassinden on the north: Also of another land of the said Thomas Forstar, lying in Halkerston's Wynd, east side the transe thereof, between a land of the late John Baty on the north, and a land of the late William Halkerston on the south. Witnesses, Sir William Watson, Gilbert Anderson, Andrew Haithwy, Thomas Rynd and William Watson, serjeant.

457. 1532 Nov. 27. Sasine on resignation by John Marlzeon, calsay maker, in favour of himself and Elizabeth Forstar his affianced spouse, of his land lying within the wester tenement of the late Thomas Butlar, west side the transe thereof, between a land of the late John Glen on the north, and a land of the late John Con on the south. Witnesses, David Kyncaid, Norman Ramsay, Henry Quhite, John Wedderburn, Edward Kyncaid, Francis Aikman, and William Watson. William Lauder is bailie.

458. 1532 Nov. 27. Compeared personally Master Adam Otterburn of Auldhame and confessed, that the £5 lands of Quhitelaw, lying in the barony of (   ) and shire of (   ), which he has from the Lord of Dundas, are now lawfully redeemed from him by Andrew Mowbray, son and heir of the late Andrew Mowbray, burgess of Edinburgh; and therefore the said Master Adam renounced the said £5 land of Quhitelaw in favour of the said Andrew Mowbray, with all right, claim of right, property and possession thereof forever. Done in the chamber of the official clerk of the burgh of Edinburgh, in presence of Master Thomas Marjoribanks, Michael Tullois, John Chancellor, ( ) Dunlop, and (   ) Dykson.

459. 1532 Dec. 3. Sasine on resignation by Margaret Currour, daughter and one of the heirs of the late John Currour, burgess, with consent of George Craik her spouse, in favour of John Henrison and Jonet Wilson his spouse, of the said Margaret's easter booth, with the penteis or shop on the north side thereof, in which John Henrison now dwells, lying within a land of the said Margaret Currour, beyond the Overbow, south side the High Street thereof, between a land of the late David Davidson on the east, and a land of the late Alexander Reid on the west; the waste land of the said late John Currour on the south, and the king's public street on the north: Together with the residue of the said land in special warrandice. With court and the oath of the said Margaret not to revoke in time to come. Witnesses, Henry Cranston, William Akinheid, Selestus Forstar, Patrick Atkin, William Craik, Andrew Quhite, Richard Wardlaw, Robert Henrison, and David Purves, serjeant. William Rynd is bailie.

460. 1532 Dec. 11. Sasine on resignation by Thomas Mosman, with consent of Margaret Forest his spouse, in favour of George

Mosman and Margaret Rutherfurd his spouse, of a land of the said Thomas lying on the south side of the High Street, in the vennel commonly called Bestis Wynd, east side the transe thereof, between a land of the late William Malcome on the north, and a land of William Rutherfurd on the south. Witnesses, John Aslowane, Thomas Rynd, Andrew Purves, and David Purves, with divers others. William Rynd is bailie.

461. 1532 Dec. 12. Sasine on resignation by Thomas Laverok, burgess, with consent of Jonet Thomson his spouse, in favour of William Pettygreif, executor of the late Master William Baillie, rector of Lestalrig, of an annual-rent of 20 merks, out of a tenement of the said Thomas Laverok lying in the Cowgate, south side thereof, between the lands of Lady Jonet Kennedy and the late Earl of Cassillis, now pertaining to the heirs of the late John Ireland on the east, and the lands of Sir John Duncan and David Heriot on the west; the croft pertaining to the Sisters of St. Kathrine of the Senis on the south, and the king's public street of the Cowgate on the north. Which annual-rent of 20 merks the said William Pettygreif forthwith resigned in the hands of William Rynd, bailie, who gave sasine thereof to Sir John Howison, chaplain, in name of the church and his successors, chaplains of the service founded by the said late Master William Baillie, and his executors and factors in the collegiate church of the blessed virgin Mary of Lestalrig. Moreover the said William Pettigreif, executor of the said Master William promised to make and deliver forthwith to the said Thomas Laverok, his heirs and assignees, a letter of reversion upon the redemption of the said annual-rent of 20 merks, as follows in the vulgar tongue:- It salbe lafull to the said Thomas Laverok, his airis or assignais till redeme the annual-rent of xx merkis quhilk he analiit to the executouris of umquhile Master William Ballie, for the payment of tua hundred merkis, to be paiit at ains or at ij termes, viz. quhenevir he or his airis paiis a hundreth merkis that thai sall haif x merkis of annuell renuncit to thame and syklyk another jc. merkis the tother x merkis of annuell redemit. Or to pay haill togidder as said is. And thereupon the said executor and Sir John Howison and Thomas Laverok asked instruments upon the reversion. Witnesses, Thomas Glendynyng, John Lauson, Alexander Purves, Adam Gibson, Thomas Knox, and David Purves. William Rynd is bailie.

462. 1532 Dec. 12. Sasine on resignation by Thomas Laverok, burgess, with consent of Jonet Thomson his spouse, in favour of David Laverok, son and apparent heir of the said Thomas, and the heirs lawfully to be procreated of his body, whom failing, his lawful and nearest heirs whomsoever, of the wester half part of the foreland of the said Thomas Laverok's tenement, lying in the Cowgate, on the south side thereof, between the lands of Lady Jonet Kennedy and a land of the late Earl of Cassillis, now pertaining to the heirs of the late John Irland, on the east, and the lands of Sir John Duncan and David Heriot on the west; the croft pertaining to the Sisters of St. Kathrine of the Senis on the south, and the king's public street of the

Cowgate on the north; containing a hall, chamber and two cellars under the same, with the penteis: Also the land called the Werkhouse lying within the said tenement, east side the transe thereof, between the barn and the cowbill stane on the north, and another small house on the south; with the use of the well or draw-well. Reserving the liferent of the said subjects to the said Thomas Laverock and his spouse. Witnesses, Master William Gibson, Dean of Lestalrig, William Pettygreif, Thomas Glendynyng, John Lauson, Alexander Purves, Sir John Howison, chaplain, Thomas Knox, and David Purves.

463. 1532 Dec. 12. Sasine on resignation by Thomas Laverock, with consent of Jonet Thomson his spouse, in favour of Ninian Laverock, son of the said Thomas and Jonet, and the lawful heirs to be procreated of his body, whom failing his lawful and nearest heirs whomsoever, of the wester half part of the foreland of the foresaid tenement lying in the Cowgate and bounded as before described, containing as specified in the sasine to David Laverok; paying yearly the annual-rents out of the said tenement to the persons whomsoever to whom they are due: Reserving the liferent of the foresaid Thomas and Jonet. Same witnesses.

464. 1532 Dec. 12. Sasine on resignation by Thomas Laverok, with consent of Jonet Thomson his spouse, in favour of Gilbert Laverok their son, and the heirs of his body lawfully to be procreated, whom failing, his lawful and nearest heirs whomsoever, of the south cellars of the said Thomas Laverok's back land, now a malt barn, with cowbill and use of the well: Also of a small land with the loft above the same, on the south side of the backland lie Werkhouse of the said tenement: Together with the kiln of the whole waste land of the said tenement, between the said Werkhouse on the north, and the croft of the Sisters of St. Kathrine of the Senis on the south: The said Gilbert paying yearly the annual-rents due out of the said tenement, to whatsoever persons have right to the same: Reserving the liferent as aforesaid. Same witnesses. William Rynd is bailie.

465. 1532 Dec. 16. Sasine on resignation by John Malcome, son and heir of the late William Malcome, in favour of Sir Robert Robertoun, chaplain, his heirs and assignees, of an annual-rent of 40 shillings, out of the said John Malcome's land, lying on the north side of the High Street, in Malcome's Close, east side the transe thereof, between a land of Thomas Paterson on the south, and the yard of John Anderson on the north. Witnesses, Robert Clerk, John Henderson, Duncan Fillane, and David Purves, serjeant. Under reversion of £30. William Anderson is bailie.

466. 1532 Dec. 19. Sasine on resignation by John Cokburn, son and heir of the late William Cokburn, in favour of John Broune in Anstruther, of an annual-rent of 40 shillings out of the said John Cokburn's tenement lying on the south side of the High Street, between a land of John Preston on the east, and a tenement of Alexander Rynd on the west; a land of William

Pacok on the south, and the king's public street on the north. Witnesses, Patrick Baron, Alexander Spens, Master John Spens, John Coldon, Alexander Kay, Alexander Pery, and Patrick Lithqw, serjeant. Under reversion of £30. John Cokburn asked (an instrument). William Anderson is bailie.

467. 1532-3 Jan. 17. William Rynd, bailie, passed to a tenement of the late James Archbukill, lying in the burgh of Edinburgh, between a tenement of the late John Irland on the east, and a land of the late John Mason on the west; and there Cristina Wyndezettis, relict of the said James Archbukill, with consent of John Young now her spouse, renounced and dimitted in the hands of the said bailie her conjunct-fee, which she had of the foreland of the said tenement: As also her conjunct-fee of a land and mansion lying within the said tenement, between a land of Robert Adamson on the south, and a land of the said John Irland on the north, in favour of John Archbukill, son and heir of the said late John Arbukill, for sasine of the said subjects to be given to him. And forthwith the said William Rynd, bailie, cognosced and entered the said John Archbukill, son and heir of the foresaid late John Arbukill, in and to the foreland, backland and mansion above specified, with their pertinents: Which foreland, backland and mansion the said John Archbukill instantly resigned in the hands of the bailie, who thereupon gave heritable sasine and conjunct-infeftment of the same to the said John Archbukill and Marjory Symson his affianced spouse: Reserving the liferent thereof to the foresaid Cristina Wyndezettis. Witnesses, James Young, John Symson, Thomas Rynd, James Styrk, William Young, and Thomas Arnot.

468. 1532-3 Jan. 23. Sasine on resignation by Robert Forstar, son and heir of the late Elizabeth Dunsyar, with consent of Alexander Forstar his father, in favour of Katrine Greg, spouse of the said Alexander, during her lifetime, and after her decease to the said Robert, his heirs and assignees, of the foreland and backland of the said Robert Forstar's tenement lying on the north side of the High Street, between a tenement of the late Archibald Napier of Merzemiston on the east, and a tenement of the late Margaret Broune on the west. Witnesses, Thomas Forstar, Andrew Rutherfurd, John McCraw, Alexander Callander, John Broun, Sir Bartholomew Robison, Thomas Arnot and Hugh Wallas, serjeants. William Lauder is bailie.

469. 1532-3 Feb. 7. Sasine on resignation by James Cant, in favour of himself and Margaret Makgill his spouse, of the backlands of his tenement lying on the south side of the High Street, between a tenement of the late Sir Thomas Halkerston, Provost of Creichton, on the east, and a tenement of the late Edward Bonkill on the west. Witnesses, John Marjoribanks, William Loch, James McGill, William Watson and Thomas Arnot, serjeants. Master David Irland is bailie.

470. 1532-3 Feb. 15. Sasine on precept from chancery in favour of Master John Chepman as lawful and nearest heir of the late Walter Chepman, burgess of Edinburgh, his uncle, of a tenement of the said late Walter Chepman lying on the south side of the

High Street, in the vennel of the Friars Preachers, west side the transe thereof, between a land of the late William Cottis on the south, and the king's common way on the north; the trause of the said vennel on the east, and the land or tenement formerly of the abbot and convent of Melrose, now pertaining to the provost of the collegiate church of Creichton, on the west. (2) Of a land and house, with pertinents, lying immediately above the pend and entrance of the said vennel, between a land of the late William Currour on the east, and the said tenement of the said Walter Chepman on the west. (3) The great yard of a tenement of the said Walter; together with the house newly built in the said yard, on the west side thereof, between the old houses and buildings in the south side of the said yard, with all their pertinents, lying between the wall of the fosse of the small yard or garden of the said tenement on the north, and the common passage on the south: Which tenement lies on the Cowgate, on the south side of the street thereof, between a tenement of Patrick Flemyn on the east, and a tenement of the late William Halkerston on the west. (4) A land and mansion previously occupied by the late John Cokburn lying within a tenement of the late Peter Marche, between a tenement of the late William Cathkin on the north, and the foreland of the said tenement on the south, a land of the Archbishop of Glasgow on the east, and a land of the late William Halkerston on the west. (5) The tavern of the fore-land of the said tenement of Peter Marche, with the cellar and back-land adjacent thereto; together with the merchant booth lying in the said foreland, immediately above the said tavern, with all their pertinents. (6) An annual-rent of 20 shillings, out of a land and houses of the said Peter Marche's tenement lying between the land and tenement of the said Archbishop of Glasgow on the east, and the land of the late William Halkerston on the west: Reserving the liferent of the foresaid first tenement and the land above the pend, with the yard foresaid and houses thereof, to Agnes Cokburne relict of the said Walter Chepman: Reserving also the liferent of the foresaid backland, tavern, booth and annual-rent of 20 shillings, to (   ) Forest, relict of the said late John Cokburn. Witnesses, John Barclay, Richard Blaklok, Alexander Spens, Robert Law, David Chepman, William Tod, Robert Spottiswode, Robert Walkar, James Cant, William Riche, William Chepman, Richard Thomson, James Gray, Thomas Mabane, and Patrick Linlithqw, serjeant.

471. 1532-3 Feb. 15. William Lauder, bailie, passed to the lands and buildings, sometime pertaining to Walter Chepman, lying upon the common moor of the burgh of Edinburgh on the north side of the church of St. Katrine of the Senis, containing one acre of land, with barn and kiln, and other houses upon the same, built and to be built, between the lands of the said common moor on the east south and west, and the North (?South) Loch of the said burgh on the north; and there the said bailie, in virtue of office, and by mandate of the provost, bailies and council of the said burgh, gave heritable state and sasine of the said acre of land, containing as above, to Master John

Chepman, burgess, his heirs and assignees. Moreover the said William Lauder, bailie, passed to another part of the arable land of the said common moor, next to the first land, lying towards the south, containing 3 acres of land with pertinents, between the Powburn on the south, and the land of the said common moor on the north, the arable lands of the said moor on the east, and the other arable acres thereof on the west; and there the bailie gave state and sasine of the foresaid 3 acres of land to the said Master John Chepman, his heirs and assignees. Witnesses, John Chepman, William Chepman, David Chepman, Robert Law, Nicholas Chalmer, John Gourlaw, Thomas Mabane, Robert Walkar, James Gray, James Greif, and Patrick Linlithqw.

472. 1532-3 Feb. 21. Renunciation by Agnes Stewart, spouse of John Vernour, in favour of Anthony Brusset, burgess, and Agnes his spouse, of the said Agnes Stewart's conjunct-fee which she has of a certain land or tenement lying on the south side of the High Street of the Cowgate, between a tenement of the late Walter Chepman on the east, and a land or tenement of William Doby on the west; the croft of the Sisters of St. Katrine of the Senis on the south, and the king's public street of the Cowgate on the north. With court, and oath of the said Agnes not to revoke in time to come. Done within the burgh of Edinburgh in the house of the said John Vernour, in presence of David Wallas, John Gray, Robert Law, Laurence Flemyn, John Wynton, Hugh Wallas and Thomas Arnot.

473. 1532-3 Feb. 21. Sasine on resignation by John Vernour in favour of Anthony Brussat, burgess, and Agnes Eldar his spouse, of the said John Vernour's tenement, lying in the Cowgate and bounded as above described. Same witnesses. William Lauder is bailie.

474. 1532-3 Feb. 21. Sasine on resignation by John Vernour, in favour of Anthony Brussat and Agnes Eldar, his spouse, of the said John's land or tenement lying on the south side of the High Street of the Cowgate, between a tenement of the late Walter Chepman on the east, a tenement of William Doby on the west, and the croft of the Sisters of St. Katrine of the Senis on the south, and the public street of the Cowgate on the north. Witnesses, David Wallas, John Gray, Robert Law, Laurence Flemyng, John Wynton, Hugh Wallas and Thomas Arnot. William Lauder is bailie.

475. 1532-3 Feb. 21. Sasine on resignation by Anthony Brussat, burgess, in favour of himself and Agnes Eldar his spouse, of (1) the said Anthony's small land and yard, lying on the south side of the High Street, in Peebles Wynd, west side the transe thereof, between a land of Robert Law on the north, and a land (   ) on the south; (2) an annual-rent of 2 merks, out of a land of Andrew Lichtoun, lying within a tenement of William Lauder, west side the trause thereof, between a land of the said William Lauder on the north, and a land of the said Anthony Brussat on the south. Same bailie and witnesses as aforesaid.

476. 1532-3 Feb. 21. Sasine on resignation by Anthony Brussat, burgess, in favour of Agnes Eldar his spouse, of his land and mansion lying within a tenement of William Lauder, bailie, on the south side of the High Street, between a land of William Adamson on the east, and a land of Mary Magdalene on the west; west side the transe thereof, between the foreland of the said tenement on the north, and a land (   ) on the south. Same bailie and witnesses as above.

477. 1532-3 March 22. Sasine on renunciation of her liferent by Marion Crukschank, relict of John Robison, burgess, in favour of Jonet Robison, daughter and heir of the said late John Robison, and on her cognition by William Lauder, bailie, as heir foresaid, in and to a certain land lying within a tenement of the late John Bruse on the south side of the High Street, between a tenement of the late Edward Bonkill in the east, and a tenement of the late Walter Blaklok on the west, lying in the lower end of the said tenement, between the lands of the late Robert Forest on the north and south, a land of the said Edward Bonkill on the east, and a land of Duncan Wicht on the west. Witnesses, William Lauder, younger, David Gardun, William Watson, Hugh Wallas and Thomas Arnot, serjeants. Reserving the liferent of the said Marion. William Lauder is bailie.

478. 1533 March 26. Sasine to James Kyle, son and heir of the late Walter Kyle, on renunciation in his favour of her conjunct-fee by Margaret Broune, relict of the said Walter, and on the said James Kyle's cognition by William Anderson, bailie, as heir of his said father, in and to the following subjects: (1) a certain land or tenement lying below the castle wall, on the north side of the High Street, between a land of the late Andrew Sym on the east, the castell bank on the north, and the king's public street on the south. (2) A certain land lying within a tenement of the late David Knox, on the north side of the High Street, between a tenement of the deceased Symon Doweill on the east, and a tenement of the late Archibald Preston on the west; west side the transe of the said tenement, between the lands of the said late David Knox on the south and north. (3) A land lying within a tenement of William Anderson on the south side of the Market Cross and the High Street, between a land of Archibald Williamson on the east, and a land of the late John Adamson on the west; east side the transe of the said tenement, betweeen a land of the late James Fairlye on the south, and a land of the late George Matheson on the north. With the said Margaret Brown's oath in court, the scriptures touched, not to revoke. Witnesses, James Weir, James Curry, James Hardgrip, John Kyle, George Kyle, John Duncane, John Litster, Laurence Broune, and David Purves, serjeant.

479. 1533 March 23. Sasine on resignation by Jonet Robison, daughter and heir of the late John Robison, with consent of Marion Crukschank her mother, relict of the said John Robison, in favour of David Gardnar and Margaret Ramsay his spouse, of the said resigner's land lying within a tenement of the late

156   PROTOCOL BOOK

John Bruse, on the south side of the High Street, between a tenement of the late Edward Bonkill on the east, and a tenement of the late Walter Blaklok on the west; in the lower end of the said tenement, between the lands of Robert Forest on the south and north. Under reversion of £20, to be paid in one day out of their own proper goods. Witnesses, George Burt, William Lauder, younger, William Burt, Thomas Scot, and Thomas Arnot, serjeant. William Lauder is bailie.

480. 1533 April 8. Sasine on precept from chancery in favour of Henry Merschell, as lawful and nearest heir of the late John Merschell, his father, of an annual-rent of 40 shillings, out of a tenement of the late Archibald Forstar of Corstorphine, lying on the south side of the High Street, between the vennel of Forstar's Wynd on the east, and a land now pertaining to William Raa on the west. Witnesses, Mungo Tennent, James McGill, James Fairly, Thomas Bertrame, James Stevinson; David Purves, William Watson and Patrick Lithqw, serjeants. Master David Irland is bailie.

481. 1533 April 11. Sasine on resignation by Duncan Wicht, in favour of Beatrix Wicht, his daughter, of the backland of the said Duncan's tenement lying on the north side of the High Street, between a land of the late James Baty on the east, and a land of the late George Halkerston on the west; west side the transe of said tenement, between his other back land on the south, and a land of David Kincaid on the north: Reserving the liferent thereof to the said Duncan Wicht. Witnesses, William Pettigreif, Michael Blythe, Alexander Paterson, John Michelson, and Thomas Arnot, serjeant. William Lauder is bailie.

482. 1533 April 11. Sasine on resignation by Duncan Wicht in favour of Elizabeth Wicht, his daughter, of the backland of his tenement lying on the north side of the High Street, and bounded as above described, lying within the said tenement, between the fore land thereof on the south, and his other back land, now pertaining to Beatrix Wicht heritably, on the north: Reserving the liferent of said backland to the said Duncan Wicht. Same bailie and witnesses as aforesaid.

483. 1533 April 11. Compeared personally Andrew Mowbray, burgess, undoubted patron of that service of the sacred chaplainry founded by the late Andrew Mowbray, his grandfather, at the altar of St. Ninian, situated within the collegiate church of St. Giles, now vacant in his hands by the death of the late Sir John Harkness, last chaplain and possessor thereof; which Andrew, of his own free will, gave granted and presented, and by the tenor of these presents, gives grants and presents Sir John Portuis, chaplain, in and to the said chaplainry service of the said altar, by delivery to him, the said Sir John, of a chalice and book, and other instruments and vestments of the said altar; and invested him in the real, actual and corporal possession of the said chaplainry and service, with all and sundry their fruits, lands, buildings, annualrents, profits, obits, oblations, emoluments, etc., thereof, conform to the tenor of the foundation of the said chaplainry

and service, during his lifetime. Witnesses to the above done within the said church of St. Giles, and at the said altar, in presence of Sirs William Wodsall, James Moffat, John Symson, John Hasty, John Clerk and Master James Murray, chaplains.

484. 1533 April 23. Compeared personally John Flucar and Jonet Balfour his spouse who constituted William Watson and Thomas Arnot, conjointly and severally, their procurators, to resign their land lying in Halkerston Wynd, east side the trause thereof, between a land of George Forstar of Strathenry on the north, and a land of the late William Halkerston on the south, in the hands of one of the bailies of Edinburgh, in favour of Patrick Sclater and Marion Murray his spouse, for sasine thereof to be given to them thereof, conform to the tenor of a charter of the said John Flucar and his spouse made thereupon; with the said Jonet's oath not to revoke. Done in the said John's house in the Canongate, in presence of Thomas Softlaw, Peter Stevinson, Patrick Ballenden, and David Purves.
The quhilk day Patrick Sclater grantis him awand till John Flucar and his spouse for thar land quhilk thai grantit that thai had sauld to him liand in Halkerston Clois the soume of xxx lib. in compleit payment thairof; and oblissis him his airis executouris and assignais till content and pay the said soume of xxx lib. to the said John Flucar his spous thar airis executouris and assignais betuix this and Mertymes day nixt to cum; and thereupon the said Patrick asked (instrument.) Done in the house of the said John. Same witnesses.

485. 1533 April 23. Sasine on resignation by William Watson, procurator, and in name of John Flucar and his spouse Jonet Balfour, in favour of Patrick Sclater, burgess, and Marion Murray his spouse, of a land of the said John Flucar and Jonet Balfour his spouse, built and waste, lying on the north side of the High Street, in Halkerston's Wynd, and bounded as described in the foregoing procuratory of resignation. Witnesses, Sir Bartholomew Robison, John Softlaw, Alexander Napier, Gilbert Dykson, and David Purves. William Lauder is bailie.

486. 1533 May 2. Sasine on resignation by Andrew Quhite, with consent of Jonet Smalem his spouse, in favour of Jonet Cornwall and Margaret Cornwall her sister, and the heirs to be procreated of their bodies, whom failing to revert to the said Andrew, his heirs and assignees, viz. to each of the said sisters one half respectively of the said Andrew's land lying within a tenement of the late Edward Bonkill, on the south side of the High Street, below the Netherbow, between a land of the late Hector Thomson on the east, a land of the late James Young on the west, a land of the laird of Ormistoun on the north, and a land of John Mure on the south: Reserving the liferent of the said land to the said Andrew Quhite and Jonet Smalem his spouse. Witnesses, James Ur, John Christeson, Henry Kirk, Adam Gallaway, James Broun, William Lauder, William Watson, Robert Law, and Hugh Wallas, serjeant. William Lauder is bailie.

487. 1533 May 19. Sasine on resignation by Robert Coupar, son and heir of the late Gilbert Coupar, burgess, in favour of Francis Spottiswode and Margaret Davidson his spouse, of the said Robert's land lying within a tenement of the late John Davidson, on the north side of the High Street, between a land of Alexander Cant on the east, and a land of Patrick Flemyng on the west; west side of the transe of the said tenement, between a land of Thomas Schort on the north, and a land of the said John Davidson on the south. Witnesses, Archibald Donaldson, William How, Andrew Galloway, John Huchon, Thomas Schort, William Watson and Thomas Arnot, serjeants. William Lauder is bailie.

488. 1533 May 30. Sasine on resignation by James Kyle in favour of Margaret Broune, of the following subjects; (1) the half part of a land or tenement lying below the castle wall, on the north side of the High Street, between a land of the late Andrew Symson on the east, and a land of the late John Windzettis on the west; the castle bank on the north, and the king's public street on the south; (2) the other half of said tenement to Alexander Affleck, attorney and in name of the said Margaret Broune in liferent; (3) a land of the said James Kyle lying within a tenement of the late David Knox, on the north side of the High Street, west side the transe thereof, between a land of the said David Knox on the north and south parts. Witnesses, John Sanderson, William Nasmyth, John Kyle, Robert Monypenny, John Flucar, George Allane, Patrick Johnston, and David Purves, serjeant. William Anderson is bailie.

489. 1533 May 31. Compeared personally Elizabeth Silver, daughter of the late Ninian Silver, burgess, and confessed that an annualrent of 10 merks was now lawfully redeemed from her by Cristian Redpath, relict of John Arres, and by John Arres son and heir of the late John: Which annual-rent the said John Arres and his spouse alienated to the said Elizabeth out of their land lying beyond the Over Bow, on the south side of the High Street, between a land of the late James Homyll, now pertaining to George Gude on the west, and a land of Nicholas Broune on the east, by delivery and payment to the said Elizabeth of the sum of £80 Scots. Done in the dwelling house of the said Ninian Silver in presence of Robert Logan of Coitfield, Henry Cranston, William Akinheid, John Hucheson, Sir George Litiljohn, John Kyle and James Kirk.

490. 1533 June 13. Sasine on resignation by Ronald Donaldson in favour of Archibald Donaldson, burgess, of an annual-rent of 2 merks, out of a land of Sir Alexander Scot, rector of Myddilbe, now pertaining to the said Ronald, lying on the south side of the High Street, near the Netherbow, between a land of the late James Bassenden on the north, and a land of Andrew Mowbray on the south. Witnesses, Walter Donaldson, Robert Donaldson, Hugh Wallace and William Watson: Under reversion of £20. William Rynd is bailie.

491. 1533 June 16. Sasine to William Bassinden, on his cognition by Master David Irland, bailie, as heir of the late James Bassinden

his father; (1) of a foreland of the said James, lying on the south side of the High Street, between a land of the late Sir Alexander Scot, Rector of Myddilbie, on the south, and the king's common ways on the east, west and north; (2) of a backland, with the caichpule, in which John Crummy now dwells, lying within the said tenement, between a land of the said John Crummy on the north, and a land or yard of Andrew Mowbray on the south. Which foreland and backland, with the catchpule, and all their pertinents, the said William Bassinden resigned in the hands of the bailie, in favour of himself and Cristina Balcasky his affianced spouse, who are thereupon seised in the same in conjunct-fee. Witnesses, William Ker, Richard Wardlaw, Thomas Purves, James Bassenden, James Balcasky, Thomas Arnot, David Purves and Patrick Lithqw, serjeants.

The quhilk day in presens of the said bailie, serjeants and witnesses, Issobell Gray the relict of umquhile James Bassinden protestit, that the giving of the sesing of the saids lands till William Bassenden sould nocht hurt hir, nor hir barnis, nor thair richtis that thai haif thairof, hir sesing, conjunct-fee and hir barnis heretage; and for remeid of law, etc., and asked instrument.

The quhilk day, in presens forsaid, John Crummy allegit he had takkis of the house he dwells in and cachepulle of termes to run, and protestit that the sesing gevin thairof till William Bassenden and his spous hurt nocht his rycht, and for remeid, and asked an instrument.

492. 1533 June 20. Sasine on charter under testimonial of the great seal, in favour of Hugh Douglas, burgess, and Marion Broune his spouse, of that waste piece of land lying in the vennel called Bestis Wynd, between the yard belonging to the provost of the collegiate church of St. Giles on the east, the waste land pertaining to John Vaiche, goldsmith, on the west, the house of the said John Vaiche on the north, and a house pertaining to John Wicht on the south: Which waste piece of land pertained to the late Andrew Cutlar, and is now in His Majesty's hands as ultimate heir. At Edinburgh 24 March in the 19th. year of His Majesty's reign. And forthwith the said Hugh Douglas, with consent of Marion Broune his spouse, resigned the said piece of land in the hands of William Rynd, bailie, in favour of Sir Henry Mow, chaplain, prebendary of the collegiate kirk of St. Giles, who is thereupon seised therein heritably, his heirs and assignees. Witnesses, Sir William Merschell, chaplain, Thomas Mosman, Robert Galbraith, William Mason, Alexander Darling and Thomas Arnot.

493. 1533 June 23. Sasine on resignation by Elizabeth Bonkill, relict of John *Lethame* (sic), of her conjunct-fee, in favour of Andrew *Lichtoun*, and on cognition of the said Andrew as lawful and nearest heir of the said late John *Lichtoun* his father, of the said John's land, lying within a tenement of William Lauder, west side the transe thereof, between a land of the said William Lauder on the north, and a land of Anthony Brussait on the south: Reserving the liferent of said land to the said Elizabeth Bonkill. And forthwith the said Andrew

Lochtoun, with consent of Elizabeth Bonkill, his mother, resigned an annual-rent of 40s., out of the foresaid land, in the hands of the bailie, who gave sasine thereof to Agnes Cokburn, relict of Walter Chepman, her heirs and assignees: Under reversion of £24. Witnesses, Master John Lauder, vicar of Kilrynny, John Chepman and Thomas Broun, Sir John Kayne and James Nisbet.

The quhilk day, in presens of the said bailie and witnesses, the said Andrew Lichtoun promittit that he sould restore and put agane all the geir that he had tane furth of his moderis hous; and oblist him that he sould tak na geir furth of the samyn in tyme tocum. And thereupon the said Elizabeth asked an instrument.

494. 1533 June 26. Sasine to James Lauson of Humby, on his cognition by William Lauder, bailie, as heir of the late James Lauson of Humby his father, of an annual-rent of 40s., out of a land of William Tod, lying on the south side of the High Street, in the vennel commonly called Snawdonis Close, in the lower end thereof, between a land of the late William Frog on the north, and a land of the late John Spens on the south: Which vennel lies on the south (sic) side of the High Street, between a land of William Adamson on the east, and a land of the late David Bell on the west: Which annual-rent of 40s. the said James Lauson of Humby resigned in the hands of William Lauder, bailie, who thereupo·· gave sasine thereof to the foresaid William Tod, burgess, and Margaret Lesle his spouse. Witnesses, Master John Gibson, Sir Bartholomew Robeson, John Twedy, John Frude, David Lauson, Thomas Arnot and William Watson.

495. 1533 June 28. Sasine to Robert Watson on his cognition by William Rynd, bailie, as heir of the late John Watson his father, of a land of the said John lying on the south side of the High Street, within a tenement of the late Master Richard Robeson, between a waste land of the said Master Richard on the south, and a land now pertaining to Nicholas Craufurd on the north; a land of the late John Adamson on the east, and St. Giles cemetery and the transe of the said tenement on the west. And forthwith the said Robert Watson resigned the foresaid land in the hands of the bailie, who thereupon gave sasine thereof to James Bannatyne, burgess of Lanark. Witnesses, David Jameson, James Pennar, Thomas Mureleyis, Robert Heriot, William Boyd, Alexander Young, notary, William Steill; Patrick Lithqw and David Purves, serjeants.

Robert Watson, the son and heir of the said umquhile John declared befor the said bailie, that he wald mak na expens apon the rasing of ony of his saidis evidentis or instrumentis furth of the common clerkis bukis na maner of way. Bot gif the said James desyrit ony he was contentit that he gart luke thame and rais thame apon his awin expens, and na uther wayis.

The saids day and witnesses the said James Bannatyne resigned his foresaid land in the hands of the bailie, who gave sasine thereof in conjunct-fee to James Pennar, attorney, in name of Margaret Gryme, spouse of the said James Bannatyne.

496. 1533 June 28. Compeared personally Robert Watson, the son and heir of umquhile John Watson, burgess of Edinburgh, and of his awin fre motif will, uncompellit or coactit, maid constitut and ordanit, be thir presentis, James Bannatyne, burges of Lanerk, and his airis, his lauchfull cessioneris and assignais as to thair awin gudis, in and to all and sundry his movable gudis of airschip, pertenand till him ony maner of way throw the deces of his said umquhile fadir, quhar wir thai may be apprehendit within the realme of Scotland: And to call all maner of personis intromettaris thairwith befor quhatsumevir juge spirituall or temporall for the samyn: Transferrand all rycht and titill of rycht thairof, fra him and all utheris his assignais, in and to the said James and his airis for evir. And that for certane soumes of money, thankis and gratitutis done till him be the said James Bannatyne for the samyn. And this to be extendit in the surest form, of consent of parties. Done in the booth of Nichol Carncors. Witnesses, William Tod, James Pennar and Thomas Bannatyne.

497. 1533 June 30. Sasine on apprising at the instance of William Sym, burgess, James Kyle, John Kyle and George Kyle, against Margaret Broune, of the following subjects, according to the amount due by the said Margaret to each of the said apprisers respectively, viz.(1)The half of that land or tenement of the said Margaret Broune, lying below the castle wall, on the north side of the High Street, between a land of the late Andrew Symson on the east, and a land of the late John Wyndzettis on the west; the castle bank on the north, and the king's public street on the south. (2)A land lying within a tenement of the late David Knox, on the north side of the High Street, in which land Adam Hestoun now dwells, west side of the transe of the said tenement, between the lands of the said late David Knox on the south and north parts. Witnesses, Robert Bruse, David Moffett, George Craik, Adam Hestoun, John Thomson, Henry Creichtoun, Patrick Levingston; William Watson and David Purves, serjeants.

498. 1533 July 9. Compeared personally David Gillaspy, and confessit and grantit that Robert Coupar burgess of the Feir is souertie for him for xiiij lib. greit arrestit of his gudis in the Feir for the pley of Myddilburgh rasit apon the haill merchandis of Scotland; and oblissis him, gif the said Robert has paiit the said soume for him be compulsioun of ony juge, that he sall content and pay to the said Robert Syk profit and retain by for the said xiiij lib. greit by the principall, as ony uther nichtbour or merchand of Scotland pais for siklyk. The said Robert asked an instrument. Done within the burgh of Edinburgh, in the booth of George Talzefeir; Witnesses, Vincent Strathauchin, notary, Nicholas Coittis, Thomas Arnot, John Kyle and John Anderson.

499. 1533 July 23. Sasine on resignation by Francis Aikman in favour of himself and Helen Creichton his spouse, the longest liver of them, and the heirs male lawfully procreated or to be procreated betwixt them, whom failing to the lawful and nearest heirs of the said Francis whosoever, of the upper hall of the

backland of his tenement, lying on the north side of the High Street, with the chambers, kitchen and loft above the same; together with the chamber of the foreland of the said tenement: Also the upper merchant booth of the said foreland, with the whole yard and waste land of the said tenement; which lies on the north side of the High Street, between a tenement of the late Margaret Broune on the east, a tenement of the late Richard Hoppar on the west, the yard of Trinity College on the north, and the King's public street on the south. Witnesses, Peter Marche, James Sym, James Lundy, William Watson, serjeant, and Dionisius Manderston. William Lauder is bailie.

500. 1533 July 24. Sasine on resignation by John Scharp, baker, in favour of himself and Cristina Forstar his affianced spouse, of his lands lying on the south side of the High Street, between a land of John Fausyde on the east, and a certain waste land on the west; the waste land of Alexander Pennycuke and another built land of the said John Scharp on the north, and the king's public street of the Cowgate on the south. Witnesses, William Liberton, elder, William Liberton, younger, David Heriot, Andrew Walkar, Adam Wilson, Alexander Robison and David Purves, serjeant. William Anderson is bailie.

501. 1533 July 30. Sasine on resignation by James Chalmers, son and heir of the late Isobel Berwyk, in favour of David Heriot, burgess, and Elizabeth Curll his spouse, of an annual-rent of 10s., out of a land of John Fausyde, lying in the end of the vennel of Forstaris Wynd, between the said vennel on the east, and a land of John Scharp on the west, a land of the late John Fresall on the north, and the street of the Cowgate on the south. Witnesses, Thomas Coupar, Robert Knox, Patrick Urry, William Quhite, John Abircrummy, Thomas Robison, and David Purves, serjeant. William Anderson is bailie.

502. 1533 July 30. Sasine on resignation by David Heriot in favour of himself and Elizabeth Curll his spouse, of all and whole the said David's lands lying on the south side of the Cowgate, between that back land of the said David and the lands of Thomas Laverok on the east, a land of the late William Harlaw on the west; the croft pertaining to the place of St. Katrine of the Senis on the south, and the fore land pertaining to Sir John Duncan on the north; with the mansion, barn and kiln, and all his other houses, biggings and lands existing within the said bounds: Excepting two lit work-houses, and the privilege of the well thereof. Witnesses, Thomas Coupar, Robert Knox, Patrick Urry, William Quhite, John Abircrummy, Thomas Robison, and David Purves, serjeant. William Anderson is bailie.

503. 1533 Aug. 8. Sasine to John Brown on his cognition by Master David Ireland, bailie, as son and heir of the late John Brown, burgess, of the said late John's land or mansion, lying on the north side of the High Street, between the fore land of the late James Baron on the south, and a land of the late William Hoppar on the north: Which land and mansion the said John Brown forthwith resigned in the hands of the bailie, in favour

of himself and Marion Cant his spouse, who are thereupon seised therein heritably and in conjunct-fee. Witnesses, Robert Bruse, John Stewart, John Baxter and William Watson. Master David Ireland is bailie.

504. 1533 Aug. 19 Sasine on resignation by David Ramsay in favour of himself and Jonet Broune his spouse, of an annual-rent of 2 merks, out of that land or tenement now pertaining to William Elphinstoun, lying below the Netherbow, on the south side of the High Street, between a land of the late Robert Merschell on the east, and a land of the late Alan Borthik on the west, a waste land on the south, and the king's public street on the north. Witnesses, Master James Edmonstoun, rector of Faulo, Alexander Murray, William Dalgleish, Andrew Ramsay, William Lauson, Alexander Lauder, Robert Doddis, Thomas Allane, and Patrick Lithqw, serjeant. William Lauder is bailie.

505. 1533 Aug. 21. Sasine on resignation by William Bell, son and heir of the late John Bell, in favour of William Lord Sinclair, of an annual-rent of 40 shillings, out of the said William's land, newly built, lying on the south side of the High Street, between a land of the late John Dalrumpill on the east, a land of the late John Vernour on the west, and the fore land of the said late John Bell on the north, and a land of the late David Bell on the south. Witnesses, Master James Murray, David Blantyre, John Guthry, Sir Thomas Mailuill, John Cowtis, Sir George Hesliheid, John Purro, and William Watson, serjeant. Sir John Cuke, chaplain is attorney for the said Lord Sinclair, and William Anderson is bailie.

506. 1533 Aug 21. The said day William Anderson, bailie, passed to a land of William Bell, son and heir of the late John Bell, newly built, lying on the *north* (sic) side of the High Street, between a land of the late John Dalrumpill on the east, a land of John Vernour on the west, the foreland of the said late John Bell on the north, and another land of the late David Bell on the south; and there Master James Murray, procurator, and in name of a noble and potent Lord William Lord Sinclair, resigned an annual-rent of 6 merks out of the foresaid land, newly built, in the hands of the bailie, who thereupon gave heritable sasine of the said annual-rent of 6 merks to Sir Thomas Mailuill, rector of Lyntoun, his heirs and assignees, in presence of the witnesses aforesaid.

507. 1533 Aug. 22. Sasine on resignation by John Con, flesher, with consent of Marion Borthik his spouse, in favour of Adam Con their son, his heirs and assignees, of the fee of the said John Con's land and mansion, in which he now dwells, lying within a tenement of the late William Cokburn, on the south side of the High Street, between a tenement of James Prestoun on the east, and a tenement of Alexander Rynd on the west, and the other lands of the said John Con on the south and north: Reserving the liferent of the said land and mansion to John Con and Marion Borthik his spouse. Witnesses, William Sym; William Watson and Thomas Arnot, serjeants. William Rynd is bailie.

508. 1533 Aug. 22. Sasine on resignation by John Con, flesher, with consent of Marion Borthik his spouse, in favour of Edward Affleck of Kilbankis and Geils Cranston his spouse, the longest liver of them, etc., of the said John Con's south land in which the said Edward Affleck of Kilbankis now dwells, lying within a tenement of the late William Cokburn, on the south side of the High Street, between a tenement of James Preston on the east, and a land of Alexander Rynd on the west. Witnesses, Adam Con and the others above named. William Rynd is bailie.
The quhilk day William Sym declarit that he had x lib. of annual of John Con's haill land, and protested the sesing gevin be the said John and his wif till Edward Afflek and Geils his wif hurt nocht him nor his annuell.
The quhilk day Edward Affleck and his wif granted thame, awand till John Con xxix sh. quhilk thai promist till pay within terme of law. John Con asked an instrument. Witnesses above written.

509. 1533 Sept. 9. Sasine on resignation by John Sprot, in favour of Philip Sprot, burgess, and Helen Litstar his spouse, of the said John's land, with fore gable thereof and two particates of land, with the space of one ell of land in the end of the yard of the foresaid land, with all their pertinents, lying on the south side of the High Street, at the Castlehill, between the land of the late John Smyth, arrowhead maker, on the east, a land of the late Andrew Mure on the west, a land of the late Thomas Ra on the east, a land of the late Alexander Bowmaker on the south; and a land of the late Andrew Mure on the west, and a land of the late James Bryson on the north. Witnesses, John Smyth, John Marjoribanks, Laurence Howy, John Cuthbertson, and David Purves, serjeant.
Under reversion containing the sum of £80. William Rynd is bailie.

510. 1533 Sept. 12. William Rynd, one of the bailies of Edinburgh, passed to the altar of St. Nicholas, situated within the collegiate church of St. Giles of the foresaid burgh, and there the said bailie gave and delivered institution of the said altar and service thereof by delivery of a chalice, book, and other habiliments and vestments of the said altar, to Sir David Purdome, chaplain, and entered him in and to the real actual and corporal possession of the said chaplainry and service thereof, with all and sundry its fruits, lands, biggings, annualrents, profits, casualties, emoluments, and all other pertinents belonging to the said chaplainry, without impediment during his lifetime, according to the tenor of the foundation thereof. The said Sir David asked an instrument. Done at the said altar in presence of Sirs John Kers, George Rogeir, John Smalem and James Hunter, chaplains, Patrick Tod, Robert Blak and George Tod, with Sir James Moffatt.

511. 1533 Sept. 11. Sasine on resignation by Alison Rouche, relict of Jasper Mayne, of her conjunct-fee, in favour of John Mayne son of the said Jasper, and on the said John's cognition by

JOHN FOULAR 165

Master David Ireland, bailie, as heir of his said father, in and to that land or tenement of the said Jasper lying on the south side of the High Street, near the Place of the Friars Preachers, west side of the transe that leads to the said place of the friars, between a land of the late John Davidson on the south, and a land of the said friars on the north; the land now pertaining to the heirs of the late Sir Alexander Jardine of Apilgirth on the west, and the king's common passage leading to the said place on the east: Reserving the liferent of the said tenement to Alison Rouche. Which tenement John Mayne resigned in the hands of the bailie in favour of himself and Margaret Martyne his spouse. Witnesses, David Kynnymond; William Watson and Hugh Wallas, serjeants.

The quhilk day in presens of the bailie Maister David Irland and witnes abone wryttin, John Mayne said that he suld preif that Isobell Mayne uther wayis callit Isobell Kar is nocht nor nevir was the dochter of umqhile Jasper Mayne his fadir; and protestit that he mycht haif tyme and place till preif the samyn. And at suld hurt him nor the laif of his sisteris and brether anent the barnis pairt of gud. Apon the quhilk Alison Rouche modir to the said Isobell askit instruments. And revoked the foresaid words utterly, and protestit for remeid quhen and quhar it efferit, and thereupon asked an instrument. Done upon the ground of the said land.

512. 1533 Sept. 26. Sasine on resignation by David Gillaspy, baker, with consent of Elizabeth Gilleis his spouse, in favour of Sir David Young, curate of St. Giles church, in name of the church, for an anniversary to be celebrated yearly and a "daill" to be made for the souls of the said David and Elizabeth his spouse, and for the souls of their ancestors and successors, and of all the faithful deceased. With court and the said Elizabeth's oath not to revoke as use is. The said Sir David asked an instrument. Witnesses, Master Alexander Levingston, Alexander Levingston, John Henrison, William Scot, William Watson, William Bowy, and David Purves, serjeant. Master David Ireland is bailie.

513. 1533 Sept. 30. Sasine on resignation by William Anderson, with consent of Jonet Merschell his spouse, in favour of a prudent man William Anderson, present bailie of the burgh of Edinburgh, his heirs and assignees, of the said William's north booth or cellar, together with the penteis beside the door thereof, and all their pertinents, of his land lying beyond the Overbow, on the north side of the High Street, between a land of James Darroch on the east, and a land of James Uddert on the west, a land of the Lord Ruthven on the north, and the king's public street on the south. With court and oath of the said Jonet not to revoke as use is. Witnesses, Thomas Arnot, Thomas Rynd and David Purves. William Rynd is bailie. Under reversion, the sum not specified and without instrument.

514. 1533 Oct. 7. Sasine to Master Alexander Dyk, on his cognition by Alexander Spens, bailie, as heir of the late William Dyk, notary public, his brother, of the said William's lands and

tenements lying on the south side of the Tolbooth, between the cemetery of St. Giles church on the east, and a tenement of the late John Spot on the west, a waste land of the late John Malison on the north, and a land of the late William Bigholme on the south. Witnesses, James Young, bailie, Gilbert Davidson, Andrew Dyk, Henry Richartson, John Mosman, Alexander Knichtson, and Hugh Wallace, serjeant.

515. 1533 Oct. 13. Renunciation by Margaret Cor, relict of Alexander Reid, now spouse to William Stevinson, in the hands of James Young, bailie, in favour of Henry Cranston lord fiar, of her liferent of that land lying on the south side of the High Street, beyond the Overbow, between a land of the late John Currour on the east, and a land of Nicholas Brown on the west, a land of the late Edward Davidson on the south, and the king's public street on the north. With the said Margaret's oath not to revoke. Done in the booth of the common clerk of Edinburgh, in presence of Robert Henrison, John Anderson and David Purves.

516. 1533 Oct. 27. Renunciation by Sir Walter Maluny, abbot of the monastery of Glenlus, in favour of Anthony Brussat, his heirs and assignees, of the land in which the said Anthony now dwells, lying within a tenement of William Lauder, west side the transe thereof, on the south side of the High Street, between a land of the said William Lauder on the north, and a land (   ) on the south: with all right, claim, property and possession which the said Sir Walter has to the said land through the decease of the late Katrine Maluny his sister, or any other manner of way. Moreover the said Sir Walter constitutes James Johnston alias Edinburgh, Thomas Arnot, Patrick Linlithqw and Hugh Wallas his procurators to take and receive possession of the said land, and in his name to raise letters of attorney from our sovereign Lord's chancery to receive the said possession; and after receiving state and sasine of the said land to resign the same in the hands of one of the bailies of Edinburgh for sasine thereof to be given to the said Anthony Brussat in the surest form. Anthony asked an instrument. Done upon the ground of the said land in presence of James Pettigreif and James Johnston.

517. 1533 Oct. 31. Sasine on resignation by William Rynd, with consent of Thomas Rynd his son and heir apparent, in favour of Margaret Weir future spouse of the said William in liferent of the following subjects: (1) The said William's land and mansion, with the houses thereof, lying in his tenement on the north side of the High Street, east side the transe thereof, between a land of the late Gilbert Trumbill on the east, and a land of the late John Lauson on the west; (2) an annual-rent of 4 merks out of another land lying within the said tenement, west side the transe thereof, in which Michel McQuhen now dwells, between the said William Rynd's lands on the south and north; (3) an annual-rent of 8 merks, out of a certain merchant booth in which John Hoip now dwells, lying in the Boothraw, on the south side of the High Street, between a land

of the late David Mailuill on the east, and the Tolbooth on the west. Witnesses, James Levingtoun, William Weir, Robert Bannatyne, John Mowat, William McCartnay, Thomas Todryk, John Sym, William Alexander, and David Purves. James Young is bailie.

518. 1533 Oct. 31. Thomas Rynd, the son and heir apparent till William Rynd declarit forsamêkle as his said fadir had put Margret Weir in the liferent of his mansion and dwelling-place for all the dais of hir lyf, tharfor he protestit in presens of the bailie James Young and utheris witnes, that the said Margret uphald and beit the said land in sclait and tymmer all tymes quhen it misteris als weill as it is now. And gif scho failis in the samyn he protestit that scho may be compellit tharto or ellis till tyne hir lyfrent. And thar apone he askit instruments. Done upon the ground of the said land and mansion.

519. 1533 Nov. 8. Compeared personally Thomas Rynd, son and heir of the late William Rynd, burgess, and confessed that an annual-rent of 8 merks out of a waste land lying in Freir's Wynd, east side thereof, between a land now of John Vernour on the south, and a land of the late Archibald Preston on the north, is now lawfully redeemed by William Uddart, by payment of £80; and therefore the said Thomas, with consent of his father renounces the same in favour of William Uddart, his heirs and assignees. Witnesses, Alexander Young, notary public, Master Henry Lauder and Thomas Rynd, and John Burgane.

520. 1533 Nov. 26. Sasine on resignation by Master Adam Otterburn, with consent of Eufame Mowbray his spouse, in favour of Thomas Otterburn their son, his heirs and assignees, of the fee of the said Master Adam's fore-land, lying on the north side of the High Street, between a tenement of the late John Mason on the east, and a tenement of the late Henry Young on the west, the land of the late Richard Hoppar on the north, and the king's public street on the south: Reserving the liferent of the said fore-land to the saids Master Adam Otterburn and Eufame his spouse. Witnesses, Master Thomas Marjoribanks, Michael Tullois, John Otterburn, James Brown, John Chancellar, and William Watson, serjeant. Alexander Spens is bailie.

521. 1533 Nov. 26. Sasine on resignation by Master Adam Otterburn in favour of Robert Otterburn his son, his heirs and assignees, of his merchant booth lying in the land in the Buithraw on the south side of the High Street, between a land of Alexander Mauchane on the east, and a land of Francis Peebles on the west. Same bailie and witnesses as aforesaid.

522. 1533 Nov. 26. Assignation by Master Adam Otterburn of Auldhame in favour of John Otterburn, his son and heir apparent, whom he constitutes his assignee in and to the ward of the land of Easter Halis, lying within the shire of Edinburgh: transferring the same, the donation thereof, and the letters made to him thereupon, from him his heirs, and all others his assignees; together with all right and title of right which he or they in

168 PROTOCOL BOOK

any way have to the said ward, to the said John Otterburn forever. Witnesses, Michael Tullois, Alexander Harlaw, Robert Smith, James Brown, elder, James Brown, younger, and John Chancellar.
The same day and witnesses, Master Adam Otterburn makis and constitutis Jonet Otterburn his dochter his lauchfull and unrevocabill cessioner and assignay in and to the marriage of the air or airis of Strahenry quhatsumevir: transferrand and giffand all rycht thairof fra him and his airis in and to the said Janet Otterburn, with all proffittis of the samyn. And this instrument to be extendit in the best and largest form that can be maid or devisit. Witnesses aforesaid.

523. 1533 Dec. 9. Compeared personally Alexander Wilkeson, burgess, and constituted William Symson his lawful and irrevocable procurator, attorney, etc., giving him power and special mandate, for him and in his name, to take possession, state and sasine of an annual-rent of £10, by resignation thereof by Alan Mosman and his spouse, out of the said Alan's land, lying in Forstar's Wynd; and after receiving sasine thereof, to resign the said annual-rent in the hands of one of the bailies of Edinburgh, for sasine thereof to be given to a chaplain in name of the church, according to the tenor of a foundation to be made thereupon: And the said Alexander promised that whatever was done by his said procurator in the premises, he would hold firm and stable under hypothec and obligation of all his goods present and to come. Done within the burgh of Edinburgh in the cemetery of the church of the Friars Minor, in presence of George Cant, William Loch, Sir Luke Bow, chaplain, and Master David Dun.

524. 1533 Dec. 9. In presens of Maister James Lauson, Provost of the burgh of Edinburgh, and James Young, balze of the samyn, Alane Mosman, burges of the said burgh, ratifiit and apprevit the decreit gevin be the Lordis of Counsall with James Lauson aganis the said Alane, and soume contenit thairintill. And als ratifiit and apprevit the apprysing of the said Alanis landis to the said James, for the soume contenit in the said decreit, and all that followit thairapon. The said James Lauson asked an instrument. Done in the booth of the common clerk, to be extended in more ample form. Witnesses, Master Francis Bothuell, William Rutherfurd, John Swan, Symon Bannatyne, and William Watson.

525. 1533 Dec. 9. Sasine on resignation by James Lauson in favour of Alan Mosman and Margaret Borthik his spouse, of the said Alan's land or tenement, now pertaining to the said James Lauson, by reason of apprising thereof, made by the said James for certain sums of money due to him, as in two decreets of the Lords of Council is more fully contained, lying on the south side of the High Street, in the vennel called Forstar's Wynd, east side the transe thereof, between a land of the late ·Sir John Ramsay, knight, on the north, and a land of the late John Foular on the south. Witnesses, Master Francis Bothuell, Master James Lauson, provost, William Rutherfurd, John Swan,

Symon Banntyne and William Watson. James Young is bailie.

526. 1533 Dec. 9. Sasine on resignation by James Lauson in favour of Alan Mosman and Margaret Borthik, his spouse, of another land or tenement sometime pertaining to the said Alan, now to the said James by reason of apprising, lying in the vennel of the Friars Preachers, east side the trause thereof, between the lands of John Gibson on the south, and the lands of William Stawis on the north. Witnesses, Sir William Bow, chaplain, and the others foresaid.

527. 1533 Dec. 9. Sasine on resignation by Alan Mosman, with consent of Margaret Borthik his spouse, in favour of Alexander Wilkieson, burgess, of an annual-rent of £10, out of the said Alan's land or tenement lying in the Forstar's Wynd, east side the trause thereof, and bounded as before described. With the said Margaret's oath not to revoke in time to come. Witnesses, Master James Lauson, provost of Edinburgh, Master Francis Bothwell, and the others aforesaid. William Symson is attorney. James Young is bailie.

528. 1533 Dec. 9. Sasine on resignation by William Symson, procurator and in name of Alexander Wilkieson, in favour of Sir Luke Bow, chaplain, in name of the church, for the sustentation of a chaplainry perpetually to be celebrated in the parish church of Saint Cuthbert's, below the castle wall, conform to the tenor of a charter of foundation to be made thereupon, of an annual-rent of £10, out of the said Alan Mosman's land or tenement lying in Forstar's Wynd, east side the trause thereof, as above described: Reserving the liferent of the said annual-rent to the said Alexander Wilkieson. Same bailie and witnesses as aforesaid.

529. 1533 Dec. 18. Sasine under testimonial of the great seal in favour of an *oratrix* or beids woman and widow, Marjorie Bassinden, relict of the late Evangelist Passeur, burgess of Edinburgh, for the good and faithful service done to His Majesty by the said Evangelist, of a waste land lying in the lower end of a tenement of John Melrose, lying on the north side of the High Street, beside the Castlehill, between a tenement of William Wallange on the west, and a tenement of John Wicht on the east, the lands of the late Archibald Wischart beside the North Loch on the north, and the waste land or yard of the said tenements on the south. Also a built land lying beside the Castlehill, on the south side of the High Street, within a tenement of the late James Barcar, west side the trause thereof, between a land of Alexander Chalmer on the south and north parts, a land of the late David Pinschenot on the east, and a land of Patrick Bartoun on the west: Which was given and granted by Margaret Brewhouse, daughter and heir of the late Peter Brewhouse to the late George, bishop of Elphin in Ireland, being in special warrandice of his land and croft lying at the Castlehill, on the south side of the High Street, between the waste land and the Castle Vennel on the west, the lands of Andrew Hathochy and the late Mathew Harvy on the south, the lands of John Sprot and his spouse and of James

Scott on the east, and the said Castlehill on the north; sold and alienated to the said bishop by Margaret Brewhouse by charter and sasine in warrandice of his lands and croft foresaid; now in His Majesty's hands as ultimate heir by reason of escheat as an inherent right of the Crown. Witnesses, William Pacok, Andrew Moncur, Alexander Pery, Robert Reynald, William Nicholson, John Cuthbertson, John Auldstoun, Thomas Arnot and Hugh Wallas. Alexander Spens is bailie.

530. 1533 Dec. 30. Compeared personally Alexander Wilkieson, burgess, and declared generally, that he by his procuratory constituted William Symson, that he might resign an annual-rent of £10 out of a land of Alan Mosman, lying in Forstar's Wynd, in the hands of James Young, bailie; and that the said bailie delivered sasine thereof to Sir Luke Bow, chaplain, in name of the church, conform to the tenor of a charter of foundation made thereupon: Which resignation so made by his said procurator in the hands of the said bailie, and the giving of a sasine thereof by the said bailie to the foresaid chaplain, in name of the Church, the said Alexander Wilkieson has ratified, and, for him his heirs and assignees has forever approved and confirmed. Alexander asked an instrument. Done beside his dwelling-house below the castle wall. Witnesses, William Symson, Alexander Smith, William Wilkieson, John Busbe, and William Watson, serjeant.

531. 1533 Dec. 30. Sasine on resignation by Alexander Wilkieson in favour of Sir Luke Bow, chaplain, in name of the church, of the following annual-rents, viz: (1)an annual-rent of 20 shillings, out of the said Alexander's tenement, lying below the castle wall,on the south side of the High Street,between a land of Alexander Chalmer on the east, and a land of Alexander Napier on the west;(2)an annual-rent of 23 shillings, out of a land of Thomas Bertrame,lying below the castle wall,on the north side of the High Street, between another land of the said Thomas Bertrame on the east, and a land of the said Alexander Wilkieson on the west: Reserving the liferent of the said annual-rents of the said Alexander resigner. Witnesses, Thomas Bertrame, and the others foresaid. James Young is bailie.

532. 1533-4 Jan. 3. Sasine to William Ramsay, on his cognition by William Sym, bailie, as heir of the late John Ramsay his father, of a tenement or great building of the said John, lying on the south side of the High Street, in Forstar's Wynd, east side the transe thereof, between a land of Alan Mosman on the south, and a land of the late John Foular on the north: Which tenement William Ramsay forthwith resigned in the hands of the bailie, in favour of Marjorie Wood, who is thereupon seised in liferent therein. Alexander Wood is attorney for the said Marjorie. Witnesses, John Mayne, George Hoppringill, William Hoppringill, Thomas Hart, John Keyr, and Hugh Wallas, serjeant.

533. 1533-4 Jan 8. Sasine on process of recognition led before the provost and bailie of Edinburgh,in favour of Alexander Napier, Lord Merzemstoun, his heirs and assignees heritably,of a land of the late Sir James Allirdes, lying on the north side

of the High Street, within the tenement of the said Alexander Napier, between the lands on the south and north. Witnesses, John Dykson, Sirs James Denniston and David Purdy, chaplains, John Hucheson, Alexander Napier of Wrightshouses, Andrew Murray, Thomas Arnot, William Watson, Patrick Lithqw and Hugh Wallas. James Young is bailie.

534. 1533-4 Jan. 20. Sasine on renunciation by Jonet Anderson, daughter of the late Thomas Anderson, in favour of William Anderson her brother, of the tenement of the said late Thomas, lying on the north side of the High Street, between a tenement of John Fischar on the east, and the lands of the late John Williamson on the west; the North Loch on the north, and the King's public street on the south. With the said Jonet's oath not to revoke. Witnesses, Alexander Young, notary, William Uddart, Thomas Uddart, James Uddart, Henry Cranston, John Cowane, William Watson and Thomas Arnot.

535. 1533-4 Jan. 20. Sasine to Alexander Adamson, on his cognition by George Cant, bailie, as brother and heir of the late David Adamson, of the said David's tenement lying on the north side of the High Street, beside the Netherbow, between the land of the late Andrew Elphinston of Selmis, now pertaining to Master Henry Spittall, on the east, and a land of Alexander Cant on the west; the lands or yard of Trinity College on the north, and the King's public street on the south. Witnesses, Sirs David Young and William Merschell, chaplains, Master David Ireland, William Adamson, Richard Gray, Thomas Arnot and William Watson.

536. 1533-4 Jan. 20. Sasine on renunciation by Master Richard Boithuell, provost of the Kirk-of-Field, in favour of William Anderson, son and heir of the late Thomas Anderson, of a tenement of the said Thomas, lying on the north side of the High Street, between a tenement of John Fischar on the east, and the lands of the late John Williamson on the west; the North Loch on the north, and the King's public street on the south. And forthwith the said William Anderson resigned his tenement foresaid in the hands of James Young, bailie, in favour of himself and Elizabeth Uddart his affianced spouse, the longest liver of them, and the heirs lawfully to be procreated betwixt them, etc., who are thereupon seised in conjunctfee in said tenement. Witnesses, Master James Lauson, provost of Edinburgh, Master Francis Boithuell, Alexander Young, notary public, William Uddart, Thomas Uddart, Robert Hoppar, John Park, Gilbert Neilson, Thomas Arnot and William Watson.

537. 1533-4 Feb. 9. Sasine on resignation by John Levingtoun, in favour of Elizabeth Levingtoun his daughter, and James Newman her spouse, of the following annual-rents: (1) an annual-rent of 20 shillings out of a land or tenement of the late Walter Chepman, lying in the Cowgate, on the south side thereof, between a land of the late John Adamson and Jonet Lamb his spouse on the east, and a land sometime of John Vernour "*le* plottok" on the west. (2) an annual-rent of 13sh.4d. out of a land of Robert Law, flesher, lying in Peebles Wynd, west

side the transe thereof, between the land of Anthony Brussat on the south, and a land of John Carnoquhen on the north. Witnesses, Robert Johnston, Roger Murray, John Burrowman, George Merschell, William Craig, Robert Knox, John Raa, Thomas Bryson, and Thomas Arnot, serjeant. William Sym is bailie.

538. 1533–4 Feb. 14. Sasine on resignation by Isobella Balfour, with consent of George Sandilands her spouse, in favour of Jonet Balfour, of an annual-rent of 2 merks out of a land of the said Jonet, lying below the Netherbow, on the south side of the High Street, between the lands of the said Isobella Balfour on the south, and the King's public street on the north. With the said Isobella's oath not to revoke. Witnesses, George Allan, John Burrowman, Henry Quhite, John Robison, Robert Henrison, Donald Reid and Patrick Lithqw, serjeant. William Sym is bailie.

539. 1533–4 March 2. Sasine on resignation by James Uddart, in favour of Cristina Towris his spouse in liferent after the said James's decease, of his land, lying on the north side of the High Street, between a land of Henry Lille on the south, and a waste land of the late Gilbert Fische on the north; a land of the late William Baron on the east, and the transe of the said tenement on the west. Witnesses, Alexander Pery, and William Watson, serjeant. Alexander Spens is bailie.

540. 1533–4 March 16. Sasine on resignation by Robert Hector, with consent of Margaret Liddaill his spouse, in favour of Henry Scot, burgess, of the said Robert's waste land, on the south side of the High Street, lying within a tenement of the late John Bruse, west side the transe thereof, between a land or mansion of the late Patrick Forous on the north, and the waste land of Henry Lille on the south; the land of the late Edward Bonkill on the east, and a land of the late Walter Blaklok on the west. Witnesses, Thomas Lyndesay, Robert Urquhart, Robert Carryk, James Thomson, Thomas Purdy, Sir Walter Cant, and James Johnston *alias* Edinburgh, serjeant. George Cant is bailie. This land is analiit under a reversion contenand lx lib. quhilk the said Robert oblissis him till pay, and redeme the samyn betuix this and Yule nixt-tocum. Falzeand thair of the said Henry till pay the remanent of xxti.lib. and sua the land to be fre to the said Henry and his airis for evir. Robert asked instruments.

541. 1533 – 4 March 18. Compeared personally William Logane in Leith, and constituted Gilbert Logane, Michael Logane and Richard Lundy his procurators, severally and conjointly, to redeem the lands of Fluris lying, etc. and premonish. . . . . .
Todryk his mother, and John Litill her spouse, to receive the sum for the redemption of the said lands of Fluris, conform to the tenor of the letter of reversion made thereupon. And likewise to forewarn them to remove themselves and their gear from the land and houses, in which they now dwell lying within the town of Leith at the feast of Pentecost next and immediately following; and finally constitutes them his procurators in all actions, questions, pleas, etc., promising to hold the same firm and stable. Done in the notary's dwelling-house in presence

of John Anderson, Andrew Quhite, John Douglas and John Quhite.

542. 1533–4 March 24. Sasine on resignation by Margaret Currour, daughter and one of the heirs of the late John Currour, with consent of George Craik her spouse, in favour of Henry Cranston and Cristina Smyth his spouse in conjunct-fee, of the land of the said John Currour, now pertaining to the said Margaret and her spouse, lying beyond the Overbow, on the south side of the High Street, between a land of the late Edward Davidson on the east, and a land of the late Alexander Reid on the west, now pertaining to Henry Cranston; the waste land of the said late John Currour on the south, and the King's public street on the north. With the woman's oath not to revoke. Witnesses, Alexander Rynd, Henry Levington, James Aikman, William Aikinhead, Henry Tyndaill, Patrick Aitkin, Maurice Coupland, Thomas Glendynnyn, William Watson and Thomas Arnot. Alexander Spens is bailie.

The quhilk day, etc., in presens of the bailie and witnes aboue wryttin Margret Currour and George Craik hir spous oblis thame thair airis, etc., till warrand and keip the said Henry Cranston and his spous, and thair airis, harmless and skaithles at the handis of all maner of personis, anent the said land, quhilk thai had analiit till him. And gif it happin ony uthir airis of the said John Currour to be liffand, and cum hame to this cuntrie, and trouble or optenis the saidis landis fra the said Henry Cranston or his airis, in that cais thai obliss thame faithfully, and thair airis as said is, till content and pay the soume of xxxv lib. to the said Henry Cranston and his airis for the said land. Because the said land was sauld for the said soume, and na better at this tyme. And als to warrand the said Henry and his land skaithles of all annuellis awand furth of the said land, of all tymes befor the dait hereof, but fraud or gyle. And thereupon asked instruments.

543. 1533–4 March 24. Sasine on resignation by John Michelson, son and heir of the late Cristina Stallis, in favour of Henry Tyndaill, burgess, and Agnes Currour his spouse in conjunct-fee, of the said John Michelson's land lying on the south side of the High Street, in the end of a tenement of William Lauder, west side the transe thereof, between a land of the late John Lethame on the north, and another land of the late Patrick Scallis on the south: Reserving the liferent of the foresaid land to Isobella Scot, relict of the said Patrick Scallis. Witnesses, Alexander Rynd, Henry Levingtoun, James Aikman, Alexander Pery, Thomas Arnot and William Watson. Alexander Spens is bailie.

544. 1533–4 March 24. Sasine on resignation by Agnes Currour, daughter and one of the heirs of the late John Currour, with consent of Henry Tyndaill her spouse, in favour of James Aikman, burgess, and Isobella Currour his spouse in conjunct-fee, of the said Agnes Currour's upper hall of the backland of the said late John Currour's tenement on the south side of the High Street, at the Castlehill, between a land of the late

174 PROTOCOL BOOK

William Adamson on the east, and a land of the late John Dee on the west: Together with the chamber, kitchen, and lofts above the same; and one cellar of the said backland, with all their pertinents. With the usual oath of the woman not to revoke. Witnesses, Thomas Michelson, John Michelson, Alexander Rynd, Henry Levington, John Litill, Alexander Pery, William Blaklok, and Thomas Arnot, serjeant. Under reversion of £52. Alexander Spens is bailie.

545. 1533-4 March 24. Bond of relief by Agnes Currour and Henry Tyndaill her spouse to James Aikman and Isobella Currour his spouse, to warrant and keep them free from all annual-rents owing furth of the land analiit to them in the foregoing seasine. And if any living heir of the said John Currour should come to this country and trouble them or obtain the said land from the said James Aikman and his spouse, in that case they oblige themselves to pay to the said James and his spouse, the sum of £52 for which sum the said land was analiit.

546. 1533-4 March 24. The quhilk day Henry Tyndaill granted him weill and thankfully paiit, be the handis of James Aikman and Issobell his spous, of the soume of fifty tua pundis usuall money of Scotland, for the hall, chalmer, ketching, lofts, and ane cellar of the bakland of umquhile Johne Currour, quhilk the said Henry and his spous analiit to thame apon the said soume; and thairfor discharges thame thairof, and thair airis forevir: Reservand alwayis till the said Henry and his spous, and thair airis, the ane reversion apon the redemyng of the said land contenand the said soume of £52. Witnesses, Alexander Rynd, in whose house this is done, Henry Levington and John Michelson.

547. 1533-4 March 24. John Michelson grantit him weill contentit and paiit, be the handis of Henry Tyndaill and his wif, of the soume of xliij lib. xiijs. iiijd., for his land quhilk he analiit to thame, liand at the fut of William Lauder's Clois, eftir the form of his chartour and instrument maid thairapone. And thairfore the said John Michelson, for him, his airis, etc., quhytclamys and dischargis the said Henry Tyndaill and his spous, their airis, etc., forevir. Same place and witnesses.

548. This prothogoll follow and suld be tane in befor the letter 6 wrytt the xxiiij day of Merche anno xxxiij, at the beginning of the secund laif befor.
1533-4 March 21. Compeared personally Elizabeth Dykson, sister and one of the heirs of the late James Dykson, with consent of Alexander Bertoun her spous, on the one part, and Jonet Dykson sister and the other of the heirs of the said late James, with consent of George Cant her spouse, on the other part; and agreed to the division of a certain tenement of land, lying within the burgh of Edinburgh, in the vennel of the Friars Preachers, west side the transe thereof, in this manner as after follows in the vernacular:-
The quhilk day it is appoyntit and fynalie aggreit betuix honorable personis, that is to say Elizabeth Dykson, eldest sister and ane of the airis of umquhile James Dykson, with

consent of Alexander Berton hir spous, on that ane pairt, and Jonet Dykson, the younger sister and the tother of the airis of said umquhile James, with consent of George Cant her spous, on the tother pairt, anent the pairtisyng and dividing of ane land and tenement liand within the burgh of Edinburgh, on the south syde the kingis streit in the Freir Wynd, on the west syde the trans of the samyne, betuix the land of Edward Bissait on the north pairt, and the land of Johne Richartson on the south pairt in this maner as eftir followis, viz. The said Jonet Dykson, with consent of the said George hir spous, as youngest sister, has dividit and set the said land and tenement in this kynd, that is to say, the nether hall, ketching and chalmer with the galriis on the west syde pertenand thairto and pertinentis, to be ane pairt and half of the said land and tenement. And the ovir hall, with the chalmer, ketching and galriis on the west syde, with the sellaris of the samyn land, to be the tother pairt and half of the said tenement; and that pairt sall hald the haill land watter ticht. Of the quhilk ij pairtis of the said land the first chois was referrit to the said Elizabeth, as eldest sister, and to Alexander Berton hir spous. And thai beand ryplie avisit thairwith nemmit and chesit to thame the said last pairt, viz. the ovir hall, chalmer, ketching, galriis and thre cellaris to pertene and remane with thame heretablie. And sua the first pairt of this division, that is to say, the nether hall, chalmer, and ketching, and galriis thairof, with thair pertinentis, to remane with the said Janet and George hir spous heretablie, in all tymes tocum. And the said Elizabeth and Alexander till keip the nether hall scaithles of watter, and of the fluring of the uthir hall, and the pertinents thairof. And heir apone bayth the saidis pairteis askit instruments. Done upon the ground in presence of William Sym, Alexander Spens, bailies, Master David Ireland, John Burroman, John Cant, Gilbert Elwand, and William Watson, serjeant.

549. 1533–4 March 21. Sasine on resignation by Jonet Dykson, with consent of George Cant her spouse, in favour of Elizabeth Dykson and Alexander Berton her spouse, of the foresaid hall, chamber, kitchen and gallery of the tenement of the late James Dykson, lying in the wynd of the Friars Preachers. Same witnesses as above. Alexander Spens is bailie.

550. 1534 March 21. Sasine on resignation by Elizabeth Dykson, with consent of Alexander Berton her spouse, in favour of Jonet Dykson and George Cant her spouse, of the said Elizabeth's part of the said tenement of the late James Dykson, lying in the vennel of the Friars Preachers, west side the transe thereof, which was possessed *pro indiviso*, viz. the nether hall, chamber, kitchen with gallery, etc. Same bailie and witnesses as aforesaid.

551. 1534 March 26. Sasine on resignation by James Dornwyk, in favour of himself and Helen Purde his spouse, of his land in the vennel of Sanct Mary Wynd, east side the transe thereof, between a land of the late Edward Bonkill on the north, and

the land pertaining to the altar of St. Severin, situated within the church of St. Giles, on the south. Witnesses, Sirs David Purde and William Adamson, William Hill, James Kynnaird, Gilbert Williamson, William Pettigreif, James Young, James Gray, and William Watson, serjeant. Alexander Spens is bailie.

552. 1534 March 27. Sasine on resignation by Master Thomas Broune, rector or prebendary of Lamlathane, in favour of Master John Chepman, burgess, his heirs and assignees, of an annual-rent of 6 merks, out of a backland of John Broune, in a tenement of the late James Baty, on the north side of High Street, between the fore land of the said James Baty on the south, and a land of the late John Bonkill, now pertaining to Edward Kincaid, on the north; a land of Master Adam Otterburn on the east, and the trause of the said tenement or close called Bonkill's Close on the west. Witnesses, John Aitchison, David Chepman, John Carnbe, William Riche, William Watson and Thomas Arnot. Alexander Spens is bailie.

553. 1534 March 28. John Broune broke the sasine given by Alexander Spens, bailie, of 6 merks annual, leviable from his land as is contained in the protocol immediately preceding to Master John Chepman, by breaking a dish as use is, protesting that the same shall not be any prejudice to him; and for remeid of law in more ample form. Witnesses, William Sym and George Cant, bailies, John Baxter, Andrew Mowbray, Master David Ireland, William Watson and Thomas Arnot.

554. 1534 April 2. Sasine on resignation by John Fischar, with consent of Isobell Wyndezettis his spouse, in favour of Thomas Fischar their son, his heirs and assignees, of an annual-rent of 9 merks, out of a land of the late John Coky, lying on the south side of the High Street, between a land pertaining to the chaplain of the service of St. Triduan, founded by the late Sir Robert Hopper, at the altar of Saint Roch, situated within the church of St. Giles, on the east, and a land of James Aikman on the west: Reserving the liferent of the said annual-rent to the said John Fischar and Isobell, the survivor of them. Witnesses, Sir Alexander Scot, provost of Corstorphine, Sir George Richartson, Bartholomew Fairlie, Andrew Fischar, John Elphinston, Andrew Henrison, Thomas Arnot and William Watson. James Young is bailie.

555. 1534 April 2. Sasine on resignation by John Fischar, with consent of Isobell Wyndzettis his spouse, in favour of Sir Alexander Scot, chaplain, provost of Corstorphine, in name of the church, for an anniversary to be celebrated yearly, for the souls of the said John Fischar and his spouse, of an annual-rent of 40 shillings, out of a land of the late Master William Blakstok, lying on the north side of the High Street, between the fore land of the chaplain of the Holy Cross, situated within the parish church of Dalkeith, on the south, and the trause of the tenement on the east, and another trause of the tenement of the said Archibald Williamson on the west. Witnesses, Thomas Fischar and the others aforesaid.

556. 1534 April 2. Sasine on precept from chancery in favour of Cornelias Haliburtoun, sister and heir of the late Thomas Haliburton, of an annual-rent of 7 merks out of a land of the late John Homyll, now pertaining to the heirs of the late James Homyll, lying on the south side of the High Street, within a tenement of William Lord Borthik, east side the transe thereof, between the waste land of the said tenement on the south, and the mansion of the said Lord Borthik on the north; a land of the late Henry Rynd, now of Alexander Rynd, on the east, and a tenement of the late Charles Levington on the west. Witnesses, Thomas Smyth, Andrew Tailzour, William Williamson, Thomas Arnot and William Watson, serjeants. George Cant is bailie.

557. 1534 April 9. Compeared Thomas Craufurd, burgess, and with consent of Helen Craufurd his daughter and heir apparent, constituted David Craufurd his procurator to resign his waste land within his tenement, between the stone wall and his other waste land on the north, and the waste land of William Elphinston on the south, in the hands of one of the bailies of Edinburgh, for sasine thereof to be given to the said William Elphinston and his spouse Katherine Curll, conform to the tenor of a charter to be made thereupon. Witnesses, Alexander McNeil, notary public, William Sym, James Dornwyk, William Stewart, James Ra, John Burrowman, William Henrison and William Watson.

558. 1534 April 9. Sasine on resignation by David Craufurd, procurator and in name of Thomas Craufurd, with consent of Helen Craufurd, daughter and heir apparent of the said Thomas, in favour of William Elphinston and Katherine Curll, his spouse, of a tenement of the said Thomas Craufurd, namely his waste land lying within his said tenement on the south side of the High Street, between the land of Thomas Scot on the east, and the tenement of William Elphinston on the west, the stone wall, etc., on the north. Witnesses aforesaid. William Sym is bailie.
The quhilk (day) in presens of the ballie William Sym, and the witnes abon wryttin, Thomas Craufurd, in his latter will and mynd, left in legacy to (   ) Craufurd and (   ) Craufurd his dochteris, the rest of the money beand in William Elphinston's hand restand awand for the waist land that he sauld to the said William, and ordanit the samen to be gevin till his said tua dochteris; and that with consent of Helen Craufurd his dochter and apperand air. And therapone Alexander McNeill askit instrument. Done in the dwelling-house of the said Thomas Craufurd in presence of William Sym, William Elphinston, James Dornwyk, and the others above written.

559. 1534 April 11. Sasine to Alexander Levingtoun, on his cognition by George Cant, bailie, as son and heir of the late John Levingtoun, burgess, in and to a tenement of the said John, lying on the north side of the High Street, between a tenement of the late Nichol Spethy on the east, a tenement of Donald Kyle on the west, a land of the Earl of Argyll on the north, and the king's public street on the south. Moreover the said bailie passed to another land of the said late John Levingtoun, lying

on the south side of the High Street, lying within a tenement of William Adamson, west side the transe thereof, between a land of the said William Adamson, on the north, and a land of Robert Law on the south; and there cognosced and entered the said Alexander Levingtoun in and to the foresaid land, under and above, by delivery to him of earth and stone as use is. Witnesses, Alexander Cant, William Tod, Robert Bishop, Andrew Edgar, Thomas Anderson, Andrew Tod, Richard Lauder, John Park, William Watson and Thomas Arnot.

560. 1534 April 16. Sasine to Isobella Ambrose on her cognition by James Young, bailie, as grand daughter and heir of the late William Merschell, in and to a land of the said William lying on the north side of the High Street, within a tenement of James Halkerston, west side the transe thereof, between a land of the late Allan Buchan on the north, and a land of the said James Halkerston on the south; and which tenement lies between a land of Duncan Wicht on the east, and a land of the late Robert Lyndesay on the west. And forthwith the said Isobel Ambrose, of her own free will, as she asserted, resigned the foresaid land in the hands of the bailie, who thereupon gave sasine and conjunct-infeftment thereof to the said Isobella Ambrose and James Broune her spouse, the survivor of them, and the heirs lawfully procreated or to be procreated between them, whom failing to the heirs of the said Isobel whomsoever. Witnesses, William Stevinson, notary public, William Aikinheid, George Gibson, Robert Spens, John Alderston, John Cannoch, William Watson and Patrick Lithqw, serjeants.

561. 1534 April 17. Sasine on process of recognition led before the provost and bailies of Edinburgh by the Friars Preachers, in favour of friar Andrew Layis, in name of the convent place of the Friars Preachers, and their successors, of the following subjects, (1) The waste land of the late Patrick Reidpethe, lying beside the Netherbow, on the north side of the High Street, between a land of the said late Patrick, newly built, on the south, and the yard of Trinity College on the north; a land of the late Thomas Turnour on the east, and a land of the late George Henrison on the west. (2) Another waste land lying below the Bow of Saint Mary Wynd, west side the High Street, between the yard of the saids Friars on the south, and a land of the late William Cody on the north; the cemetery of the said Friars on the west, and the King's common way on the east. Witnesses, William Sym, Alexander Spens, bailies, Francis Spottiswood, Robert Flemyng, John Barrowman, Alexander Pery, Quintin Wauchop, and Thomas Arnot, serjeant. James Young is bailie.

562. 1534 April 20. James Young, bailie, passed to the following subjects, to wit, (1) A tenement of the late Luke Young, now pertaining to the heirs of the late John Davidson, lying on the south side of the High Street, between a land of John Purves on the east, and a land of the late William Fausyde, now pertaining to William Tod and Walter Scot, on the west; and there John Cunynghame, spouse of the late Helen Young, re-

nounced his conjunct-fee or liferent which he has of a certain land lying within the said tenement, west side the trause thereof, between a land of the said John Davidson on the north, and a land of William Sym on the south. (2) Also of an annual-rent of 20 shillings leviable out of the foresaid land of the said William Sym lying within the said tenement, between the lands before named on the north, and a land of the late John Bell on the south. (3) Likewise of his other annual-rent out of the easter booth of the foreland of the said tenement, in the hands of the said bailie, in favour of Thomas Cunynghame, son and heir of the said late Helen Young his mother. And forthwith the said James Young bailie cognosced and entered the said Thomas Cunynghame, as heir foresaid, in and to the foresaid land excepting the south cellar thereof, and two annual-rents respectively. Witnesses, William Sym, Walter Scot, Richard Cristeson, Thomas Todryk, James Dornwyk, John Arkill, Sir Edward Edgar, Patrick Lithqw, William Watson and Thomas Arnot, serjeants.

563. 1534 April 20. Sasine on resignation by Thomas Cunynghame above designed, with consent of John Cunynghame his father, in favour of Francis Spottiswood, burgess, and Margaret Davidson his spouse, of (1) The said Thomas Cunynghame's land, excepting the cellar thereof, lying within the tenement of the late Luke Young now of the heirs of the late John Davidson, lying and bounded as before described; (2) an annual-rent of 20 shillings out of the foresaid land of William Sym within the said tenement; (3) an annual-rent of 6sh.8d. out of the foreland of the said tenement. The same bailie and witnesses as in the previous sasine.

564. 1534 April 20. Sasine on resignation by Thomas Gray, procurator and in name of Thomas Harlaw, cousin and one of the heirs of the late Robert Forous, in favour of Henry Scot, burgess, of the following subjects, (1) The said Thomas Harlaw's third part of a certain land and mansion, lying within a tenement of the late John Bruse, on the south side of the High Street, between a land of the late Edward Bonkill on the east, and a land of the late Walter Blaklok on the west; a land of the late William Ker on the north, and another waste land, now pertaining to the heirs of the late Henry Scot, on the south; (2) another foreland of the said late Robert Forous lying in the lower end of the said tenement, between the land of the said late Edward Bonkill on the east, and a land of the late Patrick Forous on the west; the street of the Cowgate on the south, and a land of the late John Robison, now of David Gardiner, on the north; (3) an annual-rent of 25 shillings out of the foresaid land of David Gardner, within the said tenement, in the lower end thereof, between the said foreland on the south, and another land of the said late Robert Forous on the north; (4) the said Thomas Harlaw's part of another backland of the said late Robert Forous, lying in the lower end of the said tenement, between the land of the said David Gardner on the south, and a land of Henry Lille on the

north. Witnesses, Nichol Carncors, Patrick Scot, John Mosman, David Dwn, David Gardner, Thomas Lynto; Thomas Arnot and William Watson, serjeants. William Sym is bailie.

565. 1534 April 20. Sasine on resignation by George Law, cousin and one of the heirs of the late Robert Forous, in favour of Henry Scot, burgess, of the following subjects. (1) the said George Law's third part of a certain land and mansion lying within the foresaid tenement of the late John Bruse, on the south side of the High Street, and bounded as before described; (2) his third part of another foreland of the said late Robert Forous, lying in the lower end of the foresaid tenement, and bounded *ut supra;* (3) his third part of annual-rent of 25 shillings, out of the land of David Gardner lying in the lower end of the said tenement, and bounded as aforesaid; (4) the said George Law's third part of another backland of the said late Robert Forous, also lying in the lower end of the said tenement, between the land of David Gardner on the south, and the land of Henry Lille and his spouse on the north. Same bailie and witnesses as in the preceding sasine.

566. 1534 April 20. Sasine on resignation by Henry Scot in favour of himself and Jonet Scot his spouse, of his third part of the land and mansion lying within the tenement of the late John Bruse, on the south side of the High Street. Also of his third part of the foreland and backland of the late Robert Forous lying within the foresaid tenement; and his third part of the annual-rent of 25 shillings; out of the land of David Gardner lying in the said tenement; and all bounded as described in the said Henry Scot's sasine of the same in folio 190. Bailie and witnesses *ut supra.*

567. 1534 April 24. Sasine on resignation by David Carnegy, burgess of Dundee, in favour of William Sym, bailie of the burgh of Edinburgh, of a land or tenement formerly of John Scharp, now pertaining to the said David Carnegy, lying on the south side of the High Street, between a land of Alexander Pennycuk on the east,and a land of James Black on the west;a land of Gilbert Welsche on the north,the Cowgate and another land of the said John Scharp on the south. Witnesses,Michael Blyth, John Burrowman,Thomas Robison,Alexander Pery;Thomas Arnot,Patrick Lithqw and Hugh Wallas,serjeants. Alexander Spens is bailie.
The quhilk day in presens of the said ballie Alexander Spens, and witnes abone writtin, David Carnegy oblissis him till freith and mak the said land fre of all annuellis awand furth of the samyn to Corstorphin, or otheris, of all termes bygane to this day; and thereupon the said William Sym askit an instrument. Attour the said William Sym oblist him, and his airis, that quhat tyme that evir John Scharp, his airis and assignais, contentis and payis to him, his airs or assignais, the soume of iiij^{xx}· lib. usuall money of Scotland, that he sall renunce and gif our the said land and tenement frelie to thame without any obstakle or impediment.

568. 1534 April 27. Sasine to William Pacok on his cognition by George Cant, bailie, as heir of the late William Pacok his

father, in and to the said William's foreland, lying on the south side of the High Street, between a land of the late John Bell on the east, and a land of James Preston on the west; a land of John Marjoribanks on the south, and the King's public street on the north. Witnesses, William Sym, Master David Irland, John Pardovyne, Andrew Tod; William Watson and Thomas Arnot, serjeants. George Cant is bailie.

569. 1534 April 27. William Pacok, the son and air of the umquhile William Pacok, sett in assedatioun till Peter Pacok, all and haill his estmost buith on the stair of his forland, for ij yeir nixt tocum eftir the feist of Witsonday nixt tocum, for vj merkis in the yeir; and promittit to warrand him the samyn durand the said yeris. Peter Pacok asked an instrument. Done in the booth of the late John Levington. Witnesses, Vincent Strathauchin, and Patrick Lithqw, serjeant.

570. 1534 May 6. Sasine on resignation by Peter Ramsay in favour of a discreet religious man, friar John Greirson, professor of theology and provincial of the whole order of the Friars Preachers within the kingdom of Scotland, in name and for the part of the Friars and convent of the place of the said order of Friars Preachers within the burgh of Dundee, and their successors, of an annual-rent of £10, out of the lands of John Scharp, baker, lying on the north side of the High Street of the Cowgate, between a land of John Fawsyde on the east, and a certain waste land on the west; a waste land of Alexander Pennycuke and another built land of the said John Scharp on the north, and the king's public street of the Cowgate on the south. Witnesses, Alexander Spens, George Cant, Alexander Pery, Robert Donaldson, Thomas Ramsay, Thomas Brown, James Gray, William Watson and Thomas Arnot. James Young is bailie.

The quhilk day in presens of the ballie and witnes abon wryttin, William Sym allegit and said, that the new land biggit be John Scharp apon the west pairt of the land that he coft fra John Sprot is a pairt of the land quhilk he now has in heretage, and suld pay the pairt of the annuell aucht furth of the haill land, safer as it extendis to; and therfor he protestit that the said new land biggit apon the said waist ground mycht releif him of the annuell awand furth of his land to Corstorphin or uthir placis, and for remeid of law quhen and quhar it efferit. The said William asked instruments. Witnesses, *ut supra.*

The quhilk day, in presens of the ballies and witnes forsaid, Peter Ramsay declarit that the time he took sesing of the x lib. of annuell, it was given to him of all and haill the lands abon writtin, without ony restriction be thame that had rycht tharto; and therfor he protestit, that he and his assignais mycht bruke the samyn without impadiment, eftir the forme of his charter and infeftment maid thar apon, and thar apon askit instrument. Witnesses *ut supra.*

571. 1534 May 7. Renunciation by William Ogill in favour of George Nicholl, burgess, of a letter of reversion made by the said George to him upon the redemption of the land previously

alienated by him to the said George, lying in Forstaris Wynd, west side the transe thereof, between a land of Thomas Ramsay on the south, and a land of the laird of Corstorphin on the north. Done in the booth of the common clerk, in presence of Thomas Gray, John Alison and James Nicholl.

572. 1534 May 22. Sasine on renunciation by Isobella Edname, relict of John Bannatyne, fuller, of her conjunct-fee in favour of Helen Keith and John Gray heirs of the said John Bannatyne, and on cognition of the said Helen and John by James Young, bailie, as heirs foresaid, to wit the said Helen Keith in the one half part of a land of the said John Bannatyne, lying on the south side of the High Street, within a tenement of the late Charles Levington, now pertaining to John Foular, notary public, on the north: Which half part of the foresaid land the said Helen Keith, with consent of Robert Gray her spouse, resigns in the hands of the bailie, who thereupon gave heritable sasine and conjunct-fee thereof to Cuthbert Dik, burgess, and Jonet Hannay his spouse. With court and the oath of the woman not to revoke in time to come: Reserving the liferent of the said half part to Isobel Edname. Witnesses, Sir John Thomson, chaplain, James Stirk, Patrik Urry, Hugh Wallas and David Purves.

573. The said day hour and witnesses James Young, bailie, cognosced and entered John Gray, son of Marion Keith, as one of the heirs of the said late John Bannatyne in and to the other half part of the foresaid land, under and above with pertinents. And forthwith the said John Gray, with consent of Patrick Urry his curator, resigned his half part of the foresaid land in the hands of the bailie, who thereupon gave heritable sasine and conjunct-infeftment thereof to Cuthbert Dyk, burgess, and Jonet Hannay his spouse. Witnesses ut supra.

574. 1534 June 3. Sasine on resignation by Alexander Mauchane, in favour of Adam Mauchane his son, his heirs and assignees, of an annual-rent of 6 merks, out of a land of William Craik lying in Buithraw, on the south side of the High Street, between a land of the late Sir John Rynd, chaplain, on the east, and a land of Alexander Mauchane on the west, also of an annual-rent of 3 merks, out of a land of the said Alexander Mauchane, lying in the Buithraw, between a land of the said William Craik on the east, and a land of the late Michael Frog, now pertaining to Master Adam Otterburn and James McCalzeane, on the west. Witnesses, Edward Kincaid, Gilbert Lauder, Alexander Pery, George Levingston, Sir John Watson and Sir John Aikman, chaplains, Hugh Wallas, Thomas Arnot and William Watson serjeants. George Cant is bailie.

575. 1534 June 13. Sasine to Alexander Malison, on his cognition by George Cant, bailie, as heir of the late Thomas Malison his father, in and to a land of the said Thomas, lying below the Castle Wall, on the north side of the High Street, between a land of the late Andrew Robison, now pertaining to Alexander Wilkeson, on the east, and a land of David Kincaid on the west, the Castlehill on the north, and the king's public street

on the south. And forthwith the said Alexander Malison resigned his foresaid land, under and above, in the hands of the bailie, who thereupon gave heritable sasine and conjunct-infeftment thereof to Archibald Wilson and Katrine Cathkin his spouse. Witnesses, Master David Ireland, George Somervell, Thomas Paterson, John Johnston, John Cannoch, Andrew Scot, and William Watson, serjeant.

576. 1534 July 1. Sasine on resignation by William Scallis and Elizabeth Brady his spouse, with one consent, in favour of John Purro, burgess, of the lands of the said Elizabeth Brady and William Scallis her spouse, lying on the south side of the High Street, in the vennel of the Friars Preachers, east side thereof, between the lands of Alan Mossman and George Gibson on the south, and the lands of John Vernour and the late William Powis on the north, the land sometime of John Anderson, now pertaining to James Ur, on the east, and a land of the said Alan Mossman and the said vennel on the west. Also of another land of the said William Scallis and his spouse lying in the vennel of the Kirk of Field, east the transe thereof, between a land of the Abbot and Convent of Jedburgh on the south, the lands of Henry Scot on the east, and north, and the said vennel on the west, in security of the first land. Witnesses, John Young, John Swayne, Patrick Scot, George Darroch, John Watson, and David Purves, serjeant. James Young is bailie.

577. 1534 July 17. Renunciation by Robert Sinclair, son and heir of the late Robert Sinclair, in favour of Archibald Leiche, son of the late David Leiche, of a land of the said David lying within a tenement of the late Symon Doweill, on the north side of the High Street, between a tenement of Alexander Cant on the east, and a tenement of the late David Knox on the west, a land of the late John Reid and the late (   ) on the south, and the lands of the late Ninian Thomson and a certain waste land on the north. Witnesses, Patrick Tennent, Andrew Dalmahoy, Martin Uddart, John Malcome and David Purves, serjeant.

578. 1534 July 17. Sasine to Robert Sinclair, on his cognition by James Young, bailie, as heir of the late Robert Sinclair his father, in and to an annual-rent of 6 merks out of the land of the late David Leiche, lying within the tenement of the late Symon Doweill, and bounded as before described. The witnesses as aforesaid.

579. 1534 July 17. Sasine on resignation by Elizabeth Hoppar in favour of herself and Patrick Tennent her spouse, of the following subjects: (1) Of a backland of the said Elizabeth lying on the south side of the High Street, between a certain foreland of the late Patrick Richartson on the north, and a land of Clement Litill on the south, a land of the late Elizabeth Scot, Lady Manerston, on the east, and a land of John Cant on the west; (2) the foreland of the said Elizabeth lying on the north side of the High Street, between a tenement of the late Richard Hoppar on the east, and a land of the late James

Baty on the west; a land of Master Adam Otterburn on the north, and the king's public street on the south; (3) the backland of the said Elizabeth Hoppar, lying on the north side of the High Street, within a tenement of the said late Richard Hoppar, between a land of the said late Richard on the south, and a land now pertaining to George Henrison on the north. Witnesses, Sir Walter Cant, Barnard Sprot, Stephen Eldar, James Litiljohn, David Irrewyn, Sir John Watson, John Preston, Peter Bynny, David Dwn; Thomas Arnot and William Watson, serjeants.

580. 1534 July 18. Sasine on resignation by Robert Sinclair, son and heir of the late Robert Sinclair, in favour of John Reid, son and heir of the late John Reid, of an annual-rent of 13sh.4d. out of a land of his said father, lying within a tenement of the late Symon Doweill, on the north side of the High Street, between a tenement of Alexander Cant on the east, and a tenement of the deceased David Knox on the west. Witnesses, John Purves, John Burrowman; William Watson and Patrick Lithqw, serjeants.

581. 1534 July 28. Sasine given by James Young, bailie, conform to a process of recognition, in favour of Alexander Levington, of a waste land and chapel, sometime pertaining to George, bishop of Elphin, lying upon the Castlehill, on the south side of the High Street, between a land of the late James Scot on the east, the lands of the said hill and the Castle Wynd on the west; the lands of the late Mathew Harvey and Thomas Haithwy on the south, and the said Castlehill on the north. Witnesses, Sir John Kyle, John Smyth, William Dyk, Walter Ramsy, Alexander Blakburn, Thomas Baron, Patrick Lithqw. Alexander Levington resigns said waste land and chapel in favour of Marjorie Bassenden who is thereupon seised in the same.

582. 1534 Aug. 11. Sasine to Margaret Davidson, on her cognition by James Young, bailie, as heir of the late John Davidson her father, of a land and bark-house, built and waste, of the said John Davidson, beside the place of the Friars Preachers, on the west side of the transe that leads to the kirk of the said Friars, between their waste land on the south, and a land of the late Jasper Mayne on the north, the land or yard . . . . . and the public street leading to the said kirk on the east. Witnesses, Alexander Young, notary public, John Somervell, John Spottiswood, and Patrick Linlithqw, serjeant.

583. 1534 Aug. 19. James Young, bailie, passed to that land of the late John Davidson, lying on the south side of the High Street, within a tenement of the late Archibald Todryk, on the east side of the trause thereof, between a land of the late Andrew Watson on the north, and a land of the Friars Preachers on the south; and there Elizabeth Spottiswood, daughter of the late Francis Spottiswood, confessed that the said land is now lawfully redeemed from her by Margaret Davidson her mother, daughter and heir of the late John Davidson by payment to her of the sum of 200 merks; and therefore renounced the said land from her and over gives all right, claim, property and

possession which she has to the same forever. And forthwith the said James Young, bailie, cognosced and entered the said Margaret Davidson, as daughter and heir of the late John Davidson, in and to the foresaid land, under and above, with pertinents. And immediately thereafter the said Margaret Davidson resigned the one half of the foresaid land in the hands of the bailie, who thereupon gave heritable sasine thereof to Margaret Spottiswood her daughter, her heirs and assignees. And in like manner the said Margaret Davidson resigned the other half of the foresaid land in the hands of the said bailie, who forthwith gave heritable sasine thereof to William Lindsay, attorney and in name of Barbara Spottiswood, her daughter, her heirs and assignees: Reserving to the said Margaret Davidson her liferent of both halves of the land foresaid. Witnesses, Alexander Young, Archibald Farnlie, Sir Alexander Cunynghame, James Styrk, John Tait, James Johnston *alias* Edinburgh, serjeant.

584. 1534 Aug. 19. Sasine on resignation by Margaret Davidson, daughter of the late John Davidson, in favour of William Spottiswood, son and heir of the deceased Francis Spottiswood, of the said John's land now pertaining to the said Margaret, lying on the north side of the High Street, beside the Netherbow, between a land of Alexander Cant on the east, and a land of Patrick Fleming on the west, a land of the late Gilbert Coupar, now pertaining to the heirs of the late Francis Spottiswood, on the north, and the king's public street on the south: Reserving the liferent of the foresaid land to Margaret Davidson. Witnesses, Masters Peter Chaplane and Martin Balfour, Alexander Young, William Lyndesay, James Bassinden, John Tait, John Hoip, James Stirk, David Purves, and James Johnston *alias* Edinburgh, serjeant. James Young is bailie.

585. 1534 Aug. 19. Sasine on resignation by Margaret Davidson above designed in favour of John Spottiswood, son and heir of the late Francis Spottiswood, his heirs and assignees, of the said Margaret's whole back lands lying within a tenement of the late John Davidson her father, on the south side of the High Street, between a land of William Lyndesay on the east, and a land of the late Archibald Todryk on the west; the foreland of the said tenement on the north, and the land of John Barclay on the south. Reserving the liferent of said back land to the resigner. Same bailie and witnesses.

586. 1534 Aug. 22. Sasine on resignation by Alan Mossman, with consent of Margaret Borthik his spouse, in favour of Walter Scot of Brankishame, his heirs and assignees, of the said Alan's tenement, lying on the south side of the High Street, in the vennel of Forstar's Wynd, east side the transe thereof, between a land of the late Sir John Ramsay, knight, on the north, and a land of the late John Foular on the south: And this in special warrandise of the lands of Borthauch, Comonsyde and Drydane, with fortalices and mills thereof, and their pertinents, before alienated by the said Alan to the said Sir Walter Scot for the sum of 325 merks. Witnesses, John Mosman, James Scot, James

Stewart, Master Michael Scot, William Mowet, David Haw, and Hugh Wallas, serjeant. William Sym is bailie.

587. 1534 Aug. 28. Sasine on resignation by Adam Mauchane, son of Alexander Mauchane, in favour of himself and Marion Litill his spouse, of the following subjects: (1) The said Adam's land, formerly pertaining to his father in fee, lying in Buithraw, and on the north (sic) side of the High Street thereof, between a land of William Craik on the east, and a land of the late Michael Frog, now pertaining to Master Adam Otterburne and James Makcalzeane on the west; (2) an annualrent of 6 merks, out of the foresaid land of William Craik, on the south side of the High Street, in Buithraw, between a land of the late Sir Alexander Rynd, chaplain, on the east, and the said land of Adam Mauchane on the west. Witnesses, William Litill, John Adamson, Alexander Litill, William Hamilton, Adam Reid, John Scharp, and David Purves, serjeant. James Young is bailie.

588. 1534 Aug. 29. Sasine on resignation by Edward Afflek and Geils Cranston his spouse, with one consent, in favour of Thomas Broune, burgess, and Jonet Craik his spouse, of an annualrent of 5 merks, out of their land lying within a tenement of the late William Cockburn, on the south side of the High Street, between a tenement of James Preston on the east, and a tenement of Alexander Rynd on the west; the land and mansion of John Con on the north, and a land of the late Sir William Broune on the south. Witnesses are Thomas Tarbet, William Makcartnay, Thomas Glendinning, John Young and Thomas Arnot, serjeant. Upon reversion of £30 under instrument. Alexander Spens is bailie.

589. 1534 Aug. 29. James Young, bailie, passed to a tenement of the late James Townis, lying on the north side of the High Street, between a land or tenement of the late Archibald Preston, now pertaining to John Mauchane, on the east, and a tenement of the late William Carkettill on the west; and there cognosced and entered John Anderson, son and heir of the late John Anderson, in and to the wester part or half of that yard and waste land lying in the lower north end of the said tenement, between a land or garden of the late William Malcome on the south, and the North Loch on the north. And in like manner cognosced and entered Elizabeth Watson, daughter and heir of the late John Watson, in and to the easter part and half of the said yard and waste land, lying within the said tenement, in the lower north end thereof, between the waste land of the tenement of the said John Mauchane on the south, and another waste land of the foresaid tenement on the north. Witnesses, John Purves, John Nicholl, Thomas Arnot and William Watson.

The same day, hour and witnesses James Young, bailie passed to the tenement of the late James Townis lying on the north side of the High Street, and bounded as above described; and there John Anderson, son and heir of the late John Anderson, with consent of Elizabeth Watson his spouse, resigned his land or building, with halls, chambers and houses thereof, lying within the said tenement, east side the transe thereof, between a land of the late John Burgane on the south, and a land sometime of Thomas Coupland, now pertaining to Thomas Paterson on the north. Likewise the said John Anderson, with consent of Elizabeth Watson his spouse, resigned their land or yard lying in the lower north end of the said tenement, as well as on the west part as on the east part, between the land or garden of the late William Malcome and the waste land of the said John Mauchane on the south, and the North Loch, also the waste land of the tenement of the said John Mauchane on the north, in the hands of the bailie, who thereupon gave heritable sasine and conjunct-infeftment of the said land or building, with halls, chambers and houses thereof; and likewise of the foresaid yard and waste land, with all their pertinents, to John Young, burgess, and Elizabeth Borthuik his spouse, the survivor of them, etc. Reserving, however, the lower hall with the chamber in which the said John Anderson now dwells, (but excepting the cellar), and the use of the half part of the said yard to the said John and Elizabeth his spouse, the survivor of them in liferent. Witnesses, John Purves, John Nicholl, Thomas Arnot and William Watson.

590. 1534 Sept. 12. Sasine on resignation by Thomas Arthour, burgess, in favour of Robert Mar, burgess, and Margaret Harvy his spouse, of the said Thomas Arthour's house, lying within a tenement of the late William Foular, on the north side of the High Street, between a tenement of the late Donald Kyle on the east, and a tenement of the late Andrew Dykson on the west; west side the trause of the said tenement, between a land of the said late William Foular on the south, and a land of the late William Fleschour on the north. Witnesses, Sir James Dennyston, chaplain, John Blythe, Alexander Pery, Archibald Ramsay, Archibald Harvy, Sir Patrick Reid, chaplain, William Watson, Thomas Arnot and Hugh Wallas.

591. 1534 Sept. 12. Sasine on resignation by William Anderson, with consent of Jonet Merschell his spouse, in favour of Thomas Gibson, burgess, his heirs and assignees, of an annual-rent of 20s. out of the said William Anderson's land lying beyond the Overbow, on the north side of the High Street, between a land of James Darroch on the east, and the land of James Uddart on the west, the land of Lord Ruthven on the north, and the king's public street on the south. Witnesses, Henry Cranston; David Purves, William Watson and Thomas Arnot, serjeants. Alexander Spens is bailie.

592. 1534 Sept. 18. Sasine on resignation by Thomas Ramsay, with consent of Marion Ramsay his spouse, in favour of John Ramsay their son, and Margaret Nicholl his affianced spouse, the surviver of them, and the heirs lawfully to be procreated between them, of: (1) the said Thomas Ramsay's land or tenement, lying on the south side of the High Street, in the vennel of Forstar's Wynd, west side the trause thereof, between a land of the late Thomas Bervyk on the south, and a land of George

Nicholson on the north; a land of George Arnot and the late David Quhite on the west, and the transe of the said vennel on the east; (2) the fee of the merchant booth in which the said Thomas now dwells lying within a certain land in Buithraw, on the north side of the High Street, between the land of Alexander Mauchane on the east, and a land of the late Francis Peebles on the west: Reserving the liferent of the said subjects to the said Thomas Ramsay and Marion his spouse. Witnesses, Master David Ireland, John Young, John Walderson, Peter Spens, James Nicholl, Stephan Thomson, George Nicholl, William Hog; William Watson and Thomas Arnot, serjeants. Alexander Spens is bailie.

593. 1534 Sept. 25. Sasine on resignation by John Litill, with consent of Marjorie Jossie his spouse, in favour of William Chamblet, burgess, and Jonet Lochor his spouse, of a land or tenement of the said John Litill, lying at the Castlehill, on the north side of the High Street, between the lands of John Smyth on the south, and a land of the late John Musche on the north, the common transe on the west, and a land of the late John Adamson on the east. Also of an annual-rent of 4 shillings, out of a certain land, lying at the North Loch, pertaining to the late John Cranston, between a land of the late John Adamson on the east, and a land of Andrew Moncur on the west. Witnesses, Vincent Strathauchin, notary public, John Smyth, Sir John Thomson, chaplain, Cuthbert Dyk, James Anderson, William Vaiche, Robert Heriot, John Wodhall, and David Purves, serjeant. James Young is bailie.

594. 1534 October 3. Sasine on precept from chancery in favour of Thomas Robertson *alias* Davy, as kinsman and heir of the late Christopher Robertson *alias* Wynton, of an annual-rent of 10 merks, out of a land or tenement of the late Andrew Harvy, now pertaining to the heirs of the late Francis Towris, lying on the north side of the High Street, between a land of the late Adam Hoppar on the east, and the land of John Fischar on the west. Dated at Edinburgh 3 October in the 22nd. year of the King's reign. Witnesses to the sasine given on the same day, Robert Graham, Thomas Gibson, Robert Spens, Thomas Cathkin, and Thomas Arnot. William Tod is attorney for the said Thomas Robertson *alias* Davy, and James Young is bailie. The said 3rd day of October, James Young, bailie passed to the land or tenement of the late Adam Harvy, now pertaining to the heirs of the deceased Francis Towris, lying and bounded as above described, and there George Forest, procurator and in name of Thomas Robertson *alias* Davy, kinsman and heir of the late Cristall Robertson *alias* Wynton, resigned his annualrent of 10 merks, upliftable out of the foresaid land or tenement of the late Andrew Harvy, and out of the backland of the said tenement, lying between a land of Henry Levington on the south, and a waste land of the said late Adam Hoppar on the north, in the hands of the bailie, who thereupon gave sasine of the said annual-rent of 10 merks to John Murray, burgess, and Margaret Talliezefer his spouse. Same witnesses as above.

APPENDIX

Source	Date	Printed
SRO Yester Writs (GD28/392)	12 Apr 1520	Foular, iii,62
SRO Morton Inventory (GD150/774)	30 Jul 1521	Foular, iii,232
SRO Yester Writs (GD28/396)	31 Jul 1522	Foular, iii,300
SRO Antiquaries Charters (GD103/30)	14 Jan 1523/4	Foular, iii,437
SRO Register House Charters (RH6/973A)	11 Oct 1525	Foular, iii,640
SRO Register House Charters (RH6/998)	11 Dec 1526	Foular, iii,761
SRO Register House Charters (RH6/1000)	11 Dec 1526	
SRO Henderson of Fordell Writs (GD172/93)	9 Feb 1526/7 (Latin text)	Foular, iii,777
Laing Charters no 330 (mis-dated) (Originals in Edin. Univ. Liby.)	5 Sep 1527 (not 1521)	Foular, iii,854
Laing Charters no 363 (Edin. Univ. Liby.)	5 Sep 1527	Foular, iii,853
SRO Register House Charters (RH6/1013)	25 Sep 1527	
SRO Henderson of Fordell Writs (GD172/94)	28 Feb 1529/30	
SRO Register House Charters (RH6/1057)	29 Jun 1530	Foular, iv,231 (dated 25 Jun)
SRO Henderson of Fordell Writs (GD172/95)	12 Apr 1530	Foular, iv,221
SRO Yester Writs (GD28/490)	30 Jul 1532	Foular, iv,425
ECA Miscellaneous Early Writs (In bundle)	3 Dec 1534	

Foular also acted as common scribe of the burgh on 19 May 1531 and 29 May 1532 when he extracted two deeds from the lost Burgh Court Book, *Edin. Recs.*, ii, 49–50, 56–57.

The last item above must have been an entry in a final, sixth protocol book, no longer extant.

INDEX

ABERCROMBY (Abircrummy), John, 162
Aberdeen, bishop of, see Spens, Thomas
Abernethy, James, 114
  Sir Robert, 98
  Robert, 134
Adamson, Alexander, 5, 10, 13, 15, 18–21, 25, 29, 31, 37, 66,100, 135, 140, 171
  David, 171
  Euphemia (Euphame), 35–6, 62, 127
  James, 113, 141
  Janet (Jonet), 5, 18–19, 23–24, 65, 76, 81, 83, 86, 123, 137–8
  John, 2, 16, 29–30, 34, 55, 57, 64, 76, 85–7, 122, 130, 135–7, 143, 155, 160, 171, 186, 188
  John, younger, 21
  Katherine, 25, 31, 52, 78
  Marion, 137, 147
  Robert, 4, 152
  William, burgess, 1, 4–5, 10–11, 13–21, 30, 35–7, 41, 45, 55, 64, 66, 73, 75, 78–9, 85–7, 90, 94, 98–101, 106–7, 120, 123, 128, 131, 135, 138, 146, 155, 160, 171, 173–4, 176, 178
  Master William, younger, 10
  Sir William, chaplain, 64, 77, 113
Affleck (Afflek), Andrew, attorney, 58, 158
  Edward, of Kilbankis, 164
  Edward, 3, 6, 12, 39, 186
Aikenhead (Aikinheid, Akinheid), Ronald, 133
  William, 30, 85, 87, 98, 132, 149, 158, 173, 178
Aikman, Francis, burgess, 26, 46, 61, 77–8, 85, 88–9, 104–5, 141, 144–5, 149, 161

James, 15, 47, 89, 99, 104, 121, 125, 173–4, 176
  Sir John, chaplain, 29, 61, 182
  Katrine, 47
Aitchison (Achinson, Achinsone), Alexander, 72
  George, 88–9, 129
  John, 57, 76, 106, 126–7, 137, 143, 147, 176
  Sir John, chaplain, 127
  Thomas, 85, 88
  William, 77, 88
Ainslie, (Hainslie), Andrew, 67
  John, 51
Aitkin, Patrick, 101, 133, 173
  William, 40, 52
Alderston, (Aldinstoun, Auldstoun), John, 119, 170, 178
Aldjoy, George, 29, 110–1
  Margaret, 97, 107
  William, 29, 135
Alexander, William, 167
Alexanderson, Hector, 40
Allan (Allane), Christian, 49
  George, 98, 158, 172
  John, 13
  Katrine, 127
  Thomas, 163
Allardyce, (Allirdes), Sir James, 170
Allison (Alison), John, 182
  Marion, 43
Ambrose, Isobella, 178
  Thomas, 98
Anderson, Alexander, 12, 17–8, 21, 54, 58, 63, 144
  Beatrix, 45, 57, 79–80, 116
  David, 129
  Gilbert, 83, 149
  James, 50, 65–6, 98, 120, 137, 139, 188
  Janet (Jonet), 141, 171
  John, burgess, 40, 50, 110, 186
  John, 6, 10–1, 13, 24, 26–7, 34, 40, 43, 50,

52-3, 64, 67, 72-4, 76-7, 79-81, 89-90, 106, 108, 110-1, 132, 134, 141, 143-4, 147-8, 151, 161, 166, 173, 183, 186-7
Lancelot alias Laurence, 139
Margaret, 17-20
Marion, 17-9
Marjory, 17-9
Thomas, 37, 48, 171, 178
Walter, 28
William, burgess, 13, 22, 34, 92, 100, 132, 135, 139, 147-8, 151-2, 155, 158, 162-3, 165, 171, 187
Arbroath, vicar of, see Foular, Master Andrew
Arbuckle (Arbukill, Archbukill), Andrew, 49
James, 152
John, 152
Arbuthnot (Arbuthnat), James, 142
Archibald, John, 116, 152
Ardochmore, 139
Argyle (Argyll), Earl of, 119, 177
Arkill, John, 179
Arkittis, John, 139
Arnfillane, 70
Arnot, George, 30, 58, 64-5, 70, 72, 90, 92, 98, 113-4, 188
John, 42
Patrick, 20, 41
Thomas, 1-2, 9-10, 12, 16-20, 22, 24, 26-8, 30, 32-3, 38-42, 45-55, 58-9, 61-2, 66-7, 69-70, 73, 75, 77, 79, 81-3, 86-8, 90-1, 93, 97-103, 105-6, 108-9, 113, 115-6, 117, 119, 120, 122, 124-5, 128-9, 133-7, 139, 142-4, 147-8, 152, 154-61, 163, 165-6, 170-4, 176-82, 184, 186-8
Arres, John, 55, 76, 89, 134-5, 158
John, younger, 89, 158
Arthur (Arthour), Thomas, burgess, 63-4, 187
Askill, Thomas, 118
Askirk (Erskirk), Janet (Jonet), 55, 134
William, 55
Aslowane, John, 160
Atkinson, John, 105
Auchinleck, Alexander, 143-4
Auld, Andrew, 43, 96
John, 114
Ayr, 66
Ayton, John, 80, 109
Thomas, 80
Master William, 80

BAILLIE (Bailze, Balze), William, 46, 85, 87, 135
Master William, rector of Restalrig, 150
Baird, Thomas, 37, 85
Balbirny, Patrick, 139
Balcasky (Balkasky), Cristina, 159
James, 37, 75, 93, 131, 159
Robert, 130
Bald, James, 37
Balfour, David, of Cauldstoun, 80
Henry, 145
Isabella (Isabel), 94, 112, 172
Janet (Jonet), 83, 157, 172
John, 19, 54, 94, 112, 126
Master Martin, 185
Balgarvy, James, 3
Ballantyne (Ballentyne), John, 141
Katherine (Katrine), 34, 66, 112, 136
Sir Patrick, chaplain, 66, 128
Ballenden, Patrick, 157
Ballingavy, Master William, 31
Bannatyne, James, burgess of Lanark, 76, 160-1
John, 10, 182
Patrick, 40, 43, 64
Robert, 167
Symon, 168-9
Thomas, 161
Barbour, James, 21, 102
Barclay (Berclay), John, 96, 148, 153, 185
John, burgess, 32-3, 43, 73, 101
Barker (Barcar), Alexander,

INDEX

8, 25, 61
James, 87, 99, 169
Janet (Jonet), 76, 89
John, 2, 8–9, 60, 137
Lancelot, 16, 87, 135
Laurence, 46
Thomas, 119
Barnard, Sir Thomas, 101
Barnet, Sir Thomas, chaplain, 106–7
Baron (Baroun), Alexander, 54, 65, 83–4, 114, 120, 128–9, 141, 145
 Andrew, 59, 73, 81, 93–4, 131
 Elizabeth, 44, 93
 James, 42, 54, 56, 58, 60, 65–6, 81, 90, 112, 136, 162
 Sir James, 8, 57, 109
 John, 81, 83
 Marion, 64–5, 81–3, 86, 123, 137–8
 Patrick, bailie, 3, 18, 35, 53–6, 60–2, 65, 67–72, 78, 80–4, 86, 90, 114, 120–2, 132, 141, 145, 152
 Patrick, of Spittalfield, 65
 Sir Robert, 65
 Thomas, 128, 184
 William, 10, 106, 172
Bartleman (Bartilmo), Henry, 101, 125, 133
 John, 4, 8
Barton (Bartoun, Berton, Bertoun), Alexander, 17, 100, 129, 174–5
 John, 61
 Patrick, 169
 Robert, of Overbarton, 47, 56–7, 79, 109, 115
 William, 50
Bass, Laird of, 78
Bassendyne (Basseildene, Bassenden, Bassendene, Bassinden, Bassindene), James, 12, 33, 41, 45, 101–2, 134, 158–9, 185
 Marjorie, 54, 68, 169, 184
 William, 149, 158–9
Bathcat (Bathket), 80
Battel Yards, 101
Baty, Agnes, 30–1, 42, 66, 68
 Helen, 30

James, 28, 30, 42, 106, 137, 139, 156, 176, 183–4
John, 149
Margaret, 30
Baxter, John, 163, 176
Bayne, David, 75, 127
 John, 9, 38, 88
Beaton, James, archbishop of St Andrews, 33, 73, 148
Bell, Adam, 108, 128
 Andrew, 128
 David, 30, 41, 160
 George, 7, 123
 Janet (Jonet), 116, 119
 John, burgess, 2, 6, 31, 41, 45, 57, 72–3, 79, 89, 108, 123, 128, 138, 141, 163, 179, 181
 Master John, 48–9
 Robert, 69
 Stephen, 111, 132–3, 142, 145–6
 William, 2, 45, 57, 123, 163
Bell's Wynd, 41, 104
 vennel of, 142
Belsches (Belses), Alexander, bailie, 25, 52, 87, 89–90, 92–3, 96–7, 99–106, 108–9, 111–3, 129
 James, 104, 109
Bennet, James, 63
Bertram (Bertrame), Andrew, 11
 James, 13–5, 17
 Thomas, 156, 170
 Walter, 50, 59
Berwick, 39
Berwick (Bervyk, Berwyk), George, 35–6
 Isobel, 162
 John, 54
 Thomas, 50, 67, 187
Best, John, 2
Best's Wynd, 9, 12, 38, 58–9, 68, 136, 142, 145, 150, 159
Bickerton (Bykkerton), Patrick, 114
Bigholme, Sir John, canon of Jedburgh, 35–6, 62
 Thomas, 58
 William, 59, 142, 166
Binnie (Bynny), Peter, 184
Binning (Bynnyng), Andrew, 76

Bishop (Bischop), Margaret, 93
Robert, 131, 171
Bisset (Bissait, Bissat), Edward, 5, 59, 79, 103, 148, 175
James, 59
John, 99
Black (Blak), James, 12, 16, 22, 145, 180
John, 84, 110, 119, 136
Robert, 63, 164
William, 63
Blackadder (Blacater), Beatrix, 61, 77
John, 140
Margaret, 80
Blackburn (Blacburn), Alexander, 184
Blackie (Blaky), Alexander, 98
Blacklok (Blacklo, Blacklok, Blaklok), James, 111
Richard, 153
Walter, 3, 18, 50, 65, 81, 86, 123, 129, 137, 155–6, 179
William, 39, 41, 54, 61, 81, 87, 89, 97, 106, 108, 136, 174
Blackstock (Blakstok), Cristine (Cristiane), 71, 96
John, 9, 24, 32, 61, 69, 76, 113, 117, 122, 147
Ninian, 49
William, 113
Master William, procurator, 71, 95–6, 113, 176
Blackwood (Blakwode), John, 129
John, burgess of Lanark, 49
Blair, Archibald, 77
George, 19
Blantyre, David, 123, 163
Blyth (Blythe), Alexander, 129
John, 187
Michael, 72, 156, 180
Thomas, 17, 58, 63, 102
Bog, Andrew, burgess, 75, 137, 146
Isobel, 75, 146
William, 137
Bolton, Robert, 19
Bonar, Andrew, 115
Master Andrew, chaplain, 51

David, 47–8, 114–5
Bonkle (Bonkill), Alexander, 3, 12, 35, 113, 141
Edward, 3, 18, 28, 52, 59, 65, 81, 86, 123, 129, 131, 137, 152, 155–7, 172, 175, 179
Elizabeth, 159–60
John, 137, 176
Bonkle's Close, 176
Boothrow, 6, 11, 18–9, 32, 51, 75, 95, 109, 147, 166–7, 182, 186, 188
Borthauch, 185
Borthwick (Borthik, Borthuik), Alan, 60, 85, 163
Alexander, 57
Andrew, 78, 94–6
Elizabeth, 17–8, 20, 139, 187
Francis, 94–6
Margaret (Margret), 128, 168–9, 185
Marion, 163–4
Robert, 72, 121
Stephen, 57, 95, 135
Thomas, 19, 72, 142
Walter, 30–1, 42, 66, 68
Borthwick, William, laird of, 10–1, 19, 41, 54, 72, 87, 94, 99, 121, 125, 142, 177
Borthwick's Wynd, 72, 121
Boswell (Boiswall, Boiswell), David, 123
David, of Affleck, 122
John, 54
Master John, 122–3
Bothwell (Boithuell, Bothuell), David, 8
Elizabeth, 110–1
Francis, 8, 9, 61, 65–6
Master Francis, burgess, 8, 25, 87, 112, 135–7, 168
Master Richard, provost of Kirk o' Field, 122, 124, 136, 171
Master Richard, younger, 112
Boutstar, Sir Alexander, monk of Dundrennan, 72
Bow, Sir Luke, chaplain, 168–70
Sir William, chaplain, 169

INDEX

Bowie (Bowy), William, 29, 94, 165
Bowmaker, Alexander, 164
Bowman, William, 63
Bowok, Sir John, 122
  William, 83
Boyce (Bois), William, 144
Boyce's Wynd, 136
Boyd, Alexander, 106
  William, 34, 160
Brady, Elizabeth, 50, 183
Braid, 119
Branwode, James, 61
Brewhouse, Margaret, 169–70
  Peter, 169
Briggs (Briggis), Marion, 18
Brighouse, 119
Brisset (Brissait, Brussait, Brusset), Anthony, burgess, 25–6, 49, 125, 154–5, 159, 166, 172
Broadfoot (Braidfut), Sir William, 4, 8
Brog, James, 109
  Robert, 33
Brounehill, Andrew, 16, 134
Brounleis, James, 73
Brown (Broun, Broune), Agnes, 139
  Andrew, 122
  Cristine, 71
  David, 99
  Master David, 11
  Elizabeth, *alias* Smyth, 88
  Elizabeth, 132
  George, 45, 79, 116
  Isobella (Isobel) *alias* Smyth, 90–2
  James, 29, 32, 157, 167, 178
  James, junior, 168
  James, senior, 168
  Master James, 122
  Janet (Jonet), 46, 65, 94, 96, 112, 163
  John, burgess, 1, 21, 24, 34, 42, 46, 59–60, 65–6, 68, 75, 80, 85, 93, 101, 112, 125, 131, 136, 152, 162, 176
  John, younger, 80
  John, in Anstruther, 151
  Katrine, *alias* Smyth, 90–2
  Laurence, 130, 155
  Margaret, 26, 33, 42, 45, 47, 61, 77–8, 85, 88, 146, 152, 155, 158, 161–2
  Marion, 38, 45, 55, 68, 134, 142, 144, 159
  Marjory, 93, 96–7, 118, 136
  Nichol, 76, 134
  Nicholas, 55, 89, 158, 166
  Robert, 108, 144
  Thomas, 40, 109, 116, 122, 136, 160, 181, 186
  Thomas, *alias* Smyth, burgess, 88, 90–2
  Master Thomas, rector of Lamlathane (*sic*), 57, 79–80, 90–2, 94, 141, 176
  William, 24, 46, 55, 93–4, 136–7
  Sir William, chaplain, 2, 8, 18, 21, 48, 57–8, 115, 186
Bruce (Bruse), Alexander, 2, 18–9, 23–4, 64–5, 80–3, 86, 123, 137–8
  Andrew, 27
  Isabella, 93, 136–7
  James, 19, 46
  John, burgess, 2, 18–9, 23, 46, 64–5, 81, 83, 86, 123, 138, 155–6, 172, 178–80
  Robert, 28, 46, 65, 90, 93, 98, 112, 136, 161, 163
  Robert, burgess, 2, 8
  Robert, of Binning, burgess, 119
  Walter, 39, 110
  William, 86, 89
Bruce's Land, 145
Bryce (Brys), James, 41
Bryson, James, 164
  Thomas, 88, 172
Buchan (Buchane), Alan, 44, 98, 178
  James, Earl of, 71
  Stephen (Stephan), 44, 98
Bulcraig, John, 54
Bulloch (Bullok), John, 51
Burgane, John, 50–1, 106, 109–10, 167, 187
Burgh Muir, 144, 153
Burn, Alexander, 131
Burrell, Andrew, 9
Burrow (Porro, Purro), John, 48, 52–3, 58, 77, 103, 163, 183

Burrowman (Barrowman, Burroman), John, 117, 172, 175, 177-8, 180, 184
Burt, George, 156
William, 156
Busby (Busbe), John, 109, 134, 170
Butler (Butlar), John, 26-7, 116
Thomas, 20, 70, 149

CADDELL (Cattall, Cattell), Agnes, 54
John, 19, 106, 113
Thomas, 54, 94
Cady, Robert, 63
Sir William, chaplain, 47, 130, 143-5
Cadzow (Cadzo), James, 35, 62
Sir Quintin, 28
Cairncross (Carncors), Nichol, (Nicholas), dean of Guild, 51, 67, 79, 86, 129-31, 161, 180
Cairns (Kairns, Kairus, Karnis) Bartholomew, 60, 88, 90
George, attorney, 9, 133
John, 143
Margaret, 143-4
Thomas, 122
Calder, David, 58
Callander, Alexander, 152
Cambuskenneth, abbot of, 82
monastery of, 15, 82
Cambusmichael, church of, 32
Cameron, James, 47, 56, 109, 115, 127
Janet (Jonet), 56-7, 109
Thomas, 98-9, 114, 124
Cameron's Land, 126
Campbell, David, 63
John, chaplain, 18-9, 104
Michael, 63
Thomas, 136
Campion (Kempioun), Sir William, 3
Cannon (Canon), Gilbert, 1, 66, 90, 104
John, 1, 66
Canney, John, 80
Sir Thomas, 32, 65, 80
Canongate, 36, 157

Cant, Agnes, 25
Alexander, 7, 9-10, 38, 117, 127-8, 147, 158, 171, 178, 183-5
Elizabeth, 25, 127
George, 52, 100, 129, 168, 171-2, 174-7, 180-2
Henry, 8-9, 25-6, 40, 52-3, 66
James, 52-3, 129, 152-3
Janet (Jonet), 100, 140
John, 1, 54, 81, 111, 139, 148, 175, 183
Margaret, 99
Marion, 163
Sir Walter, 172, 184
Caribberis, James, 32
John, 74
Carkettill (Carkettil), Elizabeth, 140
John, 142
Sir John, chaplain, 10, 18-9, 41, 57, 72, 79-80, 87, 103, 121, 125
Marion, 117
William, 110, 186
Carlowry, 124
Carmichael (Carmichell), Robert, 54
Thomas, 88
Carmuir, Master James, 42
John, 82
Katherine, 27, 53
Carnbe, John, 176
Carnegy, David, burgess of Dundee, 145, 180
Carnie (Carny), David, 118
Carnoch (Cannoch), John, 77, 123, 178, 183
Carnoquhen, John, 29, 109, 172
Carrick (Carryk), Matthew, 67
Robert, 172
Carver (Carvour), Patrick, 17, 34
Carwode, Martin, 48
William, 9
Cassillis, Earl of, 71, 150
Castle bank, 100
hill, 35-6, 48, 62, 67, 76, 78, 85, 95, 100, 116, 120-1, 135, 164, 169-70, 173, 182, 184, 188
hill, vennel of, 67-8

INDEX

vennell, 169
wall, 40, 43, 46, 52, 60, 64, 73-4, 85, 87-8, 91, 93, 98, 106, 135-6, 158, 161, 169-70, 182
wynd, 120
Cathkin, Andrew, 100
  Katrine, 183
  Thomas, 188
  William, 144, 153
Chalmers (Chalmer), Alexander, 46, 78, 85, 169-70
  David, 99
  James, 67, 162
  Nicholas, 154
  Thomas, 28
Chamblet, William, 97
Chancellar, John, burgess, 98, 120, 149, 167-8, 188
Chaplane, Master Peter, 185
Chapman (Chapmen), David, 39-40, 153-4, 176
  Master James, 105
  Master John, burgess, 55, 88, 101, 118-9, 152-4, 160, 176
  Walter, burgess, 3, 5, 39-40, 152-4, 160, 171
  William, 153-4
Charteris, John, attorney, 10, 13-4, 17, 87, 131
Chatto, Sir Andrew, 95
Cheyne (Scheyne), Nicholas, 25, 61, 112
  Master William, 30
Christison (Christesone, Cristeson), John, 157
  Richard, 179
  William, 97
Clark (Clerk), Adam, 59
  John, 32, 59, 157
  Sir John, chaplain, 135, 147
  Margaret, 31
  Master Patrick, 81
  Robert, 50, 151
  Simon, 37, 106
  William, 46, 132-3
Clarkson (Clerkson), Thomas, 107-8
  William, burgess, 90, 92, 108
Cleghorn (Cleghorne), Isobel, 64
  John, 64, 118-9
  William, 64
Cochrane, Elizabeth, 80
  George, of Bawbachlaw, 80
Cockburn (Cockbune, Cokburne), Agnes, 5, 39, 40, 153, 160
  Alison (Alesane), 12
  Edward, 29
  Elizabeth, 1-2
  James, 1-2
  John, 140, 151-3
  Marion, 87, 116, 129
  Patrick, 29
  William, 2, 11, 48, 53, 115, 140, 151, 163-4, 186
Cody, William, 178
Coksone, Robert, 18-9, 43, 47, 148
Coky, James, 38, 69
  John, 89, 99, 176
Coldane (Coldon), John, 8-13, 16, 58, 67-8, 71, 80, 82, 84, 90, 114, 120-2, 128, 132, 141, 145, 152
  Master John, chaplain, 10-1
  William, burgess, 44, 98
Collin (Colyne), Robert, 49, 66
Colquhoun, Archibald, 139
  Master James, rector of Luss, 10
  Sir John, of luss, 9
Colville (Coluill), James, 41
Common Muir, see Burgh Muir
Commonside, 185
Cook (Cuike, Cuke), George, 60
  Master George, 124
  James, 140
  John, 38, 125
  Sir John, chaplain, 163
  Thomas, burgess, 6, 75, 87, 125, 135, 142
Con, Adam, 163-4
  John, 20, 48, 115, 149, 163-4, 186
Congleton (Congilton), Master Hugh, chaplain of Kirk o' Field, 99-100
Cor, Margaret, 166
Cornwall, Janet (Jonet), 157
  Margaret, 157
Corny, Thomas, of Keldwode, 58
Corsbe, James, 33

Corstorphine, 180
Corstorphine, Lord of, 38, 132-3, 182
Cossar, Cristiane, 3
Costy, James, 100
Coupar, Gilbert, burgess, 158, 185
  Nicholas, 46
  Robert, 158
  Robert, burgess, 161
  Thomas, 93, 101, 162
Couper, Sir Alexander, chaplain if Kirk o' Field, 17, 46, 49
Coupland, Mark, 82
  Maurice, 1, 35, 54, 96, 110-1, 119, 127, 148, 172
  Robert, 9, 13
  Thomas, 5, 26, 110, 136, 187
Court, William, 109
Coutts (Coittis, Cottis), Sir Goerge, 40
  John, 51, 163
  Matthew, 58
  Nicholas, 161
  Robert, 41
  William, 153
Cowan (Cowane), Andrew, 129, 134
  Cristina, 33
  Marion, 134
  John, 9, 16, 41, 45, 171
Cowgas, Helen, 58
Cowgate, 4, 9, 14-7, 19, 22, 26-7, 29, 32, 35-6, 39, 41, 44-5, 47, 52-4, 62, 70-1, 74, 82, 98, 104-5, 108, 111, 114, 117, 124, 133, 140-3, 145-6, 150-1, 153-4, 162, 171, 179-81
Cragmylie, James, 138
Craig, Alexander, 31
  Sir Cuthbert, 67
  John, 145
  Thomas, 103
  William, 172
Craik, George, 13, 52, 149, 161, 173
  Janet (Jonet), 186
  John, 100, 109
  Philip, 51

William, 11, 54, 109, 120, 123, 136, 149, 182, 186
William, younger, 109
Cranston (Cranstoun), Elizabeth, 3, 6, 12, 101, 141
  Giles (Geills), 3, 6, 39, 146, 164, 186
  George, 129
  Henry, 85, 87, 90, 92, 98, 129, 149, 158, 166, 171, 173, 187
  James, 30
  John, 11, 101, 118, 141, 188
  Patrick, 39
  William, of Rathobyres, 3-4, 6, 20, 141
Crawford (Crauford, Cranford), David, 100, 177
  Edward, 41, 80, 82, 108
  Helen, 177
  James, 52, 104
  Master John, 93
  Sir John, chaplain, 56, 87, 93
  Nicholas, 50, 160
  Nicholas, of Oxgangs, Justice Clerk, 104
  Thomas, burgess, 62, 85, 177
Creich, David, 102
Crichton (Creichton, Creichtoun), Sir Adam, of Feldy, 131
  Helen, 161
  Henry, 161
  James, of Cranstonriddell, 4, 20, 39
  Marion, 1
  Martin, 39
  Patrick, 4-5
  Patrick, of Kinglassie, 3, 113
Crichton, provost of the collegiate church of, see, Halkerston, Sir Thomas
Cross House (Corshouse), 43, 64, 73, 142, 148
Crossmichael (Corsmichael), 70
Cruikshank (Crukschank), Marion, 155
Cruke, John, 112
Crummy, John, burgess of Linlithgow, 33, 83, 159

INDEX

Culross, monastery of, 43
Cumming (Cuming, Cummyn, Cumyn), Alexander, 22
  John, 79
  Thomas, 71
Cunningham (Cunninghame, Cunyngham, Cunynghame), Sir Alexander, 2, 99, 114, 124, 141, 185
  Gabrial, 136
  George, 83
  John, 138, 178-9
  Marion, 8
  Marjorie, 105
  Simon, 89
  Thomas, 179
  William, 80, 117, 143
Curle (Curll), Elizabeth, 162
  James, 101, 136
  Katherine (Katrine), 85, 177
Currie (Curre), Hugh, 139
  James, 139, 155
  Richard, 124
Currour, Agnes, 120-1, 173-4
  Cristine, 120
  Elizabeth, 106
  George, 120-1
  Isabella, 120-1, 174
  James, 116
  Janet (Jonet), 120-1
  John, 50, 101, 104, 120-1, 149, 166, 173-4
  Margaret, 16, 120, 149, 173
  Marion, 120
  Robert, 16
  Thomas, 106
  William, 16, 104, 149, 153
Cuthbertson, John, 164, 170
Cutlar, Andrew, 159
  Archibald, 24, 72, 83
  Henry, burgess of Haddington, 72
  John, 72
  Master Richard, vicar of Rerrick, 72

DALGLEISH (Dalgleiss, Dalglesche), Sir David, 146
  Thomas, 129, 134
  William, 163
Dalkeith, 113
  parish church of, 126

Dalmahoy, Andrew, 35, 134, 183
  John, 34
Dalry, 87
Dalrymple (Dalrumpill, Dalrymple), Alexander, 68, 114
  David, 79, 123
  John, 128, 163
  Katrine, 114
Darling, Alexander, 46, 76, 159
  Sir Philip, chaplain, 11, 76
Darroch (Darroche), George, 183
  James, 13, 16, 27-8, 93, 97, 132, 165, 187
Davidson, Agnes, 131
  David, 149
  Edward, 10, 109, 125, 166, 173
  Gilbert, 166
  Giles (Geils), 101, 125
  John, 6-10, 28, 32-3, 43, 50, 52, 73, 128, 148, 158, 165, 178-9, 184-5
  Margaret, 7, 9, 158, 179, 184-5
  William, 51, 101
Davy, see Robertson, Thomas, alias
Dawson, William, 146
Dee, Alexander, burgess, 27, 73
  Cristina (Christian), 74, 141
  Isabella, 26-7
  John, 4, 120, 174
  Marion, 9
Dempster, Henry, 32
Denholm (Dennun, Dennunn), John, 28, 98
  Patrick, 28
  Robert, 3-4, 32-3, 124
Denniston (Dennystoun), Sir James, chaplain, 10, 31, 63-4, 145, 171, 187
Dick (Dik, Dyk), Master Alexander, 142, 165
  Andrew, 166
  Cuthbert, 97-8, 182, 188
  William, notary, 17, 41, 165, 184
Dickson (Dikson, Dykson, Dyksone), Adam, 72
  Alexander, 134

Andrew, 32, 63, 81, 117, 187
Andrew, younger, 81
Elizabeth, 14, 17, 100, 174-5
George, 59, 129-30
Gilbert, 157
James, 174-5
Janet (Jonet), 100, 174-5
John, 8, 30, 68, 90-2, 100, 131, 146, 171
Sir John, chaplain, 98, 114, 124
Patrick, 39
Robert, 111
Thomas, 72, 80, 97, 129-30
William, 124
Sir William, vicar of Kirkcudbright, 72
Dingwall, Master John, apostolic protonotary, provost of Trinity College, 74, 92-3
Dobie (Doby), Janet (Jonet), 52
William, 71, 154
Dodds (Doddis), Robert, 163
Donaldson, Archibald, burgess, 7, 45, 103, 158
Duncan, 87
James, 61
John, 73
Robert, 158, 181
Rolland, burgess, 7, 42, 88, 101-3
Ronald, 64, 71, 77, 158
Walter, 103, 158
Dornwyk, James, 131, 175, 177, 179
John, 131
Dougall, John, burgess, 106
John, younger, 106
Douglas, Adam, 94
Archibald, 25
Archibald, Lord of Kilspindie, Lord High Treasurer, 2
David, 29, 98
Hugh, 144, 159
James, 3, 80
John, 144, 173
Robert, of Pumpherston, 3-4, 6
Dowell (Doweill), Sir Matthew, chaplain, 127

Symon, 24, 38, 64, 117, 121, 135, 155, 183-4
Dowy, Janet alias see Linton
Dronar, David, 80, 100
Drumbrek, William, 16
Dryburgh, Thomas, 44
Dryden, 185
Dumbarton, 116
church of, 139
Dumbarton (Dumbartane, Dumbertane), Henry, 94, 125
John, 100
Thomas, 100
Dun (Dwn), David, 180, 184
Master David, 168
John, 3, 12, 113
Dunbar, Alexander, 24-5
Gavin, archbishop of Glasgow, 78, 81, 153
James, 40
Duncan (Duncane), John, 155
Sir John, 150
Thomas, 103
Duncanson, Sir James, chaplain, 89-90, 92, 94, 100, 107-8, 111
Dundas, James, 85
Lord of, 149
William, 70
Dundrenen, monk of, see Boustar, Sir Alexander
Dunkeld, bishop of, see Hepburn, James
Dunsyre (Dunsayar, Dunsyair), Elizabeth, 33, 47, 95, 146, 148, 152
William, burgess, 33, 42, 45, 47, 77, 89, 146
Dunsyre's Close, 42

EASTER Hailes, 167
Eccles (Eklis), James, 147-8
Ecclesgreig, vicar of, see Lawson, Master Richard
Edgar, Andrew, 31, 81, 178
Edward, 179
Edinburgh, James Johnston alias, see Johnston
Edmond, Elizabeth, 94

INDEX

Edmondston (Edmonstoun), Master James, rector of Fala, 163
Ednam (Edname), Cristian, 54, 109
  Isobella, 182
  Thomas, 139
  William, 139, 145
Eglington (Eglintoun), Hugh, earl of, 103, 125
  John, 16
Elder (Eldar), Agnes, 154–5
  Stephen, 96, 184
  Thomas, 12, 110
Ellis (Heleis), James, 52
Elphinstone, Alexander, 75, 80–1, 97, 141, 147
  Andrew, of Selmis, 55, 171
  George, attorney, 116
  Giles (Geilis), 116
  James, bailie, 29
  John, 80–1, 176
  Robert, 20, 99
  Thomas, 22, 25, 38, 51
  William, bailie and burgess, 22–5, 38–42, 45, 50–1, 85, 116, 128, 132, 163, 177
Elwand, Gilbert, 175
England, 9
Erskine (Erskin), Adam, 115
Esdale (Esdaill), Robert, 130, 133
Evat, Alexander, 133
Ewin, Agnes, 145–6
  Patrick, 26
  Sir Thomas, chaplain, 30, 60–1, 132–3

FAIR, John, 42
Fairbairn (Fairbarne), Agnes, 28
Fairley (Fairlie, Fairly), Bartholomew, 176
  Master Clement, 54
  James, 44, 46, 89, 99, 145, 155–6
  John, 95, 144
  William, 29
Fairnlie, Archibald, 119
Falcon, (Falcone, Falcoun), John, 20, 36–7, 44, 90, 107
  Marion, 37–8, 107
  Thomas, 14–5, 17, 47
  William, 20, 44, 90
Falconer, Peter, 48
Farnlie (Farnle), Archibald, 185
  Sir David, prior of Monymusk, 47
  James, 61
Faulo, George, 35
Fauside (Fausyde, Fawsyde), Adam, 105
  John, burgess, 52, 70–1, 94, 132, 146, 162, 181
  John, younger, 70
  William, 7–8, 33, 43, 73, 93, 148, 178
Fenton (Fentoun), James, 35–6, 57, 62, 127
  laird of, 109
Ferguson, Andrew, 101
  John, 84
Ferrie, Barbara, 50
  David, 114
  William, 4, 6, 75, 130
Fetteresso, rector of, 122
Fillane, Duncan, 151
Finlay (Fynlaw, Fynlay), Gilbert, 61
  John, 19
  Symon, 135
Fish (Fische, Fysche), George, 51, 103
  Gilbert, 106, 172
  John, 126
Fisher (Fischar, Fyschar), Andrew, 176
  Elizabeth, 137, 147
  John, burgess, 48–9, 56, 59, 98, 109, 120, 126–7, 142, 171, 176, 188
  Katrine, 79
  Thomas, 176
Fleming (Flemyn, Flemyng), Alan, 139
  Janet (Jonet), 109, 148
  Laurence, 154
  Patrick, 7, 10, 39, 41–2, 52, 57–8, 77, 88, 102, 108–9, 153, 158, 185
  Patrick, younger, 109
  Robert, 178
  Lord, 119

Flesher (Fleschour), William, 63, 187
Flews (Fluris), 172
Flockart (Folkart), Thomas, 59
Flucker (Flucar), David, 47
  Sir David, 111
  Helen, 47
  Janet (Jonet), 16
  John, cutler, 83, 157-8
Forbes, Helen, 95
  James, 49
Foreman (Forman), John, 77, 86
Forfar, David, 52
  Isobel, 52
Forfar, rector of, see Simpson, Master James
Forres (Forous), Margaret, 62
  Marion, 142
  Patrick, 172, 179
  Robert, 63, 179-80
  William, 2
Forrest (Forest), Agnes, 9, 12, 133
  George, procurator, 188
  Katrine, 48-9, 82
  Margaret, 11, 51, 136, 149
  Robert, 155-6
Forrester (Forestar, Forstar, Forster, Fostar), Alexander, 139
  Alexander, burgess of Stirling, 32-3, 73, 146-8, 152
  Archibald, of Corstorphine, 156
  Cristina, 162
  David, 72
  Sir David, chaplain, 67
  Duncan, 83
  Elizabeth, 149
  George, 146, 149
  Master George, 29
  George, of Strathenry, 157
  James, 2, 82
  John, 46
  Katherine, 77
  Philip, burgess, 2, 45
  Robert, 32-3, 73, 146-7, 152
  Selestus, 149
  Thomas, 152
  Thomas, of Strathenry, 149
  William, 31
Forrester's (Forstaris, Forstar's) Wynd, 20-1, 38-9, 44, 71, 90, 128, 132-3, 162, 168-70, 182, 185
  vennel of, 187
Forsyth, Janet (Jonet), 30, 69
  Margaret, 97
  Robert, 147-8
  William, 30, 67, 69, 97
Fortune (Fortoun), Symon, 30
  William, 11
Foular, Alexander, 41, 138
  Master Andrew, vicar of Arbroath, 41
  Helen, 27-8
  John, 10, 24, 81, 89, 128, 168, 170, 182, 185
  Thomas, 81, 88, 90, 92
  William, 32, 58, 63-4, 81, 117, 147, 187
Foulis (Fowlis), James, 118
  Master James, 45, 51, 59, 91, 124
  William, 124
Frank, Master Thomas, procurator, 54
Freeland (Freland), Robert, 13, 15, 101
Frew, Robert, 103
Friar Preachers, 5, 7, 22, 32, 79, 107, 115, 117, 128, 148, 153, 165, 169, 174-5, 178, 184
  cemetery of, 178
  church of, 3
  convent of, 85
  vennel of, 50, 59, 156, 183
  wynd of, 21
Friars Minor, 54, 69-70, 114
  cemetery of, 168
Friars' Wynd, 128, 167, 175
Frissell (Fresall, Fressall), Cuthbert, 137, 147
  Sir David, chaplain, 50
  John, 46, 62, 65-6, 112, 136, 162
  Thomas, 46-7, 65, 112, 136
Frog, Michael, 69, 95, 182, 186
  William, 160
Frude, John, 160
Fullerton (Foularton), William, 104
Fyndgude, James, 88

INDEX

GAIT, the, 114
Galbraith, John, 13, 15, 30
   Master Robert, attorney, 12-5, 29, 51-2, 74, 91, 106, 129, 159
Galloway, Adam, 157
   Andrew, 88, 158
   James, 3
   Robert, 22
Galloway, bishop of, see Wemyss, Henry
Garden (Gardun), David, 155
Gardner, David, 155, 179-80
   John, 47, 105
Garland, John, 69-70, 102
Geddes, Sir John, 99
Gemmell (Gamyll), Richard, 131
Geychane, John, 138
Gibson, Adam, 150
   Agnes, 10
   Alexander, 108
   Andrew, 39
   George, 26, 32, 51, 53, 119, 128-9, 178, 183
   Gilbert, 31
   James, 99
   John, 20, 120, 132-3, 169
   Master John, 160
   Thomas, burgess, 71, 88, 106, 187-8
   Master William, dean of Restalrig, 151
   Sir William, chaplain, 93
Giffart, Janet (Jonet), 145
Gilbert, James, 35
   Michael, goldsmith, 106
Gill, David, 9
Gillespie (Gillaspy), David, burgess, 11, 19-20, 49, 54, 87, 94, 112, 125, 142, 161, 165
Gillies (Gilleis), Elizabeth, 19, 54, 94, 165
Gilquhammyte, Robert, 102
Gilroy (Gilry), James, 1, 3, 66
Girdwood (Gyrdwode), John, 49
Glasgow, archbishop of, see Dunbar, Gavin
Glen, Elizabeth, 84
   John, burgess, 2, 19-20, 22, 32, 84, 87, 116-7, 130, 142, 149
   Robert, 84, 87, 89-90, 111, 116, 129-31

Glendinning (Glendynnyn, Glendynnyng), James, 10
   Thomas, 74, 150-1, 173, 186
Glenluce, abbot of, see Maloney, Sir William
Goddiskirk, Agnes, 107-8
   Ninian, 51
   William, 35
Goldsmith (Goldsmyth), Sir James, 125
   Nicholas, 99, 126
Good (Gude), George, 3-4, 19-20, 61, 85-6, 113, 135, 142, 158
Gordon, Walter, 108
Gothrason, Sir Thomas, chaplain, 54
   Sir William, chaplain, 3, 33
Gourlay (Gourlaw), Alexander, 106
   James, 5
   John, 123, 154
Gowanlock, Patrick, 105
Gowrie (Gaury), Marion, 40
Graham (Grahame), Adam, 78
   Alexander, 51, 78
   Gilbert, of Knokdoliane, 139
   James, 52
   Janet (Jonet), 107
   John, 51-2, 78
   Robert, burgess, 59, 69-70, 81, 93, 97, 107, 110, 138, 188
   William, 93, 107, 113, 147
Gray, Alexander, 2, 12, 31, 38, 59, 64, 100
   David, 11
   Finlay (Fylnay), 101
   George, 8
   Isobel, 159
   James 99, 106, 116, 146, 153-4, 176, 181
   John, burgess, 24, 31, 49, 54, 59, 68, 97, 154, 182
   Richard, 17, 87, 171
   Robert, 2, 8, 12, 24, 31, 38, 54, 64, 75, 78, 105-6, 132, 142, 146, 182
   Thomas, 137, 179, 182
Greenhill (Greinhill), John, 148
Greenside, 24
Greif, James, 154
   Thomas, 22

Greig (Greg), Katrine, 152
Thomas, 97
Grier (Greir), Peter, 64
Grierson (Greirson), John, provincial of Friars Minor, 107, 114, 181
Peter, 54
Grob, John, 134
Gryme, Margaret, 160
Guild (Guld, Gulde), William, 65, 75, 113, 136
Guthrie, Master Alexander, 117
Guthry, John, 163
Gylour, Alexander, 54, 93, 112
Sir John, chaplain, 79–80, 94

HADDINGTON, 72, 83
Haithway (Haithwy), Alexander, 9
Andrew, 67, 149
Robert, 5, 9
Thomas, 59, 117, 120, 125, 184
Haliburton (Haliburtoun, Halyburton), Alison, 20, 90
Cornelius, 177
Master James, 109
Margaret, 148
Robert, 10, 12, 34–5, 59–60, 83, 98, 123
Thomas, 177
Walter, 4
William, 61
Halkerston, Adam, 126
Alexander, 26, 53, 58, 83
George, 22, 28, 32, 42, 44, 47, 56–7, 79, 98, 105, 109, 117, 156
James, 13–7, 26–7, 131, 178
John, 83
Thomas, 49
Sir Thomas, provost of Crichton, 40, 129, 152–3
William, 39, 42, 57, 66, 79–81, 83, 149, 153, 157
Halkerston's Wynd, 22, 32, 42, 49, 66, 83, 117, 149, 157
Hall, James, 60
Robert, 12
Halliday (Haliday), Helen, 29

Thomas, 70
Hamill (Homyll), James, 89, 158, 177
John, 177
Sir Patrick, 13
William, 94
Hamilton (Hamyltoun), Alexander, Bathcat, 80
Sir Bartholomew, chaplain, 49, 53, 122, 125
Janet (Jonet), 29
John, 66, 76
Patrick, 22
Sir Patrick, of Kincavill, 51
Peter, 80
Thomas, in Alderston, 6, 34
William, 16, 87, 127, 186
Hannay (Hanny), Sir Constantine, chaplain, 10–1
Janet (Jonet), 182
William, 64
Hardgrip, James, 155
Richard, 135
Hardy, Francis, 141
Harkes, John, 79, 81
Harkness, Sir John, chaplain, 156
Harlabankis (Harlaubankis), James, 46, 60–1, 143
Marion, 3, 12, 20, 99, 113
Harlaw, Alexander, 105, 137, 168
James, 100
Thomas, 179
Harper (Harpar), Sir Andrew, chaplain, 38, 55, 85, 89, 90, 107
Margaret, 85
Hart, Janet (Jonet), 50
Thomas, 170
Hartsyde, 39
Harvey (Harvy), Adam, 188
Andrew, 35, 48, 59, 188
Archibald, 187
Cristiane, 98
John, burgess, 30
Margaret, 187
Matthew, 67, 91, 120, 169, 184
Thomas, 30, 106
William, 80

INDEX

Hastie (Hasty), John, 157
Hathochy, Andrew, 169
Haw, David, 186
   James, 46
   William, 17
Hay, John, burgess, 31, 41, 45, 72, 104–5, 130–1, 141–2
   William, 26
Heatlie (Haitly), Cristina, 143
Hector (Ector), Robert, 61, 63, 128, 172
Henderson (Hendirson), Andrew, 12
   Master Henry, 108
   Master James, attorney, 27
   John, 20, 48–9, 77, 104, 151
   Laurence, 105
   Thomas, 134
   William, 12, 58, 105
Henrison, Agnes, 105
   Andrew, 176
   David, 27
   Edward, 98, 100, 105
   Elizabeth, 5–6, 11
   George, 10, 30–1, 35, 42, 53, 66, 78, 87, 89, 178, 184
   Henry, 104
   Master Henry, 21, 40, 57
   Isobel, 48–9, 77
   James, 9, 24, 27, 31, 72, 78, 88–9, 104–5, 141–2, 144
   Master James, of Fordel, 30, 107
   Janet (Jonet), 30, 34–5, 101
   John, 98, 134, 142, 144, 149, 165
   John, younger, 144
   Laurence, 141–2
   Margaret, 97
   Michael, 97
   Richard, 32
   Robert, 48–9, 58, 69, 73, 77, 82–3, 97, 148–9, 166, 172
   William, 22, 130, 133–4, 177
Hepburn (Hepburne), Adam, 146
   James, bishop of Dunkeld, 47, 98, 114, 124

Herniston (Merzemstoun), Alexander Naper, Lord, 170
Herries (Hereis), Richard, 120
Herriot, Alexander, 130–1, 146
   David, 150, 162
   Robert, 9, 160, 188
   Thomas, 79–80
Hesliheid, Sir George, 163
Heston (Hestoun), Adam, 112, 161
High Riggs (Hieriggis), 8, 64, 75, 85, 87, 97, 105, 135
High Street, 1–22, 24–36, 38, 40–70, 72–6, 78–91, 93–101, 103–123, 125, 127–73, 176–88
Hill, James, burgess, 88, 91, 148
   William, 24, 148, 176
Hislop (Heslihop), George, 120
   Sir George, chaplain, 48, 57, 76–7, 82, 97
Hog (Hoge), John, 3, 32
   Robert, 59, 111
   William, 188
Holy Trinity, college of, 12
Holyrood, abbey of, 54, 58, 119
Home (Hume), Andrew, 43, 50, 64, 73
   George, of Spott, 69
   Isobel, 43
   James, burgess, 1–2, 96, 148
   John, 71
   Robert, 32
   Thomas, 116
Hope (Hoip), Janet (Jonet), 72
   John, burgess, 71, 94, 166, 185
Hopper (Hoppar), Adam, 34–5, 49, 59, 66, 98, 112, 134, 188
   Alexander, 139
   David, 34–5, 59
   Elizabeth, 25, 139, 183–4
   George, 69
   Henry, 69, 94
   Master Henry, 139
   Isobel, 2
   James, 147
   Katrine, 45, 88
   Richard, 26, 30, 35, 61, 66, 69, 94, 112, 134–7, 139, 162, 167, 183–4

Robert, 171
Sir Robert, 176
William, 60, 88, 137, 162
Hoppringill, Edward, 76, 90, 92
George, 170
William, 170
Horne, Andrew, 51
James, 110
Thomas, 111
How, William, 4, 158
Howie (Howy), Laurence, 85, 164
Master Thomas, chaplain, 11, 12, 24
Howison, John, 35, 119
Sir John, chaplain, 150-1
Nichol, 111
Nicholas, 34, 89
William, 4
Howiston, 111
Hoy, Master Thomas, 51
Huchesone, Andrew, 31
John, 13, 63, 67, 100, 103, 122, 131, 133, 158, 171
Peter, 170
Richard, 40
Robert, 12, 31, 64, 98
Huchon, John, 158
Hunter (Huntar), Gilbert, 41, 53, 125
Martin, 123
Sir James, chaplain, 53, 164
John, 116
Thomas, 131
Huntroddis, Margaret, 133
Sir Robert, 130, 133
William, burgess, 3
Hynd (Hynde), Archibald, 9
John, 9

INCHECOK, Francis, 4, 51, 68, 74, 96, 140-1
Patrick, 43
Inglis, Alexander, archdeacon of St Andrews, 22
Gavin, 143-4
George, 22
Sir James, 47
John, 72

Mars, 26
Patrick, procurator, 22
William, 27, 53, 58
Inverleith, laird of, 106
Ireland, Adam, novice, O.F.M., 71
Christina, 95
Master David, burgess, 69, 71, 74, 89, 95-6, 113, 152, 156, 158, 162-3, 165, 171, 175-6, 181, 183, 188.
John, 71, 137, 150, 152
Matthew, 6, 26
Patrick, 127
Irvine (Irrewyn), David, 184

JACOB, John, *alias* Stevinson, 105
Jackson (Jakson), Sir John, chaplain, 122
James, John, *alias* Stevinson, 105
James the Fourth, 84
Jamieson, David, 46, 160
James, 34
John, 46
Jardine, Sir Alexander of Applegarth, 165
Jedburgh, abbot of, 50, 62, 183
canon of, see Bigholme, Sir John
convent of, 183
Johnston, Adam, 60-1, 123
Alexander, 85
George, 94
James, bailie, 2, 7, 22, 25-9, 34, 38-9, 41-2, 44-6, 50-1, 58, 60, 62, 66, 68, 72-3, 89-90, 98, 103-4, 106-9, 121, 140, 166
James, smith, 28
James, *alias* Edinburgh, 82, 146, 148, 166, 172, 185
John, 2, 8-9, 13, 22, 28-9, 31, 34-5, 41, 43, 54, 56, 58, 64-5, 68, 70-1, 76, 80-1, 83, 109, 123-4, 132, 183
Martin, 143
Patrick, 158
Robert, 52, 172
Thomas, 112, 132

William, 44, 52, 70, 87, 89, 122
Josse, Alexander, burgess, 127
  William, 133
Jossie, Marjorie, 188
Justice, 88

KAY, Alexander, 137, 152
  William, 70
Kane (Kayne), Sir John, 160
Keith, Helen, 8, 105, 182
Kellie (Kelle), Sir George, 96, 134
Kemp, Thomas, 17
Kennedy, Donald, burgess, 47, 114
  Janet (Jonet), 47-8, 114-5
  Lady Janet (Jonet), 71, 150
  John, 131, 144
  Sir John, chaplain, 18-9
Ker (Kar, Kers, Keyr, Keyre), Andrew, of Greenhead, 41
  Isobel, 145
  Sir James, chaplain, 97, 119
  John, 40, 170
  Sir John, chaplain, 32, 40, 81, 100, 106-7, 143-5, 164
  Master Matthew, 129
  Patrick, 140
  Robert, 5
  Master Thomas, notary public, 41, 55, 101
  William, 3, 18, 41, 55, 65, 81, 86, 123, 137, 159, 179
Killearn, rector of, see Sutherland, Master James
Kilpatrick, Janet (Jonet), 27
  Laurence, 27-8, 75
  Matthew, 26
Kilrenny, vicar of, see Lauder, Master John
Kilsyndie, Lord of, see Douglas, Archibald
Kincaid (Kyncaid), David, 2, 88, 99, 149, 156, 182
  David, of Coates, 105
  Edward, 2, 56, 66, 73, 76, 80, 99, 102, 105, 115, 118, 120, 123, 131-2, 139, 142, 146, 176, 182
  James, 2, 64
  John, 25
  Patrick, 45, 118, 120
  Thomas, 28, 60, 98
  Master Thomas, 74
King, James, 118
  John, 98, 119
Kinghorn, 145
King's Wall, 29, 54, 78, 91, 95, 108
Kinloch (Kynloch), David, 118
  Sir George, chaplain, 52, 99, 128, 146
  Paul, 45
Kinnaird (Kinnard, Kynnaird), James, 66, 85, 144, 176
  William, 144
Kinnew (Kynnew), Sir Alexander, 27-8
Kinnimonth (Kynnynmont, Kynnymond), David, 165
  William, 81
Kinpont (Kynpont), Andrew, 84
Kirk, Henry, 18, 157
  James, 158
Kirk o' Field, 4, 54, 57, 96, 98, 114, 122, 124, 140
  chaplain of, see Congitton, Master Hugh, and Couper, Sir Alexander
  provost of, see Bothwell, Master Richard
  vennel of, 43, 49-50, 183
Kirkcaldy, William, of Grange, 145
Kirkcudbright, 70
Kirkhop, John, 10
Knight (Knycht), Alexander, 34
Knightson (Knychtson), Alexander, 166
Knollis, James, rector of Roskeen, 104
  Margaret, 104
  Patrick, 104
  Master Patrick, 104
Knox, David, 24, 38, 64, 106, 155, 158, 161, 183-4
  Gilbert, 24-5, 122
  John, 100
  Robert, 114, 124, 162, 172
  Stephen, 5, 56, 67, 121-2, 135
  Thomas, 50-1

Kyd, Sir Robert, 51
Kyle, Donald, 63, 177, 187
  George, 155, 161
  Isobel, 7-8
  James, 121, 155, 158, 161
  John, 38, 83, 94, 108, 121, 155, 158, 161
  Sir John, 184
  Marion, 121
  Thomas, 136
  Walter, 64, 155

LAING (Layng), Adam, 71
  James, 60
  John, 111
Lamb (Lambe), Christian, 143
  Christina, 109, 143
  James, 129-30
  Janet (Jonet), 122, 171
  Robert, 17
Lamlathane, 176
Lany, Margaret, 82, 111
Lauchlane, Robert, 54
Lauder, Alexander, prior, O.F.P., 85
  Sir Alexander of Blyth, 1, 3, 12, 57, 66, 79, 90, 104, 113, 141
  Alexander, 163
  Allan, 111
  Archibald, 31
  Gilbert, 8-9, 25, 61, 66, 80, 111-2, 116, 182
  Master Henry, attorney, 28-9, 80, 83, 85, 91, 167
  James, 28
  Janet (Jonet), 41
  Master John, vicar of Kilrenny, 82
  Richard, 178
  Robert, 11, 97, 141
  Walter, 26
  William, bailie, 2-7, 10, 12-6, 59, 68, 83, 90, 101, 105, 125, 130-1, 146, 149, 152-60, 162-3, 166, 173
  William, younger, 155-7
Lauder's (William) Close),174
Lauriston (Lowreson, Lowrestoun, Lowrison, Lowristone, Lowristoun), Andrew, 106

Janet (Jonet), 38-9
John, 5-6, 56, 67, 71, 106
Thomas, 39
William, 39
Laverock (Laverok), David, 143, 150-1
  Gilbert, 151
  John, 114
  Laurence, 64
  Ninian, 151
  Thomas, 71, 91, 134, 150-1
Lavy, William, 46
Law, George, 180
  John, 46
  Robert, 25, 32, 54, 57, 99, 109, 114, 153-4, 157, 171, 178
  Stephen, 43, 96, 131
Lawson (Lauson, Lausone), David, 112, 160
  Elizabeth, 122
  George, 29, 110
  Master James, provost of Edinburgh, 8-9, 122, 168-9, 171
  James, 51, 128, 169
  James, of Humbie, 160
  James, of Humbie, younger, 160
  John, 112, 150-1, 166
  Sir John, chaplain, 2, 84
  Ninian, 41, 44
  Richard, 29, 112
  Master Richard, 108, 116
  Sir Richard, 112, 122
  Master Robert, vicar of Ecclesgreig, 138, 140
  Robert, 63
  Robert, of Highriggs, 128
  Thomas, 128
  William, 112, 163
Lees (Layis, Leyis), Andrew, 178
  Janet (Jonet), 24
Legat (Legait), Jasper, 44, 125
Leishman (Lescheman, Lichtman), John, 43, 52
Leitche (Lesche, Leiche), Archibald, 78, 183
  David, 38, 183
  George, 121
Leith, 24, 78, 83, 172

INDEX

Leith (Leithe), George, burgess, 9
  Richard, 84
Lekprevik (Likprevik, Lykprevyk), John, 10, 29, 56
Leslie (Lesle, Lesly), Margaret, 146, 160
  Robert, burgess, 55, 104
Letham (Lethame), John, 97, 141, 159, 173
  John, friar, 20
  Master John, 39
  William, 20, 48, 115-6
  Sir William, monk of Paisley Abbey, 20
Leverax, lordship of, 139
Lewis (Lowis), William, 143
Liberton (Libertoun), Henry, 51, 89, 107
  James, 52
  Robert, 70
  Thomas, 52
  William, 45, 70, 140-1, 143, 162
  William, younger, 45, 70, 140, 162
Liberton Wynd, 12, 16, 104, 107-8
Lichton (Lichtoun), Andrew, 125, 154, 159-60
  John, 125, 159
Liddell (Liddaill), Agnes, 41, 52, 74
  Janet (Jonet), 41, 52, 74
  Katherine, 74
  Margaret, 74, 172
  Marion, 63
  Sir Robert, 2
Lillie (Lille), Henry, deacon of the skinners, 12, 133, 142, 172, 179-80
  Sir Henry, 142
  John, 9
  Laurence, 97
  Sir Robert, chaplain, prebendary of Kirk 'o' Field, 17, 46, 49, 134
Lincluden, 70
  provost of, see, Stewart, Master William
Lindsay (Lyndesay), Adam, 3, 31, 116
  Elizabeth, 105
  Margaret, 137
  Robert, 3, 44, 78, 98, 178
  Thomas, 67, 172
  William, 7, 21, 27, 30-8, 40-1, 46-50, 52-3, 86, 109, 134, 148, 185
Linlithgow, 81-2
Linn (Lyn), Elizabeth, 114
  Marion, 114
  Robert, 60, 70, 76, 114
  Thomas, 111
Linton (Lynto, Lyntoun), John, burgess, 4, 51, 67
  Janet (Jonet) alias Dowy, 43, 73, 148
  Thomas, 180
  Sir William, 18
Linton, rector of, see Melville, Sir Thomas
Lithgow (Linlithqw, Lithqw), David, 87, 125, 142
  James, 76
  Sir John, chaplain, 74
  Patrick, 2, 5, 8-9, 12-3, 15, 17, 20, 22, 26, 35, 38-9, 41-2, 44-5, 50-1, 53, 55, 58, 60-1, 63-5, 69, 71-4, 78, 80-1, 85, 87-8, 91, 93-4, 96, 98-9, 101, 103-6, 108, 113-6, 123-4, 127-8, 130-1, 135-8, 140, 142, 146-8, 152-4, 156, 159-60, 163, 166, 171-2, 178-81, 184
Little (Litill, Lytill), Alexander, 109, 137, 143-4, 147, 186
  Andrew, 9, 12
  Archibald, 41
  Clement, 1, 96, 110, 127, 137, 139, 144, 147-8, 183
  Cuthbert, 107
  Edward, 9, 16, 21, 32, 81, 107, 137, 147
  Helen, 34
  John, 6, 37, 75, 103, 120-1, 172, 174, 188
  John, friar, 12
  Katherine, 41
  Marion, 186
  Richard, 11, 13, 30, 101
  Thomas, burgess, 144
  William, 113, 135, 137, 147, 186

Littlejohn (Litiljohn, Litiljohne),
  Agnes, 46
  Sir George, chaplain. 9, 53,
    89, 117-8, 158
  James, 42, 184
Litster (Litstar), Elizabeth, 16
  Helen, 164
  John, 155
Livingston (Levingston, Levingstoun, Livingtoun), Master
  Alexander, attorney, 18,
    22, 50-1, 76-7, 90, 110-20,
    129, 140-2, 165, 177-8, 184
  Andrew, 59
  Charles, 10, 25, 49, 54, 94,
    99, 111, 125-6, 177, 182
  Elizabeth, 129, 171
  Lady Elizabeth, 129
  George, 41, 182
  Henry, 52, 75, 98, 141, 173-4, 188
  Isobel, Lady Roslin, 89-90
  James, 129, 143, 167
  John, 25, 35, 49, 62, 76-7,
    106-7, 109-10, 120, 131,
    143, 171, 177, 181
  Margaret, 56-7, 79, 109
  Thomas, 59
  William, 55
Loch, John, burgess, 148
  John, younger, 148
  John, 21, 87
  Matthew, 118-9
  William, 78, 152, 168
Lochmyll, Michael, burgess, 32, 34
Lochore (Lochor), Janet (Jonet), 188
Lockhart (Lokart, Lokkart),
  John, 70
  Master John, 35
  Robert, 138-9
  William, 45, 56, 109, 118,
    122, 126-7, 147
Locksmith (Locksmyth, Loksmyth),
  John, 114
Logan (Logane), Elizabeth, 36,
    62, 69-70, 118
  Gilbert, 26, 57, 62, 172
  James, 118
  Michael, 62, 172
  Robert, of Coatfield, 24,
    117, 158

Logie (Logy), Master Gavin, 43
Lothian, official of, 132
Love (Luf), John, 97
Lumly, Alexander, 39
Lundie (Lundy), James, 162
  Richard, 29, 172
Lunn (Lun), Robert, 131
Luss, rector of, see Colquhoun, Master James

MABANE, Thomas, 55, 153-4
Mack (Mak), Adam, 38-9
  William, 38-9
  Master William, 38
Madder (Mader), John, 32
  Richard, 26
Main (Maine, Mayne, Meyne),
  Adam, 22-3
  George, 25, 28, 51
  Isobell, 165
  Jasper, 11, 164-5, 184
  John, 93, 110, 144, 164-5, 170
  Katrine, 32, 117
  Robert, 143
Mair, Alexander, 12
Malcolm (Malcome), John, 25,
    38, 103, 125, 135, 151, 183
  Thomas, 111
  William, 38, 103, 110, 136,
    150-1, 186-7
Malcolm's Close, 136, 151
Malison, Alexander, 182-3
  Master John, 35, 62, 166
  Thomas, 182
Malloch, Malice, 115
Maloney (Maluny), Katrine, 166
  Sir Walter, abbot of Glenluce, 166
Manderston, Dionysius, 162
Mar, Robert, 81, 187
Margaret, Queen of Scotland, 73
Marjoribanks, John, dean of
  Guild, 1, 10, 18, 21, 29,
    42, 66, 128, 152, 164, 181
  Symon, burgess, 108
  Master Thomas, attorney,
    11, 51, 58, 63, 108, 128,
    130-1, 136, 146, 167

Market Cross, 6, 34, 135, 155
Marlzone (Marlzeon), Christian, 111
  John, 116, 149
  Margaret, 28
Marsh (Marche, Marshe), Peter, 42, 49, 57, 77, 79, 81, 153, 162
Marshall (Marschell, Merschell, Monschell), Agnes, 28
  Finlay (Fynla, Fynlay), 52, 129
  George, 172
  Henry, 145–6, 156
  Janet (Jonet), 57, 92–3, 165, 187
  John, 156
  Robert, 60, 85, 143, 163
  William, 178
  Sir William, chaplain, 57–8, 140, 159, 171
Martin (Martyne), Sir Bartholomew, chaplain, 22
  John, 115
  Margaret, 110, 119, 165
Mary Magdalene, land of, 4, 22, 32, 59, 155
Mason, Alexander, 95–6
  James, 33
  John, 49, 69, 94, 152, 167
  Robert, 2, 4
  Simon, 18
  William, 159
Matheson, Andrew, 54
  Elizabeth, 125
  George, burgess, 44, 64, 102, 155
  John, 126, 148
  John, younger, 126
Mathew, Thomas, 123
Mathie (Mathy), Agnes, 47
Mauchane, Adam, 182, 186
  Alexander, 15, 32, 56, 87, 109, 132, 147, 167, 182, 186, 188
  George, 61
  Isobel, 61, 80, 111–2
  Janet (Jonet), 105
  John, bailie, 3, 10, 13, 20, 29, 56, 65, 67, 71, 86–7, 89–94, 97, 106–7, 113, 186–7

Maxwell, George, 8
  John, 44
  William, 75, 87
Meikle (Mekil, Mekle), Andrew, 148
  George, 148
  Sir John, chaplain, 130–1, 148
Meldrum, James, notary public, 44, 67
  John, 103
  Master William, 55, 93
Meloun, Andrew, 54
Melrose, abbot of, 52–3, 59
  convent of, 26–7, 40, 52–3, 59, 153
Melrose (Melros), David, 50, 122
  John, 122, 169
Melville (Mailuill, Maluill), David, burgess, 19, 33, 42, 47, 50, 93, 95–6, 146, 167
  Sir John, chaplain, 109
  Margaret, 42–3
  Robert, 37, 42–3, 93, 146–7
  Sir Thomas, rector of Linton, 128, 146–7, 163
Menzies, John, 40, 43, 52, 64, 74
  Marion, 64
Mercer (Merser), Robert, 104
Merlzone (Merlzon), John, 72
  Walter, 68
Merrilees (Mureleyis), Thomas, burgess, 29, 34, 127, 160
Methven, Lord, 74
Michelson (Michelsone, Micheson), David, 35, 61
  George, 35–6, 71
  John, 97, 141, 156, 173–4
  Mathew, 116, 118
  Thomas, 35, 97, 141, 174
Middelburg, 161
Middlebie (Myddilbie), Andrew, 19
Mill (Meill, Myll), Sir Andrew, chaplain, 43, 54
  James, 71
Millar, David, 108
Mite, Robert, 103
Moffat (Moffett), David, 161
  Sir James, 69, 157, 164
Moncreif, Hugh, 85

Moncur, Andrew, 60, 68, 78, 85, 100, 170, 188
Montgomery (Montgumry), Laurence, 97
Monymusk, prior of, see Farnlie, Sir David
Monypenny, Robert, 80, 158
Moris, Janet (Jonet), 53
Morison, John, 129
Robert, 13, 15
Morton (Mortoun), Robert, 17
Thomas, 113
Morton, Earl of, 59
Mossman (Mosman), Alan, 37-8, 50, 128, 168-70, 183, 185
George, burgess, 149-50
John, 55, 93, 166, 180, 185
Thomas, goldsmith, burgess, 83, 130-1, 136, 149-50, 159
Mow, Sir Henry, prebendary of St Giles, 159
William, 6, 10-1, 17-8, 20, 25, 30-1, 35, 45
Mowat (Mowet), John, 167
William, 186
Mowbray, Andrew, 2, 21, 41, 45, 51, 60, 88, 101-3, 118, 149, 156, 158-9, 176
Andrew, grandfather of above, 156
Elizabeth, 33
Eufame, 53, 167
Helen, 105
Mudy, Elizabeth, 148
John, 85
Muir (Muire, Mure), Alexander, 16, 49, 70, 129, 134
Andrew, 164
John, friar, 107
John, burgess, 28, 51, 157
Sir Patrick, chaplain, 67
William, 76
Muirhead (Muirheid), William, 108
Mulikin, John, 81
Multray, Richard, 53
Murray, Alexander, 163
Andrew, 101, 145, 147, 171
Andrew, chaplain, 54, 123
Charles, 139
Master James, prebendary of Dunglass, 120, 130, 157, 163

James, attorney, 71, 73-4
Master John, of Blackbarony, 33, 73, 101, 145, 148
John, burgess, 32, 43, 59, 84, 105, 109, 134, 140, 188
Margaret, 74, 147
Marion, 157
Patrick, 30
Peter, 71
Roger, 79, 131, 172
Thomas, 38, 101
Sir William, chaplain, 46, 57
Musche, John, 188
Myans, Helen, 38

McCALZEANE (Makcalzeane), James, notary public, 4, 75, 95, 106, 137, 142-4, 182, 186
Margaret, 137
Master Thomas, 12-3, 15, 143
McCartnay, William, 167, 186
McCracken (McCrekane), Brice, 18-9
McCraw, John, 152
McDowell (MacDowell, MakDoweill), Sir William, chaplain, 68-9, 74, 113, 129
McEwen (Mackewyn), Isobel, 116
McGauchan (McGauchane), James, 75, 87
John, 128
McGill (Makgill), James, 29, 43, 106, 141, 152, 156
James, younger, 35
Margaret, 152
Makelarsay (sic), Andrew, 70
McLennane, James, 69
Macluill, David, 18
McMillan (Mcmyllane), John, 10
McNeill, Alexander, notary public, 10, 13, 15, 21-2, 26, 30, 61-2, 107, 177
John, 13, 15, 30, 61
McQueen (Makquhen), Michael, burgess, 20, 91-2, 166
Patrick, 123, 138, 142

INDEX

McTear (McTeir), William, 85, 107

NAIRN (Nairne), Archibald, 71
Napier (Nepar), Agnes, of Order of St Katherine of Sienna, 13-4
  Alexander, of Wrightshouses, 171
  Alexander, 68, 157, 170-1
  Archibald, of Merzemstoun, 47, 60, 146, 152
  Archibald, 33, 42, 51
  Elizabeth, of Order of St Katherine of Sienna, 13-4
  Helen, 14
  Janet (Jonet), 13-5, 17, 131
  John, burgess, 13-7, 47, 59, 125
  Katrine, of Order of St Katherine of Sienna, 13-4
  Margaret, of Order of St Katherine of Sienna, 13-4
  Marion, 16-7
Nasmyth, William, 158
Neill, Robert, 158
Neilson, Gilbert, 171
  James, 50
  John, 76
  Thomas, 76
Netherbow, 2, 7, 12, 16-7, 28, 35-6, 41-2, 54-5, 57, 60, 63, 80, 86, 99, 101-2, 109, 123, 128, 131, 134, 157-8, 163, 171-2, 178, 185
Nether Liberton, 140
Newbattle, abbot of, 66
  convent and monastery of, 66
Newhaven, 115
Newman, James, 171
Nicholas, Alexander, 87
Nicholl (Nichol), Alexander, 75
  George, 59, 181-2, 188
  James, 182, 188
  John, 186-7
  Margaret, 187
Nicholson, George, 132, 187-8
  John, 8, 104-5
  Richard, cordiner, burgess, 5-6, 56, 67, 111
  William, 170
Niddrie (Nudry), Elizabeth, 73, 96
  John, 16
  Thomas, 43
  William, 43
Niddrie Wynd, 11, 21, 50, 59, 76, 89, 122, 129
Nisbet (Nesbit), James, 59, 160
  William, 2, 5, 11, 20-1, 68
Norrie (Nory), Henry, 104
Janet (Jonet), 5
  Thomas, 38
North Loch, 9, 47-9, 56, 60, 66-7, 69, 80, 98, 115-6, 122-3, 133, 137, 153, 169, 171, 186-8

OCHILTREE (Vchiltrie), John of Cannach, 148
Ogill, William, notary public, 39, 137, 181
Ogilvy, John, 16
Oliphant, Walter, 30
Ormiston, laird of, 157
Orrok, David, 73
Otterburn (Ottirburne), Master Adam of Auldhame, attorney, 2, 26-7, 30, 49, 53, 69, 76, 85, 94-6, 120, 124-5, 139, 149, 167-8, 176, 182, 184, 186
  Janet (Jonet), 168
  John, 167-8
  Patrick, 45
  Robert, 53, 167
  Thomas, 58, 68, 167
Over Bow, 3, 8, 13, 46, 55, 60, 76, 92, 101, 108, 125, 132, 134-5, 143, 149, 158, 165-6, 173, 178, 187

PADY, John, 75, 87
Paisley, monk of, see, Letham, Sir William
Panter (Panteir), Arthur, curator, 29
Pardovan (Pardouyne), John, 61, 85, 95, 119, 121, 181

Park, Alexander, 51
John, 110, 171, 178
Passer, Evangelist, burgess, 54, 67-8, 169
Evangelist, younger, 54, 67-8
Paterson, Alexander, 106, 156
Andrew, 88
Beatrix, 88, 90-2
George, 50, 90
James, 74
John, 97, 116
Katrine, 89
Luke, 50, 122
Thomas, 110, 120, 135, 151, 183, 187
Sir Thomas, chaplain, 2, 143
Paul, Robert, 72
Peacock (Pacock, Pacok), James, 3
Peter, 63, 181
William, 53, 151-2, 170, 180-1
William, senior, 180-1
Pearson, (Peirson), Andrew, 22, 44, 142
John, 29
Peebles (Peblis), Alexander, 47, 120
Francis, 32, 147, 167, 188
Peebles Wynd, 4, 6, 22, 25, 32, 49, 75, 89, 109, 117, 130, 141, 154, 171
Penicuik (Pennycuke), Alexander, 67, 145-6, 162, 180-1
John, 116
Penman, Janet (Jonet), 129
Pennar, James, 160-1
Penny, Thomas, 116
Perth, 97
Pery, Alexander, 95-6, 152, 170, 172-4, 178, 180-2, 187
Pettigrew (Pettigreif), James, 166
Margaret, 40
William, 28, 150-1, 156, 176
Pillane, Patrick, friar, 13
Pinkerton (Pinkertoun, Pynkerton), Cristina, 29-30
Elizabeth, 49
Matthew, 55, 58
Pinschenot (Pynschernot), David, 78, 169
Piper, Janet (Jonet), 1
Plewlands, 119
Pollock (Pollok, Powok), Agnes, 97
Sir Patrick, 3, 39
Pomfray, David, 70
Pope (Paip), Mr John, younger, 117
Portous (Portuis), Sir John, chaplain, 107, 117, 124, 156
Mungo, 100
Powis, James, 116
William, 183
Preacher (Prechour), Nicholas, 54
Preston (Prestoun), Alexander, 14
Archibald, 5, 24, 26, 56, 64, 67, 71, 79, 106, 110, 121, 165, 167, 186
Henry, 35, 48, 53, 62, 115-6, 127
James, 11, 29, 72, 140, 143, 163-4, 181, 186
John, 5-6, 56, 67, 71, 82, 89, 151, 184
Margaret, of Order of St Katherine of Sienna, 13-4
Simon, bailie, 53, 55-7, 59, 61, 64-6, 68, 70-4, 78, 81, 86, 96, 114, 127-8, 130-1, 133, 135, 137, 139-41, 143
Thomas, of Binning, 26, 45, 93, 136
William, 35, 61-2
Purdie (Purde, Purdome, Purdy), Sir David, chaplain, 143, 164, 171, 176
David, 8-9
Helen, 175
Robert, 52, 105
Thomas, 24, 27, 81, 86, 123, 138, 172
Purves, Alexander, 150-1
Andrew, 119, 150
David, 3-4, 9-13, 16, 19-20, 26, 28-9, 35, 39-41, 43-5, 47-8, 50-9, 63-4, 67-71, 75-6, 78-80, 82-6, 90-2, 94-7,

INDEX

99–101, 103, 107–14, 116, 118–20, 122–6, 129, 132–8, 140, 143, 147–51, 155–62, 164–7, 182–3, 185–8
Janet (Jonet), 63
John, 7–8, 12, 29, 33, 41, 58, 63, 118, 134, 138, 178, 184, 186–7
Thomas, 159

RAE (Ra, Raa), Sir George, 80
James, 177
John, 172
Thomas, 164
William, 16, 28, 43, 58, 82, 86, 98, 107–8, 127, 156
Ralston (Railstoun), Thomas, 51
Ramage (Rammage), John, 76
Ramsay, Andrew, 163
  Archibald, 35, 111, 136, 187
  David, 163
  Isobella, 87, 125
  John, 16, 49, 73, 138, 170, 187
  Sir John, 128, 168, 185
  Margaret, 155
  Marion, 147, 187–8
  Norman, 149
  Peter, 146, 181
  Robert, 71, 108
  Thomas, 5, 17, 38, 42, 132–3, 146–7, 181–2, 187–8
  Walter, 68, 85, 100, 120, 145, 184
  William, 143, 170
Raperlaw, William, 98, 114, 124
Raperlaw's Wynd, 74, 140
Redpath (Reidpethe), Cristian (Cristina), 89, 158
  John, 72
  Patrick, 178
Reid, Adam, 186
  Alexander, 41, 55, 134, 149, 166, 173
  Sir David, chaplain, 55
  Donald, 172
  James, 76
  Janet (Jonet), 10, 34
  John, 29, 183–4
  John, elder, 184

Sir Patrick, chaplain, 187
William, 86
Renfrew, 80
Renton (Ranton, Raytoun), John, John, notary public, 50, 104, 146
Renwick (Rannyk), Sir David, chaplain, 2, 99
Restalrig (Lestalrig), 24, 124, 176
  dean of, see Gibson, Master William
  rector of, see Bailie, William
Reynold, John, 131
Robert, 131, 170
Richardson (Richtson, Richartsone), Andrew, 42
  David, 134
  George, 104, 111
  Sir George, 176
  Henry, 166
  Janet (Jonet), 30, 56, 60–1, 64, 67
  John, 20–2, 90, 92, 109, 175
  Margaret, 21
  Patrick, 1, 96, 108, 110, 118, 123, 139, 143, 148, 183
  Symon, 2
  Thomas, 21, 47, 148
  Sir Thomas, chaplain, 66, 111–2
  William, 43, 85, 148
  Sir William, chaplain, 17
Richmond (Richeman, Richemant), William, 85, 98
Riddell (Riddaill), John, 16, 134
  Richard, 16
  Stephen, 57, 116
Rig, John, 44
Ritchie (Riche), William, 153, 176
Roberton (Robertoun), Sir Robert, chaplain, 151
Robertson, Christopher, alias Wynton, 188
  Cristall, alias Wynton, 188
  David, 89
  John, 129–30
  Patrick, 59
  Master Richard, 127, 129–30

Thomas, *alias* Davy, 188
Robison (Robeson, Robisone),
  Alexander, 162
  Andrew, 78, 182
  Andrew, *alias* Sclater, 93
  Archibald, 4
  Sir Bartholomew, 146, 152, 157, 160
  Cristina, 118
  David, 119
  George, 72, 75, 146
  Sir Gilbert, chaplain, 128
  Helen, 118
  Janet (Jonet), 155
  John, 134, 155, 172, 179
  Katherine, 54
  Margaret, 31, 119
  Marjorie, *alias* Sclater, 116
  Margaret, *alias* Sclater, 118
  Peter, 64
  Master Richard, 143, 160
  Robert, *alias* Sclater, 119
  Thomas, 162, 180
Roger, Sir George, chaplain, 3, 132-3, 164
  Mathew, 124
Romanes (Romannos), Sir Alexander, 126
Ross (Ros), Alexander, 58
  James, 1, 66, 90, 104
  Lord John, 51
  Lord Ninian, 51, 108
  Robert, 108
  Thomas, 19
Rouche, Alison, 22, 32, 117, 164-5
Rowat, Robert, 105
  William, burgess, 8, 105
Rowe, James, 55
Runciman (Runsyman), John, 16, 41, 108
Russell (Russall), John, 70-1
  Thomas, 4
Rutherford (Rutherfurd), Andrew, 152
  Margaret, 150
  William, 5, 134, 136, 150, 168
Ruthven, Laird of, 93, 165, 187
Rymald, Robert, 37
Rynd (Rynde), Agnes, 29
  Sir Alexander, chaplain, 186
  Alexander, burgess, 4, 11-2, 19-20, 29, 48, 51, 59, 87, 115-6, 120, 125, 140, 142, 151, 163-4, 166, 173-4, 177, 186
  Henry, 177
  James, 11-2, 51, 123
  Janet (Jonet), 82
  John, 30
  Sir John, chaplain, 6, 11, 51, 75, 109, 182
  Robert, 79
  Thomas, 73, 78-9, 81, 95-6, 113, 145, 148-50, 152, 165, 167
  William, bailie, 1-4, 8-12, 15-7, 146-52, 158-60, 163-7

ST ANDREWS, archbishop of, see Beaton, James
  archdeacon of, see Inglis, Alexander
St Cuthberts, parish church, 169
St Giles, altar of Holy Blood, 46
  altar of Holy Cross, 103
  altar of our Lady of Pity, 68
  altar of St Ann, 31
  altar of St Bartholomew and St Severin, 131, 148, 176
  altar of St Colm, 37
  altar of St Eligius, 96
  altar of St James, 45-6, 60, 88, 90
  altar of St Katherine (Katrine), 98, 114, 124
  altar of St Michael, 90
  altar of St Nicholas, 119, 164
  altar of St Ninian, 156-7
  altar of St Roche, 176
  altar of St Salvator, 22
  altar of St Sebastian, 47
  cemetery of, 35, 142, 160, 166
  chaplain of, 176
  church of, 2, 8, 11, 18, 35, 37, 39, 45, 55, 59, 60, 68-

9, 88, 90, 96, 103, 111, 114, 119, 125, 127, 131, 156-7, 159, 164-5, 176
  curate and vicar of, see Young, Sir David
  prebendary of, see Mow, Sir Henry
St John, George, Lord, preceptor of Torphichen, 69-70, 72, 114
St Katherine of Sienna, church of, 153
  croft of, 154
  prioress of, see Seton, Katrine
  sisters of the Order, 56, 71, 93, 150-1
  sister of the Order, see Napier, Agnes; Napier, Elizabeth; Napier, Katrine; Napier, Margaret; Preston, Margaret
St Mary, chapel of, 89, 100
  hospital of, 143
  land or chapel of, 129
  vennel of, 16, 43, 62-3, 96, 129, 131, 134
St Mary Magdalene, land of, 117, 125
St Mary's, Bow of, see Over Bow
Wynd, 17, 27-8, 52, 58, 69, 88, 97, 100, 143, 175
St Paul, hospital and place of, 20
St Severin, land of, 27
St Triduana, chaplain in service of, 176
Sanderson, John, 158
Sandilands, George, 172
  James, of Calder, 111
Scallis (Scawis, Schelis, Stallis), Cristiane (Christian), 97, 114, 173
  John, 50
  Patrick, 97, 173
  William, 50, 62, 75, 109, 128, 139, 183
Schaw, Alexander, 57, 90, 92
  William, 61, 108
Scheirsmyth, Janet (Jonet), 28, 124
  William, burgess, 17, 28, 45, 69, 97, 124
Scotland, Thomas, 12
Scott (Schott, Scot), Alexander, 61-2, 69-70, 111, 145
  Sir Alexander, provost of Corstorphine, 126-7, 143, 176
  Sir Alexander, rector of Middleby, 41-2, 101-2, 158-9
  Andrew, 183
  David, 97
  Elizabeth, Lady Manerston, 15-6, 96-7, 110-1, 118-9, 139, 148, 183
  Henry, 50, 61-2, 69-70, 72, 79-80, 183
  Isobella, 173
  Master James, 86, 123, 127, 138
  James, 25, 36, 61-2, 67, 120, 169-70, 184-5
  Janet (Jonet), 162-3, 180
  John, 35-6, 98-9, 127, 148
  Marion, 18, 61-2, 69-70
  Master Michael, 186
  Patrick, 1, 50, 68, 82, 180, 183
  Richard, 26, 62
  Robert, 38
  Thomas, 10, 36, 61-2, 69-70, 156, 177
  Walter, 93, 97, 118-9, 138, 145, 178-9
  Walter, of, Brankishame, 185
  William, 42, 102, 165
  Master William, 145
Scougall (Scowgall), Archibald, 122
  Katrine, 24-5
  Thomas, 116
Scrimgeour (Scrymgeour), Cristina, 81
Sellar, David, 54
Selyman, Thomas, 104
  William, 47, 115-6
Seton (Seyton, Seytoun), Henry, 54, 114
  Katrine, prioress of the order of St Katherine of Sienna, 15
  Lord, 85, 88

Sharp (Scharp), John, 35–6, 51, 71, 123, 145–6, 162, 180–1, 186
Short (Schort), James, 77
  Thomas, 158
Silver, Elizabeth, 89, 158
  Ninian, burgess, 158
Sim (Sym), Andrew, 155
  James, 21, 77, 162
  John, 167
  William, burgess, 9, 60, 72, 85–6, 88, 94–6, 98, 105–7, 109, 112, 115, 121, 142, 161, 163–4, 170, 172, 175–81, 186
Simpson (Symson), Andrew, 41, 158, 161
  Henry, 101
  James, 64
  Master James, rector of Forfar, 108
  Janet (Jonet), 44, 98
  John, 20–1, 40–1, 46, 68, 93, 143, 152, 157
  Margaret, 123–4
  Marion, 108
  Marjorie, 152
  Sir Mathew, chaplain, 21, 44, 46, 60–1
  Michael, burgess, 20–1, 44, 90
  Robert, 106
  William, 21, 44, 113, 168–70
Sinclair (Sinclar), Alexander, 138
  Master Henry, 129
  Marion, 113
  Robert, 68, 80, 183–4
  Robert, younger, 183–4
  Thomas, 24
  William, 22, 32, 117
  Lord William, 41, 128, 163
Skeill, Gilbert, 42
Slater, Andrew, 111
  Patrick, 157
  see Robison, Andrew, alias; Robison, Margaret, alias; Robison, Robert, alias
Slater's Close, 118–9
Slewman (Sleuchman), Janet (Jonet), 44
  Master Thomas, 43, 71, 113

Smalem, Janet (Jonet), 157
  Sir John, 164
Small, Adam, 123
  Connell, 87
Smart (Smert), Robert, 81
  William, 47, 104, 111, 113
Smethberd (Smeithberd), Thomas, 26
  William, 100, 113
Smith (Smyth), Albert, 45
  Alexander, 170
  Archibald, 113
  Cristina, 173
  James, 94, 168
  John, deacon or kirkmaster of hammermen, 8, 31, 68–9, 75, 85, 100, 113, 115, 120, 164, 184, 188
  Sir John, chaplain, 98, 100
  Robert, 29
  Thomas, 29, 35, 60, 62, 104, 142, 177
  William, 8, 76, 85, 100, 132, 134
Snowden's Close, 160
Softlaw, John, 83, 157
  Thomas, 61, 63, 157
Somerville (Somervell, Sommervell, Summervell), George, 183
  Lord Hugh, 26–7
  Janet (Jonet), 108
  John, 94, 106–7, 184
  Walter, 63, 108
  William, 26
South Street, 72
Spence (Spens), Alexander, in Auldliston, 139
  Alexander, 47, 94–6, 151, 163, 165, 167, 170, 172–6, 178, 180–1, 186–8
  John, 95, 160
  Master John, 152
  Peter, 188
  Robert, 58, 178, 188
  Thomas, bishop of Aberdeen, 20
Spethy (Speithy), John, 28, 69, 96
  Nichol (Nicholas), 106–7, 110, 177
Spittall (Spittaill), Master Francis, 60

INDEX

Henry, 55
Master Henry, 42, 171
Janet (Jonet), 93
John, 42, 147
Spottiswood (Spottiswod), Barbara, 185
Elizabeth, 7, 184
Francis, burgess, 7-9, 33, 158, 178-9, 184-5
John, 184-5
Margaret, 8
Sir Mungo, 18
Robert, 153
William, 185
Sprot (Spot), Barnard, 184
John, 67, 164, 166, 169, 181
Philip, burgess, 164
Sir William, chaplain, 108
Staithwy, Robert, 32, 69
Stalker, Sir Robert, chaplain, 30, 42, 53, 78
Robert, 42
Stanley (Stanelie), Robert, 50
Stanton, James, notary public, 18-9, 21, 24, 27, 74
Robert, 140
William, 88
Stawis, William, 63, 169
Steel (Staill, Steill), John, 97
Sir Robert, 10
William, 35, 61-2, 81, 160
Stevenson (Stevinson, Stevinsoune), Andrew, canon of Whithorn, 71
James, 1, 38-9, 66, 156
Leonard, 32
Mungo, 3-4, 6, 39
Peter, 157
William, notary, 10, 39, 45, 47, 59, 88, 104, 166, 178
see Jacob, John *alias* and James, John *alias*
Stewart, Adam, 45, 119, 123, 140
Agnes, 154
Alan, 30
Sir David, chaplain, 119
Henry, 74
James, 185-6
John, 17, 50, 69, 79, 163
Sir John, chaplain, 94, 116, 119, 140
Richard, 67

Thomas, chaplain of the altar of the Holy Blood, 133
William, 29, 177
Master William, provost of Lincluden, 70
Stinking Style (Stynkand Style), 32
Stirk (Styrk), James, 94, 152, 185
Sir John, chaplain, 20, 81, 123, 137-8
Stonehouse (Stanhouse), Thomas, 145
Storie (Stury), Andrew, 64
James, 40, 43, 52, 64
Stoves (Stoiffis), 44
Strachan (Strathauchin, Strathauchyne), Adam, 101
Albert, 102
Janet (Jonet), 57, 109
Margaret, 58
Vincent, notary public, 3, 12, 20, 57, 65, 67, 72, 81-2, 85, 92, 98-9, 103, 107, 109, 112, 120, 128, 130, 132, 139, 144-6, 161, 181, 188
William, 56-7, 109
Strahenry, 168
Straiton (Straton, Stratoun), Alexander, 127
David, 47, 108
Robert, 108
William, 108
Strand, the, 35
Strathearn (Strathern), Matthew, 63-4
Stway, Dougal, 99
Suerde, Adam, 48
Suffolk, 70
Summer (Somer), John, 54, 101
Sutherland, Master James, rector of Killearn, 138
Swaine, John, 122, 183
Swan, John, 112, 128, 168
Swift, Janet (Jonet), 44
John, 41, 103
Thomas, burgess, 10, 29, 44, 54, 94, 112, 126
Sydsarf, John, 32, 44
Syk, Robert, 161

TAILZOUR (Taylor), Andrew, 177

Tait, James, 144
  John, 108, 112, 134, 185
  Margaret, 64
Talzefeir, George, 75, 135, 146, 161
  James, 11, 35, 68
  Margaret, 59, 188
Tarbet (Tarbot), Thomas, burgess, 93, 103, 136, 186
Tavernar, Thomas, 47
Temple Lands, 24, 69
Temple Lands of Estirelbotill, 75
Tennent, Alexander, 80, 113, 116
  John, 49, 134
  Kentigern, 130
  Mungo, burgess, bailie, 3, 6, 12, 20, 46, 53, 55, 57-63, 66-7, 75-6, 78, 83, 90, 99, 113, 116-9, 121, 123-4, 130, 132-9, 141, 156
  Patrick, 183
Thomson, Andrew, 100
  Edward, 28, 58, 64, 88
  Elizabeth, 76
  Hector, 16, 35-6, 59, 157
  Henry, 59, 133
  James, 28, 97, 172
  Janet (Jonet), 150-1
  Sir John (chaplain), 64, 182, 188
  John, 35, 131, 161
  Ninian, 38, 183
  Richard, 153
  Stephen, 53, 74, 188
  Thomas, 132
  William, 10-1, 90-2, 106-7, 123
  Sir William, 47
Thortourhouse, 73
Tod, Andrew, 81, 123, 178, 181
  David, 12, 17, 41, 102, 120, 134, 139
  George, 164
  John, 22
  Patrick, 164
  Robert, 2, 12, 134
  Sir Thomas, 29, 34, 44, 64, 66, 71
  William, waxmaker, burgess, 3, 34, 38-9, 70, 90, 109-10, 138, 146, 153, 160-1, 178, 188
Tod's (Sir Thomas) Close, 34
Todryk, Archibald, 7, 33, 42-3, 50, 73, 148, 184-5
  Thomas, 132, 167, 179
Tolbooth, 2, 9, 36-8, 45, 68, 80, 86, 107, 136, 142, 166-7
Towers (Touris), Alexander, 4, 6, 75, 87, 98
  Andrew, of Moshouschelis, 4, 75
  Cristiana (Cristina), 2, 4, 74, 172
  Francis, 29, 59, 95, 98, 123, 135, 188
  George, 98
  George, of Bristo, 5
  James, 5, 56, 67-8, 73-4, 82, 106, 110, 186
  John, friar, 20, 61
  John, 59-60, 95-6, 98
  Margaret, 29
  William, of Elwodsyde (Elwansyde), 75, 87, 97
  William, of Moshouscheilis, 75
Trinity College, 10, 20, 26, 60-1, 88, 118, 162, 171, 178
  provost of, see, Dingwall, Master John
Tullis (Tullas, Tullois, Tullos), Henry, 58, 61, 64, 71, 79, 118
  Michael, 26, 30-1, 39-40, 53, 69, 120, 125, 149, 167-8
  Thomas, 80
Tunno, Thomas, 101, 125, 143-4
Turing, Adam, 118
  Elizabeth, 10, 25
  James, 45, 51, 60
  Janet (Jonet), 5, 10, 25, 78, 131
  Katherine, 5
  Thomas, 16-7
Turnbull (Trumbill), David, 76
  Gilbert, 166
  Katrine, 123
  Rolland, 18
Turner (Turnour), Alexander, 10

INDEX

John, burgess, 13, 29
Thomas, 178
Tweedy (Twedy), Agnes, 80–1, 141
  Alexander, 141
  John, 3, 6, 12, 104, 113, 160
Tyndale (Tyndaill), Henry, 116, 121, 173–4
  Sir John, chaplain, 20, 113, 129, 135
  John, 3, 20, 113

UDDART (Uddert, Udwert), Alison, 59–61, 98
  Andrew, burgess, 5–6, 30, 41, 50–1, 56, 73, 79, 106, 131
  Elizabeth, 171
  James, burgess, 2, 4, 6, 60, 75, 79, 155, 171–2, 187
  Martin, 183
  Robert, 4
  Thomas, burgess, 50, 79, 86, 122, 171
  William, 3, 60, 79, 86, 107, 110, 123, 167, 171
Ugstoun, 39
Unthank, Thomas, 141
Ure (Ur, Urre, Urry, Vrry),
  Alexander, 87
  George, 4, 64, 66, 87, 95, 105
  James, burgess, 1, 50, 66, 104, 157, 183
  Patrick, 69–70, 76, 98, 128, 162, 182
Urquhart, Robert, 27, 52, 86, 123, 172

VALLANCE (Valange, Vallange), William, 48, 133
Vaus, Henry, 62
  Robert, 35, 55, 143
Veitch (Vaiche), Alexander, 120
  David, 57, 134
  John, attorney, 9, 12–3, 38, 58–9, 68, 159

Thomas, 43, 96
William, 188
Vernour, John, 27, 31–2, 45, 53, 72, 79, 89, 154, 163, 167, 171, 183
  William, 26–7, 41, 123, 128
Vocat, Master David, 25, 49, 143

WAIT, Alan, 8
  John, 58
Walderson, John, 188
Walker (Walkar), Alexander, 47
  Andrew, 100, 162
  Robert, 153–4
Wallace (Wallas), Adam, 33, 42
  Andrew, 27–8, 41
  Archibald, 80
  David, 154
  Gavin (Gawin), 63, 102
  Hugh, 1, 3, 9–10, 22, 32, 34, 41, 44, 46–7, 49–51, 58, 66, 76–7, 80–1, 87, 91, 101, 104, 106, 109, 111, 113–5, 122, 128, 131, 134, 147, 152, 154–5, 157–8, 165–6, 170–1, 180, 182, 186–7
  James, mason, 29, 75, 80, 87, 111
  John, 22, 107
  Margaret, 31, 41
  Thomas, 127
  Sir Thomas, chaplain, 6
  William, 139
Wallange, William, 76, 116, 169
Wallaston (sic), 139
Wan, William, 136
Wardlaw, Alexander, 73
  Archibald, 104
  Barbara, 36–7
  Cristiane (Cristina), 36–7, 104, 107
  Sir David, 126
  Elizabeth, 36–7, 107
  Henry, of Kilbaberton, 104, 108, 127
  Isabella, 118–9
  James, 15–6, 82, 135–6
  John, 82, 95–6
  Marion, 20
  Maurice, 50

Richard, burgess, 20, 36–8, 47, 87, 90, 93, 135, 149, 159
Robert, 15–6
Thomas, 6, 36, 38, 107
Watson, Andrew, 7, 128, 184
Elizabeth, 110, 186–7
Sir James, 62–3
John, burgess, 160–1, 183, 186
Sir John, 78, 182, 184
Robert, burgess, 20–1, 44, 60, 90, 93, 160–1
Sir Thomas, chaplain, 21
William, 27, 32, 34, 42, 46, 50, 53, 73, 80, 83, 86–7, 89–94, 99, 106–9, 111, 113–4, 118, 120, 122–5, 127–9, 131, 137–43, 145–9, 152, 155–8, 160–3, 165, 167–73, 175–84, 186–8
Sir William, 149
Wauchope (Wauchop), Master David, parson of Penicuik, 25
Margaret, 122
Mungo, 97
Quintin, 178
Thomas, 127
Waugh (Wauche), John, 129, 137
Weddell (Weddaill), Alexander, bailie, 69–70
Archibald, 109
John, 97
Wedderburn, John, 149
Weilfed, John, 98
Weir, George, 94
James, 155
Margaret, 166–7
Robert, 111
Thomas, 4
William, 167
Welsh (Welsche), Gilbert, 51, 67, 145, 180
Wemyss (Wemys), David, 85
Henry, bishop of Galloway, 70, 119
Werrok, John, 54, 96
West Bow, 75, 87, 105
West Port, 8, 97
White (Quhite), Andrew, 46, 59, 61, 91, 149, 157, 173
David, burgess, 31, 90, 92, 188
Elizabeth, 31–2
Henry, 149, 172
John, 40, 55, 59, 76, 81, 134, 138, 173
Margaret, 76
Thomas, 46, 57, 61, 97
William, 28, 162
Whitebrow (Quitbrow), Sir Philip, chaplain, 34, 41, 45
Whitehead (Quhiteheid, Quhitheid), John, 130–1
Margaret, 13, 30, 41, 45, 52, 73–4
William, 131
Whitehill (Quhithill), Thomas, 42
Whitelaw (Quhitelaw), 80, 149
Whithorn, canon of, see, Stevenson, Sir Andrew
Wight (Wicht), Beatrix, 156
David, 28
Dimean, 44
Duncan, 28, 30, 98, 105–6, 137, 155–6, 178
Elizabeth, 156
John, 27, 48, 58, 76, 106–8, 159, 169
Katrine, 46
Margaret, 106
Wightman (Wichtman), Master Thomas, 74
Master William, 50–2
Wilkison (Wilkesone, Wilkesoun, Wilkieson), Alexander, 85, 168–70, 182
William, burgess, 31–2, 58, 67, 79, 85, 88, 101, 138, 170
Will, John, 52
Williamson, Archibald, 11–2, 30, 34, 64, 76–7, 103–4, 113, 116, 125, 130, 135, 155, 176
Gilbert, 129, 176
Isobel, 130
John, 30, 35, 42, 76, 94, 104, 107, 113, 116, 171
Master John, 46
Sir John, 57
Thomas, 20, 39, 57
William, 88, 177

INDEX

Willison (Willesone), Alexander, 111
Wilson, Adam, 90, 92, 134, 162
  Archibald, 63, 183
  Charles, 106
  George, 25, 51
  Henry, 89
  Janet (Jonet), 149
  John, 57, 78, 125
  Robert, 43
  William, 46
Winton (Wynton), John, 154
  see Robertson, Christopher alias Robertson, Cristall alias
Winzet (Windzettis, Wyndezettis, Wyndzettis), Cristina, 152
  Elizabeth, 126
  Isobell (Isobella), 142, 176
  John, 55, 134, 158, 161
  William, 101, 125
Wishart (Wischart, Wishert), Archibald, 48, 132-3, 148, 169
  Helen, 101
  George, 132
  Janet (Jonet), 132-3
  Thomas, 132-3
  William, 118, 132-3
Wood (Wode), Alexander, 43, 170
  Andrew, 54, 101, 125, 127, 143-4
  David, 45
  Elizabeth, 19-20, 96
  Francis, 130, 141, 144-5
  Sir James, chaplain, 93
  John, 146
  Marjorie, 170
  Thomas, 38, 55, 93, 133
  William, 119
Woodhall (Wodhall), John, 188
Woodsell (Wodsall), Sir William, 157
Workhouse, 151
Wright (Wricht, Wrycht), Adam, 76, 87, 125
  John, 112
Wrightshouses (Wrichtishoussis), 58
Wylie (Wyle), John, 95, 106

YELLOWLEES (Yelloleyis, Zaloleyis), Elizabeth, 103
James, 75
Young, Alexander, notary public, 7, 17-8, 20, 35, 48, 56, 64, 67, 86, 93, 123, 131, 134, 138-9, 160, 167, 171, 184-5
  Alison, 13, 131-2
  Connal, 88, 90, 147
  David, 5, 78, 165
  Sir David, vicar and collector, curate of St Giles, 4-5, 7, 10-1, 18, 20, 47, 81, 99, 125, 129, 131, 171
  Elizabeth, 134
  Helen, 178-9
  Henry, burgess, 20, 36-8, 69, 94, 167
  James, bailie, 28, 33, 60, 132, 152, 157, 166-71, 176, 178-9, 181-6, 188
  John, 47-9, 71, 76-7, 82, 106, 110-1, 129-30, 132-3, 152, 183, 186-8
  John, younger, 47-9, 77, 82
  Sir John, 3, 20, 28
  Katherine, 33-4
  Luke, 105, 138, 178-9
  Patrick, 46, 89
  Richard, 143
  Walter, 3-4, 20, 113, 137
  William, 93, 136-7, 152
  Sir William, chaplain, 21

ZAIR (Zare), Thomas, 22, 32, 117